I0135391

CUMBERLAND ISLAND

Cumberland Island

THE UNIVERSITY OF GEORGIA PRESS   ATHENS

FOOTSTEPS IN TIME

Stephen Doster   PHOTOGRAPHS BY BENJAMIN GALLAND

a
Friends Fund
publication

Publication of this work was made possible, in part, by a
generous gift from the University of Georgia Press Friends Fund.

Unless otherwise noted, all photographs in the book were taken
by Benjamin Galland.

© 2020 by the University of Georgia Press
Athens, Georgia 30602
www.ugapress.org
All rights reserved
Designed by Erin Kirk
Set in Adobe Garamond
Printed and bound by Versa Press
The paper in this book meets the guidelines for
permanence and durability of the Committee on
Production Guidelines for Book Longevity of the
Council on Library Resources.

Most University of Georgia Press titles are
available from popular e-book vendors.

Printed in the United States of America

24 23 22 21 20 C 5 4 3 2

Library of Congress Cataloging-in-Publication Data

Names: Doster, S. M. G. (Stephen M. G.), 1959– author. | Galland,
    Benjamin, illustrator.
Title: Cumberland Island : footsteps in time / Stephen Doster ;
    photographs by Benjamin Galland
Description: Athens : The University of Georgia Press, [2020] | Includes
    bibliographical references and index.
Identifiers: LCCN 2020001635 | ISBN 9780820357393 (hardback)
Subjects: LCSH: Cumberland Island (Ga.)—History.
Classification: LCC F292.C94 D67 2020 | DDC 975.8/746—dc23
LC record available at https://lccn.loc.gov/2020001635

"Dungeness"

On a lonely wooded isle
Where the southern summers smile
Stand a sad and stately pile
Ivy drapes its mouldering sides
And the south wind's plaintive plea
Blendeth with the chanting tides
Of the moaning sea

Ah me! Once those roofless halls
Where the silence now appalls
Rang with mirth of festivals
Where the banquet's stateliness
Filled the night with noble glee
Long ago at Dungeness
By the moaning sea

Through these doors at eventide
Shadows pale still flit and glide
Stalwart hero, fairy bride
From the graves where evermore
They are slumbering peacefully
In the forest on the shore
Of the moaning sea

The magnolia breathes its balm
And the moonlight sleepeth calm
O'er the slowly swaying palm
Owlets hoot and fireflies gleam
Silent bats dart elfishly
Through the ruin like a dream
By the moaning sea

Round about hoar oak woods brood
Guardians of the solitude
Lest the centuries intrude
For the marching ages press
And the changes yet to be
Steal on gray old Dungeness
By the moaning sea

—S. G. W. BENJAMIN

Samuel Greene Wheeler Benjamin (13 Feb 1837–
19 Jul 1914), born in Greece to U.S. missionaries,
was a world traveler, author, poet, journalist,
and diplomat appointed U.S. minister to
Persia in 1883.

Contents

List of Boxes ix

Preface xi

Acknowledgments xvii

CHAPTER I   Tacatacuru 1

CHAPTER II   San Pedro 59

CHAPTER III   James Oglethorpe 97

CHAPTER IV   The Lawless Crew 123

CHAPTER V   Land Fever and the Plantation Era 137

CHAPTER VI   The War of 1812 and British Invasion 175

CHAPTER VII   The Monarch of Cumberland Island 203

CHAPTER VIII   The Hotel Era and the Settlement on the North End 245

CHAPTER IX   The Carnegies and the National Seashore 281

Afterword 349

Selected Bibliography 355

Index 361

Boxes

Timucuan Language   26

Pareja's Catechism   45

Native Beliefs and Practices   46

Spanish Control   62

Mission Towns   64

Plants Used by Indigenous Peoples   65

Westo Raids   94

Spain's Title to Georgia   106

War of Jenkins' Ear   112

Jonathan Bryan   124

The Board of Trade   128

Oglethorpe's Men in Gray's Gang   129

Yamasee Guides Helped Free the Enslaved   132

The Townshend Acts   139

John McQueen   145

Great Yazoo Land Fraud   157

George Cockburn   192

Charles Gibbs's Buried Pirate Treasure   197

Island Shipwrecks   200

Island Lighthouses   217

Admiral Du Pont   225

Elias Clubb   254

William Hunter Burbank Sr.   261

Grant Visits Cumberland   267

Hotel Guests   274

Lee Interment   276

Stafford Lawsuits   300

Stafford Place Burned   309

Crime on the Island   341

Preface

On a clear day you can see Cumberland Island from the south end of St. Simons Island, where I grew up in the 1960s and 1970s. For me, and possibly many others on St. Simons, Cumberland was that green line with a hint of white bluffs on the horizon, often obscured by summer haze and morning mists or obliterated from sight by rainstorms. Even today, when friends talk about Cumberland's history, they mention its wild horses and the Carnegies' run of the island before the National Park Service took over. That was my assessment of Cumberland, too, even though I had visited it several times after it became a National Seashore. It was the place where feral horses wandered the grounds of the Carnegie Dungeness mansion ruins. It had a wide beach that went on forever. But it was still the island on the horizon enshrouded in a historical haze and the mists of time.

Any book about Cumberland stands in the long shadow cast by Mary Bullard's excellent *Cumberland Island: A History* (2003), also published by the University of Georgia Press. Bullard, a Carnegie descendant, left no stone unturned in her twenty years of research. She wrote several other books and monographs about Cumberland, each one shedding light on island history by her meticulous research. Mary Miller's books, with personal accounts of island life, likewise opened windows on the north end of Cumberland's past. More impressive is the fact that neither Bullard nor Miller had the benefit of Internet resources, such as historical newspapers and archives, that continue to reveal new details of Georgia's past as they are digitized and posted online, bringing into focus events otherwise lost to the historical record.

JOLLY RIVER

Tyger Island

PART
of
AMELIA I.

A T L A N T I C

Scale of Two Miles or Twenty Chains to one Inch

A resurvey of Big and Little Cumberland by John McKinnon, surveyor, certified February 5, 1802. (Courtesy of Georgia Archives, Carnegie Estate Records of Cumberland Island, acc. 1969-0501M)

These books by Bullard and Miller, as well as Larry Dilsaver's *Cumberland Island National Seashore: A History of Conservation Conflict*, blew the dust off of Cumberland, revealing a place steeped in history. What I have come to realize is that, when you step off the boat onto Cumberland Island, you walk in the footsteps of men and women who played significant roles in America's past. The fierce Timucuan chief Tacatacuru ruled over the island and surrounding area before the arrival of French explorer Jean Ribault and Spanish Florida's first governor, Pedro Menéndez de Avilés. Soon after, waves of Jesuit and Franciscan priests landed on the island's shores to establish missions. Then came James Oglethorpe, Georgia's founder, who erected forts on Cumberland in a quest to drive Spain from the area. A period of squatter communities, led by the mysterious and charismatic Edmund Gray, followed Oglethorpe's departure. Next came the plantations and Revolutionary War hero Nathanael Greene, his remarkable wife, Caty, and the "monarch," Robert Stafford. The British returned in 1815 under Adm. George Cockburn, this time as invaders of the newly formed United States of America. Another invader arrived in 1864 in the form of Adm. Samuel Francis Du Pont and the U.S. Navy. Enslaved African Americans were emancipated on both occasions. One man, Ned Simmons, was enslaved twice and freed twice in his lifetime. Then there is Robert E. Lee, Ulysses S. Grant, and Andrew Carnegie, all of whom once walked the same south-end paths thousands of visitors tread over each year.

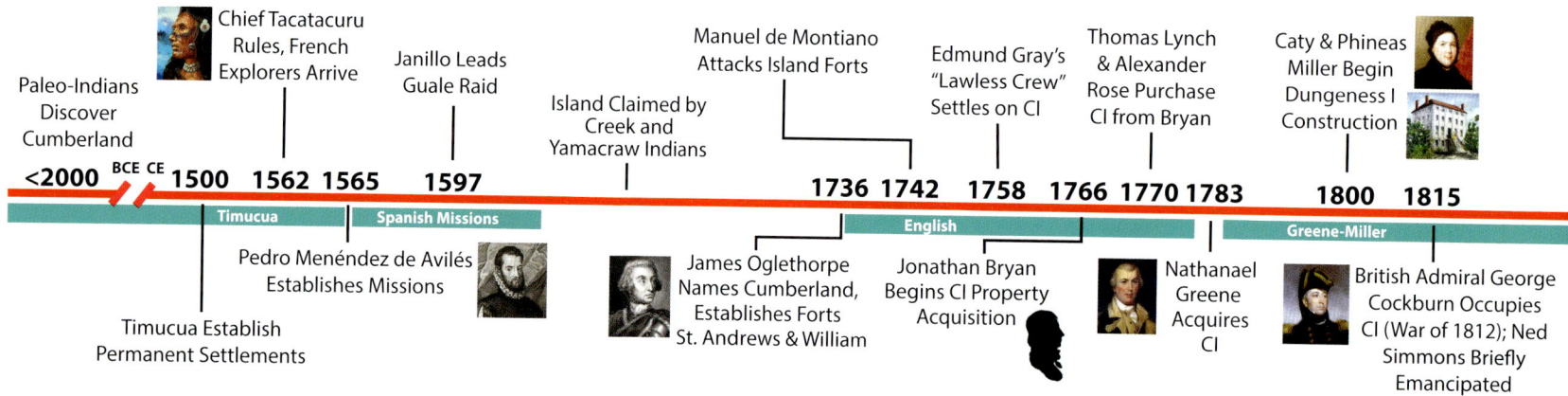

Paleo-Indians Discover Cumberland

Chief Tacatacuru Rules, French Explorers Arrive

Janillo Leads Guale Raid

Island Claimed by Creek and Yamacraw Indians

Manuel de Montiano Attacks Island Forts

Edmund Gray's "Lawless Crew" Settles on CI

Thomas Lynch & Alexander Rose Purchase CI from Bryan

Caty & Phineas Miller Begin Dungeness I Construction

<2000 ^BCE^ ^CE^ **1500   1562 1565   1597   1736 1742   1758   1766 1770 1783   1800   1815**

Timucua   Spanish Missions   English   Greene-Miller

Pedro Menéndez de Avilés Establishes Missions

Timucua Establish Permanent Settlements

James Oglethorpe Names Cumberland, Establishes Forts St. Andrews & William

Jonathan Bryan Begins CI Property Acquisition

Nathanael Greene Acquires CI

British Admiral George Cockburn Occupies CI (War of 1812); Ned Simmons Briefly Emancipated

In reading this book you might notice that history has a way of repeating itself on Cumberland Island. Hostile forces, starting with the Guale, repeatedly invaded the island. Two admirals, Cockburn (War of 1812) and Du Pont (Civil War), made their headquarters there. Two enormous Dungeness mansions were erected on the south end and met the same fate. Both Oglethorpe and the Confederate military strategists reached the same conclusion about how to best defend the Cumberland Sound. Each successive wave of owners spun the wheel of fortune in an attempt to make the island a self-sustaining, money-making enterprise, not out of greed but out of necessity. A number of entrepreneurs, going back to Jonathan Bryan and General Greene, considered developing the island by selling lots and building hotels on the north and south ends of the island. And so on it goes.

Writing a history of Cumberland is similar to writing the biography of a place. As Ralph Waldo Emerson wrote, "there is no history, only biography." The dilemma is deciding what to leave in and what to leave out, who or what to include, and how much. Some historical figures are central to Georgia history but peripheral to Cumberland's past. Mary Musgrove was one such person. Other men and women no doubt played large roles in island events but left no record in the form of diaries, newspaper accounts, or oral history interviews. My goal in writing this history was to include as many relevant and interesting events and perspectives as possible. Fortunately, digitally archived

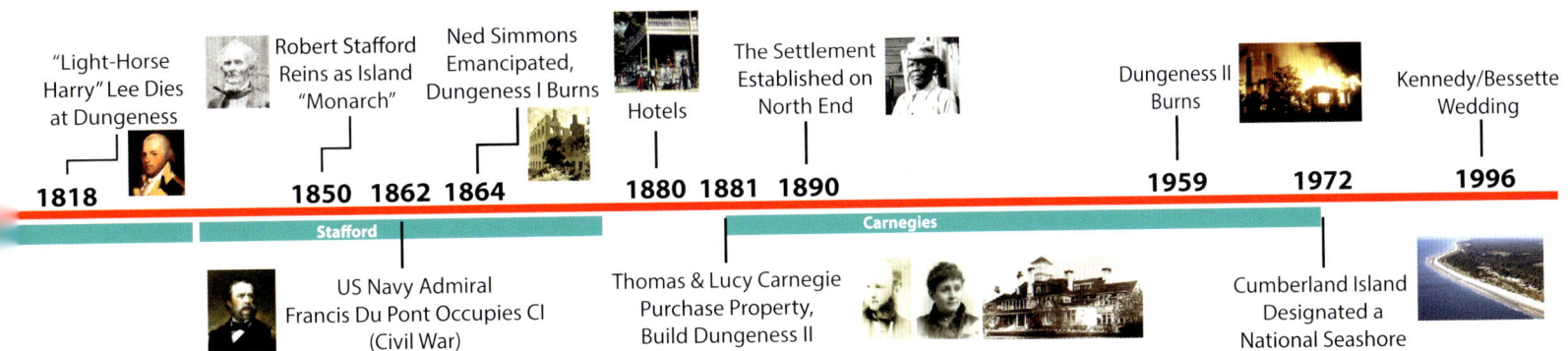

"Light-Horse Harry" Lee Dies at Dungeness

Robert Stafford Reins as Island "Monarch"

Ned Simmons Emancipated, Dungeness I Burns

Hotels

The Settlement Established on North End

Dungeness II Burns

Kennedy/Bessette Wedding

1818   1850 1862 1864   1880 1881 1890   1959   1972   1996

Stafford   Carnegies

US Navy Admiral Francis Du Pont Occupies CI (Civil War)

Thomas & Lucy Carnegie Purchase Property, Build Dungeness II

Cumberland Island Designated a National Seashore

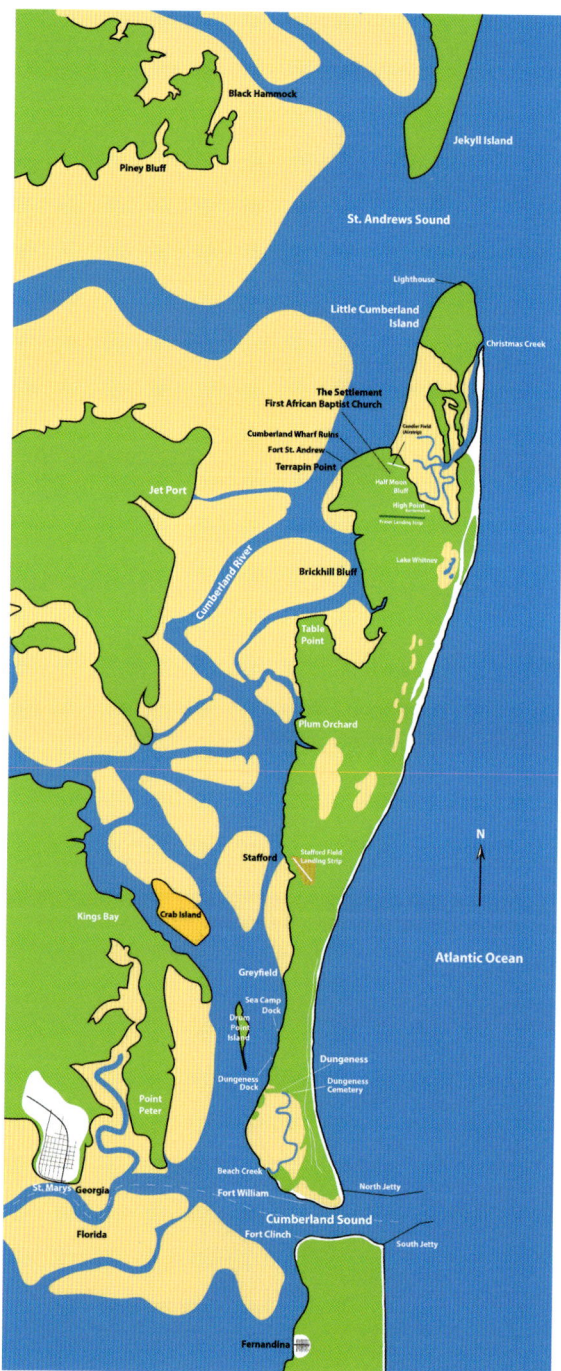

collections, such as historical newspapers, and online search tools have greatly enhanced researchers' ability to gather information once accessible only in libraries and museum archives.

Some histories are a mile long and three inches deep. Others are three inches long and a mile deep. This book is of the mile-long, three-inch deep variety. It doesn't attempt to be an encyclopedia of Cumberland Island. If it were, it could easily be a four-volume set. An entire book could be written about Native occupation alone. This book *is* an attempt to relate the main events and cast of characters that have shaped the island's history. To that end I attempted to make it an oral history, quoting eyewitnesses rather than telling the reader what they said, especially since those who were there often express themselves more eloquently than an interpreter could. Quotations therefore retain the original grammar, spelling, and punctuation of their eighteenth- and nineteenth-century writers, with my clarifying notes in brackets. To make the text more readable, I have reduced the use of ellipses that indicate text between quoted passages has been deleted. Information about sources by chapter appear in the bibliography; unless otherwise attributed, newspaper quotations are from the Georgia Historic Newspapers, a project of the Digital Library of Georgia.

Thousands of visitors come to Cumberland each year from around the world. Day hikers and overnight campers bask in Cumberland's tranquility and marvel at its beauty, leaving behind whatever worries they have on the mainland. They may be unaware of the island's history. For them, the present moment is enough—but what a history. If they only knew whose footsteps they now walk in . . .

Map of Cumberland Island and surrounding area.

Acknowledgments

I'm grateful to the following people for bringing this book to print.

First and foremost, I thank Jingle Davis, an award-winning journalist, editor, and author. Jingle was engaged in researching a book about tabby and asked me if I would write one about Cumberland Island. She had written two books in a series about Georgia's barrier islands by the University of Georgia Press. Both books, *Island Time* (St. Simons) and *Island Passages* (Jekyll), placed the bar very high for Buddy Sullivan's *Sapelo: People and Place on a Georgia Sea Island* and for this book. Her encouragement and advice came at much-needed times in the course of researching and writing this manuscript. I hope the end result approaches the standards she set.

The National Park Service staff at the Cumberland Island National Seashore, St. Marys, were exceptionally helpful in providing research material and photographs. Jill Hamilton-Anderson put me in touch with John Mitchell, who graciously accompanied Ben Galland and me to Cumberland and personally gave us the grand tour of the island, capping off a remarkable day by introducing us to Carol Ruckdeschel. John, now retired, continues to volunteer his time at Plum Orchard. Both John and Nick Roll opened the museum in St. Marys to Ben and me on several occasions. John and Nick spent hours patiently guiding me through the vaults of information and images.

I have been incredibly fortunate to work three hundred feet away from the Jean and Alexander Heard Library at Vanderbilt University, which houses an entire set of the extant *Colonial Records of the State of Georgia* and other tomes related to Georgia history, including books specifically about Cumberland Island. What I couldn't access via the library loan network, I could find using ProQuest and other online resources provided by Vanderbilt's libraries and archives. And what the main library didn't have in its archives, I could get through interlibrary loan, including Nathanael Greene's letters, the wartime correspondences and ship's logs of Admiral Cockburn, and copies of Capt. Nathan Brown's personal letters written on Cumberland during the Civil War. The University of Georgia's Hargrett Rare Book and Manuscript Library proved to be an invaluable resource for some of these documents. Many thanks also to the Library of Congress staff, the Rhode Island Historical Society reference staff, and the Georgia Historical Society reference staff. Allison Hudgins and Steve Engerrand at the Georgia Archives provided maps and historical photographs that put faces to people mentioned in the text. Mimi Rogers, curator at the Coastal Georgia Historical Society, and her staff, many of them volunteers, are always a great resource for any research involving the Georgia coast.

Judy Buchanan, Connie Brazell, and Harland Harris at the Bryan-Lang Archives in Woodbine provided a wealth of support, information, and historical images for this project. Judy initially guided me to the photographs and documents I needed. Upon her retirement, Connie became my main contact and proved equally generous with her time. The Bryan-Lang Archives house copies of all the Cumberland Island oral histories compiled by Joyce Seward and contain a wealth of historical data about Camden County and surrounding counties. For historians, genealogists, and laypeople tracing their family roots, Bryan-Lang is a key resource. For me, it was a godsend.

Daniel Tardona (Timucuan Preserve, National Park Service, Jacksonville) and Richard Vernon (National Park Service Southeast Archeological Center, Tallahassee) provided in-depth archaeological studies and striking historical images used in the first two chapters. Janet Wiley and Janelle Moore (Mission San Louis, Tallahassee) granted use of artwork by John LoCastro and Edward Jonas also used in chapters 1 and 2. Neal Adam Watson at the State Archives of Florida guided me to Theodor De Bry's engravings of Timucua culture used throughout the first chapter. Original artwork by two talented artists, Theodore Morris (losttribesflorida.com) and Martin Pate (martinpate.com), also grace the pages of this book.

The first Dungeness manor, built by Caty Greene, Nathanael's widow, was such an imposing structure that pilots' guides, used by ship crews to navigate coastal waters, listed it as a landmark. Surely many amateur and professional artists made sketches, watercolors, oil paintings, and photographs of the place. Some of those paintings went up in flames when the house burned shortly after the Civil War. Nathanael Greene's descendants are unaware of any surviving paintings of the original Dungeness House, so as of this writing all we have are photographs and watercolors of the mansion's ruins. Until now. Amy Sterling, a Nashville, Tennessee artist with a passion for re-creating images of historical structures, rendered what the mansion might have looked like at its inception based on photographs of the ruins, written descriptions of Dungeness by visitors, and similar structures located on coastal plantations.

Glynn County historian Amy Hedrick provided information about Clubb family history. Historians June Hall McCash and Patricia Barefoot also pointed me to people who were instrumental in researching this book. I am indebted to Buddy Sullivan, Dorine Brown, and Tom Dennard for contacts and information they provided. Jane Mattingly Williams interpreted the French text on Capt. André Thomas's map of Fort St. Andrews. I thank Anne Doster for her editing and constant encouragement and support during the writing of this book.

William Nightingale, a direct descendant of Nathanael Greene, provided the photograph of General Greene's portrait by Thomas Scully. Jim Bruce and Liza Marshall, Nathan Atkinson Brown descendants, sent images of Nathan and his wife as well as photos of the family sword. Sonja Olsen Kinard, a wealth of knowledge about local history, provided many useful details about life on Cumberland.

Frank Lee, a local pilot, flew coauthor Ben Galland around Cumberland Island. The amazing four-color aerial photographs in this book are the result of that flight.

Will Harlan, who wrote a book about Carol Ruckdeschel, provided her contact information. Carol graciously and patiently answered questions that I e-mailed to her. Jerald Milanich, a noted authority on southeastern Native history, once lived on Cumberland and excavated Native sites there. His insights have made this a better book.

I thank the anonymous reviewers whose comments sharpened the focus of this manuscript. One of them suggested an unconventional approach to the book, advice I agreed with and tried to implement. I hope the reviewer approves.

Deborah Oliver of Ab Initio put in a tremendous amount of work polishing the manuscript. Last but certainly not least, I thank the University of Georgia Press editors and staff, Patrick Allen, Jon Davies, Katherine La Mantia, Erin New, and Jordan Stepp, not only for making this book a reality but for continuing to publish books about the Golden Isles of Georgia.

CUMBERLAND ISLAND

CHAPTER 1   Tacatacuru

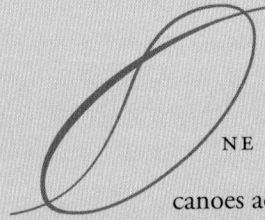

ONE SUNNY DAY four thousand years ago, Native scouts paddled dugout canoes across an expanse of water that emptied into the ocean. They set foot on an island filled with towering pine trees and majestic oaks bearing acorns, a prized food staple. The party traversed the island on foot and by water over a period of several days marveling at the variety of forest wildlife—deer, bear, wildcat—and the abundant marine life surrounding its shores, including right whales in the deep sounds just north of the island. They encountered freshwater lakes and streams, large forest communities, brackish ponds and sloughs, and salt marshes filled with grasses that could be used to make huts and communal buildings. Sassafras and other medicinal plants grew prolifically, untouched as yet by human hands. They crossed a large dune system to what seemed to be an endless beach and feasted on eggs half-buried in sea turtle nests. The scouts communicated to each other in excited tones, eager to relay the good news of their discoveries to their tribe. This barrier island would be a procurement station, a new source of food and medicinal herbs for their people.

Intertribal warfare, famine, or a powerful king expanding his domain may have catalyzed this expedition. Or it could have been the simple desire to explore new lands

This medium- to dark-gray chert spear point measures 12.1 cm (4.7 in.) tip to tip and approximately 5 cm (2 in.) at its widest point. (Courtesy of National Park Service Photo/ Darryl Herring)

Mammoth Hunter, by Theodore Morris. (Courtesy of Theodore Morris, losttribesflorida.com)

that led them there. Whatever the reason, humans had discovered the island we know as Cumberland. These hunter-gatherers were precursors of the Timucua (*tim-OO-qua*), who would permanently inhabit Cumberland not long before the arrival of the French and Spanish.

How did these people arrive in what is now the southeastern United States? One current theory is that Asian peoples, Paleoindians ("paleo," meaning ancient or before recorded history), followed herds of mastodon, mammoth, camel, and bison across the Bering Strait (connecting present-day Russia and Alaska) on a six-hundred-mile-wide land bridge called Beringia, an area the size of British Columbia and Alberta combined.

The Paleoindian period of colonization spanned a time from about 15,000 BC to 7000 BC. Recent evidence suggests the migration started twenty thousand years ago with hunters following the American continent coasts in boats along the so-called Kelp Highway that supported marine life. The Paleoindian people settled coastal areas from Alaska down the Pacific coast to South America and from there migrated inland.

Archaeological excavations indicate the Timucuan forefathers filtered into current northern Florida and southern Georgia around 11,000 BC. Whether they arrived via South America and Mexico, from the Caribbean, or from the Great Lakes area has not been determined. During that period so much water was packed into Ice Age glaciers that sea levels were some 350 feet lower than they are today, making Florida's land mass almost double its present size. Groundwater levels were also much lower then, and many of the rivers, lakes, and springs currently found in Florida and southern Georgia did not exist, making surface water scarcer for the Paleoindians.

Twenty-five miles southeast of Tallahassee lies the Page-Ladson sinkhole, an ancient watering hole beneath the Aucilla River, one of nearly thirty underwater archaeological "wet" sites on the Aucilla. Ancient sinkholes and limestone formations held water that attracted animals and forerunners of the Timucua. Paleoindian artifacts and animal bones, including a mastodon tusk found at the Page-Ladson sinkhole, suggest human occupation of northern Florida during the late Pleistocene, perhaps predating Clovis culture people who lived in North America thirteen thousand years ago (evidence of Paleoamerican communities was unearthed near Clovis, NM, in the 1920s and 1930s). If so, it pushes back substantiation of people occupying the southeastern United States by another thousand years or more.

The Paleoindians' Cumberland looked very different from the Cumberland Island we know today. The island is currently 17.5 miles long (excluding Little Cumberland Island), covering 36,415 acres (56.25 square miles), with tidal creeks, marsh, mudflats, and small freshwater lakes occupying 16,850 acres of that. Cumberland was about a third smaller when the first inhabitants arrived. It is the southernmost barrier island in Georgia and the westernmost shoreline on the Atlantic coast of the United States. The marine terrace on which Cumberland formed appeared forty thousand years ago during the Silver Bluff stage of the Pleistocene epoch (aka, the Ice Age). Geological evidence reveals the island was once farther north and much farther east than its current location. A warming period about twelve thousand years ago marked the beginning of the Holocene period. Advancing seas eroded the front of barrier islands while simultaneously depositing sand behind them, causing a rapid migration of these sea islands westward along the

Lake Whitney, ca. 1900. (Courtesy of Georgia Archives, Lucy Coleman and Thomas M. Carnegie Family Papers, acc. 1994-0003m, 94-3m_vii_151)

continental shelf to their current positions. Even today, each high tide transports sand to the west side of Georgia's barrier islands, creating shoal areas known as dividings where the incoming tides meet. Sandbars and mud banks formed at these locations present navigational problems for vessels plying inland waterways.

The rise in sea levels created a new shoreline, forming the beach, dune, and inter-dune areas of Cumberland. The inner ridge (Pleistocene) and outer dune structures (Holocene) are separated by marshland, formerly a narrow lagoon. This topography is evident on the north and south ends of Cumberland Island. During the Holocene epoch, rising seas created marshland and Christmas Creek, separating Little Cumberland from Greater Cumberland. A good portion of the southeastern section of Cumberland is Holocene land. A wide marsh flat and Beach Creek separate it from the western finger of Pleistocene land just south of Dungeness. Much of the Holocene deposits between the north and south Holocene areas on Cumberland's seafront have eroded, leaving behind a Pleistocene shoreline.

Cumberland's lakes and ponds rely on rainwater for replenishment. Lake Whitney is the largest freshwater resource on all of Georgia's barrier islands, covering forty acres with an average depth of six feet. At one time it was a popular place for duck hunting and large enough to support a small ferry that transported people from one side to the other, but no longer. Wells, eighteen feet deep or less depending on the location, have provided freshwater for island inhabitants for centuries. Much deeper wells have been

The north end and Little Cumberland, bisected by Christmas Creek.

The south end of Cumberland Island, bisected by Beach Creek.

drilled to tap the Floridan (or Coastal Plain) aquifer, where natural underground pressure creates a constant water flow. Workers drilled a 680-foot well near Dungeness in 1887, filling a 50-foot-high storage tank that supplied gravity-fed water to the Carnegie mansion and outbuildings. Similar wells supplied water towers at other homes on the island and the hotel on the island's north end. A 1965 survey found nineteen "natural and artificial ponds, outflows, and drainage fields" on Cumberland, susceptible to droughts and human alterations to the landscape. Since the 1970s, an influx of residents to Kings Bay and Camden County has reduced the rate of flow from artesian wells drawing on the underground aquifer.

Three centuries of rice, cotton, and other crop cultivation on Cumberland as well as extensive logging have dramatically altered the variety and extent of flora on the island, but the principal vegetative zones—beach, primary dunes, interdune flats, shrub zone, shrub forest, upland forests, salt marshes, and freshwater zones (wetlands)—remain intact. Sea oats, a variety of grasses (salt meadow cordgrass, bitter panic, dropseed, sandspur), beach elder (a shrub), pennywort (dollarweed), beach croton, yucca, and prickly pear cactus comprise the plant communities found in the dune and interdune zones.

Behind the dunes these plants give way to flowering weeds. Wax myrtle, dahoon holly and yaupon holly (used by Natives to make ceremonial drinks), groundsel tree, red bay, and other shrubs begin to appear behind the interdune meadows along with catbrier, pepper vine, Virginia creeper, muscadine grape, and other vines. This zone transitions to the live oak, pine, and palmetto forests that make up much of the landscape (Schoettle). Long stretches of Cumberland shore, where sand dunes and oak forests collide, have no transition zones. Dune migration to the west is attributed to cattle, horses, and feral pigs overgrazing the dune vegetation.

Spanish moss (*Tillandsia usneoides*), with its tiny flowers, drapes from tree limbs. Spartina grass (*Spartina alterniflora*, aka cordgrass), which spreads across one-third of Cumberland's salt marsh system, was used by aborigines, early European settlers, and slaves to build grass huts and is a favored food source for feral horses.

Cumberland hosts over three hundred bird species (including brown pelican, bald eagle, Canada geese, egret, heron, and mallard), seventeen species of terrestrial mammals (white-tailed deer, raccoon, opossum, armadillo, cottontail rabbit, gray squirrel), thirty-five reptile species (sea turtle, snapping turtle, alligator, rattlesnake, water moccasin, king snake, frogs, salamanders), eighteen species of amphibians, twelve brackish and freshwater fish species, and a number of invertebrates. Manatees range as far north as

Sand dunes encroaching on forest.

Man on dunes overlooking oak forest, ca. 1918. (Courtesy of Georgia Archives, Lucy Coleman and Thomas M. Carnegie Family Papers, acc. 1994-0003m, 94-3m_VII_16)

southeastern Georgia in the spring, summer, and early autumn. Little wonder early inhabitants found the island a natural larder with its abundance of terrestrial fauna and fish, crabs, oysters, and mussels.

The Timucua

The Timucua people emerged from their Paleoindian ancestors, inhabiting a region extending from a line running north of today's Georgia-Florida border to Cumberland Island, south to Cape Canaveral, then west to Tampa, and north along the Aucilla River near Tallahassee back to the Georgia-Florida border (Ehrmann). The Aucilla River, which bisects Florida's panhandle east of Tallahassee, marked the western boundary between the Timucua and the Apalachi (Apalachee), a smaller but prosperous people described by early chroniclers as "fearless." The term "Timucua" designates this region of Native Americans who spoke a similar language. The dialects within that region varied, including Mocama, spoken by tribes living on the Georgia coast. One of those tribes, the Tacatacuru, lived on Cumberland Island. Estimates of the pre-Columbian Timucua population, in what is now northern Florida and southern Georgia, range from twenty thousand to one million people. Noted anthropologist and archaeologist Jerald Milanich puts the figure at about two hundred thousand, divided into thirty independent chiefdoms. In the sixteenth and seventeenth centuries, the French and Spanish estimated the Timucuan geographical extent in a number of ways. First, the Timucua language was discernable from the Apalachi and Creek languages. Explorers often relied on an interpreter (sometimes kidnapped for the purpose) until they reached a region whose language the interpreter could not understand, and then they resorted to sign language. Second, Timucua customs and manner of dress were distinguishable from other major tribal groups. Finally, the Natives informed the newly arrived Europeans of the locations of nearby tribes and of their enemies. Modern archaeologists have identified many Timucuan sites based on the artifacts unearthed there.

Milanich extends the Timucuan speakers' northern reach to the junction of the Oconee and Ocmulgee Rivers, which converge to form the Altamaha. That would indicate the Timucua dominated an area of nineteen thousand square miles (twelve thousand in Florida and seventy-two hundred in Georgia) at the time of European contact. Their territory consisted of about thirty chiefdoms and more than five hundred villages. Each chiefdom had a main town from which the dominant chief ruled. The French and Spanish usually named a village, region, and the people who lived there after the

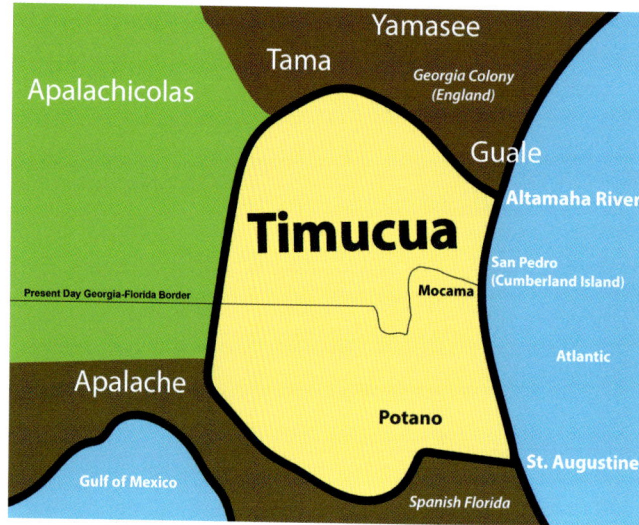

This map depicts the general geographical area of Timucua presence. Some researchers have extended the southern boundary as far south as Cape Canaveral and west to Tampa.

Council house, by John LoCastro. (Courtesy of Mission San Luis, Florida Department of State)

paramount chief who ruled their respective domains; no record survives of what the people living in this region called themselves. Archaeological evidence suggests most Timucuan villages averaged twenty-five households with a total population of around 200–250 inhabitants, possibly due to the constraint of arable land and hunting grounds in the immediate area. From these towns, other villages would sprout and grow, creating a chiefdom. The central village structure was a council house, "the great public house," large enough to hold a village's entire population. The French explorer Jean Ribault (*re BOW*; also spelled Ribaut) described a council house as "very great, long and broad with seats round about made of reeds, trimly couched together, which serve them both for beds and seats set on great round pillars painted with red, yellow, and blue." Here the chief met each morning to receive the village leaders and drink *cacina*, a potent, high-caffeine concoction made from yaupon holly (*Ilex vomitoria*) leaves (the Timucua used variations of *cacina* for different occasions). The council house at Tacatacuru was larger than others in the area and "open at the top with a skylight, round in shape and made of whole pine trees." Villages often formed alliances as mutual protection against enemies or to distribute food to areas experiencing a poor harvest. An alliance might be created by marriage or forced by a powerful chief who would demand vassal chiefs to pay tribute in food, hides, feathers, or other status symbols.

War Leader, by Theodore Morris. (Painting reproduced courtesy of Theodore Morris, losttribesflorida.com)

Cumberland Island has been known by many names. The indigenous name for it, Wissoo (also Wissoe or Missoe), translates as "the island of sassafras," a pungent plant used for its medicinal properties. Another Native name for the island was Atuluteca, also meaning "sassafras." The Timucua called the sassafras tree *pauane* and used its roots, stems, leaves, bark, and flowers for ceremonial, culinary, and medicinal purposes such as treating wounds, skin disorders, and fever. Ribault initially named the river that flows into Cumberland Sound the Seine River and named Cumberland "Ile de la Seine." The Spanish later renamed the Seine River "Santa Maria," which the British later Anglicized to "St. Marys." Spanish officials renamed Cumberland Isla de San Pedro but first knew the island as Tacatacuru (or Tacatacoru) after the island's Chief Tacatacuru, whose influence in the area was on the ascent. His subjects were likewise called the Tacatacuru.

Chief Saturiwa (also Saturiba or Satouriona), who resided on the St. Johns River, ruled a chiefdom extending from Cumberland Island to what is now St. Augustine. His main village, "a pueblo of 25 large houses, where in each one live eight or nine Indians with their wives and children, because [those of] one lineage live together," was situated on the south bank of the St. Johns River, most likely where Naval Station Mayport now lies. Chief Saturiwa, for whom the tribe was named, had authority over thirty nearby chiefs and their towns. The domain of this localized alliance extended from modern Jacksonville to the village of Saraby (also Caravay) on Little Talbot Island. Chief Tacatacuru on Cumberland would eventually replace Saturiwa in stature, and on Saturiwa's death he became the paramount chief of the region. Both the Tacatacuru and the Saturiwa spoke a Mocama (also Mocamo) dialect that differed from that of the other Timucua tribes of Florida. Mocama was yet another Native name for Cumberland Island, meaning "on the sea" or "salt water." Although the two tribes shared the same tongue, their pottery and shell midden arrangement, which inform archaeologists of the village layout, indicate the Tacatacuru were culturally distinct from the Saturiwa. Mocama speakers over time occupied the area from the St. Johns River north of Jacksonville to the San Buenaventura de Guadalquini mission on the south end of St. Simons Island and possibly as far north as the Altamaha River.

Timucua Natives on Cumberland Island occupied numerous villages. The largest one—Chief Tacatacuru's primary village—was located on the southern end of the island along the banks of the inland waterway. It extended from Dungeness property for almost a mile to north of the present-day Dungeness Wharf, where most of the population

Approximate location of the Tacatacuru
on Cumberland Island.

Villagers at River's Edge, by Martin Pate, Newnan, Georgia.

Archaic or Meso-Indian period ceramics (8000–1000 BC). Native Americans decorated pottery by scratching, impressing, or stamping designs on surfaces. (Courtesy of Southeast Archeological Center NPS)

Shell tools used to create digging, pounding, or puncturing instruments. Recovered during Brickhill Bluff excavations. (Courtesy of Southeast Archeological Center NPS)

Contact period ceramics. A carved wooden paddle was likely used to stamp a design onto this vessel. (Courtesy of Southeast Archeological Center NPS)

resided. Jerald Milanich, John Ehrenhard, and other archaeologists have surveyed the island since the 1970s. Based on the location of shell middens, ceramics, and other surface objects, they determined the location of the main south-end village and the Spanish mission of San Pedro de Mocama later established there. The Spanish located another mission, Porturiba (the Timucuan name for the nearby Satilla River, which empties into St. Andrews Sound) on the northwest end of Greater Cumberland. A second possible site for this mission is Brickhill Bluff, where in 1976 Ehrenhard identified olive jar sherds recovered there. Older ceramics at Brickhill point to aboriginal occupation dating from the Early Deptford period (ca. 500–100 BC) to the Late Mississippi period (1200 BC–AD 1600).

Smaller satellite villages subject to Tacatacuru extended across the island, mostly on the lagoon (marsh side) of the island, and onto the mainland. Shell middens containing animal bones, mollusk shells, and other waste mark the locations of these villages. Many of the middens were later dug up and used by English and American planters to make tabby or to lime agricultural fields in order to alter the soil's acidity. Burial mounds that

Beach Friends, by Theodore Morris. (Painting reproduced courtesy of Theodore Morris, losttribesflorida.com)

Detail from *Villagers at River's Edge*, by Martin Pate, Newnan, Georgia. (Courtesy of Southeastern Archeological Center NPS)

once dotted the island were also destroyed to clear land for planting. Having found evidence of Native sites on the ocean side of Cumberland, Jerald Milanich surmises these were camping locations from which Natives harvested loggerhead turtles and evaporated seawater to collect salt.

The ceramics Natives left behind and the materials they used—sand, shell, or grass, to bond with clay, a process called tempering—yield clues as to who lived on Cumberland and when. Native potters, usually females, typically rolled moist clay and sand into thin rope, then coiled the rope into the shape of a pot that was smoothed over on the inside and outside using a rock and water. The potter next pressed a wooden paddle with a design etched on it onto the pot's outer surface, then dried the pot in the sun, and finally placed it in a fire to bake. Some of the earliest cultures (St. Simons, Orange, Norwood) used plant fibers as tempering agents. Southeast Georgia saw a succession of discrete groups of people starting with Deptford culture (about 500 BC to AD 750), the Wilmington culture (AD 750 to AD 1000), and the Savannah culture, which lasted until the arrival of the French and Spanish.

Our knowledge of the Deptford period comes from their burial mounds as well as sand-tempered ceramics. Natives during the Wilmington period used crushed pottery as a tempering agent. Savannah culture aborigines produced "cord-marked, check-stamped, and complicated stamped" pottery (Milanich). All three of these prehistoric cultures were probably the forebearers of the Natives on Cumberland. At some point, they began to be influenced by peoples of northeastern Florida, as evidenced by the

Pottery from Satilla and Deptford cultures, 800 BCE–700 CE. Pottery designs change over time. Archaeologists can date most pottery based on shape and design. (Courtesy of Southeast Archeological Center NPS)

Partially restored but incomplete Native American vessel found near Mayport, Florida. (Courtesy of National Park Service Photo/Darryl Herring)

presence of San Marcos Phase pottery on the island. Early human encampments on the island were relatively modest in size, containing five dwellings occupied by small nuclear families.

Chief Tacatacuru's immediate domain included Cumberland, Amelia Island (now in Florida), and the south end of St. Simons Island. Much of what we know about the southeastern Native tribes comes from the writings of European explorers and missionaries who first encountered them. Their observations provide many fascinating clues about what the Tacatacuru of Cumberland looked like and what their customs and religious beliefs were. Though not totally accurate and at times portraying Native customs through the lens of European preconceptions, these are the only surviving written accounts. The French extensively documented the Timucua way of life in Saturiwa's province, which in turn provides insight into the lives of Natives living on Cumberland. Jean Ribault, Nicolas Le Challeux, and René de Laudonnière (*day law dun YAIR*) left behind detailed descriptions of Timucuan physical features, dress, beliefs, and customs.

Jacques Le Moyne de Morgues, an artist who accompanied Laudonnière, observed the Timucua in great detail, creating sketches of Native life later reimagined, engraved, and published by the Belgian cartographer Theodor de Bry. The remarkable Franciscan monk and linguist Father Francisco Pareja de la Orden served as a missionary on Fort George Island and on Cumberland Island. Pareja interviewed numerous caciques (*kah-SEE-kays*), as the Spanish called indigenous leaders, using a catechism or standard list of questions. His records are housed at the Archivo General de Indias in Seville, Spain (Worth, Bolton). Other names for chiefs used by the Natives included *paracusi*, *utina*, *holata* (Timucua and Apalachee), *mico* (Muskogean or Guale), *mica* (chieftainess, Guale), *inaha* (second in command), and *mandador* (order giver).

Late nineteenth- and early twentieth-century ethnologists and historians—among them Herbert Bolton, Mary Ross, John Tate Lanning, John Swanton, W. W. Ehrmann, the linguist Albert Gatschet, and the Rev. Maynard Geiger, OFM—mined the French and Spanish archives to retrieve this data. John Worth, Jerald Milanich, John Hann, and other modern historians continue to carry the torch and shed light on the historical record of Native Americans and Spanish missions in what is now Georgia and Florida.

Physical Description

Some early observers described the Timucua as a very tall race compared to the French and Spanish. However, Native skeletal measurements from excavations indicate the Timucua averaged 5'5" to 5'7". Not so tall by modern standards. Timucua men wore their hair in a raised bun, adorned with animal and feather headdresses, which probably gave the impression of greater height. Gatschet writes that "men and women generally went nude. Their bodies were well proportioned, the men were of a brown-olive color, tall stature and without apparent deformities. The majority of men tattooed themselves in very artistic devices on the arms and thighs, and to judge from Le Moyne's pictures, the chiefs at least were tattooed over the whole body."

Ribault, Laudonnière, Le Moyne, and others commented on the Natives' proclivity for painting and tattooing their bodies in red, black, and bright blue designs. Some tattoos indicated rank in the tribal hierarchy. "The forepart of their bodies and arms they also paint with pretty devices in azure, red, and black, so well and properly, that the best painters of Europe could not improve upon it. The most of them have their bodies, arms, and thighs painted with very fair devices, the painting whereof can never be taken away, because the same is pricked into their flesh. The reader should be informed that all these chiefs and their wives ornament their skin with punctures arranged so as to make certain designs. Doing this sometimes makes them sick for seven or eight days. They rub the punctured places with a certain herb, which leaves an indelible color." During time of war, "they use a sleighter colour of painting their faces, thereby to make themselves shew the more fierce; which after their warres [wars] ended, they wash away againe."

"They trussed up their long black hair," writes Gatschet, "in a bunch resting on their head, and covered their privates with a well-dressed deerskin. Women wore their hair long, reaching down to the hips. Both sexes were in the habit of wearing their finger nails long." Le Moyne reveals a practical reason for growing long nails: "they let their nails grow long on fingers and toes, cutting (scraping) the former [fingernails] away, however, at the sides (with a certain shell), so as to leave them very sharp, the men especially; and when they take one of the enemy, they sink their nails deep in his forehead, and tear down the skin so as to wound and blind him." "Women were seen to climb the highest trees with agility," Gatschet continues, "and to swim over broad rivers with children on their backs. When they became pregnant, they kept away from their husbands, and during their periods were careful to eat certain kinds of nutriments only; they drank blood to render their sucking [sic] children stronger and healthier."

Early European observers described the Timucua as hawk-nosed, muscular, and agile people with ruddy (olive or red) complexions, though the women were generally lighter complexioned from their habit of rubbing bear grease into their skin. Timucua men wore breechclout made of deerskin or woven from palm leaves and even plant roots, "consisting of a belt about the waist and a skin or a piece of cloth passed between the legs and between the belt and the body, the ends being allowed to fall down in front and behind." The skins might be painted yellow, red, black, or another color according to each man's taste. Women wore a short skirt made of either moss (*guano*) or animal skin that covered their breasts and private parts, "the knot saddling the left side above the thigh." The moss garment was usually smoked over an aromatic fire to exterminate insects, especially red bugs (*Trombicula alfreddugesi*), also known as chiggers or harvest mites. A chief might wear painted deerskin cloaks, bearskin, and bird plumes. Women wore hats fashioned from intertwined palm leaves. Tribal doctors and men of status often wore animal skins with the heads still on.

Ribault noted that Native men pulled out the hair from their bodies except for their heads, which was very black, worn hip-length, and "trussed up, with a lace made of

Woman of the Sacred Clay, by Theodore Morris. (Painting reproduced courtesy of Theodore Morris, losttribesflorida.com)

herbs, to the tops of their heads and fastened after the form of a diadem [a crown or headband]." The hair, thus styled, also served as a quiver to hold arrows when at war. Bird feathers were often used to adorn their heads, especially when men went into battle.

Shells were often used as currency among the tribes. Men and women adorned themselves with jewelry, including shell necklaces, fish-teeth bracelets, anklets made from pearls, and belts made of balls the color of silver. Men also wore "round, flat plates of gold, silver, or brass, which hung upon their legs, tinkling like little bells," used particularly in dances. Men and women wore shell ornaments above the elbows, wrists, ankles, below the knees, and around their throats. In pre-Columbian times a wide indigenous trade network extended from the Great Lakes to the Gulf of Mexico and from the Atlantic to the Mississippi River. Some of the Timucua gold first seen by Europeans came from this network, including gold from the Cherokee mines of northern Georgia. Spanish vessels sailing in flotilla from Havana to Spain carried precious metals from Caribbean and Mexican mines; those blown off course by storms and seasonal hurricanes and wrecked on the southern East Coast might have been the source of the gold and silver accumulated by the North Florida tribes.

Timucua men occasionally had about their necks gorgets made of gold, silver, or copper mined in the Appalachians. These were round or oval gold and silver plates about the size of a small platter, worn to protect the back and breast during war or for ornamentation during peacetime. Ribault describes one Native wearing "a round plate of red copper, well-polished, with a small one of silver hung in the middle of it, and on his ears a small plate of copper, with which they wipe the sweat from their bodies." Another writer mentions that "the Floridians have pieces of unicornes hornes [unicorn horns] which they weare about their necks." The horns most likely

Worked shell gorget with eight-pointed star and scallop design, found at Kauffman Island midden in Lake Kerr, Florida. (Courtesy of National Park Service Photo/Darryl Herring)

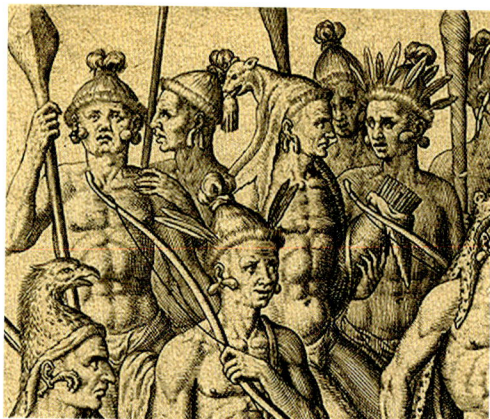

Theodor de Bry engraving of Timucua with metal objects embedded in their ears. (Courtesy of the State Archives of Florida)

Native American bead necklace, made from gastropod shells. Strung on modern thread. Found at Kauffman Island midden in Lake Kerr, Florida. (Courtesy of National Park Service Photo/Darryl Herring)

came from bison, which were abundant in northern Florida and southern Georgia at that time.

Unlike tattooing, body piercing was largely confined to the soft ear lobe, passed through with the claw of a bird or "small oblong fish-bladders, which when inflated shine like pearls, and which, being dyed red, look like a bright-colored carbuncle [gem]." As did other cultures, the Timucua prized beads made from green and red stones or the bones of fish or other animals. Bracelets made of fish teeth were common.

Europeans traded with the Timucua for gold, silver, copper, lead, and turquois stones. The French obtained "a great abundance of pearls, as fair pearls as are found in any country of the world," which the Natives gathered from freshwater mussels or oysters. The pearls were "blacke by meanes of roasting them, for they do not fish for them as the Spanyards doe, but for their meat."

Dwellings

Ribault describes a Timucua village he encountered near the mouth of the St. Marys River: "their houses are made of wood, fitly and closely set up and covered with reeds, the most part after the fashion of a pavilion." Le Challeux and Le Moyne add more details in their descriptions, attesting to the sturdiness of Timucua constructions. "Their dwellings are of a round shape and in style almost like the pigeon houses of this country [France], the foundation and main structure being of great trees, covered over with palmetto leaves, and not fearing either wind or tempest. The chief's dwelling stands in the middle of the town, and is partly underground in consequence of the sun's heat. Around this are the houses of the principal men, all lightly roofed with palm branches, as they are occupied only nine months in the year; the other three being spent in the woods. When they come back they occupy their houses again, and if they find that the enemy has burnt them down, they build others of similar materials. Thus magnificent are the palaces of the Indians. Their houses are not many together, for in one house an hundred of them do lodge; they being made much like a great barne, and in strength not inferior to ours, for they have stanchions and rafters of whole trees, and are covered by palmito-leaves, having no place divided, but one small roome for their king and queen."

Gatschet confirms Le Moyne's observation that the Timucua vacate their villages at a certain period each year and provides additional descriptions of their dwellings: "During the three or four months of the rainy season they retired to the woods and lived there in huts covered with palmetto leaves. They did so evidently to avoid the burning rays of the subtropical sun. The ordinary settlements of the Timucua were a conglomerate of huts surrounded by strong palisade fences, not unlike the kraals [African village of huts usually enclosed by fencing] of the Kaffirs [ethnic groups in Africa who speak Bantu languages]. They seated themselves on coarse benches made of nine poles or canes running parallel, the benches forming half circles; there they held their councils of war and peace while the women prepared food for them or let the cassina [*Ilex cassine*, or dahoon

Theodor de Bry engraving of a Timucua village. Not all villages were walled in. There is no evidence that villages on Cumberland Island were enclosed in this manner. (Image courtesy of the State Archives of Florida)

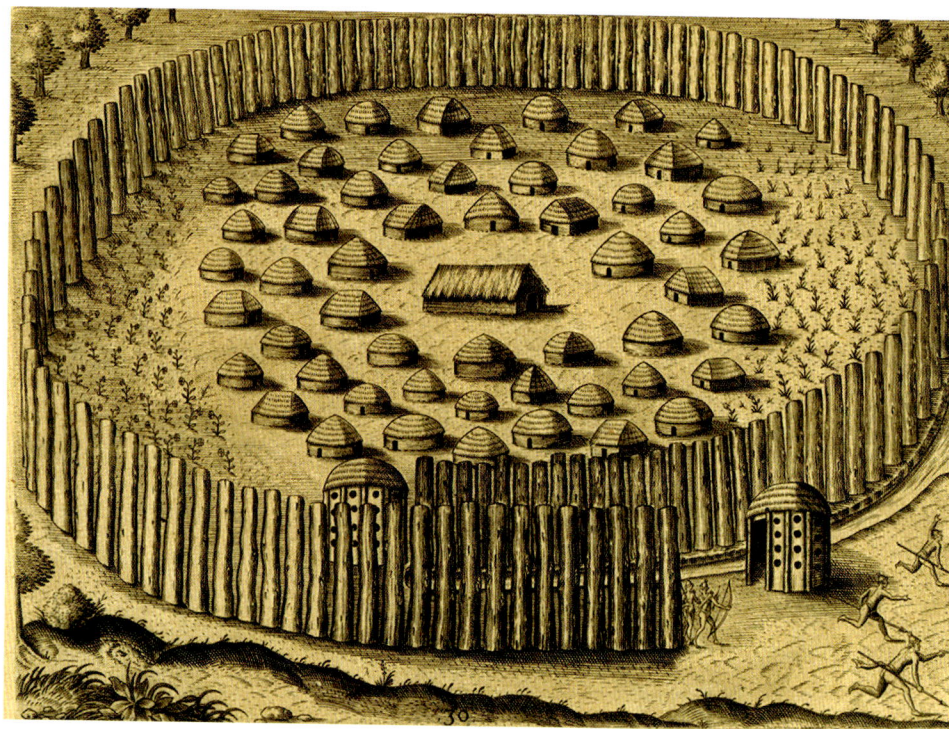

holly] drink make the round of the assembled warriors. They were adept in the art of manufacturing fans, hats and other tissues from palmetto leaves and also moulded large earthen vessels in which water was carried."

An obvious question anyone living in or visiting South Georgia might ask is how the Timucua slept with mosquitoes, horse flies, wasps, and other biting insects prevalent at certain times of the year. Two things keep mosquitoes at bay: wind and smoke. Several writers offer insights into ingenious methods, including smudge fires, the Timucua employed to sleep unmolested by these pests. "They are often bothered by little flies," wrote one observer, "which they call in their language *maringous*, and it is usually necessary for them to make fires in their houses, absolutely under their beds, in order to be freed of these vermin; and they say that they bite severely, and the part of the skin affected by their bite becomes like that of a leper. In the middest of this house is a hearth, where they make great fires all night, and they sleepe upon certain pieces of wood hewn in for the bowing of their backs, and another place made high for their heads, which they put one by another all along the walles on both sides."

Social Structure and Councils

Timucua chiefdoms were organized into hierarchies based on matrilineal descent—that is, kinship to the mother or the maternal line of the high-ranking clan. When a male chief died, his oldest nephew from his eldest sister of the same clan (not his own son) became the next chief. Both male and female chiefs came from the White Deer clan. Pareja's notes on Timucuan lineages shed light on a layered, aristocratic tribal social organization: "I begin with the pedigrees of the upper chiefs and their progeny," Pareja wrote. "The upper chiefs (*caciques*), to whom other chiefs are subject, are called *ano parucusi holata ico* (or *olato aco* or *utinama*). From this class comes a councilor who leads the chief by the hand and whose title is *inihama*. From him comes another class, that of the *anacotima*. The *cacique* seeks the advice of these second councilors when he does not require that of the *inihama*." Several more castes, "held in high consideration," descended from the *inihama* and did not intermarry. "Of a further line derived from the upper chief all members call and consider each other as 'nephews.' This is the line of the White Deer, *honoso nayo*. In the provinces of the 'Fresh Water' and Potano, all of these lineages emanating from the chief are termed people of the Great Deer, *quibiro ano*. Families sprung from former chiefs are *oyorano fiyo chuluquita oconi*, or simply *oyolano*. The lower pedigrees of the common people are the 'Dirt (or Earth) pedigree,' *utihasomi enatiqi*; the Fish pedigree, *cuyuhasomi*, and its progeny. Another strange lineage is that of the Buzzard, *apohola*. Still another pedigree is that of the *chulufichi*; from it is derived the *arahasomi* or Bear pedigree. From the acheha derives itself the Lion family or *hiyaraba*, the Partridge line or *cayahasomi*, and others. In some districts these lineages are of low degree, while in others they rank among the first."

Native chiefs relied on their councilors (the *inihama* and *anacotima*) for advice, assembling on certain mornings of the year, Laudonnière tells us, "in a great common house, whither their king repaireth and setteth down upon a seat, which is higher than the seats of the others where all of them, one after another, come and salute him, and the most ancient begin their solemn salutations, lifting up both their hands twice as high as their face, saying, '*Ha he ha!* And the rest answer, '*Ah ah!* As soon as they have done their salutation every man sitteth down upon the seats, which are round about in the house. If there be anything to entreat of, the king calleth the *lawas* [or *laüas*], that is to say their priests and the most ancient men, and asketh for their advice. Afterward, he commandeth cassine to be brewed, which is a drink made of the leaves of a certain tree. They drink this cassine very hot; he drinketh first, then he causeth to be given thereof

Timucuan Language

Pareja's translation of the Timucua language provides some insight into kinship relations, which were essential in the community: *Chirico viro* and *chirico nia* (terms used by a mother or father speaking of their son or daughter, respectively). *Ahono viro misoma* (my elder son). *Ahono nia misoma* (my elder daughter). *Ahono viro pacanoqua* (my intermediate son). *Ahono nia pacanoqua* (my intermediate daughter). *Ahono viro iubuacoli* (my youngest son). *Ahono nia iubuacoli* (my youngest daughter). *Itina* (my father). *Itaye* (your father). *Oqe itimima* (the father of that one). *Ytorina* (my grandfather). *Ytora naribuana* (my great-grandfather). *Ytora muluna* (my great-great-grandfather). *Siqinona* or *nisiqisama* (the one who begot me; name given to the father after his death). *Naribuana* (my old man; name given to father's brother after his death). *Hue sipire* (the second stepfather). *Ysona* (my mother). *Ulena* (my child). *Yacha* (name given to a mother without children or kindred). *Yquinena* (she who gave me milk; name given to one's mother after her death). *Neba* (mother's brother). *Nibe* (father's sister). *Nasi* (son-in-law). *Nubo* (daughter-in-law). *Qiena* (my child; used by men only). *Quisotimi* (name given to third cousins, father's sister's child, or to a stepdaughter or stepson). *Ama* (children of father's sister). *Eqeta* (children of father's sister). *Üti nocoromale* (those who are natives of one country). *Hica nocoromale* (those who are of one town). *Paha nocoromale* (those who are of one house). *Hica nicorobale* (we who are of one town). *Paha niocoralebale* (we who are all of one house). *Ano quela niyahobale* (we are of one lineage, caste, or generation). *Ano quela chichaquene?* (of what lineage are you?). *Ano quelemalema, ano pequatamale* (master and servant, master and vassal).

to all of them one after another in the same bowl, which holdeth well a quart-measure of Paris. This drink hath such a virtue that as soon as they have drunk it, they become all of a sweat."

Le Moyne later adds more details to the elaborate proceedings surrounding all significant issues affecting the community: "They decide upon nothing until they have held a number of councils over it, and they deliberate very sagely before deciding. Meanwhile the chief orders the women to boil some casina, and which they afterwards pass through a strainer. The chief and his councillors being now seated in their places, one stands before him, and spreading forth his hands wide open, asks a blessing upon the chief and the others who are to drink. Those who cannot keep it down, but whose stomachs reject it, are not intrusted with any difficult commission or any military responsibility, being considered unfit, for they often have to go three or four days without food; but one who can drink this liquor can go for twenty-four hours afterwards without eating or drinking. In military expeditions, the only supplies which the hermaphrodites carry consist of gourd bottles or wooden vessels full of this drink [Laudonnière includes parched corn

Council house ceremony. Original oil painting by John LoCastro. (Courtesy of Mission San Luis, Florida, Department of State)

among the provisions]. It strengthens and nourishes the body, and yet does not fly to the head as we have observed on occasion of these feasts of theirs."

From these accounts by Laudonnière and Le Moyne, we learn that Timucua chiefs often relied on the counsel of their leading men, a politically astute approach that empowered others without ceding ultimate power. It is also evident that the close proximity in which the Timucua lived to one another and shared food and drink allowed European-borne diseases to quickly spread throughout the tribe. Lastly, the cassina drink used during celebrations, which caused drunkenness, was not the same concoction as the one distributed at tribal councils or on military expeditions. The potency and ingredients used in this drink likely varied between tribes or even between villages within the same tribe, according to the ceremony being performed.

Though Timucua Natives were bound by a mutually intelligible language, they were never united politically or ethnically, and they didn't consider themselves to be subtribes of a larger, extended group. In fact, they were often at war with one another, forming temporary alliances led by special war chiefs to conduct expeditions against a common foe. More permanent alliances were formed through trade, marriage, and military

Theodor de Bry engraving of a Timucua king assembled with his council of elders and priests to deliberate affairs of importance. (Image courtesy of the State Archives of Florida)

force. Attacks by Native warriors, using clubs, spears, and bows and arrows, have been described as furious. The French and Spanish well understood the ancient maxim that "the enemy of my enemy is my friend," exploiting that knowledge to align themselves with tribal chiefs in territories they wished to control, though maintaining those alliances proved to be difficult at times.

Local Alliances and Warfare

Hernando de Soto and his men are the first Europeans on record to travel through Timucuan territory in Florida. De Soto's route north from Tampa Bay in 1539 placed him at times in the heart of the Timucua before moving northwest to enter what is now Southwest Georgia. On the way he made enemies, made slaves of those who rose up against him, and executed many others. Twenty-three years later, on May 1, 1562, Jean Ribault reached the St. Johns River—which the Natives called Alata—on the eastern edge of the Timucua region, whereupon he named it the Rivière de Mai (River of May).

His intent was to establish a Huguenot colony. The chief on the north bank of the St. Johns met Ribault with gifts and quantities of fish. Ribault next visited Saturiwa, described by one writer of the day as "very old," though de Bry's engravings depict a much younger leader. Saturiwa met the French on the south bank of the St. Johns with caution, perhaps due to previous unrecorded experiences with other Europeans or because of the mistreatment of western Timucuan tribes by de Soto. But the French soon won him over despite having already erected a stone marker on his land.

After less than a week's stay, Ribault then stopped at a Timucua village near present-day St. Marys, which his men visited. Ribault next stopped at an island north of there, possibly Cumberland Island, where he "met another Timucua chief as affable as all the others had been" (Hann). This was probably Chief Tacatacuru. Ribault continued north along the coast where he founded Charlesfort (named for Charles IX of France) on present-day Parris Island, South Carolina.

In 1564, René de Laudonnière, who had accompanied Ribault on the first expedition as second-in-command, sailed up the St. Johns River with three hundred Huguenot colonists fleeing persecution by French Catholics. This time Saturiwa greeted the aliens warmly. Jacques Le Moyne de Morgues, an artist accompanying Laudonnière, would provide much of the early written records of Timucuan customs and culture. He also is credited with producing a series of sketches depicting scenes of Timucuan life, later published by the engraver Theodor de Bry. Jerald Milanich and others have since cast doubt on the accuracy of the de Bry sketches as either modified or created by another artist based on Le Moyne's written accounts. Regardless of their provenance, the sketches can still offer visual clues about Timucuan dress, customs, and events witnessed by the French.

What happened next to the French illustrates the geopolitical maneuverings that began almost immediately on Laudonnière's arrival and the skill with which the indigenous people used the Europeans for their own purposes, just as the French and later Spanish attempted to manipulate the Timucua. Saturiwa presented Laudonnière with a silver ingot, which naturally aroused the Frenchman's curiosity. When he asked about its origin, Saturiwa informed him that the silver as well as quantities of gold had been taken from an ancient enemy, the Thimagona, several days' journey upriver. The word "Timucua" might be derived from "Thimogona" or "Tymangoua" (Milanich). Laudonnière offered to assist Saturiwa on an expedition to fight this enemy, but Laudonnière was more eager to align himself with the Thimagona, whose access to precious metals made them a

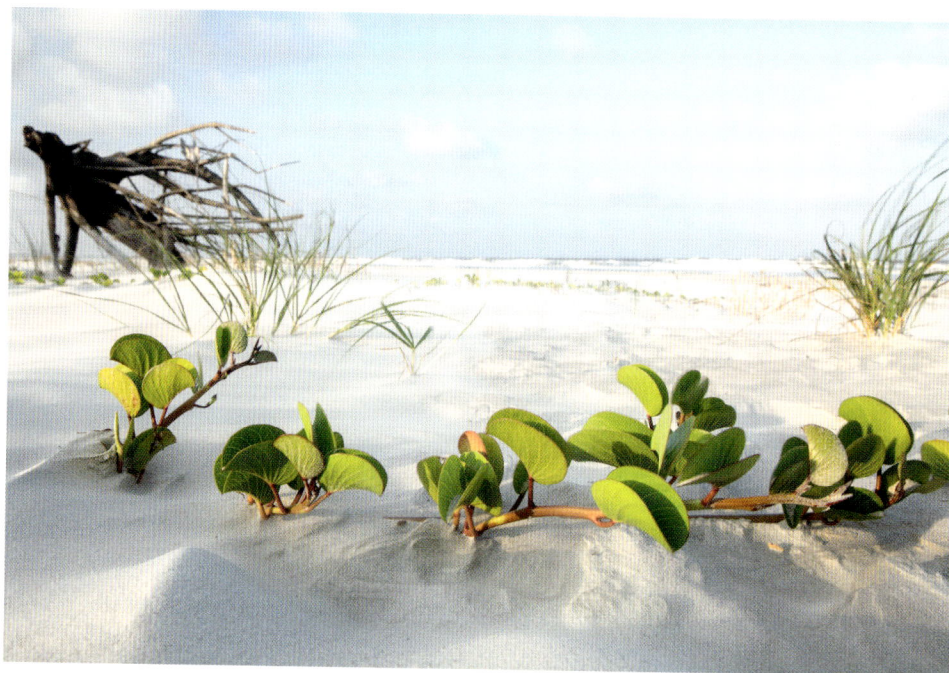

more powerful ally in his eyes. After all, Spain had derived much of its wealth and power from the silver and gold mines of Mexico and South America. Now, the French, led by Laudonnière, envisioned an opportunity to tap into a new source of mineral wealth, one that de Soto had somehow overlooked. That temptation would prove to be the downfall of the French. Instead of forging strong alliances with the various Timucua tribes, Laudonnière played one group off of the other—Saturiwa, the Thimagona, the Potano—in an attempt to secure food and improve his chances of establishing a colony during the first winter without aligning himself with any of the tribes.

After meeting Saturiwa, Laudonnière sailed up to the St. Marys River and then to the Satilla, where he met Chief Tacatacuru, which he described as one of the "tallest and best-proportioned men possible" (Hann). On the Satilla, the French found at the Timucua town of Iracana, a place reputed to have the prettiest women of the region, a number of Native leaders assembled to enjoy themselves. Tacatacuru, accompanied by his beautiful wife and five daughters, made a presentation of his bow and arrows as a sign of loyalty to the French. His wife made presents of small silver balls, which the Europeans took as further evidence that precious metals were prevalent among the Natives.

While Tacatacuru on Cumberland and Saturiwa prepared for war, Laudonnière began erecting Fort Caroline on the south bank of the St. Johns, land that Saturiwa generously set aside for the purpose. Some of the gold Laudonnière sought might have come from North Georgia through trade with other tribes. Most of the gold and silver they saw, however, likely came from Spanish shipwrecks. Tales of vast quantities of gold among the Timucua were just that, fabrications by chiefs maneuvering for French support against their enemies.

Two months after Laudonnière's arrival, Saturiwa sent word that he was ready to attack Paracousi Outina, head chief of the Thimagona, with five hundred warriors. Laudonnière had already formed an alliance with Outina and began to renege on his earlier promise to join Saturiwa's raid. The Outina region covered a section of the St. Johns River, extending west to present-day Clay and Putnam Counties in Florida. Saturiwa, accompanied by Tacatacuru and warriors living on Cumberland Island, proceeded with the expedition. The plan called for five of the chiefs to continue by canoe with half of the men while Saturiwa moved stealthily overland the final eight or ten leagues for a surprise dawn attack.

Ten of the forty-two illustrations attributed to Le Moyne concern warfare, a topic in which the Timucua were well-versed. "A chief who declares war against his enemy does not send a herald to do it," Le Moyne writes, "but orders some arrows, having locks of hairs fastened at the notches, to be stuck up along the public ways." Both Laudonnière and Le Moyne describe the ceremony that took place when Saturiwa along with Tacatacuru went to war with Outina. "When he (Saturiwa) was sitting down by the river's side, being compassed about with ten other paracoussies, he commanded water to be brought him speedily. A fire was lighted on his left and two great vessels full of water were set on his right. This done, looking up into heaven, he fell to discourse of divers [many] things, with gestures that showed him to be in exceeding great choler [anger], which made him shake his head hither and thither, and to turn his face toward the country of his enemies and threaten to kill them. Then the chief, after rolling his eyes as if excited by anger, uttering some sounds deep down in his throat and making various gestures, all at once raised a horrid yell, and all his soldiers repeated this yell, striking their hips and rattling their weapons. He cried out thrice, 'He Thimogona!' And which was followed with five hundred Indians which cried, all with one voice, 'He Thimagona!' He oftentimes looks upon the sun, praying to grant him a glorious victory of his enemies; which, when he had done, by the space of half an hour, he sprinkled with his hand a little of the water, which he held in a vessel, upon the heads of the paracoussies, and cast the rest in a rage and despite [contempt] into a fire and added, 'As I have done with this water, so I pray that you may do with the blood of your enemies.' Then he poured the water in the other vase upon the fire and said, 'So may you be able to extinguish your enemies and bring back their scalps,' which is the only and chief triumph of their victories."

Laudonnière writes that the Timucua who went to war painted their faces red or black "and [stuck] their hair full of feathers, or down, that they may seem more terrible." Le Moyne adds they were "in the habit of painting the skin around their mouths a blue color." They covered their bodies with bear grease for ceremonial reasons and for protection from the sun's heat and biting insects, according to Laudonnière.

When Tacatacuru, Saturiwa, and their men went to battle, they "preserved no order but went along one after another," Le Moyne recorded. "On the contrary his enemy, Holata Outina, whose name means 'king of many kings' and who was much more powerful as regards both wealth and number of his subjects, used to march with regular ranks, like an organized army, himself marching alone in the middle of the whole force, painted red."

Tacatacuru's young men ran ahead "on the wings [periphery] or horns of his order of march," acting as advanced scouts. "These are able to follow up the traces of the enemy by scent as dogs do wild beasts; and when they come upon such traces they immediately return to the army to report." Instead of using trumpets or drums to direct troops, as the French did, Tacatacuru used heralds, "who by cries of certain sorts direct them to halt or to advance or to attack or to perform any other military duty." The Timucua didn't usually engage in battle after sunset. Instead, Tacatacuru's men encamped in squads of ten, "the bravest men being put in squads by themselves. When the chief has chosen the place of encampment for the night in open fields or woods, and after he has eaten and is established by himself, the quartermasters place ten of these squads of the bravest men in a circle around him. About ten paces outside of this circle is placed another line of twenty squads; at twenty yards further, another forty squads, and so on, increasing the number and distance of these lines, according to the size of the army."

Timucua combat tactics were described by another writer clearly impressed with their success: "The Indians are exceedingly ready with their weapons and so warlike and nimble that they have no fear of footmen; for if these charge them they flee, and when they [the enemy] turn their backs they are presently upon them. They avoid nothing more easily than the flight of an arrow. They never remain quiet but are continually running, traversing from place to place so that neither crossbow or arquebuse [arquebus, a long gun or musket] can be aimed at them. Before a Christian can make a single shot with either,

Theodor de Bry engraving of Chief Saturiwa performing ceremonies prior to an expedition against an enemy. (Image courtesy of the State Archives of Florida)

Theodor de Bry engraving of Chief Outina with his army on a military expedition. (Image courtesy of the State Archives of Florida)

Wood and iron smoothbore matchlock arquebus, approximately .75 caliber. Inlaid bone decoration. German, 16th century. Purchased from an antique dealer in the 1950s, not original to the site. (Courtesy of National Park Service Photo/Darryl Herring)

an Indian will discharge three or four arrows, and he seldom misses his object. Where the arrow meets with no armor, it pierces as deeply as the shaft from a crossbow."

As one chronicler asserts, "Their bows are very perfect. The arrows are made of certain canes, like reeds, very heavy, and so stiff that one of them, when sharpened, will pass through a target. When they strike upon armor, break at the place the parts are put together; those of cane split and will enter a shirt of mail." Quivers were made of skins, but the men often used their hair to hold arrows. "It is wonderful how suddenly they take them into their hands in order to shoot at a distance and as straight as possible."

Le Moyne and the other French chroniclers depict Native battles as quite different from traditional European conflicts. Le Moyne was writing from firsthand experience, having joined the expedition against Outina and received a leg wound. "All their military operations consisted either in secret excursions," he writes, "or in skirmishes as light troops, fresh men being constantly sent out in place of any who retired. Whichever side first slew an enemy, no matter how insignificant the person, claimed the victory, even though losing a great number of men. Any who fall are instantly dragged off by persons detailed for the purpose who, with slips of reeds sharper than any steel blade, cut the skin of the head to the bone. Then, if they have time, the[y] dig a hole in the ground and make a fire, kindling it with some [embers] which they keep burning in moss done up in skins and carry around with them at their belts, and then dry these scalps to a state as hard as parchment. They are also accustomed after battle to cut off with these reed knives the arms of the dead near the shoulders, and their legs near the hips, breaking the bones when laid bare, with a club, and then to lay these fresh broken and still running with blood, over the same fires to be dried. Then hanging them and the scalps also to the

Theodor de Bry engraving of a sorcerer leading a postbattle victory celebration. (Image courtesy of the State Archives of Florida)

ends of their spears, they carry them home in triumph. They never left the field of battle without shooting an arrow as deep as they could into the arms of each of the corpses of the enemy."

The returning warriors participated in postbattle ceremonies, assembling "in a place set apart for the purpose to which they bring the legs, arms, and scalps which they have taken from the enemy, and with solemn formalities fix them up on tall poles set in the ground in a row. Then they all, men and women, sit down on the ground in a circle before these members while the sorcerer [shaman], holding a small image in his hand, goes through a form of cursing the enemy, uttering in a low voice a thousand imprecations. At the side of the circle opposite him there are placed three men kneeling down, one of whom holds in both hands a club with which he pounds on a flat stone, marking time to every word of the sorcerer. At each side of him the other two hold in each hand the fruit of a certain plant, something like a gourd or pumpkin, which has been dried, opened at each end, its marrow and seeds taken out, and then mounted on a stick and charged [filled] with small stones or seeds. These they rattle after the fashion of a bell, accompanying the words of the sorcerer with a kind of song after their manner. They have such a celebration as this every time they take any of the enemy."

Laudonnière adds that the victors "assemble all their subjects, and for joy, three days and three nights, they make good cheer, they dance and sing; likewise, they make the most ancient women of the country to dance, holding the hairs of their enemies in their hands, and in dancing they sing praises to the sun, ascribing unto him the honor of the victory."

Tacatacuru's and Saturiwa's warriors invaded the Thimagona town and captured twenty-four prisoners, after which they "retired themselves immediately to their boats," Laudonnière wrote, "and began to sing praises unto the Sun, to whom they attributed their victory. And afterwards they put the skins [scalps] on the ends of their javelins. They divided their prisoners equally to each of the paracoussies [allied chiefs] and left thirteen of them to Saturiwa, which straight away dispatched an Indian to carry news before of the victory to them which stayed at home to guard their houses, which immediately began to weep [perhaps out of joy or relief]. But as soon as night was come, they never left dancing and playing a thousand gambols in honor of the feast. The next day the Paracoussy Saturiwa came home, who, before he entered into his lodging, caused all the scalps of his enemies to be set up before his door, and crowned them with branches of laurel, showing by this glorious spectacle the triumph of the victory which he had obtained. Straightaway began lamentation and mourning [the chroniclers don't explain the reason for this ritual], which as soon as the night began were turned into pleasures and dances." Swanton writes that prisoners were often tortured to death, but Laudonnière convinced Saturiwa to return his captives to Chief Outina. Saturiwa complied to maintain good relations with the French, and he continued to supply the inhabitants of Fort Caroline with maize and other foodstuffs, though at times all he could provide was fish.

Laudonnière's relations with Outina soon soured, and he took the chief as a prisoner in exchange for food. That only compounded problems as the Thimagona simply installed a new chief, one of Outina's infant children, and enemy tribes offered to supply the French with food in exchange for executing Outina. With supplies running low, some French colonists seized a ship and turned to pirating in the Gulf of Mexico. Matters deteriorated to the point that Laudonnière was on the verge of abandoning Florida altogether when Jean Ribault returned in August 1565 with reinforcements and orders to assume command of the colony. He offered Laudonnière a coregency over the colony, which was rejected.

Marriage, Mourning, and Burial Ceremonies

Community members holding principal positions, including chiefs and their wives, were carried in litters for certain ceremonies and occasions of state. Le Moyne describes one such event in which a woman sitting on a raised seat covered with a decorated skin was borne on the shoulders of four men and protected from the sun by an arrangement of green foliage. Two men blowing on reed flutes marched before them. Two more men carrying large feather fans attached to long poles walked alongside each side of the litter, presumably to cool the woman and keep away flying insects. The litter bearers carried "crotched" sticks in one hand, which were stuck into the ground when they halted. The litter handles fit into the crotches.

Le Moyne describes the elaborate ceremony in which marriage to a chief was consummated: "When a king choose to take a wife, he directs the tallest and handsomest of the daughters of the chief men to be selected. Then a seat is made on two stout poles and covered with the skin of some rare sort of animal, while it is set off with a structure of boughs, bending over forward so as to shade the head of the sitter. The queen elect having been placed on this, four strong men take up the poles and support them on their shoulders, each carrying in one hand a forked wooden stick to support the pole at halting. Two more walk at the sides, each carrying on a staff a round screen elegantly made to protect the queen from the sun's rays. Others go before blowing upon trumpet made of bark, which are smaller above and larger at the farther end and having only two orifices, one at each end. They are hung with small oval balls of gold, silver, or brass, for the sake of a finer combination of sounds. Behind follow the most beautiful girls that can be found, elegantly decorated with necklaces and armlets of pearls, each carrying in her hand a basket full of choice fruits and belted below the navel and down to the thighs with the moss of certain trees, to cover their nakedness. After them come the bodyguards.

"With this display the queen is brought to the king in a place arranged for the purpose where a good-sized platform is built up of round logs, having on either side a long bench where the chief men are seated. The king sits on the platform on the right-hand side. The queen, who is placed on the left, is congratulated by him on her accession and told why he chose her for his first wife. She, with a certain modest majesty, and holding her fan in her hand, answers with as good a grace as she can. Then the young women form a circle without joining hands and with a costume differing from the usual one, for their hair is tied at the back of the neck and then left to flow over the shoulders and back; and they wear a broad girdle below the navel, having in front something like a purse, which hangs down so as to cover their nudity. To the rest of this girdle are hung ovals of gold and silver, coming down upon the thighs, so as to tinkle when they dance, while at the same time they chant the praises of the king and queen. In this dance they all raise and lower their hands together."

Wives whose husbands succumbed to disease or died in battle took part in another ceremony as explained by Le Moyne. "The wives are accustomed to get together on some day which they find convenient for approaching the chief. They come before him with great weeping and outcry, sit down on their heels, hide their faces in their hands, and with much clamor and lamentation require of the chief permission to marry again at the end of the time appointed by the law. The chief, sympathizing with them, assents, and they go home weeping and lamenting, so as to show the strength of their love for the deceased. After some days spent in this mourning they proceed to the graves of their husbands, carrying the weapons and drinking cups of the dead, and there they mourn for them again and perform other feminine ceremonies. After coming to the graves of their husbands they cut off their hair below the ears and scatter it upon the graves, and then cast upon them the weapon and drinking shells of the deceased as memorials of brave men. This done they return home but are not allowed to marry again until hair has grown long enough to cover their shoulders."

"Polygamy is permitted among them," writes Laudonnière, "yet few have more than one wife at a time, possibly on account of the expense of supporting them, for he is accounted a good [huntsman] that provides well for one. It is common with them, however, to repudiate their wives, if disobliged by them or tired of them. The rejected woman, if with child, generally revenges herself for the affront by taking herbs to procure an abortion—an operation that destroys many of them, and greatly contributes to depopulate them."

"When a king dieth," writes Laudonnière, "they bury him very solemnly and upon his grave they set the cup wherein he was wont to drink, and round about the said grave they stick many arrows and weep and fast three days together without ceasing. All the kings which were his friends make the like mourning, and in token of the love which they bear him, they cut off more than one-half of their hair, as well men as women. During the space of six moons (so they reckon their months), there are certain women appointed which bewail the death of this king, crying with a loud voice thrice a day; in the morning, at noon, and at evening. All the goods of this king are put into his house, and afterwards they set it on fire so that nothing is ever more after to be seen. The like

Theodor de Bry engraving of women whose husbands have died in battle or from illness. They sit, weeping before their chief, asking him to avenge their husbands' deaths, to provide for them in their widowhood, and to permit them to remarry. (Image courtesy of the State Archives of Florida)

is done with the goods of their priests, and they bury the bodies of their priests in their houses, and then set them on fire."

Gatschet adds that on the death of a *holata*, or chief, "a thorough abstention from food was ordered for three days; the deceased was buried ceremoniously, on the top of a terrace-mound, a smaller mound erected over his grave, and a large conch or marine shell, which had been his drinking cup, placed over this monticule [mound]. The conch was then surrounded by a circle of arrows stuck perpendicularly into the soil, at two-or-three feet distance from the conch."

Transsexuals or "two spirits"—tribe members who assumed the dress, social status, and role of the opposite sex, carried heavy loads for the tribe, and brought food to the storehouses—were acknowledged by the community as having a special role in ceremonial tasks. Le Moyne incorrectly refers to them as hermaphrodites—persons who have both male and female sex organs or other sexual characteristics. "Hermaphrodites," he

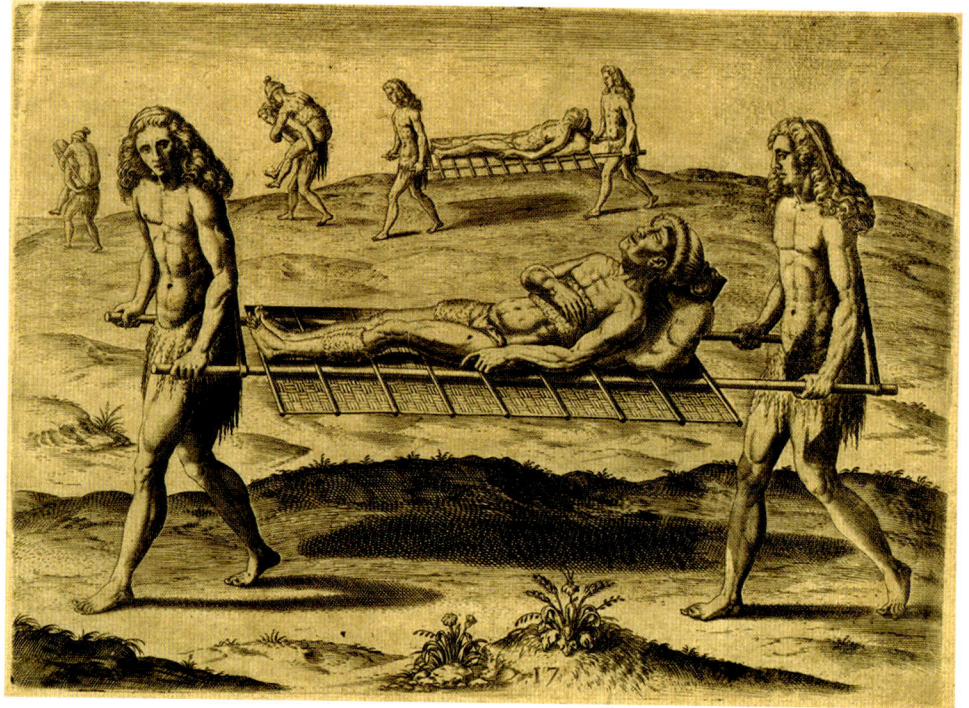

Theodor de Bry engraving of transsexuals transporting wounded warriors. Stretchers were made of two stout poles covered with a mat of woven canes. (Image courtesy of the State Archives of Florida)

writes, "partaking in the nature of each sex, are quite common in these parts and are considered odious by the Indians themselves, who, however employ them as they are strong, instead of beasts of burden. When a chief goes out to war the hermaphrodites carry the provisions," which included a potent concoction of *cacina*. Its nicotine effect sustained warriors for up to two days without food. "When any Indian is dead of wounds or disease, two hermaphrodites take a couple of stout poles, fasten cross-pieces on them, and attach to these a mat woven of reeds. On this they place the deceased with a skin [animal skin] under his head, a second bound around his body, a third around one thigh, a fourth around one leg. Why these are so used I did not ascertain, but I imagine by way of ornament as in some cases they put the skin on one leg only. Then they take thongs of hide, three or four fingers broad, fasten the ends to the ends of the poles, and put the middle over their heads, which are remarkably hard and in this manner they carry the deceased to the place of burial. Persons having contagious diseases are also carried to places appointed for the purpose on the shoulders of the hermaphrodites who supply them with food and take care of them until they get quite well again." Another source notes that hermaphrodites "were specialized workers of the charnel house industry. They helped with initial preparation and burial of dead bodies and then with reburial preparation of bodies as they were reburied years later. Such duties included scraping flesh from bone and rearticulating bones."

Healers

Conjurers or shamans (also called wizards) served a number of functions in Timucua society, including that of priest and doctor. They derived their power from knowledge of medicinal plant properties and the mysterious black arts (which Europeans attributed to devil worship), coupled with an impressive use of theatrics. Laudonnière writes: "They have their priests to whom they give great credit because they are great magicians, great soothsayers, and callers upon devils. These priests serve them instead of physicians and surgeons; they carry always about with them a bag full of herbs and drugs to cure the sick who, for the most part, are sick with the pox [a disease, like syphilis, that leaves skin lesions]." Ribault mentions the Natives gave him "roots like rinbabe [rhubarb], which they hold in great estimation and make use of for medicine."

Le Moyne sketched a ceremony he saw a shaman perform to foretell the outcome of a pending battle. Both he and Laudonnière attest that the predictions came true. "The sorcerer made ready a place in the middle of the army and seeing the shield which [a Frenchman's page] was carrying, asked to take it. On receiving it, he laid it on the ground and drew around it a circle upon which he inscribed various characters and signs. Then he knelt down on the shield and sat on his heels so that no part of him touched the earth and began to recite some unknown words in a low tone and to make various gestures as if engaged in a vehement discourse. This lasted for a quarter of an hour, when he began to assume an appearance so frightful that he was hardly like a human being; for he twisted his limbs so that the bones could be heard to snap out of place, and did many other unnatural things. After going through with all this he came back all at once to his ordinary condition, but in a very fatigued state, and with an air as if astonished; and then, stepping out of his circle, he saluted the chief and told him the number of the enemy and where they were intending to meet him."

Le Moyne describes the shaman's methods of caring for sick patients, such as by bloodletting, a practice employed by European doctors in the medieval to early modern

Theodor de Bry engraving of Chief
Outina consulting a sorcerer before battle.
(Image courtesy of the State Archives of
Florida)

eras. "Their way of curing diseases is as follows: They put up a bench or platform of
sufficient length and breadth for the patient and lay the sick person upon it with his
face up or down, according to the nature of his complaint, and cutting into the skin
of the forehead with a sharp shell, they suck out blood with their mouths and spit it
into an earthen vessel or a gourd bottle. Women who are suckling boys or who are with
child come and drink this blood, particularly if it is that of a strong young man as it is
expected to make their milk better and to render the children who have the benefit of
it bolder and more energetic. For those who are laid on their faces they prepare fumiga-
tions by throwing certain seeds on hot coals; the smoke being made to pass through the
nose and mouth into all parts of the body and thus to act as an emetic, or to overcome
and expel the cause of the disease. They have a certain plant, whose name has escaped
me, which the Brazilians call *petum* (*petun*) and the Spaniards *tapaco* [tobacco]. The
leaves of this, carefully dried, they place in the wider part of a pipe and setting them on
fire and putting the other end in their mouths they inhale the smoke so strongly that it

comes out at their mouths and noses and operates powerfully to expel the humors. In particular they [the Timucua] are extremely subject to the venereal diseases, for curing which they have remedies of their own, supplied by nature."

A Timucua shaman was not above injuring someone or using "the skin of a viper and that of a black snake, along with part of the black guano (a kind of palm tree) and other herbs" to cause that person to die. The shaman would not "eat fish, cut his hair, or sleep with his wife" until the victim was dead. If he did not die, the shaman's incantations might "react on the wizard himself and kill him." Witchcraft might also be used to attract a lover by use of certain songs and by placing (it is not recorded how) an herb into the intended's mouth. Lastly, a woman might fast or bathe in certain herbs to win back her husband's affections.

Belief System

In addition to ceremonies, the French and Spanish observed what they considered to be superstitious behavior on the part of the Timucua, but the surviving documents do not suggest a genuine curiosity about or an understanding of the Natives' belief system—unsurprising, given that the Spanish clergy, at least, were in the New World to convert the Natives. What survive are scattered descriptions from their Roman Catholic or Huguenot perspectives.

From Pareja's catechism we learn that warriors bathed in herbs before setting out on an expedition, that chiefs could exact tribute and labor from their people, and that as punishment they sometimes had the arms of laborers broken, perhaps for theft or indolence. We also learn that the presence of certain animals, a red owl or a snake, were omens that portended misfortune. A lightning strike or a crackling fire might be a sign of impending war. Belching could be a sign either of abundant food or death. Body tremblings and twitches could be an indication of an approaching visitor. Trembling eyes portended sorry and weeping. If someone's mouth twitched, it might mean people were talking about him, or a feast would soon take place, or he could experience adversity. Food taboos were common, as Swanton informs us: "The first acorns or fruits gathered were not eaten. The corn in a cornfield where lightning had struck was not eaten, nor the first ripened corn. The first fish caught in a new fish weir was not eaten, but laid down beside it so that a great quantity of fish would come into it with the next tide. When a man fell ill a new fire for his cooking was made and a new house was built, perhaps as a temporary structure to

Great horned owl effigy carved by Native Americans from the heart of a southern yellow pine. Unique human eye inside bird's eye. Carbon dated to AD 1300. Found in St. Johns River near Hontoon Island in 1955. (Courtesy of National Park Service Photo/Darryl Herring)

protect his main dwelling, since it was customary to burn the houses of chiefs and shamans upon their deaths. Some people who became ill attributed it to witchcraft and used herbs to counter whatever magic was being used against them."

Laudonnière informs us that a pregnant woman lived in a house separate from her husband, and men "would not eat food touched by a menstruant woman." Of marriage he writes that "every [man] hath his wife, and it is lawful for the king to have two or three, yet none but the first [wife] is honored and acknowledged for queen, and none but the children of the first wife inherit the goods and authority of the father." Laudonnière was likely misinformed on this last point. As both Hann and Milanich point out, the Timucua were matrilineal, so heirs to a chief would have been his eldest sister's children. If they were too young to rule, the mantle might pass to the deceased chief's brother.

The Timucua's celestial objects of deification were the sun and moon. Le Moyne recounts an annual rite performed by Chief Outina, whose "subjects were accustomed every year, a little before their spring—that is, in the end of February—to take the skin of the largest stag they could get, keeping the horns on it; to stuff it full of all the choicest sorts of roots that grow among them, and to hang long wreaths or garlands of the best fruits on the horns, neck, and other parts of the body. Thus decorated, they carried it, with music and songs, to a very large and splendid level space, where they set it up on a very high tree with the head and breast toward the sunrise. They then offered prayers to the sun, that he would cause to grow on their lands good things such as those offered him. The chief, with his sorcerer, stands nearest the tree and offers the prayer; the common people, placed at a distance, make responses. Then the chief and all the rest, saluting the sun, depart, leaving the deer's hide there until the next year."

The types of ceremonies and the manner in which they were carried out varied from tribe to tribe. Pareja writes about "the ceremony of the laurel," a ritual he claims was "performed to serve the Demon." Manmade objects, like the stone column erected by Ribault in 1562, were also revered. Ribault may have borrowed the practice of placing stone markers from the Portuguese, who marked territory on Africa's west coast in this manner. Laudonnière found the stone three years afterward topped with "crowns of bay and at the foot thereof many little baskets full of mill [corn], which they call in their language *tapaga tapola*. Then, when they came hither, they kissed the same with great reverence and besought us to do the like."

Le Moyne, as usual, is more descriptive in his account and notes that even the chief, the main object of reverence among his subjects, bowed before the stone: "On approaching they [the French] found that these Indians were worshipping this stone as an idol;

Pareja's Catechism

Franciscan missionaries who couldn't speak Timucuan used Father Pareja's Catechism—a bilingual confessional consisting of a series of fixed yes-no questions—to question non-Spanish-speaking Timucuan natives. The questions reveal a probing of the intimate relationships and certain religious beliefs and rites, such as Devil worship, practiced by the Timucuans.

Did you forbid to eat of the new maize or other new fruit, before the conjurer [shaman] had tasted it? Did you consent to your slaves sleeping together? Did you cause any conjurer to search by diabolic arts for something stolen or lost? Did you desire the chief's death to succeed him? The ceremony of the laurel, performed to serve the Demon, did you perform it? Did you order laborers to be punished so as to have their arms broken, not for the sake of work, but for being angry? When somebody was crazed, did you believe his words would become true? Did you believe that it was a sign of somebody's arrival, or that something new would happen, when a jay was chattering to another bird? Did you believe that by making a new fire in a separate pot, the sick would recover? When a woman was in travail, did you think it sinful to approach a fire just burning? [*The Timucuans used fire as a symbol of purity.*] When flooding a new fish-pond, did you desire that the conjurers pray over it, believing that many more fish will enter it? Did you outrage your consort [*spouse or companion*] by affronting terms, by insults, by scoffing, or by laying hands on? Have you gratified too much the desires of your sons, allowing them their own will without punishment and correction, and leaving them their liberty? Did you permit any married or other person to have sexual intercourse in your house or elsewhere? Did you kiss a woman? How often? How often each woman?

Theodor de Bry engraving depicting Athore, son of Saturiwa, showing René de Laudonnière the stone monument placed by Ribault. (Image courtesy of the State Archives of Florida)

Native Beliefs and Practices

As in most cultures, the Timucua had folk beliefs and religious practices, though it can't be known whether everyone in the society believed them or whether they were always practiced as described by observers. Swanton enumerates some of these practices. For instance, relatives would not eat corn sown by the deceased or from the field in which it had been sown. Relatives bathed after a funeral and refrained from eating fish for a period of time. Prayer, or a formula—a set form of words used during a ritual or ceremony— was repeated by the shaman for the first corn, the first flour, the first wild fruits, and for the first chestnuts and palmetto berries of the season. Deer hunters brought the antlers of other deer and repeated formulae over them. Arrows were laid on the ground before a hunt while the shaman repeated formulae over them, and it was customary for the shaman to receive the first deer taken. Similarly, fishing expeditions were preceded by a shaman repeating formulae and once again after the fish were caught. It was also customary for the shaman to receive half the fish, though the first fish caught were smoked and placed in a storehouse. Formulae were spoken prior to turtle hunts. Some believed no more game would be killed in a hunt if the lungs and liver of a slain animal were thrown into cold water for cooking. A hunter who merely wounded his prey repeated a formula over the next arrow so that it would inflict the mortal wound. Bones of animals captured in a snare or trap were hung from the roofs of houses in the belief that animals would not enter the snare or trap again if the ceremony were omitted. No more fish or eels would enter a man's fish weir if he inspected it immediately after having intercourse with his wife. A woman would not eat fish or venison during her monthly period, and she must also not make a new fire while she was menstruating. A woman was not to eat fish or anoint herself with bear grease for several months after giving birth. Gamblers rubbed their hands with herbs for good luck. Runners took herbs in the form of a drink to ensure victory.

and the chief himself, having saluted it with signs of reverence such as his subjects were in the habit of showing to himself, kissed it. His men followed his example, and we were invited to do the same. Before the monument [there] lay various offerings of the fruits and edible or medicinal roots, growing thereabouts; vessels of perfumed oils, a bow and arrows, and it was wreathed around from top to bottom with flowers of all sorts, and boughs of the trees esteemed choicest."

Work and Play

Deerskins, sometimes painted with images of animals, were prepared, "not with iron instruments, but with shells, in a surprisingly excellent manner; indeed I do not believe that any European could do it as well," Le Moyne writes. Ribault says the Natives used "certain stones, oyster shells, and mussels" to make "spades and mattocks [similar to a pickax]," bows and arrows, and short lances. Natives captured by de Soto's army were

Photograph of archaeologists uncovering dugout canoe on Cumberland Island (ca. 1930?). (Courtesy of the Cumberland Island National Seashore Museum NPS, Mary Bullard Collection)

Photograph of dugout canoe remains. (Courtesy of the Cumberland Island National Seashore Museum NPS)

Dugout canoe. (Courtesy of National Park Service Photo/Darryl Herring)

Theodor de Bry engraving of Timucua men tilling the soil with hoes made of shells or fish bones, and women, preceded by a worker with a pole to create a hole, sowing grain, bean, or millet seeds. (Image courtesy of the State Archives of Florida)

Theodor de Bry engraving of Natives in a dugout canoe depositing crops in a public storehouse. (Image courtesy of the State Archives of Florida)

known to have filed through their irons at night "with a splinter of stone," indicating they had the means to cut through very hard substances.

The Timucua used stone axes to clear land for planting crops and may have used controlled burns to clear forest undergrowth, still a common forestry management practice today. Canoes were made by hand from single cypress or pine tree trunks using fire to burn away the interior wood and axes to hollow out the remainder. Some were large enough to carry up to twenty men, who, Ribault contends, stood while paddling. Le Moyne illustrates rowers using short paddles with wide blades.

Dogs were the only domesticated animals recorded by missionaries and early European explorers and do not seem to have been used as beasts of burden. Their contribution to the community may have been as watchdogs. However, a letter from de Soto suggested turkey and deer domestication as well. One of Laudonnière's lieutenants reported that a chief presented him with two young eagles reared in his house.

The Apalachee ball game, similar to one played by the Timucua, held much religious and social significance and was an integral

Laudonnière writes about youthful pastimes: "They exercise their young men to run well, and they make a game among themselves which he winneth that hath the longest breath [can go the longest without stopping]. They also exercise themselves much in shooting. They play at the ball in this manner: They set up a tree in the midst of a place, which is eight or nine fathoms high [about 50 feet], in the top whereof there is set a square mat made of reeds or bulrushes, which whosoever hitteth in playing thereat winneth the game." Foot races were sometimes fixed with the use of herbs that could cause a rival runner to faint. Men played a game called chunkey in which the contestants used spears to move a flat stone disk across a field.

Food Provisioning

The Timucua were skilled hunters, but they also relied on fishing and agriculture.

Le Moyne says of deer hunting that "they manage to put on the skins of the largest [deer] which had been taken with the [deer] heads on their own heads, so that they can see out through the eyes as through a mask. Thus accoutered they can approach close to the deer without frightening them. They take advantage of the time when the animals come to drink at the river, and, having their bow and arrows all ready, easily shoot them, as they are plentiful in those regions."

Laudonnière describes the construction of their bows and arrows: "They make the string of their bow from the gut of the stag or of a stag's skin, which they know how to dress as well as any man in France, and with as different sorts of colors. They head their arrows with the teeth of fishes, which they work very finely and handsomely." Another writer describes arrow heads made of "vipers teeth, bones of fishes, flint stones, piked points of knives, gotten of the French men. Some of them have their heads of silver."

Timucua fishing methods included spearing fish from a boat and the use of weirs, "built in the water with great reeds," according to Ribault, "so well and cunningly set together after the fashion of a labyrinth, with many turns and crooks, which it was impossible to construct without much skill and industry." One Spanish writer notes the Timucua on San Pedro (Cumberland Island) "sustained themselves the greater part of the year on shellfish, acorns, and roots." French and Spanish observers listed the types of fish and shellfish in the Timucua diet, which included trout, mullet, "turbots" [possibly grouper], crab, lobster, and crawfish. The Natives saved fish grease to spread on food much as other cultures use butter. Le Moyne details how turtles and alligators were

Theodor de Bry engraving of Native hunters covered in the skins of large stags, stalking prey. (Image courtesy of the State Archives of Florida)

hunted: "They put up, near a river, a little hut of cracks and holes, and in this they station a watchman, so that they can see the crocodiles (or alligators) and hear them a good way off; for when driven by hunger they come out of the rivers and crawl about on the islands after prey, and if they find none they make such a frightful noise that it can be heard for half a mile. Then the watchman calls the rest of the watch who are in readiness, and taking a portion, ten or twelve feet long, of the stem of a tree, they go out to find the monster, who is crawling along with his mouth wide open, all ready to catch one of them if he can; and with great quickness they push the pole, small end first, as deep as possible down his throat. Then they turn the crocodile over on its back, and with clubs and arrows pound and pierce his belly, which is softer; for his back, especially if he is an old one, is impenetrable, being protected by hard scales."

Oysters were an important part of the coastal Timucua diet, especially for those living on barrier islands like Cumberland, where oyster beds were plentiful. The oyster shells were deposited around their villages, leaving large shell middens.

Theodor de Bry engraving of Natives preserving meat with fire and smoke. (Image courtesy of the State Archives of Florida)

The Timucua preserved meat with fire and smoke by constructing a grate mounted on four forked stakes four or five feet off the ground with a slow-burning fire beneath. They placed the game on the grating and let the smoke harden and preserve the meat for future use (a technique not much different than that used to preserve mullet today.) "In this process," Le Moyne adds, "they use a great deal of care to have the drying perfectly performed to prevent the meat from spoiling, as the picture shows. I suppose this stock to be laid in for their winter's supply in the woods, as at that time we could never obtain the least provision from them." The illustration Le Moyne refers to shows fish, deer, an alligator, a small animal the size of a fox, and a snake being smoked over a rack made of wood. It's more likely that the animals were skinned, gutted, and butchered before being smoked.

Corn, the Timucua's major food crop, grew to a height of seven feet with ears a foot long. "They sow their maize twice [a] year—to wit in March and in June—and all in one and the same soil," Laudonnière informs us, allowing the ground to lie fallow the remaining six months, from September through February. However, Le Moyne states the crops were planted later in the year, closer to December. It's possible he observed a crop other than beans or corn being planted that late in the year, for Ribault records other plant foods grown by the Timucua, including gourds, citrons, cucumbers, peas, and many other fruits and roots unknown to us." "They have fine pumpkins, and very good beans," Laudonnière writes. "They never dung [fertilize] their land, only when they would sow they set weeds on fire, which grow up the six months, and burn them all." Modern farming uses the same technique to replenish soil nutrients and rid the area of pests.

"The Indians cultivate the earth diligently," says Le Moyne, "and the men know how to make a kind of hoe from fish bones, which they fit to wooden handles, and with these they prepare the land well enough as the soil is light. When the ground is sufficiently broken up and leveled, the women come with beans and millet, or maize. Some go first with a stick and make holes in which the others place the beans or grains of maize. After planting they leave the fields alone as the winter in that country is pretty cold for about three months, being from the 24th of December to the 15th of March; and during that time, as they go naked, they shelter themselves in the woods. When the winter is over, they return to their homes to wait for their crops to ripen."

Laudonnière says of the harvest that "when the land is to be sowed, the king commandeth one of his men to assemble his subjects every day to labor, during which labor the king causeth store of that drink [cassine] to be made for them. At the time when the maize is gathered, it is all carried into a common house where it is distributed to every man, according to his quality [rank]. They sow no more but that which they think will serve their turn for six months. For during the winter they retire themselves for three or four months in the year into the woods where they make little cottages of palm boughs for their retreat and live there off fish which they take, of disters [oysters], of stags, of turkey cocks, and other beasts which they take," including wildcats, brown bears, lizards, and alligators.

The Natives depended on stored food for survival during colder months, assigning guards to the stores and meting out a harsh penalty for sleeping or inattentive watchmen who allowed granaries to be destroyed by their enemy. Their winter diet also included wild berries, nuts, and herbs. The woods yielded a variety of fruit- and nut-bearing plants—mulberries, raspberries, grapes, pinocks (a small green fruit), chinquapins, acorns—that, in addition to roots, supplemented their diet. When food was scarce, they resorted to eating insects, worms, roots, and dirt or clay. Pareja's catechism reveals they also occasionally ate coal, dirt, broken pottery, fleas, and lice, possibly as remedies for ailments.

The Timucua cooked by boiling, roasting, or broiling over hot coals. The French received from the Natives "grains of maize roasted or ground into flour, or whole ears of it" and "little cakes" the Timucua carried with them when traveling, described as "victual of bread, of honey, and of meal, made of maize, parched in the fire, which they keep without being marred a long while." They also took preserved fish "dressed in smoke" on their excursions away from their towns or villages. Le Challeux describes another use for corn: "The method of using it [corn] is first to rub it and resolve [grind] it into flour; afterward they dissolve it [in water] and make of it porridge [migan], which resembles the rice used in this country; it must be eaten as soon as it is made, because it spoils quickly and can not be kept at all."

Le Moyne informs us that corn, preserved game, and fruits, gathered twice a year, were stored in "roomy low granaries built of stone and earth and roofed thickly with palm-branches and a kind of soft earth fit for the purpose. These granaries are usually erected near some mountain [possibly meaning a mound or hill] or on the bank of some river so as to be out of the sun's rays in order that the contents may keep better." It is not clear if there were separate storehouses for each type of food or separate rooms within a single storehouse. And though the Natives apparently took from the storehouses' food supplies "as need may require without any apprehension of being defrauded," several writers tell us the Natives were less honorable with French articles. "They are, however, the greatest thieves in the world, for they take as well with the foot as with the hand. They steal without conscience and claim all that they can carry away secretly."

Le Moyne writes of animal food storage: "At a set time every year they gather in all sorts of wild animals, fish, and even crocodiles; these are then put in baskets and loaded upon a sufficient number of the curly-haired hermaphrodites, who carry them on their shoulders to the storehouse. This supply, however, they do not resort to unless in case of the last necessity. In such event, in order to preclude any dissension, full notice is given to all interested; for they live in the utmost harmony among themselves. The chief, however, is at liberty to take whatever of this supply he may choose."

The Natives relied on earthen and wooden pots, dishes, pans, gourds, and baskets woven from palm leaves to store food and water. Laudonnière writes of a chief who kept in his house "a great vessel of earth made after a strange fashion, full of fountain water, clear, and very excellent" along with a small dipping or drinking cup made of wood. Shells were also used as drinking vessels. Baskets and mats woven from palm leaves were in common use. Some baskets might have a strap so they could be steadied across the forehead of the bearer.

Le Moyne's description of Natives preparing an ordinary social feast brings to mind the modern Lowcountry boil. "They employ cooks who are chosen on purpose for the business," he writes. "These first of all make a great round earthen vessel, which they know how to make and to burn so that water can be boiled in it as well as in our [metal] kettles, and place it over a large wood fire, which one of them drives with a fan very effectively. The head cook now puts the things to be cooked into the great pot. Another pounds on a stone the aromatics that are to be used for seasoning; while the women are picking over or preparing the viands [food items]."

Hernando de Soto's expedition to Florida in 1539 did not mark the first time a Spaniard visited America's southeast territory. In 1521 Lucas Vázquez de Ayllón, a wealthy sugar planter from Santo Domingo, explored the eastern coast, kidnapping seventy Natives for sale in Hispaniola. Four years later he landed near modern Georgetown, South Carolina, then traveled forty or forty-five leagues by land and boat to establish a colony in either Georgia or South Carolina. The exact location hasn't been substantiated, though contemporary scholars place it on or near Sapelo Island. This enterprise ended after three months of harsh winter, hunger, disease, and conflict with the local Natives. Spain considered all of the territory from modern Florida to Georgia and South Carolina as part of La Florida, which included portions of Alabama, Mississippi, and Louisiana. Other aborted attempts to plant settlements—de Luna and Villafañe at Pensacola and Santa Elena (Parris Island, South Carolina)—forced King Philip II in 1561 to abandon further plans to colonize "inhospitable Florida" (Bolton).

But Spain could not abandon Florida for long. Ribault had sailed onto the St. Johns River in 1562 and claimed the land for France before planting a colony near Port Royal. René de Laudonnière built Fort Caroline on the St. Johns in 1564. The French presence posed a grave threat to Spain's gold- and silver-laden flotillas sailing the Gulf Stream from Havana, as the French in Florida would be the first to reach and salvage Spain's shipwrecked vessels. King Philip had to act.

Two main Spanish institutions oversaw development of the New World colonies. The Casa de Contratacíon (Board of Trade) regulated commerce and emigration, created maps and charts, and trained pilots. The Consejo de Indias (Council of the Indies) directed administrative, legislative, and judicial matters. The council made lists of candidates for leadership positions from which the king selected governors. Philip II chose a Spanish navy captain, Pedro Menéndez de Avilés, as *adelantado fronterizo* (representative of the king stationed on the frontier) and governor of La Florida. Governorships typically ran for six years, with an annual salary of two thousand ducats, part of which came from "produce of the soil." The king sent Menéndez, Spain's ablest seaman, to exterminate the French intruders and colonize the coasts. The new governor landed at St. Augustine in 1565.

CHAPTER II San Pedro

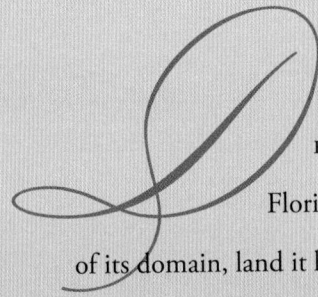

*D*ESPITE THE FRENCH PRESENCE, Spain considered all of
Florida and much of the Georgia and South Carolina coasts as part
of its domain, land it had claimed since de Soto's 1539 expedition. One week after
Ribault's return to Florida in 1565, six Spanish ships under Menéndez's command
anchored at the mouth of the St. Johns River. As *adelantado*, Menéndez was charged
with destroying Fort Caroline and routing the French. After a brief skirmish with
French ships that fled, he retreated farther south and established a settlement near
the Timucua village of Seloy, naming it San Agustín (now St. Augustine) in honor of
Saint Augustine of Hippo. Ribault then set out, against Laudonnière's advice, to attack
the Spanish, leaving behind a lightly guarded Fort Caroline on the St. Johns River. At
the same time, under cover of a hurricane, Menéndez marched his men over land to
the St. Johns River for a surprise attack on the French fort. Laudonnière, half dressed
and with sword in hand, rushed out to rally his men, but the Spaniards overwhelmed
them. Le Moyne was still recovering from the leg wound he had sustained in the campaign against Outina, but he escaped by crawling over dead bodies, leaping into the
ditch surrounding the fort, and then fleeing to the safety of three French ships

anchored nearby. Unfortunately, he left behind the majority of his original sketches depicting the Timucua. The Roman Catholic Spanish hanged most of the remaining Frenchmen from trees with the inscription, "Hanged, not as Frenchmen, but as Lutherans [heretics]."

Menéndez renamed Fort Caroline as San Mateo (now St. Matthew) and returned to St. Augustine. Meanwhile, Ribault and the remainder of the French sailed south to attack St. Augustine but were shipwrecked by the storm farther south of their target. There the consequences of Laudonnière's alienation of Chief Outina and his allies came back to haunt the French with a vengeance. The Thimagona not only refused to ferry the stranded Frenchmen across the inlet, but they informed Menéndez of their whereabouts, resulting in the Spanish massacre of Ribault and 350 of his men at what is now known as Matanzas Inlet (*matanzas* is Spanish for "slaughters"), twenty-six miles south of St. Augustine between modern-day Crescent Beach and Marineland, Florida.

Despite the takeover of a new power, Saturiwa and Tacatacuru, whose first loyalty was to the French, maintained an aloofness toward the Spanish, which Menéndez reciprocated. Memories of de Soto's treatment of the western Timucua may have influenced their thinking. Their opinion of the new Spaniards degraded further when soldiers stationed at San Mateo mistreated Natives living nearby. When the Spaniards killed several Timucuans, including three prominent men, open hostilities with Saturiwa and Tacatacuru began. Saturiwa's warriors had orders to kill any Spaniard who ventured outside the fort for food. Two messengers captured by Saturiwa's men were brought before the chief who ordered their breasts split open and their hearts removed. In time the Timucua would kill a hundred or more of Menéndez's men and set the Spanish settlement at St. Augustine on fire. The typical Spanish response was to raze Timucuan crops, destroy their fish weirs, homes, and storehouses, and deprive them of their canoes, forcing the hostile Natives to relocate farther away or settle for peace.

Decades before California's missions were established and connected by the famous El Camino Real (the Royal Road), Spain had created a network of missions extending west of St. Augustine across northern Florida to what is now the Alabama border. The original El Camino Real in North America connected these Florida missions. The Spanish authorities also established a series of coastal missions on barrier islands at existing Native villages, extending northward from St. Augustine to present-day South Carolina. The historian John Worth used the prevailing seventeenth-century conversion of 2.63 miles per league to determine distances from St. Augustine to outlying missions, allowing him

Pedro Menéndez de Avilés, La Florida's first governor. (Courtesy of the Library of Congress)

Conjectural view of Mission San Luis prior to archaeological investigations at the site. San Pedro on Cumberland Island would have had a similar arrangement of the garrison, mission, and Native village. Illustration by Edward Jonas. (Courtesy of Mission San Luis, Florida Department of State)

Spanish Control

Menéndez treated La Florida as his personal fiefdom. After his death, the territory reverted to royal control with a governor and captain general appointed by the king. An annual *situado* (subsidy) of supplies and money for salaries came from Havana by boat, though it was often in arrears for several years, creating discontent. There were originally 300 official positions attached to San Agustín, including government officials, soldiers, and priests, with one-half to two-thirds being able-bodied fighting men. This number rose to 1,000 by 1740 but averaged 400 until 1763. The soldiers stationed at presidios were rotated out of Havana, but their small number relative to the size of the territory meant the survival of Florida rested heavily on the missions and missionaries. A *situador* (agent) supervised the flow of goods and money to San Agustín. With the *situado* chronically late, residents relied on the *sabana*, exploiting the Native system of agriculture. The Royal Havana Company replaced the *situado* in the mid-eighteenth century but also failed to supply the presidios with food and supplies. In response, San Agustín turned to foreign merchants, smugglers, and privateers. After 1740 the majority of legal and illegally smuggled goods were supplied by English traders.

Four officials facilitated governmental operations in La Florida. The treasurer oversaw the distribution of monies from the annual *situado*, and accountants kept records of the payments. The governor annually sent a ship to Mexico, then known as New Spain, to collect this money. The treasurer received writs from the governor and other officials to pay suppliers, soldiers, and private citizens from the subsidy. The factor's duties included directing the distribution of supplies and munitions and providing a receipt of deliverance to each supplier. The *escribano* (notary) kept voluminous records of all official meetings, governor visits to missions and Native villages, correspondences with friars, accounts of shipwrecks, explorations, trials, and legal disputes. Much of what we know about events during the mission era come from a notary's pen.

to place their approximate locations on the mainland and the barrier islands. Two of those missions were located on Cumberland Island in 1565. The southernmost mission on Cumberland, San Pedro de Mocama (also called San Pedro de Tacatacuru), was situated on the inland side at present-day Dungeness Dock.

Within a few years, Menéndez established outposts at deep-water ports from Tampa Bay, around the coast of Florida, and north to Santa Elena on present-day Parris Island (Port Royal Sound). Menéndez had practical reasons for placing fortified missions on barrier islands, as they helped protect the four hundred married Spanish couples he brought to settle La Florida from Native attacks and gave them access to supply ships carrying much-needed provisions to maintain the nascent colony. More importantly, they would occupy strategic ports on the Florida and Georgia coasts, as stipulated by Menéndez's contract with King Philip II. His first settlement on the Georgia seaboard was a garrison of thirty men on Santa Catalina (now St. Catherines Island), where an aged chief named Guale (*Wal-lie*) reigned. This region would come to be known as Guale. Jesuit Brother Domingo Agustín, a "born linguist," translated the Catechism and prepared a Guale grammar in the Yamasee tongue within six months of arriving on the coast. The Spanish presence there would continue for another hundred years.

Menéndez was, as Herbert Bolton writes, "a soldier of God as well as of the King." But his desire to establish missions in the province was driven by practical concerns. He had a legal and moral responsibility to convert the Natives to a Christian religion, he needed a labor force to support Spain's colony, and he depended on allies to protect the residents living at St. Augustine and Santa Elana (Milanich). In September 1566, three Jesuit priests sailed from Havana on a Flemish ship to Florida at Menéndez's request to do God's work among the Timucua. The ship's crew, unfamiliar with the Florida coast, passed by St. Augustine and dropped anchor farther north at or near St. Simons Island. Father Pedro Martínez and a number of sailors went ashore seeking directions. While they were there, a storm blew the ship out to sea, leaving the shore party behind. After ten days they sailed and rowed south on the inland passage and came ashore on September 29 near Chief Tacatacuru's village on the south end of Cumberland Island, where they attempted to take food from Native fishermen. (Hann indicates this incident may have occurred farther south, near the St. Johns River.) This attracted more villagers, and fighting ensued. Martínez and three others were killed, while the remaining sailors, some wounded, escaped to the boat and continued their journey south. For this, Menéndez called for Chief Tacatacuru to be executed.

Tacatacuru's and Saturiwa's antipathy toward the Spanish only increased after more killings occurred on both sides. The two chiefs continued to harass the forts at San Mateo and St. Augustine, with the Spanish retaliating by burning villages and crops. A skirmish took place at the bar of Tacatacuru, the mouth of the St. Marys River, with the Spanish escaping by sea after hordes of Cumberland Island Natives attacked. Menéndez, aided by Guale allies, planned to attack the village of Tacatacuru on Cumberland Island in response, but the plan was scrapped.

In 1567 the French Catholic nobleman Dominuque de Gourge led (at his own expense) an expedition of three ships and two hundred men against the Spanish to avenge Menéndez's sacking of Fort Caroline and the massacre of Ribault and his men. Tacatacuru and Saturiwa Natives joined de Gourge's raid on San Mateo. The contingent set out at night, with the Natives taking forest paths and the French traveling by water. They demolished two outlying blockhouses before launching the surprise attack that

Mission Towns

The Spanish placed missions in the main towns of Timucuan chiefdoms with a twofold objective: to save souls and to secure loyal subjects who could provide free labor to support the fledgling colony. Spain's *Ordenanzas* of 1563 gave colonial governors the authority to use Natives as free laborers. *Repartimientos* gave Spanish officials the right to used forced labor for a certain amount of time on public projects like road or building construction. *Encomiendas* gave individuals a block of land and the right to use indigenous labor on that land. In exchange for this labor, the Natives were to be taught the Spanish language, receive religious instruction, and be given protection from enemy tribes and pirates.

A *doctrina*, a mission with a church and resident priest or priests, were usually planted at these towns to teach Natives Catholic religious doctrine. *Visitas*, mission stations without a resident friar, were established in satellite villages and were "visited" by priests. The principal *doctrina* buildings were the church, the *convento* (the friars' living quarters), and a kitchen for meal preparation. A typical church was 60 feet long and 30 feet wide with wattle-and-daub walls (a lattice of sticks covered with clay or mud). When dried, the walls could be plastered with murals painted on them. Some churches had vertical board wall construction, and some were open air, like a pavilion. Wrought-iron nails and spikes held the structures together. Most were supported by large posts made of pine trees anchored deep into the soil. To protect the posts and walls from rot, shells and clay were used as filling. Church roofs were made of thatched palm. Fences or low walls enclosed the mission buildings. Timucuans who converted to Christianity were buried either in the mission cemetery (*campo santo*) or in the floor of the church. Timucuans buried the traditional way were placed in graves on their sides in a fetal position. Most mission Natives were buried face up with arms folded on the chest, sometimes clutching a cross, rosary, or other religious object. Large brass bells called the community to church services and religious feasts. Natives living "beneath the bell" destroyed these symbols of Spanish and Catholic authority when they rose up in rebellion.

overwhelmed the soldiers stationed there. In retribution for the earlier executions of Frenchmen, the Spanish prisoners were killed and hung from trees with the inscription "not as Spaniards but as murderers."

By 1568 the mission at San Pedro de Tacatacuru on Cumberland Island was one of four remaining coastal posts (along with Santa Elena, San Mateo, and St. Augustine) that Menéndez established his first year in Florida (1565). In 1569, he placed a garrison or presidio at San Pedro on Cumberland Island. The presidio's purpose was to prevent more trouble from the Tacatacuru and to maintain a network of communication and supply lines with the Spanish outposts from St. Augustine to Santa Elena. We don't know what happened to Chief Tacatacuru. It's probable he died in battle or by natural causes, as the Spanish would have documented trying and executing him.

Plants Used by Indigenous Peoples

Schoolchildren are taught that squash, beans, and maize (corn) were staples of the East Coast Native American diet. But these three plants weren't the only edible flora available to the region's indigenous people. A priest born in Florida, Alonso de Leturiondo, wrote about aboriginal foods around 1700. He identified three starchy roots (*ache, zebaca,* and *pinoco*), which could be deadly if not prepared properly: "if they do not process them well, the people swell up, as two Indians burst open four years ago because they did not properly prepare the small fruit of the *pinoco*." He observed the root of the *ache* was similar to yucca. "The removal of this root or tuber," he wrote, "requires a lot of work because it grows in swamps full of water and the entire tuber has so many roots, like a horse's mane" requiring strong levers to dislodge. But the work was worth it as the resulting flour was "whiter than that from wheat, and by pounding it in a hand mortar and throwing water on it, the pungency and poison are removed." He found that *ache* made a bread tastier than that made from maize. But if not processed correctly it created a black dough, and if the poison was not removed "the mouth is set on fire and [the person is] in danger of bursting." Laudonnière

described a similar root called *hassez* used by the Timucua living on the St. Johns River and on Amelia Island.

Plentiful on the Georgia coast, acorns (*vellota amarga*) represented a large part of the diet for the Timucua on Cumberland Island. They scoured oak forests in the winter when maize supplies ran low and made bread from the foraged acorns. Leturiondo, a parish priest in St. Augustine, described the process of eliminating the bitterness and impurities, which involved removing the husks, grinding the acorns in a hand mill, and burying the meal in pits for a week or longer. The processed meal was made into loaves and laid out on wooden spits placed over a fire, making a sweet-tasting bread.

Some of the medicinal herbs Leturiondo wrote about included royal and white *itamo*, indigenous to Tama in Central Georgia, and *chitubexatic*, a remedy no one traveled without. "However deep and numerous the wounds might be," he claimed, "they are cured, purged, cleansed and healed in a very few days with this herb." Laudonnière informs us that smilax, a shrub that can form dense thickets, was used as a cure for syphilis.

The following year, 1570, Menéndez reduced the number of soldiers stationed at San Pedro. The garrison there was not well supplied, and the presidio fell into disrepair, ceasing operations about 1573.

Disputes with soldiers and military officials, health problems, and Native rebellions doomed the Jesuits' efforts. One priest, Juan de Rogel, blamed the mistreatment of Natives by Spanish soldiers for undermining the Jesuits' efforts. But he and other men of his order also viewed the indigenous people as rude savages unwilling to give up "their devils" and convert. By 1572 the Jesuits' work in La Florida came to an end.

Franciscan Missions

After the withdrawal of Jesuit priests from La Florida, Menéndez traveled to Spain and sought another religious order to take their place. The Spanish Crown responded by sending eighteen Franciscan friars in 1573. Menéndez never returned to Florida. He died in Spain a year later. His nephew, Pedro Menéndez de Márquez, assumed many of his responsibilities before the new governor, Diego de Velasco, arrived. Pedro, also an able seaman who trained under his uncle, served as La Florida's governor from 1577 to 1589.

Early Franciscan attempts to convert the Timucua were plagued by the same problems that forced the Jesuits to withdraw. Eleven more Franciscan friars arrived in 1595 as part of a renewed effort to establish and maintain missions in La Florida. Father Francisco Marrón, in consultation with Domingo Martínez de Avendaño, then governor of La Florida, assigned these friars to various missions. Father Baltasár López was sent to San Pedro de Mocama on Cumberland Island. López was from the city of Burgos in northern Spain. Though he "suffered much among the Indians" and was condemned to death on three occasions, he came to know the Timucua and their language well, gradually winning them over. Father Francisco de Pareja served as pastor at mission San Juan del Puerto (Port of the St. Johns River), on the inland side of Fort George Island at the mouth of the St. Johns. At times, during López's visitations to inland tribes, Pareja served at San Pedro de Mocama. Some historians believe Pareja wrote his dictionary of the Timucuan language during his time on Cumberland Island.

At the age of twenty-six, San Pedro's cacique in 1597, Don Juan, was already thoroughly indoctrinated into the Catholic faith and Spanish culture and proved to be a faithful ally to the Spaniards. He and other Timucua men cut their hair short "in the style of the Spanish once they converted to Christianity" (Milanich). Under Don Juan, the practice of tattooing slowly died out. He was the antithesis of Chief Tacatacuru, who had waged war with Spain from his Cumberland stronghold. Don Juan's support of the Franciscans in his domain earned him letters of praise from both the friars and Gonzalo Méndez de Canzo (also Cançio or Cancio), Florida's governor from 1597 to 1603, who lauded his devotion to spreading the faith and his loyalty to Spain. Governor de Canzo sent letters to the Council of the Indies in Madrid, which authorized a payment of two hundred ducats to Don Juan, and he petitioned King Philip II to show the cacique official recognition with a formal document, which the king approved. The Franciscan brothers later recommended that Don Juan receive rations and a salary, as a soldier would, to reward and retain his allegiance—a prudent move considering San

Pedro's importance as a major caciquedom and maritime town, the largest north of St. Augustine. Again, both the council and King Philip II approved the request.

Father López greatly influenced Don Juan and the cacique's favorable treatment of the religious and the military. It was he who nurtured Don Juan from an early age, and it was López who petitioned the Spanish government on his behalf. Don Juan repaid Spain in kind many times over by providing food for the military in times of famine and sending warriors when the presidio at San Pedro was in danger of attack. He brought other chieftains to Christianity, aided the religious in his territory, and saw to it that all infants born in his domain were baptized. At one large gathering he decreed that any Native who refused to become a Christian should leave his caciquedom.

A garrison was reestablished at the Franciscan mission on the south end of Cumberland at San Pedro de Mocama, with the soldiers residing in separate quarters. Jerald Milanich made an archaeological survey of the Timucuan village of Tacatacuru in 1970 along with William Bullard of the Florida State Museum. Based on Spanish documents, shell deposits, ceramics, and other archaeological evidence, they determined that the location of the village and the mission "is on the inland waterway side of the island bordering tidal marshes and Cumberland Sound" running from the Carnegie estate of Dungeness on the south end and continuing north of the Dungeness Wharf, with the northernmost section, three hundred yards or so, constituting the main occupied area of the village. The thirty feet of water there would have been sufficient for Spanish brigantines bringing troops and supplies from St. Augustine to dock. The shell midden formations "suggest a village laid out on an elongated, rectangular grid plan." Milanich was unable to locate the site of the large mission church raised by Governor Canzo in 1603. As of this writing, its location remains a mystery.

Father López made several trips inland from the mission on Cumberland Island, traveling over 160 miles to visit Native officials who had paid homage to Spanish officials. He was away on one such visitation in September 1597, with Father Pareja serving at San Pedro in his absence, when the Guale rose up in armed rebellion. The revolt began at the mainland mission of Tolomato, near modern St. Catherines Island, where Father Pedro de Corpa had publicly reprimanded Don Juanillo, heir to the *mico* (Guale for cacique), for polygamy. Father Corpa instead gave the title of head *mico* to Juanillo's uncle, Don Francisco. Corpa believed a chief who defied fundamental Christian tenets would undermine the Franciscans' efforts to proselytize other Natives. To Juanillo, the Spanish were interlopers and occupiers, interfering with Native affairs. Like Tacatacuru, he chose to defy European authority and left Tolomato to lead a contingent of like-minded men

San Pedro
de Mocama

Dungeness

Beach Creek

Approximate location of Mission San Pedro de Mocama.

determined to blot out the Christian movement overtaking their land. Juanillo's revolt expanded from eradicating the missions in Guale to waging war against enemy tribes and the missionaries among them. They murdered Father Corpa and four other friars and took a sixth Franciscan hostage before setting their sights on Cumberland Island.

The Guale planned to attack San Pedro de Mocama on the Feast of St. Francis (October 4), when the Christian Natives would be celebrating. Juanillo appointed officers, then assembled men, bows and arrows, and other weapons for the assault. Twenty-six canoes carrying four hundred warriors crossed the sound between Jekyll and Cumberland and proceeded along the Puturiba River (Cumberland River) to the south end of the island. The expedition presumably traveled at night so as not to be seen by anyone at Puturiba, the mission on Cumberland's north end, and arrived at San Pedro just before daylight. Two canoes got there ahead of the main body and put ashore, most likely north of the present-day Dungeness dock. They surrounded the home of Antonio López, a Christianized Native and village leader. The remaining Guale canoes had approached San Pedro's marina but aborted the attack upon seeing a Spanish brigantine lying at anchor there.

When the strangers approached the López house, a dog began to bark. López's father-in-law, Jusepe (Maynard Geiger, a prominent Franciscan historian writes that Jusepe was a son-in-law) went outside to quiet the dog, believing it was barking at Don Juan's horse. Jusepe was pierced from behind by four arrows in the shoulders and one in the arm. Despite these wounds he ran back inside the house to raise the alarm. He still had the presence of mind to take up his bow and arrow but was too injured to pull the bowstring. In the semilight, López escaped through a nearby cornfield and found Don Juan, who raised a general alarm for battle. Father Pareja heard blood-curdling cries of "War! War!" from the door of the church, where he was preparing for the day's festivities. He immediately sent a messenger to Father Chozas at Puturiba and rushed to Jusepe's bedside to hear what might be his last confession.

Meanwhile, the raiders in the first two canoes retreated posthaste across the river to the mainland with Don Juan and his men in hot pursuit. They caught up with the fleeing attackers, killed two, and took their scalps, "even though their hair was short, indicating that they were Christians" (Hann). One of the dead men was the *mandador*, or cacique's lieutenant, on Asao (located at that time on the mainland near present-day Darien, Georgia). Don Juan's men found in one of the captured canoes the habit and capuche (hood or cowl) belonging to Father Francisco de Verascola, the "Cantabrian

Giant" who had been murdered at Asao. Though Don Juan instructed his subjects to bring other captured raiders to him alive for questioning, another raider was captured and killed at a nearby village.

The proximity of Don Juan's home to Antonio López's and the report that Jusepe thought the dog was barking at Don Juan's horse implies the cacique lived nearby. Did the invaders surround the wrong house? Did they intend to kidnap Don Juan or kill him outright before attacking the mission? Regardless of their intentions, if not for a barking dog, the surprise attack on San Pedro and its outcome might have been much different.

In light of the pursuit by Don Juan and the presence of the Spanish brig, the main body of Guale raiders turned their canoes north toward their own province. Some warriors paused north of San Pedro long enough to pierce a wooden cross with five arrows, one for each Franciscan that had been murdered. The canoes continued north, passing by Puturiba located on the marsh side High Point on Cumberland's north end (the Sidney Lanier Bridge in Brunswick is visible from this section of the island). This time the invaders were spotted by Christian Natives, who informed Father Pedro Fernández de Chozas, the eighty-year-old friar stationed there. Juanillo may have intentionally bypassed this mission on the way to San Pedro de Mocama the night before to avoid raising an alarm across the island ahead of his approach. Chozas counted eleven enemy canoes filled with warriors. He reported that the *mico* of Asao defiantly called out to him, "What do you think? We have killed five friars and only one remains alive, for he was a lay-brother. What are you going to do? Come into our territory." He then lifted a hat and further taunted Chozas, saying it belonged to Father Verascola. (It may have actually belonged to one of the other murdered friars, as Don Juan claimed to have recovered Verascola's habit.) Another priest had once observed that "Indians are past masters when it comes to arrogance." These words must have burned in Father Chozas's ears as the warriors paddled on toward Bejessi (also Bejesse), a village perhaps on Little Cumberland. (Another source places Bejessi at High Point and Puturiba farther south at Brickhill Bluff.)

Chozas was from the province of Castile, Spain, and came to Cumberland Island in 1595, where he "taught the Indians the art of singing for which they esteemed him." Like his fellow Franciscans, he was an intrepid missionary, accompanying Father Verascola in 1597 to Georgia's interior (Tama) where he "barely escaped death from the hands of an Indian chief." He had returned to Cumberland Island in time for the Gualean revolt.

"Since I had no other arms," Chozas later stated, "I clothed myself with those of the Church and commenced to celebrate the Mass of my glorious and seraphic Father, St.

Francis, for it was his feast day." The messenger Don Juan sent from San Pedro arrived after Mass and informed Chozas of the attack on the south end. There is no explanation for why the invaders left the *doctrina* at Puturiba unmolested on their retreat to Guale or what happened to the other canoes laden with warriors. The fact that the eleven canoes Chozas saw, negotiating a winding river, outpaced a man on foot to Puturiba, indicates they may not have gone the entire distance to the south end of the island with the other canoes.

The taunting by Asao's *mico* may have taken place at or was possibly repeated at Bejessi. Hann writes that the Asao chieftain confronted a "Mocama interpreter named Nysiscas" near this village who challenged him to put ashore: "The chief contented himself with displaying Fray Verascola's hat and arquebus [a portable matchlock gun] the friar used to hail passing canoes when he needed a ride to visit one of the villages under his jurisdiction" (Hann). Father Chozas was informed the Guale warriors would be back to kill the Christian Natives on Cumberland.

Later in the day, Father Chozas went to San Pedro and delivered a letter to soldiers on the brigantine for the governor in St. Augustine. He also sent Father Verascola's habit recovered by Don Juan as proof of the massacre that had occurred in Guale. Chazos requested "six or more soldiers" to be dispersed among the three villages on Cumberland and an investigation into the murders of his fellow priests. He also asked for new vestments and a chalice, which he had left on a previous trip at Tolomato, one of the despoiled missions. He further proposed sentinel duty for the soldiers near the villages, if they could tolerate the Native diet of *tortas* (cakes made of corn or acorns), *hacha* (a thin stew), and shellfish.

Florida's governor and captain-general at that time, Gonzalo Méndez de Canzo, began his naval training as a young man under Pedro Menéndez de Avilés. He was perhaps best known for defeating Adm. Francis Drake at San Juan, Puerto Rico, in 1595. He was now forty-four years old and appointed by the Spanish king to govern Florida. Three days after Chozas posted his request, on October 7, 1597, at ten in the morning, the brigantine reached St. Augustine. Governor Canzo responded quickly to the call for help, dispatching six soldiers to San Pedro under Juan de Santiago with strict orders prohibiting anyone, including Don Juan, from leaving the island. Santiago and his men reached San Pedro three days later. Canzo rose from a sick bed to lead 150 men on October 16, arriving at San Pedro by October 18. San Pedro would be his base of operations for capturing and questioning hostiles, recovering the murdered friar's possessions, and conducting an inquiry into the revolt.

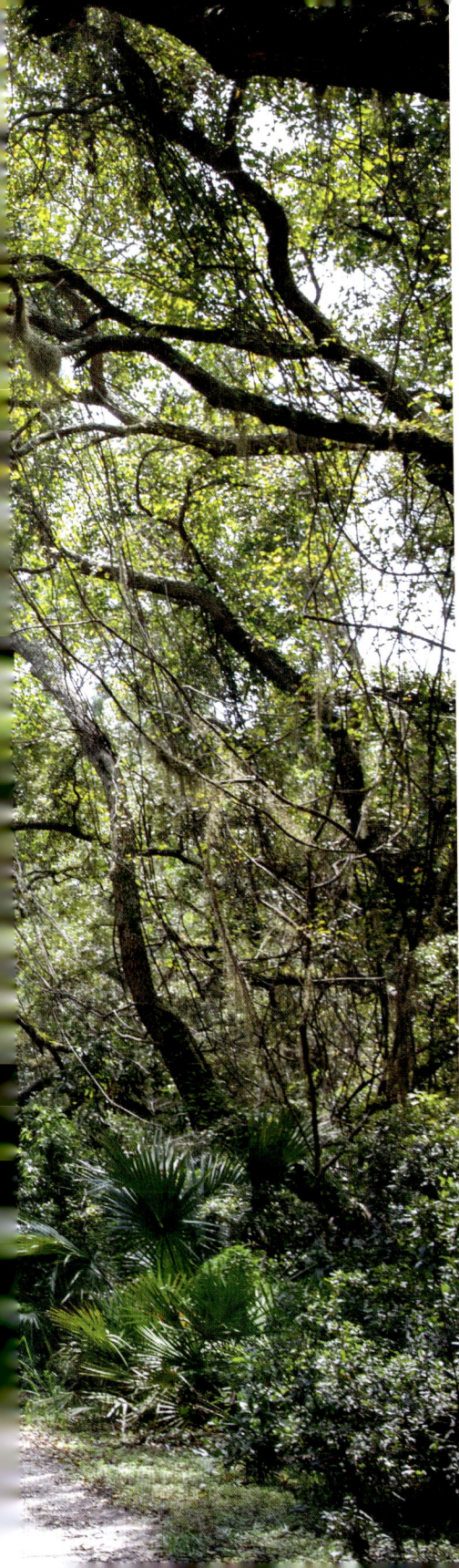

The governor immediately set about recording the testimonies of Don Juan, Antonio López, Jusepe, who still lay in bed recovering from his wounds, one of the Guale prisoners, several other officials, Father Chozas, and Father Pareja. On October 24, three weeks after the attack on San Pedro, Canzo left for Guale, where he visited the missions that had been attacked. On this expedition, Canzo exhumed the murdered friars' bodies in order to give them Christian burials. His men burned crops and villages belonging to the elusive rebels who had escaped to the interior.

By November 11, Governor Canzo and his men were back at San Pedro to transplant the remaining friars closer to St. Augustine and away from danger. He met with Don Juan and other leading Natives of the town at the church, where he offered to remove them to San Juan del Puerto on Fort George Island at the mouth of the St. Johns River, farther away from their enemies in Guale. He sweetened the offer by reducing their annual tribute from one *arroba* (bushel) of corn per married man to six *mazorcas* (six head) of maize for one year. Tributes or tithes were paid with larger, white "principal" maize, also called bread-corn, as opposed to smaller early corn, which ripened in two months, or a yellow and flinty hommony-corn. To Canzo's surprise, Don Juan and the others agreed to relocate. Canzo made the same offer to the caciques of Puturiba and Tocohaya, another Native settlement on Cumberland. They, too, consented to the move farther south.

The priest still held hostage by the Guale, Father Ávila, was released after ten months of depravation and abuse in exchange for Gualean Natives still captive in St. Augustine. As the only Spanish eyewitness to the atrocities, Governor Canzo called on Ávila to testify in court. However, Ávila kept silent lest he violate Church Law prohibiting clerics to voluntarily testify against anyone as it "might lead to punishment by death or mutilation of the guilty." Though he had suffered at the hands of his captives, the mandates expressed in the sacred canons called for him to show mercy. To do otherwise would undermine the work of all the friars in La Florida. Canzo did interrogate seven captured Natives, four of whom were young boys. Lucas, the son of a Guale chief, testified that Father Rodríquez at Tupiqui was murdered for forbidding Natives to practice witchcraft and polygamy. Canzo put Lucas on the rack to get a full confession. Though Lucas repeatedly denied direct involvement in the murder, Canzo sentenced him to the gallows, where he was hanged "until he died a natural death and his soul went out of his body."

Canzo's fire-and-sword response to the uprising had the desired effect. He instituted a policy of enslavement for all "the Indians who should be captured" in the Guale province.

Fortunately for the Gualeans, Spanish officials with authority over Canzo reversed the policy. Canzo released the Native slaves and published an emancipation proclamation. By May 1600, the Gualean *micos* were weary from the loss of crops and habitations. Hunger, a great motivator, brought them to St. Augustine seeking a return to normalization with the Spanish government. They asked for forgiveness and pled ignorance in their actions for being "a barbarous people and of little understanding" of the seriousness of their crime. Had Spanish subjects revolted in a like manner, they could have been burned at the stake. Governor Canzo considered the Guale to be "novelty seekers, who in order to cover up their cunning and deceitfulness, invent a thousand lies." Nonetheless, he accepted their excuse and restored relations with several caveats, including free passage for anyone with the governor's credentials traveling through their territory, providing manpower when requested by the governor, and a return to the Roman Catholic faith. They must also promise never again to "raise the *macana* or war club." In addition, Canzo wanted Juanillo and his followers brought to justice. Soon after this meeting, the *mico* near present-day Darien led five hundred warriors twenty-one miles inland, where they attacked a fort held by Don Juanillo, his uncle, Don Francisco, and their followers, including women and children. Both men were killed. Juanillo was beheaded, and part of his scalp was given to a Spanish sergeant, who presented it to the governor in St. Augustine.

Canzo, like other Florida governors, ruled over a vast region populated by indigenous people. St. Augustine was the only municipality in that territory inhabited by Europeans. He considered his territory to include the land south of the Chesapeake Bay and west to the Mississippi Valley. The wiser Spanish government administrators realized that maintaining good relations with the Natives through the missions, rather than by military force, was the key to their success. The caciques and *cacicas* (female chiefs) were integral to maintaining favorable relations with the tribes. To this end, the Spanish plied them with gifts—flour, maize, clothing, trinkets, even horses—and lowered the tributes, such as maize and manpower, required of each village to maintain the colony.

Father López regarded some government officials as opportunists who saw La Florida as a stepping-stone to grander appointments. Typically, these men lacked knowledge about the territory over which they had authority, and their methods were counterproductive—if not destructive—to Spain's desire to establish a colony and the friars' labors to proselytize Natives. Governors might come and go, but the friars were there for the duration.

In a letter from San Pedro to King Philip II, López wrote: "While Governor Domingo Martínez de Avendaño was ruling, the subjugation of the Indians was going on so steadily that we were led to thank God for it. We rejoiced in the increase which this land promised for the salvation of souls." Then Governor Canzo arrived, "a man without experience and unwilling to take advice." López describes Canzo's actions as "a wall" that hinders the friars' mission work, "together with a lack of respect which is shown us by the governor." Former governors, he noted, recognized that "respect for priests is the key by which blindness of the natives is unlocked." Indeed, on a visit to Cumberland Island, Governor Avendaño had knelt and kissed the vicar's hand in the presence of the assembly in a show of respect for a higher authority that the Franciscans represented. Because of this act, the Natives regarded friars "as gods in the land." López felt that Canzo had single-handedly undone the esteem with which the religious were held to the point that "there is a decrease of respect so notable that we your chaplains deplore it with tears of the soul." Canzo even attempted to turn the reliable Don Juan against the Franciscans: "And to this *cacique* Don Juan, whom I nurtured with such great labor, the governor told things that are against the honor of the priests in such extravagant terms that though he is an Indian, he was scandalized [appalled]."

Tensions between Canzo and the friars arose on several fronts. Father Pareja petitioned the governor to use more force in punishing "the wicked and recalcitrant" Natives who broke laws and ignored Christian duties such as going "into the interior among the infidels where they are accustomed to stay for a year or two without hearing Mass" or failing to return at all. The caciques also asked the governor to punish rebellious subjects, for once they converted to Christianity they disobeyed their commands. "Now," Pareja wrote, "the *caciques* do not dare to carry out these laws for fear of the governor who does not want the Indians punished even though the offenses are public and notorious." The lack of social order slowly turned Timucuan society into a dysfunctional vestige of its former self. The tension between missionaries and government officials was made clear in one of Pareja's later writings. "We [the religious] are the ones who are bearing the burden and the head; we are the ones who are conquering and subduing the land."

Father Baltazar López, Don Juan, and Don Juan's subjects were back on Cumberland by the Feast of Ascension (Holy Thursday, the fortieth day of Easter) 1598, rebuilding San Pedro and the other villages and planting maize crops that soon flourished. López returned to the place "where Christianity first took root," he declared, to minister at San Pedro, its satellite villages, and towns much farther inland. By then he had served

Bird's-eye view of a typical Spanish mission. Illustration by John LoCastro. (Courtesy of Mission San Luis, Florida Department of State)

as a missionary for seventeen years, most of that time on Cumberland Island. He had traveled hundreds of miles to visit interior villages and knew the terrain well. The nearly eight hundred Christians in seven villages between San Pedro and St. Augustine fell under his care. Each village was three or four miles from a church. On the island of Napoyca (Napuica), possibly Point Peter near St. Marys, two villages—Santo Domingo (population 180) and Santa María de Sena (112)—had their own churches. All of the Christian Natives converged on San Pedro to celebrate feast days, Holy Week, and Easter, participating in processions and hearing Mass and sermons.

The Asao *mico* who taunted Father Chozas kept his vow to return with force despite the other Gualean *micos*' promises never "to raise the *macana*" again. Warriors from that province raided three villages on Cumberland Island on October 11, 1598, burning them to the ground and killing several people. Don Juan sent word to Governor Canzo requesting more soldiers. Canzo responded with sixteen men but provided no provisions for them, which meant they relied on the locals for their food. He later followed up with fifty more soldiers and provisions and sent expeditions into Guale to burn more villages, seize canoes and stored food, and destroy crops—a predictable yet effective punishment that forced the remaining Guale rebels to sue for peace.

Father López's conversion of the Timucua during his tenure had been a slow, gentle, yet systematic approach, requiring much patience. "In the beginning," he wrote, "I was with them for four years catechizing them, so that I would ascertain their dispositions for the reception of baptism as well as to become acquainted with them. They received our holy faith so well that it is increasing, and they embrace with greater devotion what is taught them." By the time of the Guale rebellion, no pagans remained at San Pedro or the other villages in his domain. López points out that none of towns south of Guale ever rebelled against the Spanish authorities, and they even provided maize for Spaniards at the San Pedro presidio.

"Their friendship for the Spaniards," he wrote, "their subjection to the government and their love for Christianity have always been on the increase. According to these signs I can testify without scruple of conscience, that not only those who are already Christians will remain such, but that very many others will become such, for many pagans of the interior come to these Christian towns, seeking baptism from us. And those who have come in have done well." Even so, López and other friars relied on Native "fiscals" [officials] to ensure converted Natives attended church and "live as Christians." San Pedro, perhaps due to its size, had two fiscals working for the friar.

Caciques from interior regions came to St. Augustine requesting the religious superior and the governor to send Father López to their towns to instruct the Natives. López made numerous such visits, reporting "very little difficulty in their embracing the doctrine and law of God, as well as some good indications of their future reception of Christianity."

López, like Father Pareja, lamented the governor's lack of discipline in correcting Natives who he termed "mischief-makers," thinking it undermined the missionaries' work and ran counter to the king's wishes. "Without the favor and protection of the government," he wrote, "which the king has frequently commanded to be given by the governors to the religious [friars] among the Indians, there is difficulty in administering baptism in the Indian villages, owing to their great distance from St. Augustine. Moreover, there are some Christian Indians who are fugitives in the interior, and although they have not numbered more than four, a remedy could be applied; for it belongs to him who governs to punish and threaten, while it is the part of the religious to be kind fathers to the natives in order to win their love."

In other words, the Spanish thought the carrot-and-stick approach brought Natives to Christianity and kept the peace. Correcting wayward Natives who strayed from the faith was one thing, but ongoing abuse of the locals by Canzo's soldiers deeply offended the Franciscans and hindered their efforts with the indigenous population. In 1598, Canzo had ordered a raid on Ais tribesmen (near modern Cape Canaveral) for murdering several of his messengers. He also brought terror to the Sorruque (also Surruque) Natives twenty leagues south of St. Augustine for past crimes "in order that they may be an object-lesson to others." According to Father López, "seventy innocent victims"—men, women, and children—were slaughtered in that unprovoked attack.

In 1599, Father López wrote another letter to the Spanish king, accusing Canzo of using his position as governor to accumulate wealth so he could leave a rich man at the end of his appointment. "It is necessary," López wrote, "to apply a remedy as well as to inform your Majesty of his deception." López also agreed with Pareja that the presidio at St. Augustine should be relocated to Guale, land more suitable for raising crops and cattle than the sandy soil and marshes surrounding St. Augustine. A hurricane in September 1599 flooded the capitol. A more sheltered location in Guale would be less susceptible to such storms. The inhabitants would have access to clay to make bricks and tiles, and trade with the local indigenous people would provide much needed food for the presidio. Moving the fortification north would also provide more protection for the friars and Christian converts and give Spain better access to the northern region of Tama, the interior of Middle Georgia, where there were reports of mineral deposits.

Canzo, perhaps on their advice, seriously considered the move and proposed to Philip II adding another base of operations in Tama. But the king died before the plans could proceed, and his successor, Philip III, was more inclined to reduce outlays of cash for La Florida, already a drain on Spain's treasury, than to increase its military footprint—a policy of retrenchment instead of expansion. Had Spain followed the friar's and governor's advice and relocated its main fortification to the port of Darien, Sunbury, or Savannah, there would have been no "debatable land" later that century. Spain's title to the region south of the Savannah River after the arrival of the English would have been unquestioned, and there would have been no place for James Oglethorpe to settle. In short, the Georgia colony might never have existed. But St. Augustine still served as an important lifeline to missions that had spread west along El Camino Real from the Florida coast to the panhandle. Its location also ensured faster response times to salvage wrecked ships bearing gold and silver.

San Pedro's cacique, Don Juan, died on June 6, 1600, receiving extreme unction at the hour of his death. The governor lauded him as "the most valuable cacique of the territory." He was succeeded by his niece, Doña Ana, whom López described as "head chief and head of all the rest of the maritime villages down to St. Augustine."

After the Guale uprising, the debate over restoring the missions and colonizing the interior deepened. Would it be more expedient to relocate Christianized Natives to Cuba and other Caribbean islands? Should the presidios on islands like Cumberland be replaced by a coast guard to prevent the French or English from colonizing Spain's territory? An inquiry by Cuba's governor, initiated by the king, affirmed that the Franciscans' work had been fruitful and that maintaining a presence on the Georgia islands was necessary to protect Spain's ventures in New Spain. Plans to restore the missions began in St. Augustine.

Canzo visited Georgia's missions in 1603, determined to replace the church on Cumberland, which had succumbed to decay, with a much grander and imposing edifice equal in size to the one at St. Augustine to "stimulate religious zeal and serve as a model for the entire seaboard, (lifting) San Pedro to a position of spiritual as well as temporal primacy on that frontier." By then San Pedro served three hundred Christian Timucuans in addition to converts living at other villages on the island. Canzo sent Father López orders to gather building materials for the new structure ahead of his visit. Perhaps he failed to inform López of the building's scale, or perhaps the good friar thought the scope of the project was too ostentatious. Perhaps, too, López regarded Canzo's actions as political—an attempt to buy their favor or discredit their accusations about him. Regardless, when Canzo arrived with his builders, it quickly became apparent that the timbers and nails were insufficient. The governor ordered more shingles and timber from the local forests and sent for more nails from St. Augustine before continuing his tour north into Guale.

Canzo returned to San Pedro on February 19 after two weeks. The province was now officially reinstated and under Spanish protection. Ten "powerful chieftains" from Cascangue and Los Pinales, districts subject to *cacica* Doña Ana, arrived on Cumberland to meet with Canzo, who plied them with gifts and entertainment and "implored the heathen to accept Christianity and to render obedience to Father López" (Ross). In

Villagers gathering at a Franciscan Church for a ceremony. Original oil painting by Edward Jonas.
(Courtesy of Mission San Luis, Florida Department of State)

return for their allegiance to the cross, the crown, and the young chieftainess, Canzo pledged to protect their districts.

San Pedro's new church was formally dedicated on March 10, 1603, with a prolonged and grandiose oratory in which the governor recapped his role in the program to restore mission churches on the coast. When he asked López if there was anything else the mission required, the friar was curt and unemotional in his reply, declining further assistance from the governor. His reaction may have been due to Canzo's grandstanding during the previous month or to his long-standing opinion of the governor, including the slaughter of Sorruque innocents, which could not be whitewashed with the construction of new church.

Canzo asked López "to console the chieftainess Doña Ana, because she was a young maiden" who was at that time ill in bed, having missed the ceremony. The governor then went to her house himself and repeated his speech, presenting the church to her, complete with a summary of his part in bringing about its construction. The young *cacica* accepted Canzo's gift to San Pedro but in the next breath registered a complaint against Juan de Quevedo, a warrior to whom her uncle, Don Juan, had entrusted "pearls and buttons" as part of her inheritance. On Don Juan's death, Quevedo vanished from the district with the heirlooms. Canzo promised to bring the warrior to justice. In concluding their interview, he encouraged Doña Ana to keep the peace with Guale and to promote the sassafras trade, a nod to the importance of that crop to the governor. After returning to San Pedro in 1598, the island Natives had revived the sassafras trade in earnest; Canzo approved a frigate delivering supplies from Havana to stop in 1602 at San Pedro, where it loaded 12,500 pounds of sassafras for export to Spain for medicinal and commercial uses.

Father López's curious reaction to the church's dedication might also be explained by illness, for soon after that visit, his name disappears from the rolls. There are no records of the date and location of his death. He was remembered as "one of Florida's earliest and most valuable missionaries" (Geiger). Despite Canzo's grand gesture on Cumberland, the Council of the Indies terminated his term as governor due to the numerous complaints by friars and others and perhaps to extinguish his plans to extend the colony into Middle Georgia. He returned to Spain in October 1603 with his wife and son and two packages of maize seeds that would be cultivated in the northern province of Asturias.

His replacement, chosen by King Philip III, was Pedro de Ybarra (Ibarra), a military general from Spain's Basque region whose salary totaled 2,000 ducats a year. Unlike Canzo,

Ybarra was inclined toward kindness in his treatment of the indigenous population, especially the Ais and their allies south of St. Augustine, who could assist survivors of Spanish shipwrecks and alert the governor to pirate activity. But the governor's relations with the friars became strained at times, resulting in his declaration that their sole purpose was to convert the Natives; in particular, in the words of Geiger, they were "not to meddle in governmental affairs but were to attend strictly to their religious duties and to inform their religious superior of their needs." Ybarra at times believed the friars had exceeded their authority with the Natives, as evidenced by the 1598 Guale revolt. "I am governor and not they," he wrote. In November 1604 he sailed north to the Timucua and Guale provinces bearing blankets, felt hats, textiles, mirrors, beads, axes, hoes, and knives as gifts for the Native chiefs. Besides maintaining friendly relations, he wanted to eliminate discord among the tribes and to determine if the populace were being treated fairly by their caciques and the Spaniards.

When Ybarra stepped ashore at San Pedro on Saturday, November 13, 1604, he was greeted by the new *cacica*, Doña María Meléndez, who had succeeded the deceased Doña Ana. Doña María's marriage to a Spanish soldier (named Clemente Vernal) might have had something to do with her ascendancy to San Pedro. She had been *cacica* of Nombre de Dios at St. Augustine during Canzo's time as governor. He had described her as "a very good Christian" who aided soldiers at the presidio in 1591 when they needed food. At his request, the Council of the Indies had petitioned the king to acknowledge her efforts in a letter and grant her clothing and other articles, which the king approved (Geiger). Her house on Cumberland soon became a rendezvous point for chiefs traveling to and from St. Augustine, and she "was zealous in her efforts to draw them to the faith."

Father Pedro Ruíz, who accompanied Ybarra (as he had on Canzo's previous trip), was assigned to replace Father López at San Pedro, at least until a new group of friars from Spain arrived. Ybarra held a conference with Doña María, her son, Asencio, and a number of caciques subject to her. Ybarra invited the Natives to report any grievances against the Spaniards and to inform him of enemy presence. He also urged them to respect Spain's missionaries, informing them that "his Majesty" did not wish to take their lands and only desired that they become Christians, in order to "save their souls and on dying, enter into heaven. This alone," he told them, "moved the king to preserve the presidio of St. Augustine and to spend many ducats a year for its maintenance."

Another Native delegation, eleven caciques from the Los Pinales district, soon arrived at San Pedro to meet with Ybarra. He repeated his speech with promises to send

missionaries to their villages. Until then, Father Ruíz would guide them in spiritual matters. The governor encouraged them to place crosses at the entrances of their homes and along the road to their villages as signs of their conversion to Christianity. A delegation from Yufera, on the interior, arrived to hold a private audience with Ybarra. It consisted of the *cacica* of that district, her husband, and her heir. She claimed independence from any other cacique or *cacica*, including Doña María, a blood relative.

A year later in 1605, the same year Cervantes published *Don Quixote*, seven young missionaries arrived from Havana after a hazardous journey. Ybarra's friendly overtures toward the chiefs south of St. Augustine helped to ensure their safe passage when their frigate was forced ashore. He assigned one of the Franciscans, Father Juan Baptista de Capilla, to San Pedro, replacing Father Ruíz. That same year Father Capilla prepared for a pastoral visitation by the Cuban bishop, "His Very Reverend Lordship, Master" Don Fray Juan de las Cabezas Altamirano. The previous episcopal visitation to La Florida had occurred in 1528. In light of the 1598 uprising and the recent restorations of missions along the coast, official sanctification by the bishop himself seemed appropriate. Cabezas Altamirano, whose bishopric included La Florida, Cuba, and Jamaica, leapt at the chance to see how the northern part of his province fared.

The bishop arrived on Cumberland Island in mid-April with four guards and six interpreters. Ross notes: "Not infrequently a mere creek or small stream formed the dividing line between two peoples. In the case of Guale and San Pedro, Ballenas or St. Andrews Sound [between Jekyll and Cumberland Islands] appears to have been the separating waters." *Cacica* Doña María was not in attendance during this visit. However, on April 13 and 14, Doña María's son, five chieftains under her rule, and 308 Natives were confirmed by Cabezas Altamirano in San Pedro's church. The bishop gave an address in which he reminded the Natives the debt of gratitude they owed to the king of Spain "for the expense he had incurred for the expansion of the missions." Bad weather prevented Cabezas Altamirano's departure for Guale until April 18. After a successful visitation as far north as St. Catherines Island, the bishop returned to San Pedro on May 7 for a few hours to confirm applicants absent during his visit two weeks prior.

Father Capilla would go on to become the first provincial of Santa Elena, by 1612 a separate missionary province. Father Pareja spent most of his time as a missionary serving at San Juan del Puerto on the north side of the St. Johns River. In his later years he was "guardian of the convent of San Agustín," where many of his scholarly works were written. He died in Mexico in 1628.

Bishop Cabezas Altamirano's sanctification of the missions marked what Ross describes as the "dawn of the golden era of Spanish Georgia. For three-quarters of a century it continued; and then the Anglo-Saxon came up out of the Caribbean and hammered at the Gualean gate." It was indeed a golden age, considering the number of new missions that would be established in La Florida before the intrusion by Native slave raiders and the English later that century. But it also ushered in a golden sunset on Spain's waning influence over this part of its empire.

Two shipwrecked survivors supply more details about Cumberland Island during the mission period. The first is Andrés de San Miguel, a young Spaniard traveling southward along the Georgia coast on his way to St. Augustine in 1595. The other account takes place a century later, this time from an Englishman traveling north on the same coast to Charleston. Both were in ships separated by storms from their convoys and blown ashore.

Father Andrés de San Miguel—1595

The account of Andrés de Segura, better known as Father Andrés de San Miguel, a Carmelite lay brother, was translated by historian John Hann (2001) and covers the two-year odyssey of a teen, later a priest, sailing from Spain to the New World and back. Father Andrés wrote about his journey years after the event with inaccuracies that make it difficult to pinpoint several locations he writes about. Nevertheless, it provides valuable ethnographic information about the Timucua people and their culture during the era of the Spanish missions.

Young Andrés's ship, *Our Lady of Mercy*, joined a fleet bound for Spain bearing silver mined in South America. Flotillas, or fleets, sailing to and from Spain, generally avoided the high seas during hurricane seasons and winter storm seasons, but delays prevented Andrés's flotilla from leaving Cuba until March 1595. A storm separated *Our Lady of Mercy* from the fleet, and while those in charge of his ship cowered below decks awaiting its eminent destruction, the ship's purser took command, forcing anyone he could to man pumps that kept the vessel afloat. After the four-day storm abated, the officers came out of hiding long enough to determine the ship was sinking and commandeer the only lifeboat. This left the remaining passengers and crew to their own devices. Here again, the purser took charge and oversaw the construction of a boxlike, makeshift sloop that transported Andrés and thirty other survivors to shore near the mouth of the Altamaha River, most likely on Wolf Island or Little St. Simons Island.

The survivors spent ten days there tormented by mosquitoes and cold air at night, surviving on raw oysters, palm tree shoots, grasses, and pools of fresh rainwater before their rescue by Guale Natives. They persuaded their rescuers to part with cake made of parched corn and other pieces made of ground live oak corn "and made a fire using a smoldering log they carried in their canoe, on which they roasted oysters." The Natives agreed to take the Spaniards to their village, Asao (prior to its relocation on St. Simons Island) on the Altamaha River near present-day Darien. Here, they bartered with what little they still had from the wreck—rosaries, blankets, and sewing needles—for several Castilian roosters and parched corn cakes "two fingers thick," yellow and red pieces of cake made of ground live oak acorns, "sharp-tasting and bitter and which the men had trouble eating." Apparently feeling sorry for the bedraggled survivors, the Natives didn't ask payment for the thick parched-corn gruel served in deep earthenware bowls.

While at Asao, Andrés witnessed ceremonies involving the use of the *cacina* drink, the odor of which he compared to lye water. "Both Indians and Spaniards drink it in the morning," he recalled, "and they say it helps prevent the [kidney] stone, and that because of the drink there is no Indian who has it because it makes them urinate a great deal." He witnessed a game of chunkey played by the leading men of Asao, after which everyone gathered in the council house where they downed large quantities of *cacina* from half-gallon stone jars filled with the drink. "Each Indian took one of these in his hands," Andrés recalled, "and with great reverence they went about giving [the jars] to those who had played, who were each seated on a bed, and each one took and drank his. As a result of this their bellies became like a drum. And as they kept on drinking their bellies continued to grow and swell. They carried this on calmly for a while. And we [were] waiting to see how this fiesta would come to an end, when we noticed that, on opening their mouths with very great calmness, each one began ejecting by way of them a great stream of water as clear as it was when they drank it, and others, on the ground on their knees, went about spreading the water that they ejected to one side and the other with their hands." To expedite purging, Andrés was told, the men fasted before the ceremony and added seawater to the concoction.

The Native's preparation of *cacina* leaves was similar to ancient Chinese methods of tea leaf processing. They plucked the leaves from the yaupon holly (*Ilex vomitoria*) or the dahoon holly (*Ilex cassine*), placed them in clay jars, and toasted the leaves over a fire.

The dried leaves were broken up and crushed into a powder, then doused with water and heated to a boil, and finally filtered and served hot. The potency varied depending on the amount of water used. One Spanish bishop said it tasted bitter and "worse than beer." Don Alonso de Leturiondo, a parish priest born in St. Augustine, deemed it "a very healthful and medicinal drink" without the "drawback of intoxication as does other beverages of New Spain."

The Natives often traveled with nut meal, maize flour, dried persimmons, and blueberries or a similar combination of ingredients, which they mixed with fresh water at a stream or lake to make a nourishing drink called *tolocano*. A de Bry engraving alludes to the use of tobacco by the Timucua for medicinal purposes. Some documents mention its use in pregame rituals the night before athletic endeavors such as ball games. They may have even sold bundles of tobacco to the Spaniards.

After four days, Andrés and his companions departed Asao and set out from Wolf Island, in pirogues manned by Guale Natives, bound for San Pedro on Cumberland Island. They reached San Pedro, according to Father Andrés, later that afternoon. The distance is about forty miles as the crow flies, but much longer on the winding inward passage rivers. Oglethorpe's scout boats could make the trip from Savannah to St. Simons, a distance of about eighty miles, in two days, so Father Andrés's assertion that his guides covered half that distance in the same day is probable only if the wind and tide conditions were favorable.

Upon reaching San Pedro they were greeted by "the Spaniards," Andrés writes, "whom the governor maintained there and by many Christian Indian men and women who lived there, but without mass or sacraments," implying it was not a mission. Hann points out numerous errors in Father Andrés's recollections, and this is one. Mission San Pedro de Mocama was established on Cumberland in 1587, some eight years before Father Andrés's arrival. Father Baltasar López served as the mission friar, and it is likely he was visiting other Native villages on Cumberland or on the mainland during Father Andrés's visit.

Andrés continues: "They all received us one by one and embraced us with signs of love and joy and brought us to the council house, which was bigger than those that I have spoken of [at Asao], and it was open at the top with a skylight such as can be made in a council house, round in shape and [made] of whole pine trees. They gave us *atole* [a gruel made by boiling maize flour in water or milk] for supper as the daily ration. And if we ate a hen it cost us four reales. At last we ate by a set rate."

He describes the process to prepare the flour for this gruel and corn cakes. "The hand is the guide for the rammer which is more than two yards in height, and the rammer moves upward and the thin end remains in the [deep and narrow] mortar." Cakes, two fingers thick, made from this flour were cooked under the embers.

Andrés and his companions stayed at San Pedro fifteen days. He next describes the Timucuan chief, Don Juan, and his wife, who had been absent from the island. Both spoke Spanish and dressed as Spaniards. Spanish officials often gained favor with chiefs by giving them clothing, and sometimes whole outfits—a shirt, breeches, silk doublet, and a hat (Milanich).

"He and the chieftainess were Christians and spoke the Castilian language very well. He had a very good carriage and countenance, of great strength. He was named don Juan and dresses well in the Spanish manner. And when the chieftainess went out she wore a cloak like a Spanish lady. When we learned that they were arriving at the river-bank, we all went to give them a welcome. All those among their vassals who learned of their coming, who were many, flocked to the same reception. On jumping on land, he took the path toward the council house once he had spoken to us and all of us with him. But the Indian men and women [and] the big and little children began as great a wailing in a high voice as if they had dropped dead before their eyes. And they went along following them thus and crying to the council house, where he sat down on the bench made of tree branches, and all the Indians, got down on their knees before him continuing their crying, while he listened with great calmness and seriousness until, from fatigue he got up and left. And the Indians, on ceasing their crying, got back to their feet and left, drying their tears. Those who were absent because they had not been present at the reception and those from the distant villages came later. When there were many assembled, the chief came and, seated on the cot, the Indians went down on their knees before him and performed their wailing until he rose and left. They returned to their houses. The coming to weep was continued in this manner for many days. Later, while I was in St. Augustine, I went to the river every day to fish, and from there I would hear someone begin to cry in a high voice every afternoon, and that the whole village would soon follow in the same tone. And when I asked the reason, I learned that their [previous] chief had died, and that accordingly they had to cry for a whole year."

Andrés writes that he and others visited other villages on Cumberland not far from San Pedro. Along the way he spied "patches of ground with blackberries [that were] very short and woven together and so loaded down with berries that the ground covered by them was dappled red and black."

A Spanish village in La Florida.
Illustration by John LoCastro.
(Courtesy of Mission San Luis,
Florida Department of State)

After fourteen days a boat sent from St. Augustine "arrived and in it a little wheat flour, which the governor sent us. And that night the soldiers kneaded it and cooked it under the embers and pulled out a very good bread, because the experience they have in this has made them masters. With this we ate bread, and we took our leave of all that people, and we embarked and also our [Guale] chiefs and the Indian pilot. We set out before it was daylight, and before we left this river for the sea, they showed us the site where the Frenchman had their fort, and they [the Spaniards] call in San Mateo. It will be fourteen or fifteen leagues from St. Augustine. An old soldier told me the story of how they expelled them [the French] from there." Hann notes that Father Andrés references Fort Caroline on the St. Johns River, constructed in 1564 by the French under René de Laudonnière.

Father Andrés would go on to serve as an architect, designing and building major structures for his order in Mexico and playing a significant role in draining the Valley of Mexico, where Mexico City would be built.

Jonathan Dickinson—1696

The Quaker merchant Jonathan Dickinson, born in Jamaica in 1633, left that island following a devastating earthquake in 1692. He, his family, and ten slaves set sail on the schooner *Reformation*, bound for Philadelphia, where he intended to resettle. A storm shipwrecked the vessel on the Florida coast near modern Hobe Sound (a state park there is named after him). He wrote a journal about the ensuing ordeal as he and his fellow survivors trekked north, harassed by Jobe and Ais Natives who despised the English. However, they were treated well in St. Augustine, where they were provided canoes, escorts, and supplies to continue the journey north. The following account of their brief stay on Amelia and Cumberland Islands is from *Jonathan Dickinson's Journal*.

> *The 10 month, 2; the 4 of the week.* [December 2, 4th day of the week, 1696]
> An hour before sunset we got to the town called St. Mary's [a mission town on Amelia Island]. This is a frontier and a garrison town: the inhabitants are Indians with some Spanish soldiers. We were conducted to the war-house, as the custom is, for every town hath a war-house. Or as we understood these houses were for their times of mirth and dancing, and to lodge and entertain strangers. This house is about 81-foot diameter built round, with 32 squares, in each square a cabin about 8 foot long of a good height being painted and well matted. The center of this building is a quadrangle of 20 foot being open at the top of the house.
>
> In this quadrangle is the place they dance having a great fire in the middle. One of the squares of this building is the gateway or passage in. The women natives of these towns clothe themselves with the moss of trees, making gowns and petticoats thereof which at a distance or in the night look very neat. The Indian boys we saw were kept to school in the church, the friar being their schoolmaster. This is the largest town of all. About a mile from this is another town called St. Phillips.
>
> *The 7; the 2 of the week.* [December 7, 2nd day of the week, 1696]
> This morning we put on shore having passed an inlet of the sea, and here we dressed some victuals and got a little sleep until the tide served. Some of our Indians went out a-hunting for deer and hogs of both which the Spaniards said there was plenty, and when the tide served we were to go to the northernmost end of this [Amelia] island and stay for the hunters. One of the Indians brought a deer which he throwed down amongst the other Indians, and he went out again to hunt to the north end of the island, where we were to rendezvous for this night. We set forward about ten o'clock and got to the place appointed

an hour or two before sunset, it being a fine lofty wood. We employed ourselves in getting firewood for the night and moss to lie on, of both which we got plenty, having a large oak to lie under.

The Indians brought in several hogs and deer, of which we had part, so that we fared richly; having a pleasant night's repose; we got up to be gone about an hour before day.

Dickinson's party left Amelia in "seven large canoes provided to carry us being in all about sixty persons; eighteen of us [his family and slaves] and 6 of Smith's company, seven Spaniards and thirty odd Natives, which were to row the canoes and be our pilots."

> *The 10 month, 8; the 3 of the week.* [December 8, 3rd day of the week, 1696]
> This day having rowed from the last place [Amelia] until two hours before sunset we put on shore at a place where had been an Indian settlement; it being on a high bank, from whence we had a prospect of the sound. Here we employed ourselves to go and fetch bushes to make shelter against the wind and dews of the night, and in cutting of dry grass to lie on, and getting of wood which was at considerable distance. But we resolved to have it if labor would purchase it. Those that were not employed in these services were providing of water and victuals, for we had always enough to do. We had a pleasant night and rested well.

This camp, "where had been an Indian settlement" on a high bank with a view of the sound, was most likely the northwest section of Cumberland, Terrapin Point, where the village of Puturiba had been located.

> *The 10th month 9; the 4 of the week.* [December 9, 4th day of the week, 1696]
> This morning about sun-rising we saw a canoe of Carolina Indians agoing to the southward a-hunting; they kept the western side of the sound, being fearful of us. We had a canoe manned with Indians and Spaniards to go after them to speak with them, being desirous to get them to carry letters to inform of our coming, not knowing but we might alarm the out-settlement of Carolina.

Father Chozas had the same vantage point when he saw warrior canoes on the way back to Guale after the 1597 rebellion and attack on San Pedro. Dickinson's account of 1696 continues.

> This canoe of ours pursued the other, but the Carolina Indians put on shore, run into a marsh and fired at our people. The Spanish Indians who could speak the Yammaw's [Yamasee or Yamacraw] language, called unto them, and told them their business, withal entreating them to come unto them; but they answered that they were going a-hunting for

the season, therefore desired them to be gone, for they would not come near them: thus our people returned unto us. The Carolina Indians went their way, and we prepared to go forward. We having the Casseekey [cacique] of St. Wans [St. Johns] with us sent him away last night, to see if he could meet any of the Yamasee Indians of Carolina, he being acquainted with and related to them: but this canoe passed him, we set forward and rowed all the day till about an hour before sunset, and then we put on shore at an Indian field which was overgrown with sedge, it being low wet land. Here we made our accustomed provision for lodging, lying this night in a wood, having dressed victuals for this time and tomorrow; and having rested well this night, about day-break or sooner we left this place.

Dickinson and his party reached Charlestown on December 26, 1696. Three months later they sailed for Philadelphia, where he prospered, eventually serving two terms as mayor there. He died in 1722, ten years before James Oglethorpe brought the first settlers to Georgia.

A new mission named San Buenaventura de Guadalquini was planted on the south end of St. Simons between 1606 and 1609 and became part of the Mocama missions, consisting of San Juan and San Pedro. Passengers traveling between the three missions were ferried by Natives living there. The two hundred thousand Timucua in 1500 had been reduced by European-borne diseases and overwork to fifty thousand by 1595 (some estimates halve that number). San Pedro's decline in population began with epidemics that seized the province from 1612 to 1617, killing half the Timucua mission Natives, "a very great harvest of souls," Father Pareja wrote. One interior friar baptized eight hundred dying Natives at his mission. Milanich notes that people who succumb to smallpox, the plague, or measles "die quickly, before the diseases can etch evidence on human skeletons," leaving behind little archaeological evidence. Other contagious diseases—chicken pox, bubonic plague, dysentery, diphtheria, influenza, malaria, scarlet fever, typhoid, typhus, and yellow fever—killed their victims quickly and were too lethal to spread to other regions. Spanish documents record an epidemic that originated in Seville, Spain, that came to La Florida by ship, striking down Natives, friars, and two Florida governors. A smallpox epidemic lasting from 1654 to 1655 once again ravaged half of the Timucua population.

By the mid-1600s, the entire Timucua population numbered fewer than twenty-five hundred. The Golden Age of Spanish missions in Florida and Georgia saw a 98 percent decline in Native population from 1595 to 1700. By that year only about a thousand

Timucua remained. The Timucua chiefs' status deteriorated commensurately with the reduction in the number of their subjects and the loss of satellite villages under their control. By then much of the mission activity in Florida had extended from St. Augustine to missions in the Apalachee region of west Florida.

A new Franciscan mission, San Phelipe (Felipe) de Atuluteca (the aboriginal name for Cumberland) was established on Cumberland at Table Point or Brickhill Bluff in about 1670. (One historian placed it on the former site of San Pedro.) At the mission were Natives who relocated from the Newport River estuaries on the mainland between St. Catherines Island and Sapelo Island. The new inhabitants had fled the English and their Native ally raiders. By 1683 Spain realized the futility of defending poorly garrisoned missions and abandoned Cumberland Island and the missions north of it. After a 1684 pirate raid on Cumberland, many of the San Phelipe inhabitants relocated to a new mission, San Phelipe III, on Amelia Island.

Raids by pirates and predatory Native groups also led to the decline of Spanish missions in Georgia. The Westos, encouraged and aided by the English, aggressively raided villages, capturing indigenous men, women, and children and selling them into slavery. Fifty or more Yamasee under Chief Altamaha, toting English shotguns, attacked the mission on St. Catherines Island in February 1685. Yamasee and Apalachicola warriors backed by the English continued their assault on Spanish missions until 1706. As Natives of Georgia's Spanish missions retreated south to the relative safety of St. Augustine, South Carolina Yamasee—later under attack from the English—fled Georgia's interior to territory under Spain's protection, including islands formerly held by the Timucua and Guale. San Pedro de Mocama, once the largest mission north of St. Augustine, became home to Yamasee.

Eventually all of the Georgia coast Timucua would be herded south to St. Augustine and relocated to Cuba and other Spanish colonies. San Pedro last appears on the rolls of Florida missions in 1675. Milanich notes the passing in 1767 of the last Timucuan to leave Florida, Juan Alonso Cabale, who died in the Cuban village of Guanabacoa, now a suburb of Havana. Cabale was born in a Florida mission with a Spanish name. His wife was a Yamasee. After almost fourteen thousand years of living off the land in Florida and southern Georgia, four thousand years on Georgia's barrier islands, and just over two hundred years of Spanish rule, the Timucua were an extinct race.

Swanton speculates that some of the Timucua may have survived in Seminole settlements or in Volusia County, south of St. Augustine. John Worth writes that within four

Westo Raids

Westo raiders attacked Guale and Timucua missions in the early 1650s. Their goal was to enslave Native men, women, and children in order to barter for guns, ammunition, steel hatchets, blankets, and glass beads with English colonists in Virginia and South Carolina. The Westos, so called by Carolinians, were known to the Spanish as the Chichimeco. Some historians equate the Chichimeco with the Ricahecria, who left Virginia in 1656 and relocated to the Savannah River near Augusta from 1660 to 1680. Another source indicates they were driven from the Northeast by the Iroquois, who monopolized the gun trade there. The firearms provided by the English gave them a military advantage over the Yamasee (Middle Georgia), Guale (Coastal Georgia), and Timucua who still relied on bows and arrows. The Carolinians originally befriended the Westos, who served as a barrier to the Spanish, but by 1680 Charleston sought to destroy the Westos after deeming them an obstruction to the lucrative deerskin trade.

years of Spain's first contact (1517) with southeastern Natives, they were being transported to Cuba. Approximately three hundred were brought to Cuba as slaves prior to that. Between 1513 and 1564, Spain launched seven major expeditions from Cuba to the mainland of the southeastern United States; Havana served as a home base for these Natives, who were used as interpreters and guides. With the establishment of St. Augustine in 1565 as a permanent colony, immigration of southeastern Natives, including the Timucua, to Havana increased. Many of them were settled along with Central America Native immigrants in Guanabacoa.

Other Florida mission Natives were brought to Havana for trials and incarceration in the seventeenth century. Two Timucuans were confined for seven years at Havana's El Morro prison for their participation in a 1628 insurrection. The Timucuan chief, Don Thomás de Medina, was arrested and sent to Havana to be tried in 1681 on the charge of sodomy. The migration of Natives to Cuba continued through the mid-1700s, including eighty-nine mission Natives residing at Nombre de Dios (St. Augustine) and Tolomato (eight miles north of St. Augustine) who were resettled at Guanabacoa in 1763. Worth notes that the southeastern Natives survived long enough to marry Cubans of mixed African or African Native ancestry: "there were at least a few survivors who may have living descendants today," and "it may eventually be possible to identify genetic traces of this Native American ancestry among living Cubans or Cuban-Americans."

The adage that nature abhors a vacuum applies to the indigenous occupation of the southeastern United States. The Timucua, who once controlled much of Northeast

Florida and Southeast Georgia, were supplanted by the Yamasee and the Creek and their remnants, the Seminoles. Spain's slow retreat from the Carolinas to St. Augustine left the door wide open for the English to enter, which they eagerly did. The land between the St. Johns and Altamaha Rivers became disputed territory, a fifty-mile swath of land neither Spain or Britain wished to settle for fear of sparking a new war between the two countries.

Then came Oglethorpe.

CHAPTER III   James Oglethorpe

*T*HE BRITISH ENVISIONED the last of its thirteen colonies as a buffer between Carolina, Spanish Florida, and French-held Mississippi. In 1717, Sir Robert Montgomery proposed to create a colony named the Margravate of Azilia between the Savannah and Altamaha Rivers; however, the baronet's dream never left the planning stage. Sixteen years later, James Edward Oglethorpe led the first wave of settlers to a bluff overlooking the Savannah River. He was, at age thirty-six, uniquely qualified for this particular project. Young and energetic, Oglethorpe came from a well-to-do and well-connected family with an estate in Godalming, south of London, and land in nearby Haslemere. Young Oglethorpe attended Eton, Corpus Christi College, a military academy at Lompres, France, and was barely out of his teens when he received his military tutelage in Germany and Hungary during the 1716–18 Austro-Turkish War under the brilliant general and statesman Prince Eugene of Savoy. That experience would serve him well in the untamed wilderness between Charleston and St. Augustine, where Spanish, Native, and French forces hostile to the British awaited.

James Oglethorpe inherited Westbrook Manor (Godalming, Surrey, England) in 1718. The house is now home to the Meath Epilepsy Charity. (Courtesy of Bryan-Lang Historical Archives)

Oglethorpe had already achieved national prominence for his prison reform efforts while a member of Parliament. One unintended consequence of releasing debtors en masse from prison was the resulting surplus of unemployed men. Fueled by humanitarian zeal, Oglethorpe and a social network of like-minded philanthropic visionaries established a board of trustees and a charter to send carefully vetted, skilled tradesmen and their families to America. The new colony, Georgia, was named for charter grantor King George II and would be funded mainly through annual subsidies from Parliament.

There was no obligation on Oglethorpe's part to go to Georgia. He was, after all, just another trustee ineligible to hold office or own property in the new province, or to receive pay for his work. In addition, he had an English estate to maintain and a position in Parliament to uphold. Nonetheless he was the logical choice to help establish the colony, and when he accompanied the first wave of 115 settlers consisting of forty families aboard the *Anne* in late 1732, all eyes turned to him for leadership. As a young man, he had made it a goal to meet the important personages of his day. Now fate had presented the opportunity to become one himself. The ship landed briefly at Charleston on January 13, 1733, before sailing to Port Royal, where Oglethorpe left the colonists to survey a location for the new settlement. One of the South Carolinians who showed him

James Oglethorpe (1696–1785) was the leading figure and driving force behind the founding of the Georgia colony. He established Fort St. Andrews and Fort William on Cumberland Island. (Courtesy of the Cumberland Island National Seashore Museum NPS)

Yamacraw Chief Tomochichi and his nephew, Toonahawi. Tomochichi was an important ally who helped Oglethorpe establish the fledgling colony. Legend credits Toonahawi for naming Cumberland Island after Prince William Augustus, Duke of Cumberland, the youngest son of King George II. The Yamacraw reintegrated with the Lower Creek following Tomochichi's death in 1739. (Engraving ca. 1734–35 by John Faber Jr.)

the way was Jonathan Bryan, a young scout who would play an increasingly larger role in Georgia's growth throughout his life. The site Oglethorpe chose, Yamacraw Bluff, was renamed Savannah.

There, he met Mary Musgrove, the daughter of a Creek mother and an English trader father, and the wife of John Musgrove, also an English trader. Mary (her Creek name was Coosaponakeesa) interpreted for Oglethorpe in his meetings with the local Yamacraw *mico*, Chief Tomochichi (Tomachetchie) and played a vital role in the Georgia colony's early days, using her connections to ensure peace between local tribes and the English. When the English marched on Spanish Florida, she was instrumental in sending Muskogee Creek warriors to join the fight.

After Oglethorpe negotiated use of the land at Yamacraw Bluff, the colonists were transported there by smaller crafts in early February 1733. He immediately set about establishing a ring of farming and cattle-raising communities around the town to sustain the colonists and to serve as early-warning stations in the event of enemy attack. Farther south, forty men were appointed to "clear a path from Barnwell's Bluff [Fort King George on the Altamaha River] to Savannah." Oglethorpe envisioned a village every six miles and a ferryboat at every river crossing, supplemented with forts and outposts that he placed on the Ogeechee River and on the barrier islands. In 1721 South Carolina had already established Fort King George on the Altamaha River, near present-day Darien, as one of several outposts designed to intercept Spanish invaders from the south and French forces from the west and to warn Charleston of imminent threats. At the time, everything south of the Altamaha and north of the St. Johns River was deemed the Debatable Land, territory claimed but unoccupied by Spain.

Naming Cumberland Island

On his return to England in 1734 to raise more funds for the colony, Oglethorpe took a number of Yamacraw Natives with him, including Tomochichi, his wife Senauki, and his nephew, Toonahowi (Tuanahooy or Tuanouie). There young Toonahowi, heir to the Yamacraw chiefdom, met Prince William Augustus, Duke of Cumberland, George II's youngest son, who was about the same age. The "dark-eyed, black-haired child of the wilderness and the fair-haired, blue-eyed child of generations of royalty" became fast friends. Before departing for the colony, the duke presented Toonahowi with a gold watch.

Back in Georgia, Oglethorpe made regular reports to the Trustees, though not always as often as they would like. Malcontents, so-called "grumbletonians," also wrote to the Trustees to voice their complaints. He established a new town and fort on St. Simons in 1736, naming it Frederica in honor of King George's son, Frederick, Prince of Wales, heir to the throne. (Prince Frederick predeceased his father, but Frederick's son became King George III, the unlucky monarch when Georgia and twelve other colonies broke away from British rule.) In March of that year, Oglethorpe set off down the coast in two scout boats, the *Carolina* and the *Georgia*, along with a pirogue transporting Capt. Hugh Mackay, thirty Highlander indentured servants, Lt. Hugh Mackay Jr. (Capt. Mackay's nephew), and his ten rangers. Accompanying them in canoes were Tomochichi, Toonahowi, and forty Yamacraw warriors. Oglethorpe intended to trace the southernmost branch of the Altamaha River, hoping to fix the boundary between Spanish Florida and British Georgia on the St. Johns River. (Afterward, some creative

Philipp Georg Friedrich von Reck's 1736 sketch of Fort St. Andrews. Von Reck made two journeys to Georgia with Salzburger emigrants who settled at Ebenezer, near Savannah. His drawings and watercolor sketches were discovered in the Royal Library, Copenhagen, in the 1970s. (Courtesy of Bryan-Lang Historical Archives)

mapmaking by one cartographer showed a nonexistent Altamaha River branch extending to the St. Johns River, clearly intended to support the British claim of land south of Darien.)

On this scouting mission to survey the "frontiers to see where His Majesty's dominions and the Spaniard's join," Oglethorpe also set about building fortifications on the islands. He left the Highlanders under Hugh Mackay's oversight to construct a fort on the northwest side of Cumberland Island at what is now Terrapin Point, near or on the Spanish mission that once stood there. Oglethorpe had outlined a four-pointed-star configuration design on the bluff, each point being a bastion that allowed men to fire in several directions. "I called the New Fort St. Andrews," he wrote, "and the Island it stands the Highlands," presumably because of the high bluff on which the fort stood and/or in honor of the Scots who would build and garrison it.

Tomochichi informed Oglethorpe he and his men "would go to hunt buffalo as far as the Spanish frontiers." Oglethorpe suspected their true intention was to attack and kill the Spanish out-guards on the St. Johns in retaliation for a Yamasee ambush on one of Tomochichi's hunting parties the previous year. He told the chief he would accompany him on this so-called buffalo hunt. Oglethorpe's unstated objective was to reconnoiter "as far as the utmost extent of his dominions towards Augustine. We shall then know how far the lands possessed by the English confederate Indians extend." He wrote,

"Tomochichi is willing that we should settle upon any place within his lands provided the Lower Creek Nations agree to it." The chief considered all coastal lands south to St. Augustine (including Cumberland Island once occupied by the Timucua) part of his nation's domain.

Perhaps Oglethorpe originally intended to call the island the Highlands. But in a letter to Thomas Pelham-Holles, the Duke of Newcastle, dated April 17, 1736, Oglethorpe writes that "there are three beautiful islands upon the seacoast, the first the Indian king's [Tomochichi's] nephew Toonahowi, who was in England, called Cumberland, saying that the Duke had given him a watch to show him to use time and that he had obtained leave of the Creek Nation to give his name to that island, that through all times his benefactor's name might be remembered." In an August 1739 letter describing the colony's boundaries, Oglethorpe mentions "the islands of Frederica [St. Simons], Cumberland & Amelia to which they have given the names of his Majesty King George's Family out of Gratitude to him."

Did Toonahowi really suggest naming Cumberland after the duke? Or did Oglethorpe plant the seed, all the while intending to name it after the duke as a political expedient to curry the king's favor? His tendency to designate places in honor of British royalty was prudent given that the colony's charter was granted by the king and continued to exist under his good graces. There is a certain poetic majesty to naming the colony's mainland after George II, the patriarch, and its golden barrier islands after his offspring. Frederica soon became the largest British fortification in North America. Amelia, an island Oglethorpe thought superlative, bore the name of the king's second daughter. The duke, having the largest island on the coast named for him, should have had no reason to feel slighted.

Francis Moore, who came to Georgia on Oglethorpe's second voyage to the colony, records that they came to an "island, which the Indians formerly called Wissoo, in English Sassafras. This is over against Jekyl island on the south; the northwest end rises fifty feet or upwards above water, like a terras [terrace], a mile in length, covered with tall pines. The western extremity of this hill commands the passage for boats from the southward as the northern end of the island does the entry for ships. Here they met with some bark huts, which our friendly Indians had some time since built for lodging when they hunted here. They saw a great many deer and a wide savannah lying at the foot of the hill, extending near two or three miles, so that from the western point they could discover any boat that came from the southward for several miles. Mr. Oglethorpe, upon the extreme western point of the hill, the foot of which is washed on the one side by the bay and by the channel that goes to the southward on the other, marked out a fort to be called St. Andrews, and gave Captain Hugh Mackay orders to build it."

Another English writer referred to the prominence on which the fort was built as "1st Bluff." The Spanish knew this site as the Point of Bejecez on San Pedro or the Isle of Whales. Another source indicates the Scottish Highlanders asked Oglethorpe to name the fort Saint Andrews after the patron saint of Scotland. Oglethorpe's placement of Fort St. Andrews at Terrapin Point rather than the north end of Little Cumberland may have been for the pragmatic reason that his cannons would be out of range of enemy ships entering the wide sound between Cumberland and Jekyll. Placing the fort where the inland waterway narrowed improved its strategic value.

The expedition continued south the next day, passing the Clothogotheo, most likely the St. Marys River, where they landed on another island, which Oglethorpe named Amelia "in memory of Her Highness the Princess Amelia." Once they reached the St. Johns River, it was not an easy task to prevent the Yamacraw warriors, who foamed at the mouth with rage at the sight of enemy on their land, from seeking out and attacking Spanish sentries. Tomochichi and his men spied an English envoy, Major Richards, at night returning with others from St. Augustine and "would have cut them into pieces, taking them for Spaniards," if not for Oglethorpe's intervention.

After their reconnaissance south, Oglethorpe stopped at Cumberland to inspect Fort St. Andrews and was pleased at the progress Mackay and his men had made. The fort was already "in a state of defense," an anonymous letter writer recorded. "[Oglethorpe] thanked the Highlanders for their diligence and offered to carry any of them back that cared to leave the place. But not one of them would do so, saying that whilst there was danger they would stay though they should lose their next harvest."

Francis Moore provides more details about the fort, which he found in a state of "forwardness; the ditch being dug and the parapet raised with wood and earth on the land side, and the small wood was cleared fifty yards around the fort. Besides it was very difficult to raise works here, the ground being a loose sand; therefore, they used the same method of support it as Caesar mentions in the wars of Gaul [Western Europe], laying trees and earth alternately." This earth construction was not meant to be permanent. The fort, manned by Capt. Hugh Mackay commanding twenty men, mounted ten eight-pound cannons to protect the inland passage.

The logic behind Oglethorpe's claim to the land he had just surveyed was explained by the unidentified writer: "The country as far as Saint John's River was conquered from the Spaniards in Queen Ann's War and was in possession of our allied Indians at the

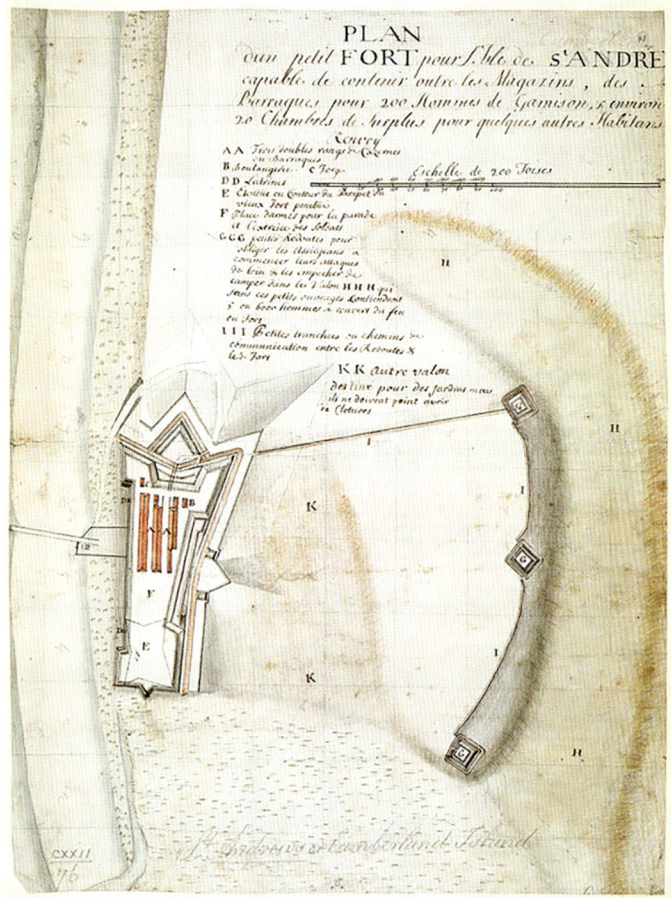

Fort St. Andrews, as drawn by Captain André Thomas ("Plan d'un petit fort pour l'Isle de St. André"). (Courtesy of the Norman B. Leventhal Map and Education Center) The French text (translation by Jane Williams) reads:

> Small fort for Island of St. Andrew capable of accommodating, in addition to the magazines, some barracks for 200 men of defense, and about 20 surplus rooms for some other inhabitants.

AA	Three double rows of barracks
B	Bakery
C	Forge
D	Latrines
E	Extent or contour of parapet of the old punctuated fort
F	Place of arms for the parade and the exercise (practice) of the soldiers
G	Small redoubts to force the opposing forces laying siege to the fort to begin their attacks from afar and to prevent them from camping in the valley.
H	That without these little works there would be 5 or 6,000 men hidden [and able to] to fire on the fort.
I	Small paths or roads of communication between redoubts and fort.
J	[Blank]
K	Other valleys/swales intended for gardens but must not have fencing.

Treaty of Utrecht. Therefore by the articles of that treaty, which says that all territories in America shall remain to those who are in possession of them, these lands being in possession of the Indians who are allies to Great Britain and have since made them over to the King, they belong to the King of Great Britain."

Oglethorpe confirmed this in his April 17, 1736, letter to the Duke of Newcastle: "The Indian king Tomochichi went down with me to the utmost limits of the King of Great Britain's dominions to put us in possession of all the lands held by their Nation from this island to the Spanish frontiers."

When Spain, alarmed by the British presence, demanded the Georgia colonists retreat north as far as the Edisto River in South Carolina, Oglethorpe declared that "I cannot deliver up a foot of ground belonging to His Majesty to a foreign power. I will alive or dead keep possession of it 'till I have His Majesty's orders." He doubted Spain had the firepower to force his removal and added that the land he had just inspected "are the keys of all America."

In June 1736, Oglethorpe reported to the Trustees a skirmish with Don Ignatio Cob, who was scouting the coast with thirty handpicked men and thirty Yamasee Natives to assess the English settlements and dislodge them if they were found to be poorly defended. After being chased out of St. Simons Sound by cannon fire from Delegal's Fort on the south end of St. Simons Island, the Spaniards attempted to enter the inland passage at Cumberland but were successfully challenged by the Scots at Fort St. Andrews. Cob and his men rowed out to sea; that night they reached the St. Johns River, where they joined forces with a hundred dragoons under Don Pedro de Lamberto. Oglethorpe was present at Fort St. George on the St. Johns, across the river from Lamberto's men, and anticipated an attack. To delay the assault until reinforcements arrived, Oglethorpe deceived the Spaniards into thinking his troop strength was greater than it actually was, perhaps a trick he learned as an aide under Prince Eugene of Savoy. He wrote that he sent "two carriage and two swivel guns to be carried into the woods, that the Spaniards might not distinguish where they were, and fired and charged the swivel guns so often as to make a salute of seven and with the carriage guns I fired five shot in answer. The swivel guns (by reason of the smallness of their report) seemed like a ship at a distance."

The hoax worked. Oglethorpe later learned the Spaniards "concluded from the guns that there was a new strength arrived." That night he had "several fires made in the woods" two or three miles away, to give the impression of a large encamped force, deploying a military ruse dating to ancient times (e.g., Gideon versus the Midianites, Judges 7:19–20). The Spaniards retired to St. Augustine "fatigued with over labor, [and] spread much dismal accounts, magnifying our strength and diligence, in order to save their reputations," he recorded. The Spanish governor called a council of war and sent a contingent under a flag of truce to meet with the English and inquire about their claim to land south of the Altamaha. Oglethorpe met them aboard a man-of-war in the sound between St. Simons and Jekyll. "After dinner," he wrote, "we drank the King of Great Britain's and the King of Spain's health under the discharge of the cannon from the ship." This was a cue for fortifications located on St. Simons at Delegal's Fort, Fort Frederica, Darien, and Fort St. Andrews to answer with cannon fire. After their volleys

Spain's Title to Georgia

England's intrusion into Georgia prompted Spain to reestablish its legal claim to La Florida "as far north as 32°30', inclusive, where lies the harbor of the island of Santa Elena" (Parris Island, South Carolina). The Spanish government chose Antonio de Arredondo to draw up this historical proof (*demostración historiographica*). He was an engineer sent from Havana in 1736 to Frederica, where he protested the establishment of the new English colony on land claimed by Spain. By 1742 he was chief of staff in Spain's attack on the colony. As a mapmaker, engineer, soldier, and diplomat, Arredondo was well positioned to make the case for Spain's title to the land.

ceased echoing over the water, "Don Pedro smiled and said no wonder Don Ignatio made more haste home than out."

Oglethorpe sailed for England in late November 1736 to make his reports, to convince the Trustees and Parliament of the need to expand fortifications south of the Altamaha, and to raise another regiment to guard the southern territory. While in England, Oglethorpe met with Britain's de facto prime minister, Robert Walpole, and King George II. The Trustees were leery of overspending Parliament's allocation for the colony and overly cautious about offending Spain by trespassing on the disputed territory. Oglethorpe convinced the king, Parliament, and Walpole of Spain's military buildup and its intention to reclaim Georgia. He made them see, too, the strategic and commercial value the colony held for Britain. Oglethorpe also convinced King George II to appoint him a colonel in the army and give him a regiment of British soldiers to take back to Georgia. His efforts paid off, and with Walpole's assistance, he raised a new regiment, the Forty-Second Regiment of Foot, to staff Fort St. Andrews.

Up to that time, Oglethorpe had been a civilian with limited military experience, primarily as an aide to Prince Eugene. Nevertheless, he got what he wanted: a rank in the regular army and a regiment. Oglethorpe was given the title of "General and Commander in Chief of all and singular his Majesty's provinces of Carolina and Georgia" and "Colonel of the Forty-Second Regiment of Foot." During the pending hostilities with Spain, he held a brevet field commission as general in order to command all allied forces, including Carolina Rangers, and Native allies.

On May 6, 1738, the doctor at Frederica, Thomas Hawkins, reported to the Trustees that "two have died at Saint Andrew's of the dropsy," a term for edema (body swelling), which can be caused by congestive heart failure, kidney disease, liver damage (cirrhosis), or long-term protein deficiency. Some soldiers at Fort St. Andrews later complained about inadequate food provisions. Also on May 6, two ships, the *Amy* and the *Whitaker* arrived at Savannah. On May 24, Capt. Hugh Mackay Sr. accompanied five "pettiaguas" (pirogues) loaded with 150 passengers, members of the Forty-Second Regiment of Foot and their families, as they sailed to Fort St. Andrews. Adjutant Hugh Mackay Jr., Captain Mackay's nephew, had already been on Cumberland overseeing seventeen Highland indentured servants construct a settlement named Mackay's Town, or Barriemackie (or Barrimache), "two Camps of Cleft [clapboard] houses in which 500 Men, and their officers are conveniently lodged," and laid out along regular rows. This settlement was located near Fort St. Andrews on the north end of Cumberland, possibly at present-day

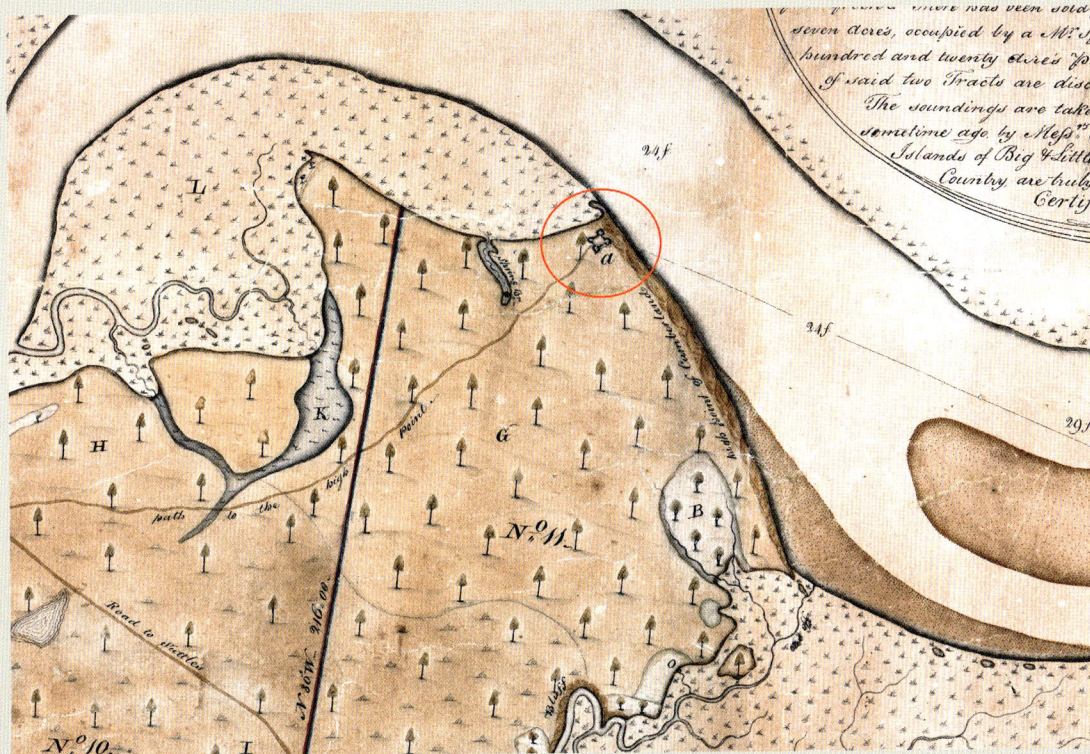

Detail of McKinnon Map showing location of Fort St. Andrews. (Courtesy of Georgia Archives, Carnegie Estate Records of Cumberland Island, acc. 1969-0501M)

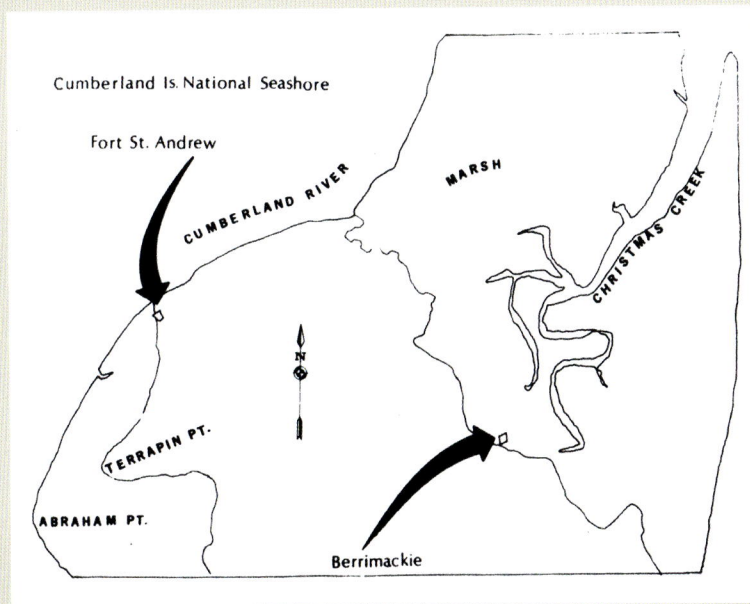

Map from 1975 displaying locations of Fort St. Andrews and Barriemackie at present-day High Point. (Courtesy of Southeast Archeological Center NPS)

High Point. Oglethorpe returned from England three months after their arrival. On November 1, 1738, he went to Cumberland to inspect his new regiment, little suspecting the hornet's nest that awaited his arrival.

Mutiny at St. Andrews

About 250 of the Forty-Second Regiment men formerly belonged to the Twenty-Fifth Regiment of Foot stationed on Gibraltar. Many of them were undesirables the commander of the Twenty-Fifth was glad to be rid of. They had been removed from civilized Europe and their Spanish paramours to this outpost on the frontier bordering Spanish Florida. They had been denied additional wages for food, a perk they enjoyed on Gibraltar, and they had not received the extra pay promised for their voyage to Georgia. To add insult to injury, rum—an anesthetic that lessened the monotony of military life—was prohibited in the colony of Georgia. By the time General Oglethorpe arrived with his new company to be stationed on Cumberland, matters had come to a head. Most of what we know about what occurred next comes from his report to the Trustees, in which he positions himself as the hero of the day.

He inspected the regiment at dawn, outside of the fort and possibly at Barriemackie, then "went up to the fort to breakfast at the commanding officer's barrack." Soon a large crowd of the discontented men gathered outside demanding to speak to him. "As I came out," Oglethorpe wrote, "I immediately suspected from the behavior of the people that there was some bad design on foot." Seeing that the crowd outnumbered the fort's guard, he "nimbly" walked out of the gate, followed by the malcontents, to get them out of the fort where ammunition was stored. He and his officers were unarmed, wearing only their swords. The general "whispered an order to the officer of the guard to secure the fort" and then turned to confront the men and asked for their grievances. Some of them made what Oglethorpe thought were unreasonable demands, and the confrontation quickly escalated. The ringleader insisted that their beds and provisions be provided gratis. "I told him to go to his quarters," Oglethorpe wrote. "He said they were cold ones [barracks], that they would not be so answered but would have their provisions and cried out, 'Now, it's your time!'"

Oglethorpe seized the man and pulled him inside the fort's outer barriers. Another man shouted, "You shall then take us all!" Captain Lieutenant Desbrisay, Oglethorpe's assistant company commander, grabbed this man and pulled him inside as well. With the mutineers hot on their heels, Oglethorpe and Desbrisay carried the two men inside the fort and ordered the barriers to be closed. The mob tried to enter, but "Captain Mackay and Mr. Mackay strove to stop them at the moat bridge." In the struggle, a soldier named Ross took Captain Mackay's sword and injured his hand. Several Highlanders nearby came running with broadswords drawn. By the time Oglethorpe delivered his prisoners to the guard and returned to the barriers, the frustrated mob had run back to their camp, crying "To arms!" Oglethorpe ordered the Highlander holding Ross down not to injure him. The Scot let Ross go, and he ran off to join his companions.

"I then considered whether it was best to stay in the fort and let the mutineers make themselves masters of the camp," Oglethorpe recounted in his written report, "or go and hinder their assembling. I was sure that all those who came over with me [the soldiers who recently arrived from England with Oglethorpe] were well affected and yet believed that if the mutineers were once masters of the camp, they might force them to join with them." The general's newly raised men, it turns out, were indeed intimidated by the Gibraltar veterans. This was a crucial moment for Oglethorpe and the colony. If the insurrectionists were allowed time to gather themselves, the tide might turn in their favor. If they seized control of the fort, their only option as one historian put it, "would have been to cast their lots with the Spanish in St. Augustine." Their knowledge of the colony's southernmost fortifications and manpower would have been of vital importance to an invading enemy.

"I therefore thought it was better to take one bold step," Oglethorpe wrote, "and go into the midst of the camp at once than suffer the innocent men and their families to fall into the hands of the mutineer." Desbrisay had already followed the mob into the camp, returning with news that the men from Captain Mackay's company were gathering and loading their muskets. Oglethorpe ordered the quarter guard, Highlanders, and scouts to follow him to the camp. Without waiting for them, he and Desbrisay ran into the camp, "hoping that my presence might awe them and prevent mischief." Captain Mackay was close on their heels.

When the general reached Barriemackie, he saw "a great many men with their arms" crowding the streets. One man, hiding behind a hut five yards away, leveled his weapon. "I stept back and called to him, 'Down with your arms.' At which he cried, 'No, by God, I'll down with you!' On which I rushed forward. He fired, the bullet whizzed above my shoulder, and the powder singed my clothes. At the same time I heard another shot fired, and the bullet whizzed by me and struck the mutineer." This second shot came from a musket Mackay had seized by force from another soldier. Oglethorpe's assailant, unawed by his commanding officer's presence, stepped forward to club him with the musket. "I closed in with him with my sword," Oglethorpe recorded, "and, seizing his firelock with my left hand, tore it from him, saying, 'Wretch, let go your arms, I will not kill you, I'll leave you to the hangman.' And did not touch him with my sword. At the same time another presented at me and missed fire. I ran and seized his piece, which he immediately let go, and ran away."

Oglethorpe, brandishing the seized musket, informed the remaining mutineers he would shoot anyone who resisted and would pardon those who dispersed. After a few tense moments, the men yielded. The mutiny had ended. "Then turning 'round," he wrote, "I saw several of the officers coming down the street to me, and the mutineer who had fired at me on the ground and a Highlander going to strike with his broadsword. I called to him to hold, which he accordingly did."

Desbrisay had also seized a musket, which had been aimed at him but misfired. He and Mackay, "slightly wounded in his hand" from the fracas at the fort, joined Oglethorpe. All three now carried muskets. "I then walked through all the camp," the general wrote, "and, calling out to the Sergeants, obliged all the men to keep their quarters and sent an officer down each street to go into their huts and examine their arms, who found 25 of them loaded with ball and most of them had been loaded before I reviewed them in the morning." The uprising had been a planned, not spontaneous, affair.

Later that day Oglethorpe assembled the men without their weapons. Among them, he wrote, was "the mutineer whom I had left prisoner in the fort, for the guard at the fort had let the two prisoners go and had told the officer that the men were in the right, for that they were not to starve." Oglethorpe had the man seized and locked up with four other ringleaders (another source indicates there were a total of six). The general once again asked the men to state their grievances. "They said they had none but that the King's pay was not sufficient to keep them without provisions [food] and that they had provisions at Gibraltar as well as pay and that Colonel Cochran had not paid them their sea pay during the time they were at sea." The Gibraltar soldiers had been accustomed to having provisions "from the King besides their pay." They were to receive six months' worth of provisions on Cumberland, after which the rations would cease to be free, and that time was about to expire. The men reminded Oglethorpe of the bonus pay for sea travel they were due. Lieutenant Colonel Cochran (or Cockran) had withheld their sea allowance. Oglethorpe reprimanded the men for their actions "and declared, upon their

showing the utmost grief, a pardon for all except the five ringleaders that were prisoners." The five were removed to Fort Frederica for a court-martial.

That evening and the next morning, Oglethorpe personally interviewed each man
"without any officer present." He was wise enough to know that some of the men would
not speak their minds in a crowd. But there was, in fact, one officer present—General
Oglethorpe himself. More than a few were no doubt intimidated meeting one-on-one
with this personage—a member of the British Parliament, de facto governor and military leader of the Georgia colony—especially knowing the fate their doomed ringleaders
faced. The general wanted "to know if they had any grievances, but they all said, No,
their officers treated them well and they had been constantly paid, except their sea pay."
Oglethorpe ordered Cochran to pay the men what was due to them. He later saw to it
that they were provided with provisions and shoes costing £6 per annum for each man.
The five ringleaders were found guilty and executed by firing squad.

Animosity between Cochran and Mackay had been brewing for some time, in particular over Cochran's apparent endeavors to profit by trafficking goods to soldiers, a
practice Oglethorpe strongly discouraged. Their rivalry erupted into an outright fight
between the two men when Cochran attacked Mackay "with a heavy stick." General
Oglethorpe ordered a court-martial to determine who was at fault. Due to Cochran's
rank, the trial was held in England. Both sailed there to stand before the military court.
Nine months later, Mackay returned to Georgia vindicated. Cochran was "removed" to
the Fifth Marine Regiment at Gibraltar.

The significance of the 1738 mutiny at St. Andrews is twofold. First, it sheds light
on Oglethorpe's character, corroborated by eyewitnesses: intelligent, quick-thinking,
decisive, fearless, coolheaded under fire, a man of action (some might say reckless),
shrewd, strict, yet fair and merciful. He displayed these qualities throughout his life,
particularly during the Spanish invasion, which leads to the second point. The mutiny
on Cumberland Island occurred four years before Spain attacked Georgia with the
intent of eradicating the English colony once and for all. Had the first mutineer who
fired on Oglethorpe hit his mark or the second man's musket not misfired, the colony's
fate might have been very different. During the 1742 invasion he personally led a charge
that repulsed an advance party of Spanish soldiers at Frederica's gates. He compelled
deserters fleeing an intense firefight at Bloody Marsh to return and make a stand. And he
outwitted Spanish Florida's governor and invading military leader, Manuel de Montiano,
after a Frenchman fled to the Spanish side by sending a letter that caused the Spaniards

War of Jenkins' Ear

The 1713 Treaty of Utrecht, which concluded the War of Spanish Succession, granted Great Britain a thirty-year contract to sell African slaves to Spanish colonies. This consent (*asiento*) also allowed British merchants to export 500 tons of merchandise each year, opening the door for illegal smuggling to Spanish ports. As a result, hostilities between the two countries continued through 1729. In that year, the Treaty of Seville gave Spain the right to board British merchant vessels to verify that the *asiento* right was not being abused. In 1731, Captain Robert Jenkins steered the ship *Rebecca*, with a cargo of sugar from Jamaica, on a legitimate return trip to London. His brig was seized off the coast of Florida by a Spanish privateer, Juan de León Fandiño, commanding a coast guard patrol boat, *La Isabela*.

Fandiño reportedly accused the English of illegal smuggling and lopped off Jenkins's left ear with the admonishment "go and tell your King that I will do the same if he dares to do the same!" The incident, seized upon by British politicians and Britain's South Sea Company as a reason to ramp up the slave trade in Spanish America and improve Caribbean commercial opportunities, led to renewed open conflict with Spain eight years later. In 1742, Spain invaded St. Simons Island in response to Oglethorpe's siege of St. Augustine two years earlier. The Spanish were repulsed by the English and retreated to St. Augustine after firing on Fort William on the south end of Cumberland Island. The conflict would be absorbed into the broader War of Austrian Succession, which ended with the Treaty of Aix-la-Chapelle in 1748. British historian and essayist Thomas Carlyle coined the conflict the War of Jenkins' Ear more than a century later. In Spain it is known as Guerra del Asiento.

to doubt the turncoat's estimate of British forces. Had St. Simons come under Spanish control, Savannah might have been a much more vulnerable target.

Less than four years after its construction, Fort St. Andrews needed repairs. In a letter to the Trustees dated December 29, 1739, Oglethorpe requested £400 to make improvements. In expectation of a Spanish counterattack, Oglethorpe dispatched Colonel Cook for more work on the fort. Thomas Eyre, Cook's assistant, wrote the fort consisted "only of small straight trees cut into lengths of fourteen foot and set close to one another upright in the ground." Other observers described the fort as "pallisaded with flankers and defended by eight pieces of cannon" with "only a rude quadrangular house, surrounded with logs or puncheons [short posts]." By the time of the Spanish invasion, the fort had an observation tower. With the outbreak of war with Spain (War of Jenkins' Ear) in 1739, Oglethorpe dipped into his own funds to make repairs at Fort St. Andrews and to "make another little one [fort] on the south end of that island." That same year, he put ashore on Cumberland and Amelia Islands "a stud of the Trust's horses and mares and the colts bred out of them," thus beginning what became an inexpensive, free-range horse farm.

Fort William and the 1742 Spanish Invasion

Oglethorpe erected a new outpost on Cumberland's south end and named it Fort William. While some historians assume it was named for Prince William Augustus, Duke of Cumberland, there is no clear evidence to support that claim. James Oglethorpe consistently referred to it as Fort William in his letters. It may have been named after Colonel William Cook, who laid out the fort and used cedar trees harvested from an upstream grove on the St. Marys River for its construction. The modest plans for Fort William infer it would not be appropriate to name it after a royal family member, as was the case for Fort Frederica, one of the most expensive fortresses the British built in the colonies at that time. The name Fort Prince William first appeared in documents in the mid-1760s, about the time Jonathan Bryan purchased the southern end of Cumberland Island. Bryan owned land in Prince William Parish in South Carolina, named after the Duke of Cumberland, and may have assumed the fort had been named for the duke.

After two unarmed Highlanders stationed at a small outpost on the north end of Amelia Island were decapitated and their bodies mutilated by Spaniards, Oglethorpe led a first-strike expedition into Florida. Some of his men slaughtered "a great number of Spanish cattle" and "killed their horses within sight" of Fort Picolata, located on the east bank of the St. Johns River, almost parallel with St. Augustine. Oglethorpe made several raids into Florida early in 1740, burning Fort Picolata and capturing Fort Saint Francis de Pupa, which stood on the west bank of the St. Johns a few miles farther north (the two forts were connected by a ferryboat). In May 1740, he laid siege to St. Augustine but withdrew in July after unsuccessful attempts to dislodge the Spanish at the Castillo de San Marcos.

After the failed siege of St. Augustine, both companies and the civilians at Barriemackie were removed to Frederica, leaving twenty troops at Fort St. Andrews. The garrisons at Fort St. Andrews and Fort William were relieved monthly by detachments of troops stationed at Frederica and Darien. Fort William was the last fort Oglethorpe constructed south of the Altamaha River. Its siting at South Point (the south end) and its twin eighteen-pound cannons—far bigger than the eight-pounders at Fort St. Andrews or indeed elsewhere in the region—on movable platforms allowed the English to challenge enemy ships entering the sound between Cumberland and Amelia Islands. Spain launched a major counteroffensive in May 1742 when Governor Manuel de Montiano

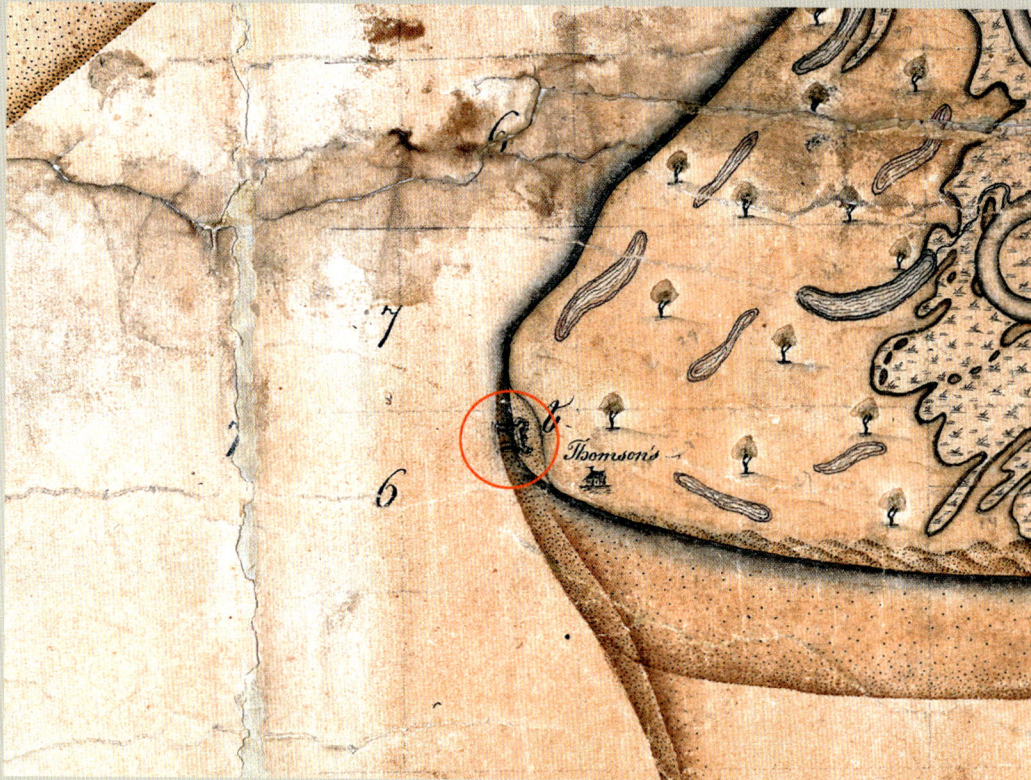

Detail of McKinnon map showing location of Fort William. (Courtesy of Georgia Archives, Carnegie Estate Records of Cumberland Island, acc. 1969-0501M)

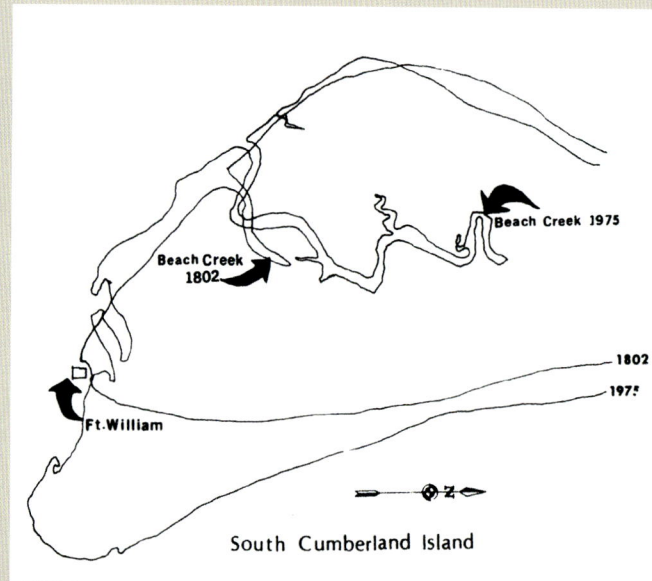

Map displaying approximate location of Fort William, 1975. (Courtesy of Southeast Archeological Center NPS)

Fort William

Approximate original location of Fort William, photographed in 2019. The current location has likely significantly shifted over time.

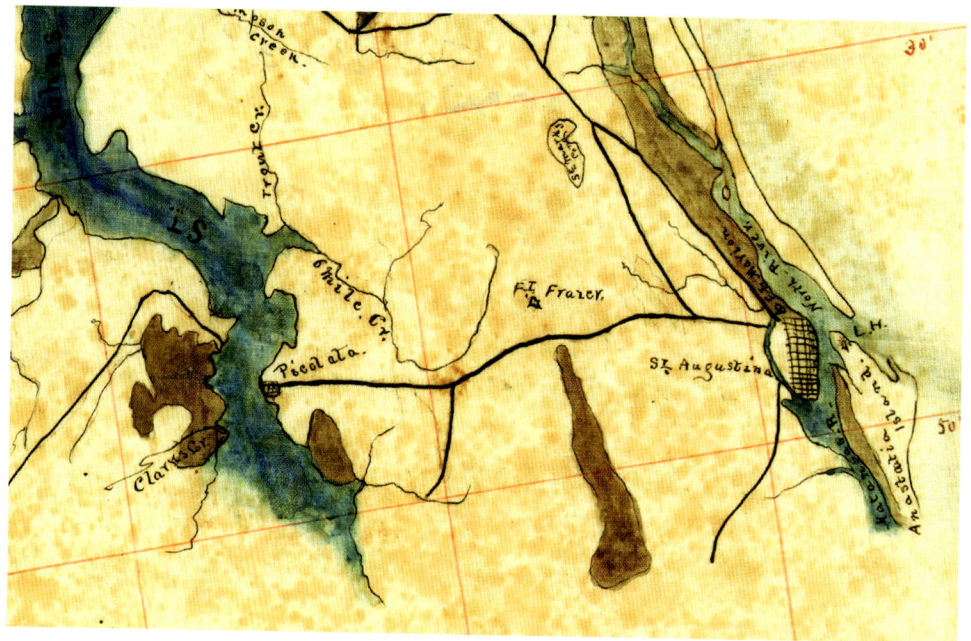

Map displaying location of Fort Picolata,
destroyed by Oglethorpe in 1740.
(Courtesy of the Library of Congress)

embarked from St. Augustine with a fleet of fifty-two schooners, sloops, galleys, half-galleys, men-of-war, and pirogues carrying almost two thousand soldiers.

Thomas Eyre didn't think highly of either of the island forts' ability to deter enemy ships, having written two years earlier that "these garrisons are of no manner of service in defending the water passage, the rivers being so wide that an enemy might pass without danger from the largest guns in England." On their own, that might have been true. However, Fort William, working in tandem with a ship anchored in the harbor, did repulse an attack. On June 21, 1742, fifteen of Montiano's vessels (another account indicates nine boats), consisting of four half-galleys, two schooners, and numerous pirogues, separated from the Spanish fleet seeking shelter from high winds and rough seas and entered the Cumberland Sound. The schooner *Walker*, commanded by Capt. George Dunbar and carrying fourteen guns and ninety men, lay at anchor southwest of the fort near the Amelia shore. The *Walker* had been sent there only the day before "to help defend that place in case of being attack'd." Fort William, along with the *Walker*, both having larger caliber cannons than the Spanish vessels, repelled them as they attempted to enter the sound, firing "so briskly on them that they [the Spanish] sheered off as fast as they could," Francis Moore later wrote. The Spaniards sailed to the north end of Cumberland, anchoring out of range of Fort St. Andrews's cannons.

Montiano had instructed several boats "to post themselves in the river between the Fort of St. Andrew and Frederica" to prevent communication between Cumberland Island and Oglethorpe. However, a scout boat dispatched from Fort William the following day safely arrived at Frederica to report the attack. That same day, men on the rigging of a merchant ship at St. Simons spied the Spanish boats at anchor north of Cumberland. Oglethorpe expected the Spanish to attack Cumberland, not realizing St. Simons was the main objective. He planned to move a large contingent of the Forty-Second Regiment back to Cumberland. In the meantime, he deployed Capt. William Horton on Jekyll with his company of grenadiers and a party of Native warriors. The general then left St. Simons at about three that afternoon, leading three scout boats and two companies of regulars. As they crossed the St. Andrews Sound, six Spanish galleys gave chase. Oglethorpe's two lead scout boats "fired very hotly at them and they at us," a ranger later recorded. Lt. William Tolson, commanding the third scout boat in the rear, watched the cannon exchange. As white cannon smoke billowed across the water obscuring his view, he thought the lead boats had been destroyed and diverted his boat for safety in the Satilla River. Observers on St. Simons saw smoke belching from the swivel guns and likewise concluded Oglethorpe was either dead or captured. As a result, his orders to further reinforce Cumberland with men were ignored, a fortunate thing for the defense of St. Simons as events played out.

Oglethorpe and his crew fought their way through enemy fire and escaped the engagement with only one casualty. They reached Fort St. Andrews, where he ordered his men to spike the cannons and abandon the fortification. In the haste and confusion, several cannons were not disabled, scores of hand grenades were left behind, and more than fifty horses were left corralled instead of being turned loose. The general and his men then left to reinforce Fort William, bringing much-needed stores and artillery along with "some four-pounders and swivel guns."

After failing to contact the main fleet, the Spaniards in St. Andrews Sound hauled anchor and sailed for St. Augustine. Oglethorpe observed them sailing south the following day and assumed the crisis had passed, at least for Fort William. He sailed to St. Simons on the *Walker* on June 26, leaving behind a scout boat and two hundred men. Five days later, thirty-six ships and boats flying Spanish colors came into view off the coast of St. Simons. By then it was obvious that St. Simons had been the main objective, not Cumberland. Most of the reinforcements at Fort William returned to Frederica.

On July 5, 1742, Montiano's fleet, carrying fifteen hundred soldiers, punched through a gauntlet of British shore batteries on St. Simons and numerous ships and boats in the sound between St. Simons and Jekyll. Montiano made several failed attempts to capture Fort Frederica before aborting his invasion of Georgia and South Carolina. (For a fuller account of the invasion on St. Simons Island, see Jingle Davis's *Island Time*.) To show something for his efforts, Montiano aimed his sights on the Cumberland Island forts. On July 15 his men burned Fort St. Andrews, and, recalling the slaughter of Spanish livestock during Oglethorpe's previous expeditions, destroyed the horses still penned there. That evening the Spaniards spied a British boat cross the sound from Jekyll and land on Little Cumberland's northern tip. The boat, commanded by General Oglethorpe, put ashore a messenger who evaded Spanish patrols and ran the length of the island to hand Lt. Alexander Stewart a simple message: defend Fort William from Spanish attack "to the last extremity" until the general arrived with reinforcements. Stewart and his men were heartened by the news that "the Spaniards were drove off of St. Simon's which put new life in the people."

Montiano thought Oglethorpe's boat had disembarked a band of Yamacraw. They had caused much dread among his men on St. Simons, and he didn't want a repeat on Cumberland. By nine o'clock the next morning his forces had abandoned the island. His haste in leaving may have contributed to his decision to slaughter Oglethorpe's horses. Montiano divided the fleet, sending his sloops and large schooners south along Cumberland's eastern shore while he led fifteen half-galleys and pirogues down the inland passage. His objective was Fort William. By then only about sixty British and a detachment of rangers were stationed on the south end. The wind died down around 6:30 later that day. Apparently, the Spanish flotilla had not yet traversed the river to the south end (possibly due to a low tide and sandbars blocking their way at the dividings), instead anchoring for the night. At ten o'clock the next morning, Montiano ordered a land assault and attempted to put ashore two hundred men from rowboats on the beach west of the fort. Anticipating this line of attack, Stewart had positioned eight rangers behind sand dunes who prevented the landing with hot musket fire. Montiano overestimated the English force behind the dunes and called off the landing.

The Spanish then attacked Fort William by water. Montiano's transports anchored offshore in the ocean were unable to assist. The Marquess de Casinas, aboard one of these ships, recalled that "the number of rounds rose to more than seventy and we heard besides a few discharges of musketry, lasting an hour." The battle actually lasted about three hours, with the loss of two Spanish galleys and little damage to the fort. Several British soldiers were wounded by splinters as cannon bursts struck the fort's observation tower. Governor Montiano realized his small-caliber ship guns were no match for the eighteen-pounders at Fort William and sailed out of the inlet for St. Augustine, ending Spain's final attempt to take by force the territory they had claimed since the 1500s. The final episode in this saga between Spain and England unfolded on Cumberland Island's south shore.

Oglethorpe arrived and paused at Fort William the next day before sailing south to locate Montiano's fleet. He ordered the fort rebuilt in anticipation of a second Spanish invasion that never came. The new construction included a wall or "rampart twelve foot high, and about fifteen foot thick, of sand, supported by puncheons" in the shape of a pentagon. A distinguishing feature of the new Fort William was a triangular structure (a ravelin) built on the fort's front, facing the sound. Designed by Colonel Cook, it housed the two 18-pound cannons set on movable platforms "by which two men will be capable of doing as much service with such cannon as ten men with cannon mounted in the common manner."

General Oglethorpe paused to disembark five hundred men for "refreshments" at the fort in early March 1743 on another expedition into Florida. It would be the fort's last involvement in a military action. Alexander Stewart was promoted to a lieutenant for his bravery in the face of Montiano's attack and became the fort commandant. Another battery was added to the fort's defenses in 1748. However, Britain's war efforts had shifted to the northern colonies bordering French-held Canada when France entered the War of Jenkins' Ear. By the time that war ended, Oglethorpe had returned to England for good and his Georgia regiment had disbanded. Only a small garrison of six men and a corporal remained at Fort William until 1765, receiving their provisions from Savannah.

The French and Indian War (1754–63) ended with the signing of the Treaty of Paris, which handed Spanish Florida over to the British. James Wright, Georgia's royal governor, asked for and received King George III's permission to extend the colony's south boundary to East Florida's northern border. The new demarcation shifted Georgia's border from the Altamaha to the St. Marys River, in large part due to the continued presence of Fort William on Cumberland's south end, an investment that would prove to be more

Map from 1766 by Daniel Paterson of the Georgia-Florida border and British fortifications in the colonial southeast. (New York Public Library Digital Collections)

significant as future events unfolded. After the Revolutionary War, the 1783 Treaty of Paris fixed the Georgia-Florida boundary along the thirty-first parallel North and the St. Marys River. A separate treaty between England and the Spanish government ceded East and West Florida back to Spain, keeping the boundary issue alive. And though the Adams-Onís Treaty transferred Florida to the United States in 1819, the border controversy wasn't officially resolved between the two states until 1872. Ultimately, the border remained on the St. Marys River. If not for Fort William, the boundary might have remained fifty miles farther north on the Altamaha.

Frederick Ober, an American naturalist, visited Cumberland Island in 1880, writing that Fort William "is placed on the extreme southern end of Cumberland in a map of the island made in 1802. Even then the fort was half submerged at high water, and at the present day its site is far out in the channel. The water of the river mouth is constantly encroaching upon the land, and the ruins of a house once standing upon the southern

Lady Oglethorpe playing a harp. (Courtesy of Bryan-Lang Historical Archives)

point may be seen, it is said, beneath the water at low tide. Old Fort William has been seen within the memory of residents of St. Mary's, but likewise beneath the waves."

James Oglethorpe sailed for England in 1743 to face a hearing on misconduct charges brought against him by Colonel Cook. The charges were dismissed, but he never returned to the colony he founded with his own finances and his own sweat and blood. King George II promoted him to brigadier general that same year. The following year, Oglethorpe was reimbursed more than £66,000 in expenses incurred by mortgaging his English properties in the building and defense of the Georgia colony. He married Elizabeth Wright, an heiress, and became a close acquaintance of leading minds of the day, among them Samuel Johnson, James Boswell, and Oliver Goldsmith.

On March 30, 1745, Oglethorpe was made major general and served under the Duke of Cumberland. Later that year, just three years after the Spanish invasion of Georgia, he led a force against Bonnie Prince Charlie's invading army, but the duke accused him of failing to pursue Jacobite rebels at Shap, England, who escaped under cover of darkness. (Members of Oglethorpe's immediate family had expressed loyalty to the Jacobite cause, which may have influenced the duke's thinking.) The duke, for whom Oglethorpe had named Cumberland Island, publicly rebuked the general for "lingering on the road." Oglethorpe was acquitted for his actions by a military court. However, his career as an active British officer was over. In 1755 he petitioned King George II to reactive his regiment, with Oglethorpe at its head, should war break out with Spain. The king denied his request. "So resentful was the general," one historian wrote, "that he feared he might not be able to control his hot temper if he met Cumberland and that the encounter might lead to a challenge from one of the Duke's subordinates."

The duke earned the moniker the Butcher for his treatment of Jacobite soldiers and civilians after the Battle of Culloden (Scotland) in 1746. One can only imagine what the Georgia Highlanders of Glynn and Camden Counties thought of him. One correspondent, identified only as W.G.M., published an August 17, 1871, editorial in the *Atlanta Daily Sun* advocating renaming Cumberland Island after its former aboriginal name: "Cumberland Island was so named more than a century ago by an Indian in honor of the Duke of Cumberland who made the Indian a present, thus displacing some Indian name, Missoee. The latter should be restored. When the English Duke grew up to manhood, he led the English army in Scotland in the 'rebellion' of 1745; and his name is coupled in history with atrocious cruelties then and there practiced on a conquered people. Away with 'Cumberland!'"

CHAPTER IV   The Lawless Crew

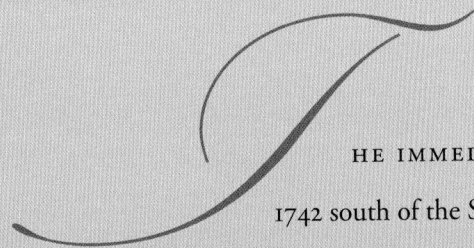

*T*HE IMMEDIATE AFTERMATH of Spain's final retreat in 1742 south of the St. Marys River marked the beginning of a new era in Georgia. Just as the footprints of Cumberland Island's indigenous people and the Spanish quickly vanished, the British presence also declined. With Oglethorpe's departure, the threat of enemy attack from St. Augustine all but gone, and slavery not yet introduced (slavery was allowed in Georgia starting January 1, 1751, providing cheap labor to work the land), many white residents abandoned what they considered to be the failed Georgia Trust experiment.

Meanwhile, events in Europe continued to shape the future of American colonial expansion. The 1748 Treaty of Aix-la-Chapelle restored Spanish and English territories to their preconflict boundaries—*status quo ante bellum*, or the state existing before the war. As such, Cumberland Island remained part of a disputed territory claimed by both the Spanish and the British. At this point, the white population in Georgia was concentrated along the South Carolina border from Augusta to Savannah and on the coast south of Savannah to Cumberland Island. Native treaties confined white settlers to an area thirty miles inland from the coast. These were the days before the

Jonathan Bryan

Jonathan Bryan, the youngest child of Native trader and planter Joseph Bryan and Janet Cochran Bryan, was born near Port Royal, South Carolina, in 1708. Some accounts of Oglethorpe's arrival in Georgia have Bryan either among those accompanying him in 1733 from Port Royal or among the group who greeted Oglethorpe on Yamacraw Bluff. Either way, his connection to Georgia's founder was assured almost from day one. That same year Oglethorpe, who described Bryan as "a very brave young man who himself with four of his Negroes worked for us gratis some Months," recommended that the Trustees grant him 500 acres in Georgia. In his year-end report to the Trustees, Oglethorpe wrote that Bryan and Colonel Bull of South Carolina "came up again in the midst of the Sickness to assist us with 20 slaves whose Labour they gave as a free Gift to the Colony."

great push into Georgia's interior during the early to mid-1800s with the advent of land lotteries and the rise of King Cotton. Though most colonists remained in and around Augusta and Savannah, Cumberland Island was not entirely abandoned. Georgia's government shied away from offering land to settlers in the disputed region, but a few entrepreneurs already had their eyes on it, betting that England's claim to the land would eventually win the day.

One such optimist was the extraordinary Jonathan Bryan, who played a significant role in Georgia's development from an inchoate colony under the Union Jack to statehood under Old Glory. He led the vanguard of land acquisition south of the Altamaha and was instrumental in developing Cumberland into an island of plantations. One historian describes Bryan as "energetic and physically strong, adventurous and astute; at various times a scout, surveyor, negotiator, soldier, planter, entrepreneur, politician, religious advocate, and patriot; knowledgeable about the myriad aspects of agriculture, sagacious in matters of law and diplomacy; acquisitive when it came to land, and adaptable in social settings."

Three years after Oglethorpe's 1733 landing at Savannah, the colony contracted Bryan to cut a road through woods and swamp from his South Carolina plantation to the Darien settlement on the Altamaha River. As a lieutenant in a company of South Carolina Gentlemen Volunteers, Bryan joined Oglethorpe's unsuccessful 1740 expedition against the Spanish in St. Augustine. Later that year Bryan recorded in his Bible that Rev. George Whitefield's influence brought about his "conversion from corruption to Christianity."

Bryan owned several plantations near Port Royal and expanded his empire by moving into Georgia in 1752, acquiring Walnut Hill, a rice plantation on the Savannah River. He would eventually own four other plantations near Savannah: Monmouth, Dean Forest, Seven Oaks, and Brampton. His vision of settling much of southeast coastal Georgia, known as the Altamaha Project, appealed to South Carolina planters who saw great potential for exporting rice, cotton, indigo, and other crops. Charleston merchant John Laurens estimated the Altamaha, Turtle, Satilla, and St. Marys Rivers could "load 300 Sail of Vessels per Annum" within twenty years of establishing plantations there.

In August 1753, Bryan set out for a monthlong journey to explore Georgia's coast on a voyage of "Discovery and Observations through the Colony of Georgia, as far to the Southward as we should think proper to proceed." In fact, he was scoping out the region for land to raise cattle and to plant indigo, corn, and rice. Joining him were two fellow planters William Simmons and John Williamson (Bryan's brother-in-law), and the German-born cartographer, military engineer, and surveyor William Gerard De Brahm.

This would be De Brahm's third visit to the coast. Bryan's journal of this voyage reveals he possessed clean, bold penmanship and a firm grasp of the English language, indicating he had received a decent education by a tutor, if not at school.

Bryan's boat was most likely a thirty- or forty-foot pirogue with ten oarsmen, possibly enslaved Africans. The boat was likely also fitted with sails. He stopped in Savannah, where he obtained an order from the Trustees' designated president, Patrick Graham. (It would be another year before the Trustees relinquished their charter and Georgia became a Royal Province with a governor appointed by the king of England.) Graham ordered a scout boat to provide extra protection on Bryan's journey into disputed land, still under threat by the hostile Spanish and their Native allies.

The voyagers stopped on St. Simons Island at Frederica, by then largely abandoned, a place "so very different from what I once knew it, that I could scarcely refrain from Tears," Bryan wrote. He penned an elegy in his journal, which included the lines, "O Frederica! had thy Founder known, The Calamitous Days that were to come, How soon thy walls defenceless should remain, And those lofty Towers level'd to the Plain."

Capt. Raymond Demere, a French Huguenot who served under Oglethorpe during the Spanish invasion of 1742 and who was now the commanding officer at Frederica, received Bryan warmly. Bryan and his men were treated to "Fruit & Punch," game, and fish. Demere, no stranger to land acquisition (he would one day own a plantation on St. Simons, six hundred acres on Jekyll Island, and hundreds of acres in surrounding areas), likely approved of Bryan's mission out of personal interest.

Bryan presented President Graham's order to another host at Frederica, Capt. Daniel Demetre, who commanded the ten-oared *Prince George*, the scout boat used in Bryan's expedition. Like Demere, Demetre had acquired property through grants and purchases, including fourteen hundred acres on Sapelo Island in the Newport District, and lots in Savannah and Hardwick. After presenting the order to Demetre, the scout boat was "in a little Time" cleaned and made ready for Bryan's use. He described the *Prince George* as outfitted with "two Swivel Guns on her Bow, and ten clever hearty Fellows double armed, which with our own boat, we thought sufficient to oppose any thing we should meet with in St. Johns River." Manning the boat were members of the Georgia Marine Company whom Oglethorpe once described as "a hardy kind of Men thoroughly acquainted with all the Water Passages and row by Night and Day." Oglethorpe had also considered them to be excellent scouts: "They can live by fishing and shooting. They are as contented in Woods as in Houses." That description fit Bryan as well, who was as used to living in primitive conditions as he was in a plantation house.

Silhouette of Jonathan Bryan. (Courtesy of the University of Georgia Press)

The men lived off the land, hunting and fishing as they traveled south, enduring sweltering heat and humidity, rainstorms, and—as anyone who lives south of the Fall Line knows—an "Abundance of Torments" in the form of biting insects, including swarms of gnats and mosquitoes at night that could only be abated by smoke, an ocean breeze, or getting away from the shore into open water.

Bryan and his men approached the north end of Cumberland Island the morning of August 23, 1753, seventeen days after setting out from South Carolina. Rowing by boat from Savannah to St. Simons was at least a two-day journey during Oglethorpe's time, but Bryan and his crew were not just exploring the barrier islands—they were inspecting the land along the rivers flowing inland as well. He described Cumberland as "a fine high island about twenty two Miles long and three or four miles wide, it is Separated from the Main by Rivers and Marshes, about two or three Miles distant from the Main Land. On this Island General Oglethorpe built a Fort about two miles from the North End [of Little Cumberland] to secure the Inland Passage, and two of his companies belonging to the Regiment were lodged there, and a good many of the Soldiers who had Familys were settled in a Village on the Side of a Creek, which runs into the Island. And towards the South End of the Island were Setled above twenty Familys whose Plantations are now all deserted and left desolate, so that there is not an Inhabitant on the Island."

Bryan found Fort St. Andrews on the north end in ruins and abandoned save for "two hunters who supply'd us with Bears Flesh and Venison." De Brahm, who had been ill for several days, possibly from heat exhaustion, returned to St. Simons in Bryan's boat. Bryan, Simmons, and Williamson joined Demetre's party and continued south, making notes about the land as they proceeded. At noon they ran into a "very hard Thunder Squall" that lasted thirty or forty-five minutes. They put ashore about four o'clock in the afternoon on a bluff of the St. Marys River on the mainland where Bryan could view Fort William on the south end of Cumberland. He described the area there as "very open and Grassy (so that a Person may see Miles before him, only here and there a Hill of oak land) with fine Springs of water. These lands are full of wild cattle and Buffalo. This is the last River in Georgia, and the next River to St. John's River." The buffalo were a by-product of the Native American practice of clearing land with fire for hunting and planting crops. The open land, soon overtaken by grasses, attracted migrating buffalo herds. William McIntosh, grandfather of Thomas Spalding, claimed to have seen thousands of buffalo between Darien and the Sapelo River in the 1700s. The names of Buffalo Swamp and Buffalo River (Glynn County) and Buffalo Ford (Camden County) are reminders of the region's forgotten past.

On Friday, August 24, Bryan and his men landed at Fort William, situated on the southernmost point of Cumberland Island, where they found it manned by a corporal and six men. He described the fort as "one of the compleatest pieces of Fortification in any of these parts (tho small) and used to contain, before the Regiment was broke, a Fort Major, and Fifty men to defend it. It was attacked by the Spaniards with Seventeen small vessels (viz) Galleys, Shorebacks, and Settees and one Thousand Men, at the Time of the Spanish Invasion, and bravely defended by the commanding officer with thirty-two men. I saw some of the Shot Holes which had penetrated through the Tower from the nine Pounders on Board the [Spanish] Galleys. The only damage being of wood the Splinters wounded some of the soldiers, which was the only damage they received in four Hours attack. This place of defence was greatly damaged by the last Hurricane and in a ruinous Condition, and now quite neglected, as all the other Fortifications are throughout Georgia." Bad weather prevented Bryan from venturing farther south, and he began the return journey north that afternoon, stopping at Frederica to collect De Brahm, who had recovered his health enough to travel.

It's curious that Bryan's journal lacked details about the environs he visited, other than the forts, especially Cumberland Island in which he would one day become heavily invested. Perhaps he wanted to keep certain knowledge about the region to himself. As Virginia Steele Wood and Mary Bullard wrote in their book about Bryan's journal, "He saw South Georgia's great rivers as conduits of trade . . . their mouths and sounds guarded by the southern barrier islands." He also would have recognized the shipbuilding value of the pine and oak. In fact, oak harvesting on Cumberland by Spanish crews and pirates had already begun. Thirty years later, a fledgling U.S. Navy would issue contracts for lumber crews to supply much-needed southern live oak (*Quercus virginiana*) for its ships.

On August 6, 1754, a year after Bryan's voyage of discovery, King George II appointed him to Georgia's Royal Council, a group of about a dozen who advised the royal governor, sat in Georgia's general assembly, and operated as a court of appeals. The following year, another extraordinary man made his way into the disputed region and settled a small colony of followers on Cumberland Island. In doing so, Cumberland Island became a crucial pawn in an ongoing chess game to establish a border between Spanish Florida and the English colony of Georgia.

The Board of Trade

The Board of Trade—an advisory body in England that recommended laws to Parliament and the Privy Council (the king's private council) for governing the colonies, and ensured American colony profitability for the mother country—also nominated and instructed Georgia's colonial governors. Some board members also sat on the Privy Council; in essence, their wishes on the matter concerning the debatable land were those of the king.

The Lawless Crew

Edmund Gray came to the Augusta, Georgia, area in 1750 by way of Virginia accompanied by "debtors" and "outlaws," settling forty miles west of Augusta in the vicinity of Brandon, present-day Wrightsborough. The name "Edmund Gray" appears on the 1749 Lunenburg County (Southern Virginia) "Tithable" table—a list of free Caucasian males sixteen or older who paid taxes to support the colony's government, and their enslaved people. According to this document, Gray owned no slaves. In 1755 he served as a representative for Augusta in the Georgia Commons House of Assembly. One of the hot issues debated by the assembly was the use of land grants to attract settlers to the colony. Gray objected to the method for valuing land, thereby finding himself at odds with Georgia's first royal governor, John Reynolds. Gray appealed to the king on this issue and "bolted the Assembly" with seven of his adherents until His Majesty's decision could be known. Without a quorum, the House could not act. Gray next published a letter to the "Freeholders of the Province," sounding the alarm of royal authority overextending itself in Georgia and urging them to go to Savannah in support of his cause. He was accused of establishing a shadow government, and the House labeled the letter "of a Seditious Nature and the Consequences of it dangerous." Under Reynolds's leadership, Gray and his faction were expelled from the assembly on January 27, 1755.

The following day, Governor Reynolds wrote to the Board of Trade of the sedition "about a fortnight ago, by the instigation of one Edmund Grey [sic], a pretender Quaker, who fled from Justice in Virginia, and is a person of no property here, but has an artful way of instilling Jealousy of their Liberties into the People's minds, and without the least scruple, supports his assertions with any Falsehoods that may serve his purpose." Reynolds further accused Gray of scheming to monopolize the Native trade and "introducing such sort of Government here would suit best with that." When the assembly sent for the ringleader, Gray, to appear before them, they learned he had "gone up the River" with his followers. He and his "gang" fled to the neutral territory south of the Altamaha to "that part of Florida called New Hanover," some thirty miles inland on the "Great Setilly [Satilla] River," settling on the north side of the river on William's Bluff on neutral ground.

He and his followers laid out a town, cleared the surrounding area for farming, and drew up regulations for governing themselves. Forty-one men of diverse national origin—Scotch, English, Spanish, and *mestizo*—signed the compact (six of them by an

Oglethorpe's Men in Gray's Gang

At least ten men who served under James Oglethorpe had remained in the area and joined Edmund Gray's gang of squatters. The names of these men—Oliver Shaw, Henry Bedford, John Williams, William Ross, Thomas Carr, John Duncan, William McKintosh, James Westley, Daniel Mackay, and John Carrol— appear on both Oglethorpe's regimental musters and the list of New Hanover residents. Their intimate knowledge of the land and waterways would have been a great asset to Gray, whose settlers were soon trading with Creek Indians and even provisioning St. Augustine with beef, pork, and produce, which they transported over land and by boat. One of Gray's adherents, Ephraim Alexander, operated a trading post that did business with the Creeks. Gray's settlers likely helped supply food to troops stationed at Frederica on St. Simons and Fort William on Cumberland. In addition, Gray's men might have done business with privateers.

"X"). The rules stipulated how land should be allotted and surveyed, the price per acre, tax requirements for building and maintaining a fort, selling cattle, and harvesting trees. Commissioners, whose tenure lasted twelve months, enforced these regulations. The settlers knew that their land claims would be worthless once England and Spain decided who controlled the territory, and many of them later applied for land grants when it became clear the British, and Georgia in particular, would gain control of the region.

The settlement, to one outside observer, became a refuge for "All persons incapable or unwilling to satisfy their Creditors, as also Men guilty of criminal Actions would resort both from the English and Spaniards." And although Gray and his band were referred to as a lawless crew by denouncers, the settlers considered themselves British subjects desirous and deserving of the favor, protection, and rule under His Majesty, King George II. The governing compact provided for formal applications to the royal governors of either South Carolina or Georgia (both laid claim to the territory) for incorporation into one of those colonies.

In his January 28 letter to the Board of Trade in London, Reynolds strongly advised the board to extend Georgia's southern boundary. "The Spaniards do not pretend to the Land to the Northward of the Mouth of the St. Juan's [Johns] River," he wrote, "which lies 30 degrees 20 minutes North Latitude." (The center of the mouth of the St. Johns River is actually 30°24′ N. The latitude Reynolds recommended is five miles farther south, in present-day Atlantic Beach.) After visiting the Georgia-Florida border he sent an alarming letter to the board dated April 7, informing board members that "boats full of Men are daily passing over to the South of the Altamaha River. They are People of Edmund Grey's Gang. They are said to be a Lawless Crew, who live like Indians by Hunting only." Yet in the next paragraph Reynolds suggests that if the board objects to fixing the southern boundary on the St. Johns, "perhaps there might be None [objection] to fixing it to the most Southern Settlement of any British Subject, Inclusive, between this and Augustine." The most southern settlement fitting that description happened to be New Hanover on the Satilla. Gray had become a pawn in the English and Spanish dispute over the debatable territory.

British and Spanish relations remained fragile. Neither the British Crown nor its royal governors wished to antagonize Madrid by officially recognizing new settlements in the disputed region. After all, a relatively minor incident off the Florida coast involving a Spanish privateer and a British merchant ship captain had created a spark that had grown into the conflagration known as the War of Jenkins' Ear (1739–48). They also did not want to provoke the Creeks, who claimed "the Lands above the flowing of the Tides," about thirty miles inland.

The Spanish governor sent a force of men by horse with a document demanding that the settlers abandon the territory. This became known to Gray when a Creek Indian named Otthelter entered New Hanover and informed him that the Captain of the Spanish Horse would soon be on the nearest bluff opposite the town with thirty-three men and "expected a Boat sent to fetch him over, that they were coming as friends only to deliver a Message from the Governor of St. Augustine." The captain, along with ten men, "with their Swords only," and an interpreter, were brought across the river by one of Gray's settlers, Ephraim Alexander, and several Creek allies. After sitting for a while, Gray wrote, the captain "declared he was sent by the Governor of Saint Augustine to acquaint the English Inhabiting that River to remove from thence for that the King of Spain would not suffer those Lands to be settled and Produced a Paper wrote in Spanish containing his Instructions." Neither Alexander, another settler named Goodbe Bryant, nor Gray, "the only Englishmen there," could read the Spanish document, though they well understood the verbal order to vacate the land. Gray told the captain he would consult Georgia's governor on the matter and "conduct ourselves according to the Orders we should receive from our Superiors." During the course of their meeting, the Spanish officer informed Gray that Georgia and Carolina would be invaded by French and Creek forces in a few months. Gray duly reported all of this to the commanding officer at Frederica. The Spaniards tarried for three days, conducting trade at Alexander's store, before setting off for St. Taffeys, a Creek Indian town south of there.

Reynolds returned to England to answer "scathing" remarks about overstepping his authority levied against him by Jonathan Bryan and others. His replacement, Henry Ellis, was the next royal governor to address the issue of Gray's settlement. Ellis, an explorer and slave trader originally from Ireland, wasted no time visiting Gray in early 1757. He wrote to the board on May 5, 1757, about the Spanish visit at New Hanover, which so terrified Gray "that he removed to Cumberland's Island, when after a short stay he returned." He also reported that Ephraim Alexander's Native trade extended down to the "Bay of Apalachee," where the Florida peninsula joins the mainland. "By Gray's management," Ellis wrote, "this fellow [Alexander] has prevailed upon some of the chiefs of these people to go to Augustine & threaten the Spaniards with War, if for the future they presume to molest or disturb those [Gray's] settlers."

Gray informed Ellis that the Spanish governor, Alonso Fernández de Heredia, as a consequence of the Native chiefs' demands, now urged Alexander to relocate his trading post on the north bank of the St. Johns River under Spanish protection, "promising to furnish them amply with goods from New York." A man referred to as Fish (probably Fisher), an agent of a New York trading company, provided the garrison at St. Augustine with supplies and would presumably do the same for Gray and Alexander. "A Trading House being Settled there under the Protection of the Spanish Government would seem like a Tacit acknowledgement of their Right to the Lands," Gray wrote to Ellis. Such an arrangement would constitute recognition of Spain's authority in the disputed territory.

Gray advised Ellis to preempt Spain by first issuing a trading license to him and Alexander. The governor initially thought it "a dangerous experiment," fearing it would "afford an opportunity to the Spaniards of practicing on these Savages [British Native allies], bringing them to change sides." He also thought Gray might eventually turn traitor. "I have proposed to him to fix upon the River St. Marys," Ellis wrote, "opposite to Fort William & assured him all manner of countenance so long as he behaves well. To this he has agreed and I have granted him a license to trade with the Indians who inhabit thereabouts." It is not clear if "opposite Fort William" meant on Cumberland Island, on Amelia Island, or in the vicinity of St. Marys on the mainland. It may well have been on Cumberland, because Alexander soon moved to the island to manage the post. A note in the Colonial Records states the council unanimously approved the measure to give "Alexander a License to trade with the Indians on the said River St. Mary." Of Fort William itself, Ellis observed on his visit, "the works are of no great extent but admirably contrived to be maintained by a small garrison."

Ellis believed Gray had truly changed spots from that of renegade legislator to merchant. "He is a shrewd sensible fellow," Ellis wrote, "& affects an austerity of manners by which he has acquired a considerable influence among the people of this colony & made some impression upon the Indians & if he can be managed may prove an useful instrument in many respects." The board wanted Gray's gang removed from the debatable land, but Ellis held a more practical and nuanced view. He intended to use Gray and Alexander, frequent visitors to St. Augustine, as a source of "early intelligence, a kind of advanced party," gathering information about Spanish movements and intentions. He saw Gray's gang as a barrier to incursions by the Spaniards and their Native allies and as a proponent who could help assure Native ally loyalty to England. From Cumberland, they could intercept escaped enslaved men and women (at times guided by Yamasee Indians) fleeing to freedom in Florida. "They will also be useful in taking up deserters from his Majesty's & the provincial Troops' many of whom fly to the Spaniards & are received and incorporated with the Troops of that Nation. They will likewise contribute

Yamasee Guides Helped Free the Enslaved

The Yamasee were very familiar with the lay of the land between Charles Town (San Jorge) and St. Augustine. In the 1660s, they sought refuge in Florida after being subjected to bondage themselves by raiding Westo Natives working for the British, then migrated back to South Carolina around 1680, where they became actively engaged with other slave-raiding tribes, capturing up to fifty thousand southeastern Natives for sale to South Carolinians. By the time of Oglethorpe's arrival, Yamasee allegiance had shifted yet again to the Spanish (following the 1715–17 Yamasee War). They not only assisted enslaved men and women fleeing to Florida but joined former slaves in raiding expeditions on South Carolina plantations. Florida Governor Antonio de Benavides offered monetary rewards for English scalps and "every live Negro" the raiders brought back.

to the suppressing a practice carried on by some people here & in South Carolina of furnishing the Spaniards at St. Augustine with abundance of Cattle & other provision by Land & thro' the Island passages by water." The possibility of salvaging shipwrecks might have been a further inducement for establishing settlements on the island.

Gray and his men had already proven themselves to be trustworthy sentinels of Spanish intentions, but they had another adversary to worry about. The French and Indian War (1754–63), an extension of the Seven Year's War (1756–63), pitted Great Britain against France and Spain. The war derives its name from the British colonists' main combatants—French forces occupying New France (the large area from eastern Canada to the Great Lakes down to New Orleans and Mobile), and their Native American allies. After traveling to Creek territory, several of Gray's men came ashore at Fort William to report rumors of a possible attack. One of the men, John Williams, told the fort commander a Frenchman had inquired about British defenses at Fort William and Frederica. Williams, a former ranger under Oglethorpe, grossly inflated the actual number of British soldiers, telling the Frenchman, "500 French would soon make themselves masters of those places."

On November 9, 1757, Governor Ellis enumerated to the board his reasons for allowing the New Hanover settlers to remain south of the Altamaha. Though he acknowledged many of Gray's followers "had taken shelter from their Creditors in the Neutral Islands," he concluded his argument by saying the settlement "may serve to give this Colony a sudden strength & prosperity not obtainable by any other measure." But "Ellis had made a *faux pas*," the historian Herbert Bolton writes. By issuing Gray a license to trade, he had violated the neutral ground, an act the Board of Trade quickly condemned as "an open defiance of his Majesty's lawful authority," one that might "disturb the peace and friendship which at present so happily subsists between his Majesty and the King of Spain . . . as it may be considered by the Spanish governor of St Augustine as an open Declaration of the Right of the Crown of Great Britain to those lands." Ellis's jurisdiction did not extend to the St. Marys River, and placing a trading post there was tantamount to declaring England's claim on the land. The board referred the matter to William Pitt, the virtual head of government in Britain at that time. The order was given in June 1758 for Gray and his followers "to remove immediately" from New Hanover.

Gray and his band apparently complied, at least temporarily. He established a settlement of about two hundred people on Cumberland Island, probably at Brickhill Bluff, where the land rises a few feet above water level. The twenty-four-foot depth at

English ceramic artifacts produced between 1749 and 1800. Excavated at Brickhill Bluff in 2007. (Courtesy of Southeast Archeological Center NPS)

Partially restored English ceramic teapot. (Courtesy of Southeast Archeological Center NPS)

the landing allows vessels to dock at the bluff, where goods can easily be loaded and unloaded. The high marsh grass between the bluff and the inland passage helped to shield Gray's boats from view. Nearby "Indian old fields" were already cleared and ready for planting rye and other crops. It was a good location to start a settlement.

Excavations at Brickhill Bluff have revealed previous occupations by Natives and later the Spanish. Tin-enameled pottery found there has been identified as delftware, an early English ceramic type produced between 1749 and 1800. Other pottery unearthed at the site date from 1779 to 1840, indicating a continued presence of settlers, some of whom may have been part of Gray's gang.

Governor Ellis went to Cumberland Island soon after the command from Pitt arrived on his desk in Savannah. "While I was at Cumberland," he wrote on May 20, 1758, "I saw & had much discourse with Mr. Gray. He is a very unintelligible character, shrewd sagacious & capable of affording the best advice to others but ridiculously absurd in every part of his own conduct. He is now settled upon that Island with his family & engaged in a small traffick with the Spaniards."

The governor next reveals a piece of intelligence, possibly to impress the board with the need for an "advance party" to be the eyes and ears of Britain in that vicinity: "With him I found a person lately come from St Augustine who informed me that a new Governor & 200 fresh Troops from Havannah were just arrived there & that the Spaniards persisted in their design of settling a new Colony in the environs of that Castle [Fort San Marcos]; & that they were preparing to build two or three other Forts on the River San Juan." The intelligence was accurate. The new Spanish governor, Lucas Fernando Palacios y Valenzuela, oversaw a population expansion of newly arrived settlers from the Canary Islands and constructed a stone fort on the gulf side of Spanish Florida.

The British government ordered both Georgia and South Carolina governors to appoint commissioners to "give orders in His Majesty's name to the Inhabitants of the settlements to remove from thence before a certain day which the commissioners might assign in their own discretion." In a gesture to comply with the Board of Trade's wishes, Ellis joined Governor Lyttleton of South Carolina in sending a commissioner from each colony by scout boat with instructions for Gray to vacate the area and stipulating a deadline. Simultaneously claiming and disclaiming the neutral territory was a delicate balancing act worthy of the most astute administrators, and both governors rose to the occasion. Each desired the territory for future expansion, but neither was willing to lay outright claim to the land due to the political fallout that would occur if doing so caused hostilities between Spain and England to erupt.

Governor Lyttleton offered to give the New Hanoverians land in South Carolina "in the same manner they are granted to the rest of His Majesty's subjects." In other words, they would have to apply for it just like anyone else. But Gray refused to relocate, claiming Spain would view such a move as acknowledging its right to the debatable territory. Ellis cautioned that forced removal might encourage Gray and his followers to "go over to the Spaniards," where "they might establish good relations between them [St. Augustine] and the Creeks." Like Reynolds before him, Ellis proposed extending the demarcation between Spanish Florida and British Georgia from the Altamaha to the St. Johns River as the "line of partition between us and the Spaniards." By doing so, Ellis argued, "mischiefs of persons unawed by government would be averted."

South Carolina sent Maj. Henry Hyrne as their commissioner. Georgia sent James Edward Powell. The two set out from Savannah on January 26, 1759, stopping at

Frederica to secure from the commanding officer, Captain Goldsmith, a pilot who first took them to New Hanover on the Satilla. There they found Gray, who appeared at last to consent to the Crown's wishes for removal with assurances from the governors that the settlers were eligible to "obtain Lands to sit down in either Province." However, Gray couldn't vouch for the rest of settlers, whom he described as "a set of people not very capable of Reasoning," and expressed his fear that some might go over to the Spaniards. Gray negotiated an extension for another twenty-eight days.

Hyrne and Powell then traveled downstream to Cumberland Island, where they met with twenty-one inhabitants and offered them the same terms. Those in attendance "professed themselves determined to obey His Majesty's orders" on the condition that they be allowed to abandon the island when the grain was ripe for harvesting—yet another extension. Goldsmith followed up by going to New Hanover and Cumberland Island in early March to verify that the king's orders were being obeyed. He reported that the people of New Hanover "had quitted the place." The Cumberland settlers "had likewise left their Habitations save only one man to take care of their effects they had not time to carry off; and the Fields of Rye which grow there in great plenty."

Georgia's governors had once seen Gray's rapport with the Creeks as a threat, but after the French turned former Cherokee allies against the English, Ellis sought out Gray for help. In spring 1759, Ellis asked Gray to lead Creeks against the enemy Cherokee warriors. That April, Gray led a war party into Savannah, carrying Cherokee scalps. In September 1761, Ellis's successor, James Wright, renewed Gray's trade license but restricted the permit to Cumberland Island.

Despite Goldsmith's earlier report, not all of Gray's followers had left the area. Some moved south to nearby Amelia Island and Talbot Island (both now in Florida). Ephraim Alexander was still on Cumberland, managing the trading post in 1763 at the end of the French and Indian War. Eighty men, women, and children occupied former Gray settlements as late as 1766. Others lived in the general area of current-day St. Marys, Georgia. A number of squatters would remain on the island to work for Cumberland's new owners who obtained grants from Georgia's land office.

CHAPTER V   Land Fever and the Plantation Era

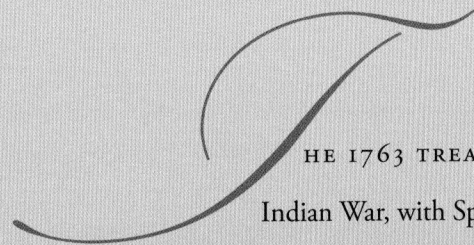

*T*HE 1763 TREATY OF PARIS brought an end to the French and Indian War, with Spain ceding East Florida and the debatable land to Great Britain. The ink had barely dried before South Carolina governor Thomas Boone issued land grants for a half million acres south of the Altamaha River, an area South Carolina still claimed title to, including Cumberland Island. The legal basis for this claim hinged on the fact that the territory from the Savannah River to the Altamaha River originally belonged to South Carolina. In fact, South Carolina had established Fort King George on the Altamaha before Oglethorpe's arrival. A heated debate between the two colonies erupted over whether this southern territory should be reunited with South Carolina. Georgia's third and final royal governor, James Wright, vehemently objected to the Board of Trade. The board not only decided in favor of Georgia's claim to the territory, it extended the colony's border to the St. Marys River.

Soon after, Georgia's colonial government created a land office with the stated purpose of encouraging new settlers, increasing the population, and cultivating vacant land. It implemented a headright system to allocate land to "free white" applicants based on the number of their dependents, indentured servants, and slaves they owned: two hundred acres for the head of the family, fifty acres for each additional white family member, and fifty acres for every "negro. . . . the property of such white person or family." Applicants could purchase more land, however, at the governor's discretion. The governor and Royal Council members met in Savannah on the first Tuesday of each month—"Land Tuesday"—to hear petitioners who applied for land grants. Georgia's legislature (General Assembly) consisted of two houses: councilors (the upper house) appointed by the king, and representatives (the lower house) elected by the populace.

A surveyor-general was appointed and charged with bestowing grants and surveying the land requested by each petitioner to validate their claim. Now that Britain had legal title to the area south of the Altamaha, many affluent and politically connected Georgians and South Carolinians rushed to snatch up their piece of the pie, which included parcels on Cumberland Island. One of the first to apply for land grants on Cumberland was Jonathan Bryan. By 1760 he was married with eight children, owned 113 slaves, and had already been granted 4,575 acres in Georgia. But his desire for more land had only been whetted. In 1766 the governor and the Royal Council, on which he sat (he had been appointed to Georgia's first Royal Council in 1754), granted Bryan sixteen hundred acres on Cumberland Island, now part of St. Mary Parish, which had been created by an act on March 25, 1765. His position on the Royal Council enabled Bryan to acquire quality land and more of it than what he was entitled to by freehold.

The following year the council granted Bryan another two thousand acres on Cumberland, but Governor Wright refused to authorize this. Bryan's interest in Cumberland Island was likely, as Wright surmised, more speculative than a desire to produce crops for export. Bryan probably had hopes of selling his island property to wealthy British investors who hired superintendents to manage their far-flung plantations. To circumvent this minor setback, he purchased additional acreage from other landholders, including relatives who petitioned for land and then promptly sold it to him. He bought fifteen hundred acres on Great Cumberland Island from a relative, James Cuthbert, in January 1769. He was already a principal landowner in Georgia, and the sale gave him almost total ownership of the two Cumberland Islands. In the ten years following his 1753 excursion into Southeast Georgia, Bryan accrued enough land to "have easily walked from Savannah to Darien and spent every night of his journey on one of his own settlements."

Other men of note to purchase land grants on Cumberland were Rev. James Bulloch, James Cuthbert, John Cuthbert, Lachlan McIntosh, Angus Mackay, Patrick Mackay,

The Townshend Acts

The Seven Year's War (1756–63) was a "world war" in that it involved the major European powers and many of their colonies. The conflict left Great Britain with a massive debt and an expanding empire to maintain. Parliament levied a sugar tax on the colonies in 1764, followed by the infamous Stamp Act in 1765, which was later repealed. In 1767, chancellor of the Exchequer, Charles Townshend, introduced into Parliament a series of acts to raise revenue. Many American colonists, including Jonathan Bryan, passionately objected, claiming Parliament had no authority to impose direct taxes on them. The Townshend Acts, with the exception of the tea tax, were repealed in 1770. The destruction of East India Company tea in Boston Harbor—the Boston Tea Party—in 1773 inspired Sons of Liberty patriots in Savannah. On May 11, 1775, young Savannahians, including John Milledge and Joseph Habersham, surrounded the Royal Magazine and "successfully appropriated a large quantity of gunpowder and applied it to the purposes of the war." They sent barrels of the powder to the Continental Army in Boston just in time for the Battle of Bunker Hill on June 17, 1775. Jonathan Bryan had served on a committee in 1759 overseeing construction of the magazine "sufficient to contain five hundred barrels of powder," and may have had a hand in the heist.

James Habersham, John Smith, Thomas Williams, and Peter Vandyke. Like Bryan, most of the early grantees saw the land more as an investment than a place to develop large agricultural tracts. But Georgia law required grantees to improve their land either by clearing it for planting or for raising cattle. Establishing sawmills, gristmills, wharves, ferries, and lumberyards, and raising a church or an orphanage qualified as improvements.

Unlike many contemporaries his age in Savannah, Bryan strongly opposed the tax acts imposed on the American colonies by Britain. He called the Stamp Act "the most detestable act of paramount will." His growing disdain for laws imposed as a result of the Townshend Acts and his personal disregard for Governor Reynolds came to a head in September 1769, when Bryan presided over a meeting in which colonists drew up resolutions demanding redress.

The document resulting from this meeting presaged the preamble to the U.S. Constitution and the Declaration of Independence by twenty years. It begins: "We, inhabitants of Georgia, finding ourselves reduced to the greatest distress and most abject condition by the operation of several acts of the British Legislature by means whereof our property is arbitrarily wrested from us contrary to the true spirit of our Constitution and the repeatedly confirmed birthright of every Briton." The resolutions that followed promoted American manufactures, called for restrictions on imports from Great Britain, Europe, and East India, and called for a ban on slaves transported from Africa and the West Indies. Britain's slave trade was then at its peak. From 1751, when owning slaves became legal in Georgia, to 1775, Great Britain had shipped more than 832,000 enslaved Africans to the Americas; at least 210,470 of them disembarked in Georgia and the Carolinas. In 1769 alone, British slave ships brought 5,000 Africans to those two provinces. That same year, New England slavers brought 243 Africans to Georgia and the Carolinas. Once news of the resolutions opposing British trade reached the king's ears, he instructed that Bryan "should be immediately suspended from his seat at the Council Board, and removed from any office he might hold in Georgia." The Royal Council obliged by striking Bryan from its ranks, though he remained a member of Georgia's assembly for another three years.

The following July (1770), he ran an advertisement in the *South Carolina Gazette* offering Cumberland Island for sale. The ad describes his ownership as "containing 11,750 acres" and another 750 acres belonging to Lachlan and George McIntosh, "which they have also offered for Sale." Another 200 acres at South Point where the ruins of Fort William stood and 160 acres on the north end where Fort St. Andrews's remains slowly crumbled into the river, were "reserved by the Government for Use of Fortifications." Bryan described the island as "well-watered, and very fine Range for the Stock—The North End very pleasant, with Pine and the best Sort for cutting Lumber—from the Middle to the South End, the land is very good for planting Corn, Cotton, or Indigo, and great Conveniency for setting up Indigo Vats upon the many springs which vent themselves though the Island. The Navigation will admit Vessels of any Burthen from one Inlet to the other within Land; and the Island abounds with great quantities of Live-Oak, of the best kind for Ship Building."

One month later (August 6, 1770), a planter named Thomas Lynch and a merchant named Alexander Rose, two Charlestonians, purchased Bryan's holdings for £1,100. As tenants-in-common, Lynch and Rose had an undivided half-interest in the nine tracts totaling 10,870 acres (not 11,750 as advertised) on Cumberland and Little Cumberland. The McIntosh properties were not included in the sale. The two new landowners petitioned the governor and council to acquire Fort William and Fort St. Andrews land but were denied this request. At the same time, Lynch and Rose complained of "loose people" who were illegally harvesting timber on Cumberland. Lynch came from a wealthy South Carolina family but wore "his clothes in the plainest order." He served in the First and Second Continental Congresses and was active in opposing the Stamp Act of 1765. His son, Thomas Jr., was a signer of the Declaration of Independence. Lynch's heirs would maintain their interest in Cumberland until 1798.

Realizing he could no longer acquire land under Governor Wright's administration, Bryan instead focused on leasing fertile Creek land in northern Florida, the "Apalachee Old Fields," to farm, raise cattle, and start new towns. In some respects, Bryan had followed in Edmund Gray's footsteps. Both had been dissatisfied with the direction his government was taking, both sought land south of the province on which to build new settlements and trade with the Creeks, and both found themselves at odds with the administration then in power. But they differed greatly in one respect: Bryan had been a key figure Georgia's founding and growth since the day James Oglethorpe arrived. He, perhaps more than anyone in the colony, had more to lose in opposing British authority. By then he was among the wealthiest men in the southern colonies, owning thousands of acres and hundreds of slaves.

With Spain and France removed from the southeast region, the Creeks could no longer play the European powers off each other and had few trading options. Governor Wright spearheaded a plan to withhold trade from the Creeks in order to force concessions, which included giving up land to the British. Suddenly, Bryan's proposal gained appeal to the Creek nation. He offered them £100 in presents and one hundred bushels of corn per annum in exchange for a ninety-nine-year lease on five million acres in northern Florida. In exchange, the Creeks would have access to textiles, tools, weapons, and other goods through his contacts in East Florida or by smuggling if necessary. The territory Bryan leased formed a triangular swath of Creek land extending from the Okefenokee Swamp southwest along the Suwanee River to the Gulf and due west of the Okefenokee to the Apalachicola River, then south to the Gulf, an area covering twelve of northern Florida's modern counties. Georgia's governor feared the worst. He knew Edmund Gray had led three hundred people south of the Altamaha. Two Charlestonian merchants familiar with Bryan's project declared that "half the settlers in Georgia would follow him [Bryan] into his Province," a prospect that would undermine Governor Wright's efforts to settle the Oconee region. A depopulated province on the governor's watch would not look good back in England. Bryan's unexplained absences from Georgia's Commons House to pursue commercial interests finally brought about his dismissal from that body in 1773 by a vote of eighteen to six.

In November 1774 he set off for Seminole towns in Florida, seeking their approval for the land lease. Patrick Tonyn, East Florida's British governor, was aware of Bryan's opposition to the royal government and considered him a dangerous subject. When Tonyn heard Bryan had been seen on the St. Johns River, he sought a warrant for his arrest for trespassing, even though his chief justice advised that Bryan had broken no laws. The governor argued that anyone who defied Georgia's government and "gone through all the Indian towns making them presents" had to be guilty of something. He sent a provost and water bailiff to arrest Bryan, but Bryan had already made good his escape to the safety of Cumberland Island.

The American Revolution put an end to Bryan's land-lease scheme. Britain's defeat and withdrawal from the region placed the Creeks in an increasingly perilous position as the new nation's thirst for more land pushed settlers farther inland. Over time the Creeks would be seen not as trading partners but as impediments to an insatiable demand for land on which to grow cotton, a demand created in part by a new set of actors who would leave their mark on Cumberland Island.

Nathanael Greene

Lynch and Rose's plans for Cumberland Island were never fully realized. They may have exported rice and indigo from the island for a time, but the American Revolution interrupted their efforts. Rose's holdings passed through several hands before they came into the possession of Revolutionary War hero Gen. Nathanael Greene. Greene was born in August 1742, one month after Florida governor Don Manuel de Montiano's failed invasion of St. Simons and assault on Fort William.

A Rhode Island Quaker, Greene became a state legislator in 1770 and eagerly took up the cause for independence. He married the vivacious and independent Catharine (Caty) Littlefield of Block Island, Rhode Island, who proved to be a force of nature in her own right. Greene distinguished himself early in the war as quartermaster general by improving the efficiency of the department's ability to gather and distribute supplies to the American forces. Despite a pronounced limp acquired in childhood and repeated bouts of asthma, he took part in a number of battles, including Monmouth and the New York campaign, and he accompanied George Washington at Trenton. His service and leadership abilities led to Greene's rise to the rank of major general in the Continental Army. Caty often visited him at military camps, where she became fast friends with George and Martha Washington. The Greenes spent the winter of 1778 with Washington at his camp in Pennsylvania. Caty, "a radiant glow in the gloom of Valley Forge," developed a lifelong friendship with the general and Martha during that bleak winter. The Greenes' first two children, George (born 1775) and Martha (also known as Patty, born 1777), were named in honor of that friendship. The Greenes would have three more offspring: Cornelia (1779), Nathanael (Nat) Ray (1780), and Louisa Catharine (1784). One child,

Thomas Scully portrait of Nathanael Greene. (Courtesy of William Nightingale, General Greene descendant)

Catharine (1785), died in infancy, and another lived for only a short time after a premature labor induced by a fall (1786).

The traditional view of Valley Forge presents images of hungry American soldiers in tattered clothing huddled around campfires, which is accurate. But it is also true that officers' spouses could join them at camp if sufficient quarters were available. The Greenes initially found lodging in a tiny cabin built for officers but moved in late winter three miles from camp to Moore Hall, the home of local patriot William Moore. There, Caty charmed and befriended other members of Washington's staff, including Alexander Hamilton, the Marquis de Lafayette, Aaron Burr, Henry Knox, Henry "Light-Horse Harry" Lee, and "Mad" Anthony Wayne. Another officer, Gen. Lachlan McIntosh, once a property owner on Cumberland Island, was also present at Valley Forge. It might have been through Macintosh that Greene first heard about Cumberland and its vast oak and pine forests.

At a gathering hosted by the Greenes soon after Caty's twenty-fifth birthday and the birth of her third child, she and General Washington danced "upward of three hours without once sitting down," Nathanael wrote, a testament to both her stamina and the founding father's physical endurance. Nathanael certainly recognized his wife's beauty and gregarious nature; despite considerable speculation about Caty's fidelity, no proof has come to light to tarnish her reputation. In one letter to her during the war, he wrote about a popular novel of the day whose female character had strayed from her marriage vows. How, he not very subtly wondered, could such a woman embrace her husband after his return from a long journey and look him in the eye?

Later in the war, as commander of the Southern Department (1780–83), Greene faced open revolt and desertion by emaciated, threadbare soldiers and officers owed back pay for their services. The fledgling government was on the verge of bankruptcy and lacked the funds to properly support its troops (a problem the South would later face under a newly formed Confederate States of America). Greene's men began to pillage Charleston when British civilians evacuated in December 1782. Because Charleston merchants refused to accept devalued American currency, Greene turned to a private contractor, John Banks, a young broker with Hunter, Banks & Company, a trading company founded in Fredericksburg, Virginia. Banks procured the necessary clothing and provisions for Greene's men but began speculating in other business ventures and ran up debts. Soon, he could no longer comply with his contract to Greene. The local merchants recommended that Greene guarantee Banks's debts in order to extend him more credit. Greene signed promissory notes that made him accountable for payments to the creditors if Banks defaulted. Banks, prone to shady, speculative schemes, not only defaulted on his obligations but died in 1783, leaving Greene with a massive, £30,000 debt and a war still to finish.

Greene's dealings with Banks tainted his reputation, and other debts incurred to equip and supply Greene's army plagued him and his wife for decades. After the war ended, they appealed to Congress for reimbursement but initially received no relief. However, Congress did appropriate money for Greene to hire Phineas Miller, a recent Yale graduate, to serve as his secretary. Miller's job was to help Greene unravel his complex tangle of legal and financial affairs.

One silver lining to this financial fiasco resulted in his acquisition of Cumberland Island. It involved a loan Greene guaranteed for Banks and Ichabod Burnet, a Greene aide de camp. Alexander Rose's undivided half-interest in the Cumberland Island tracts were sold off and acquired by John McQueen, a Charleston merchant who speculated in British Loyalists' coastal properties confiscated by the states. By 1783, McQueen was in debt and transferred his Cumberland Island interest to Hunter, Banks & Company, in which Burnet was a secret partner. Banks and Burnet offered Greene their land interest on Cumberland as security for a loan he backed for them. (Another source states that Banks and Burnet deeded the land to Greene for £5,000.) Remarkably, both John Banks and Burnet died that year. After their deaths, Greene acquired inheritance rights waivers from both Banks's and Burnet's heirs and assumed the undivided half-interest ownership of nine tracts of land on Greater Cumberland and Little Cumberland Island in Camden County. (The county had been formed in 1777 when the Georgia Constitution combined St. Mary Parish with St. Thomas Parish and land ceded by the Creeks, naming the county for Charles Pratt, first Earl of Camden.) Greene was now a co-owner with the heirs of Thomas Lynch of roughly half of the entire island, "excluding the sites of Forts St. Andrew and William, comprising 10,870 acres more or less." This tenancy-in-common arrangement interfered for years with efforts by the co-owners to realize large-scale agricultural development of the island.

Greene, who earned the sobriquets the Savior of the South and the Fighting Quaker, already owned large tracts of land in New Jersey and Rhode Island and was awarded more land after the revolution by grateful North Carolina, South Carolina, and Georgia legislatures. North Carolina gave him twenty-four thousand acres of land in present-day Tennessee. In the aftermath of war, he and other "elite gentlemen" depended on awards by appreciative legislatures to claw their way out of debt and achieve a measure of financial independence. Georgia handed him Mulberry Grove, a former silk and

John McQueen

John McQueen was born in Philadelphia in 1751 and raised in Charleston (then Charles Town) by his parents, John McQueen and Ann Dalton McQueen. He speculated in land, acquiring thousands of acres in Middle Georgia and South Carolina before the Revolutionary War. As a captain in the South Carolina Navy, he often carried dispatches from George Washington to Marquis de Lafayette in France. He continued to speculate in land and timber after the war and moved in 1784 to the Cottage, a small plantation near Thunderbolt, east of Savannah. He journeyed to France again in 1786 and dined with Lafayette and Thomas Jefferson, then minister to France. Though he was involved in Georgia politics, his financial fortunes continued to deteriorate. By 1789 he owed back taxes in Chatham County and, leaving his family behind, fled to Florida. There he joined the Roman Catholic Church, swore allegiance to the king of Spain, and changed his name to Don Juan McQueen. He owned a sawmill and sold timber, once again becoming a large landowner. In 1791 he led an expedition against the British adventurer William Bowles, who had established a Seminole state in northern Florida and had declared war on Spain. In 1802 he commanded troops in another expedition against Creek Indians. McQueen remained in Florida, where he died in 1807. He is buried in St. Augustine.

rice plantation at Joseph's Town, a settlement established under James Oglethorpe near Savannah: "A beautiful plantation where the river with a sharp turn strikes the high land and forms a bold bluff, overlooking the rich rice fields that lie before it." The property had been confiscated from its previous owner, Georgia's lieutenant governor, John Graham, a British Loyalist. Though land rich, Greene was money-poor. He sold his South Carolina estate but still struggled to pay the debts amassed during the war. "I am not anxious to be rich," he wrote Caty, "but wish to be independent. I never owned so much property as now, and yet never felt so poor and unhappy."

He, like Jonathan Bryan, Lachlan McIntosh, Rose, Lynch, and others, saw Cumberland Island's potential but had not yet brought to bear the capital, manpower, and technology to transform it into a profitable enterprise. "I find it a valuable property," he wrote to Caty after visiting the island, "and had I funds to improve it to advantage it might be one of the first commercial objects on the Continent. The island is twenty miles long and a large part of it excellent for Indigo. The situation is favorable for trade, the place healthy and the prospects delightful. On the seaside there is a beach eighteen miles long, and level as a floor. It is the pleasantest ride I ever saw."

But Greene soon learned that British Loyalists who had evacuated Florida (East and West Florida were ceded by Britain to Spain when the Revolutionary War ended) were illegally harvesting trees on his island property and shipping them to the West Indies.

A large number of Loyalists set up temporary camps in shelters on the south end of Cumberland. Many of them cut and sold timber to shipmasters lying at anchor nearby. In September 1784, Greene wrote a friend: "A party of Refugees to the number of two or three hundred are cutting down the timber, and four or five Vessels are loading with it. If some measures are not immediately taken to put a stop to these depredations the Island will soon be rendered of little value." John Bowman, a Scottish lawyer whose wife, Sabina, had inherited the other half of Cumberland from her father, Thomas Lynch, suggested to Greene that "a Person be procured to go to Cumberland in the feigned character of a Refugee" to collect the names of the freebooters harvesting Greene's timber and the names of ships hauling it away and their destinations, so Greene could lay legal claim to the harvested wood.

Greene appealed for help from Georgia governor John Houstoun, who replied that he was "really at a loss how to protect against these lawless people. Their insolence so great as would render it unsafe for any but a pretty strong force to go against them." Houstoun reached out to His Excellency Don Vincente Manuel de Zéspedes (Cespedes), the Spanish governor in St. Augustine. Zéspedes rightfully asserted he had no control over British subjects "on territory not under my sovereign's jurisdiction." Houstoun also wrote Patrick Tonyn, the departing British governor of East Florida. Tonyn instructed the agent of the British Transports Shipping at St. Marys to inquire about the illegal activity and to avoid dealing with timber poachers. This may have done the trick, for many of the refugees had left Cumberland by the following spring. Live-oaking is a dangerous and backbreaking endeavor, made more unbearable in hot weather, which may have contributed to their departure. Either way, the illegal tree harvesting diminished, though it didn't completely halt.

Next, Greene turned to his friend, the Marquis de Lafayette, to interest French officials in southern timber. The French naval minister, the Marquis de Castries, believed Northern Europe produced the best timber for shipbuilding but wanted to see samples of Cumberland wood. In August 1785 he dispatched a French vessel from the West Indies to collect a cargo of Cumberland Island live oak. Either Greene—in Newport, Rhode Island, at the time—was not informed of the plan, or the communication was lost and the frigate left with an empty hold. Greene wrote de Castries a letter of apology and urged him to send another ship. Nathanael had moved to Georgia by then and promised that with a month's notice he could "have a Cargo of Lumber provided in readiness." In December 1785, Lafayette suggested that Greene "send a Small Cargo, particularly of knees-crooked Timber, *Bois courbes de toutes Espece* [curved wood of many different tree species] to any French port." There is no record of samples being sent.

After visiting Cumberland in March 1785, Greene continued traveling south on the inland passage to St. Augustine with Col. Benjamin Hawkins, a North Carolina member of Congress who had served as George Washington's chief French interpreter during the war. They traveled to the St. Johns River in a canoe powered by oar and sail, outfitted with an awning for protection from the elements and "mattresses to sleep on," then rode on horseback from the south bank of the St. Johns to St. Augustine. Greene met with Governor Zéspedes to discuss trade and to recruit British settlers for development of his Cumberland Island property. The boundaries between East Florida and the United States were not fixed at the time. Zéspedes was suspicious of Greene's motives, fearing American representatives were being sent to gather intelligence as a prelude to the annexation of the Spanish province, which the British had only recently returned to Spain. Like several of his predecessors, the governor contemplated relocating East Florida's capital farther north. In this instance, he pressured the Spanish court to move it to Amelia Island, whose harbor was, he argued, "the deepest and easiest to enter on the whole North American coast between Mexico and New York." He planned to turn St. Augustine—Fort San Marcos in particular—into a state prison.

Zéspedes extended to Greene and Hawkins every hospitality but kept a wary eye on them during their four-day visit. "We were introduced to his Lady and daughters," Nathanael wrote Caty, "and compliments flew from side to side like a shuttlecock in the hand of good players. You know I am not very excellent at fine speeches. My stock was soon exhausted; but what I lacked in conversation I made up for in bowing." Dinner lasted five hours, a "truly elegant" affair serving mostly French cuisine. Nathanael declared himself "not unlike a stuffed pig and almost in condition of the Country tenant who said he would rather fight than eat any more."

Greene lodged with George Fleming, an Irishman, while Hawkins stayed with a Dr. Quin. A captain and fifty men were sent to guard Greene's quarters as a mark of his military stature, but he declined their services, claiming he was now a civilian. Instead, several sentinels were posted for his "protection" from displaced British Loyalists waiting to be evacuated. Tributes paid by the governor to Greene, a leading figure in America's recent victory over Britain, might have aroused some of the Loyalists to violence. Zéspedes's sentinels also allowed him to keep a wary eye on his guests' movements and any visitors they received. Greene, attuned to the sensitive relations between the two countries, declined to visit St. Augustine's fortifications, "for fear of exciting Jealousy."

While in St. Augustine, Greene courted investors and had already discussed plans with New York businessman James Seagrove to make Cumberland Island a commerce center for Spanish colonies and Georgia settlements. He also met Francis Phillip Fatio, a merchant and Swiss transplant who owned a plantation on the St. Johns. The two contemplated a venture involving trade with Cuba and Spanish East Florida. Greene and Hawkins originally intended to leave East Florida by March 19, 1785, but didn't depart until November. On the return trip, Colonel Antonio Fernández, commanding a troop of mounted dragoons, escorted them to the St. Johns. Fernández traveled by boat with Greene and Hawkins via the inland waterway to the St. Marys River where a thirteen-cannon salute (presumably for the thirteen states) by Don Pedro Vásquez, the commodore commanding his Catholic Majesty's ships at that station, received them. They were entertained overnight on the commodore's brigantine. The final leg to Cumberland Island on the commodore's barge was capped by another thirteen-gun salute, ostensibly as a sign of their esteem for Greene. But he saw it as another insult to British Loyalists waiting aboard twenty ships in the harbor for transportation to the Bahama Islands and Nova Scotia. This military escort may have been Zéspedes's way of restricting their movements in East Florida and demonstrating that he had the necessary means to defend his province.

Greene's excursion to Florida proved to be unfruitful, for he failed to recruit settlers. He and Hawkins spent the next four days examining Cumberland's resources with local residents Henry Osborne, described by one acquaintance as "an ambitious Irish lawyer intent on feathering his nest in Georgia," and Alexander Semple, a storekeeper on Cumberland's north end. A letter to Greene from a Philadelphia shipbuilder, Benjamin Eyre, implicated Semple in attempting to sell illegally cut Cumberland Island live oak. Eyre also reported that business was "very dull" in Philadelphia, as elsewhere in the postwar economy, and that "liveoak will not command cash." Not the news Greene wanted to hear.

Osborne owned most of the public land on the island's South Point. The following month he wrote to Greene urging a "final determination respecting the settlement of Cumberland." The British transports at St. Marys would depart, and the refugees "would soon go on board if not assured of a settlement on Cumberland and persuaded to stay," Osborne informed him. Some of the departing refugees were non-Loyalists who simply did not want to live under Spanish rule, which would have obliged them to swear allegiance to the Spanish Crown and refrain from holding Protestant religious services. Greene hoped to entice this group to settle Cumberland. But to attract settlers, he also he needed investors to prop up the enterprise and had a hard time finding them in the cash-strapped postwar economy. When he wrote to Greene of the precarious financial situations facing businessmen in Philadelphia and New York City, Jeremiah Wadsworth, a friend and confidante, put it this way: "money is nowhere to be found for land." Nathanael's efforts to find buyers for his timber coincided with the Panic of 1785, a financial crisis that lasted until 1788. In the midst of a postwar economic downturn, it's little wonder he looked to do business with France and the Spanish provinces. He sought, without success, a loan from Holland, using Mulberry Grove as collateral. Greene learned the hard way that the only British settlers willing to work on Cumberland did so to illegally harvest its timber. If Greene were to tame the island, it would have to be done with slave labor.

Cumberland's natural resources, its stands of oak and pine, were a significant reason for Greene's continued interest in the island. France had exhausted its own supply of ship timber, and with the Anglo-French War (1778–83) underway, importing lumber from the Baltic was hampered by a British blockade. The French looked to the United States to supply its shipbuilding needs, and Greene remained in high hopes of supplying the French navy with timber. In mid-April 1785 he wrote to the French chargé d'affaires in America, the Marquis de Barbé-Marbois, extolling Cumberland's abundant natural resources: "The whole of it [the island], except for a few old fields is covered with the best of live oak and red bay timber. Both of which are of the best quality for Ship building. The size of the oak is fit for the first rate line of battle ships." Greene allayed any concerns the French might have of moving the timber from shore to ships by pointing out that "vessels of any burthen may lay close to the banks of the Island in almost every part of it."

In his letter, Nathanael mentions several other items of interest. He states that horses thrived on the island but not horned cattle. "There is now on the Island not less than two hundred horses & some mules." These animals may have been the progeny of Oglethorpe's island "stud" or possibly left by Edmund Gray's followers. Greene had ambitious plans to settle Cumberland, writing, "I am going to lay out a town towards the south end of Great Cumberland; and many people have spoke for lotts." Fatio, his acquaintance in St. Augustine, recommended leasing the lots rather than selling them. Greene tried, without

Restored Greene Cottage. The original tabby structure was erected ca. 1800.

success, to entice some of the Loyalist evacuees who were on Cumberland at the time of the illegal tree harvesting to remain and form a permanent settlement. However, some refugees continued to trickle to Cumberland in the mid-1780s, driven from the mainland by Native raids during the Oconee War, a result of tensions between Natives and white settlers encroaching on their lands. A number of new settlers established a community at Indian Springs, where Greyfield is now located.

In a letter to Nathanael on May 20, 1785, President Washington wrote: "It gives me real concern to find by your letter that you are still embarrassed with the affairs of [John] Banks. I should be glad to hear that the evil is likely to be temporary only, [and] ultimately that you will not suffer." Greene's grand plans were driven by the crushing debt and related legal matters that constantly weighed on his mind. In a letter to Caty Greene a year earlier, he wrote of pending ruin and of his "mind being tortured with painful anxiety" about legal matters surrounding his financial straits. "If I get clear," he stated in a more reflective and hopeful moment, "it will be a lesson to be careful how I engage for others in future." True to his Quaker upbringing, Greene believed a valuable moral lesson would make this difficult interlude worthwhile.

Caty Greene

In October 1785, the Greene family moved from Rhode Island to Mulberry Grove, fourteen miles upriver from Savannah, adjacent to Richmond, an estate granted by Georgia's legislature to "Mad" Anthony Wayne, their old friend and comrade in arms whose name is enshrined in place-names in Georgia and around the country. Caty expressed doubts to a visitor about using slaves to farm the land in Georgia. "I am not determined in my own mind," she told him, "whether enslaving the Negroes is right or not."

Nathanael had initially wrestled with the issue of slavery. In the midst of America's fight for freedom, he had written to Caty that "the injury done my Country, and the Chains of Slavery calls me forth to defend our common rights. The cause is the cause of God and man. Slavery shuts up every avenue that leads to knowledge and leaves the soul ignorant of its own importance; it is rendered incapable of promoting human happiness, piety or virtue; and he that betrays that trust is guilty of spiritual suicide." In a November 1783 letter to Warner Mifflin, a Quaker, he wrote, "on the subject of slavery, nothing can be said in its defense." But then Greene sidestepped Mifflin's suggestion that he set an example, as a man of prominence and influence, and refuse to use slaves on his Georgia plantations. Greene replied that slaves "are, generally, as much attached to a plantation as a man is to his family; and to remove them from one to another is their great punishment." In addition, the Greene family had part interest in the *Flora*, a British frigate raised from the bottom of Newport Harbor; Nathanael had, before the war's end, already suggested to his cousin, Griffin Greene, that the *Flora* "might make a profitable voyage" bringing African slaves to Charleston. Given the debts accumulated by the end of 1783, Nathanael was now prepared to use the slave trade, and slave labor, to secure financial stability and even improve it if possible. Nathanael instructed his plantation overseers to "take care to have the Negroes well clothed and properly fed," and it appears he wanted to keep married slave couples together.

Greene contemplated growing grapes for wine production on Cumberland, writing on April 4, 1786, that a "Mr. Eustace who formerly had the vineyard in Virginia for making wine has lately been to Cumberland and says it is the first place upon the Continent which he has seen for raising Grapes for making wine." There was no elaboration for the basis of this claim, nor was it pursued further. He had planned to move to Cumberland in July, but after meeting in Savannah with a creditor, E. John Collett, to discuss debts Greene had guaranteed for John Banks, Nathanael visited a neighbor (William Gibbons) on his return to Mulberry Grove. He and Gibbons inspected a rice field under an "intensely hot" sun, and Greene complained of "a pain in the head" after leaving. Within a few days, on June 19, 1786, at the age of forty-three, he was dead. Although his death was attributed to heat stroke, one of his symptoms, an inflamed and swollen forehead, indicates that an infection may have played a role. On August 8, 1786, less than a month after General Greene's death, the General Assembly divided Washington County, creating "a tract of Country which shall be called and known by the name of Greene County" and designated the county seat to be named Greensborough. Meanwhile, Caty was left to manage the estate and his debts.

In the wake of Nathanael's death, the Marquis de Lafayette insisted that Caty send her son, George Washington Greene, to France at Lafayette's expense to live in the marquis's home and study with his son. George Washington, too, asked Caty to send young George to Mount Vernon for his education. However, since Lafayette asked first, her son went to France. Within a few years, with the help of her plantation manager, Phineas Miller, Caty turned Mulberry Grove into a flourishing enterprise, though not enough to satisfy creditors, who carted off furniture and her cherished phaeton. With the assistance of old friends from the war, such as Henry Knox, secretary of War, and Alexander Hamilton, secretary of the Treasury, she continued to petition Congress for redress. The latter pointed out to Caty the flaw in her case: Nathanael Greene had neglected to inform the government of his intent to endorse the IOUs at Charleston during the war. Whether Congress would have approved his request in a timely manner—if at all— is questionable. But Hamilton was adamant that a legal technicality should not allow Greene's family to become impoverished. "I love you too well not to be very candid with you," Hamilton wrote. "When will we have the pleasure of seeing you this way? I need not tell you the pleasure I should take in it."

George Washington honored Mulberry Grove with his presence when he stopped to visit Caty during a tour of the southern states in 1790. He visited her twice during his stay in Savannah, a testament of their continued friendship. Caty visited Philadelphia, then the seat of government, in 1791 to pursue the matter of compensation for Nathanael's debts to its conclusion. With Alexander Hamilton's and Anthony Wayne's help, she persuaded Congress to indemnify the Greene estate. In April the government decided in her favor. The first installment of the $47,000 involved in her case was awarded to Caty, with the balance to be paid over the next three years. Alexander Hamilton signed the check.

The First Cotton Gin, by William L. Sheppard. (Courtesy of the Library of Congress)

Illustration of Catharine Littlefield Greene with Eli Whitney from "Recollections of Washington and His Friends," *Century Magazine*, January 1878. (Courtesy of the University of Georgia Press)

Although the windfall was timely, it would not be enough to pay off all of the debts that had accrued since the war's end.

She hired a newly minted Yale graduate in 1792 to tutor her youngest children. One day at a Mulberry Grove Plantation party, he overheard upland planters complain about the arduous task of removing seeds from short staple cotton plants. Seeds of the long staple Sea Island cotton, which grew primarily on the coast, were relatively easy to separate by hand or by passing through a gin comprised of two wooden revolving rollers. James

Hamilton Couper was already using a contraption called Eve's Horse Gin, invented in the Bahamas by Joseph Eve in the 1780s, to separate Sea Island cotton seeds. The longer, silkier, and high-tensile cotton fibers grown on the coastal barrier islands were valued by New England and European manufacturers, who used them to weave fine thread, lace, and sheer garments. Farther inland, however, the cotton bolls were smaller with shorter, coarser strands. Separating the seeds was a time-consuming task.

The Greenes' tutor, Eli Whitney, put his mind to the upland-cotton problem and, with a little input from Caty, came up with a solution in ten days—a new type of cotton gin using iron combs (saws) that extracted seeds from the fibers before they reached the rollers. His invention proved to be both a boon and a bane for the southern states. This new cotton gin, a product of Yankee ingenuity, opened up the expansion of cotton farming deep into Georgia's interior and across the south, giving rise to King Cotton and its insatiable demand for slave labor. The fate of slavery would later be decided by a bloody civil war that cost thousands of lives and wrecked the southern economy, which required generations to recover in many parts of the South.

Not long after Whitney took up his tutoring job with the Greenes in Georgia, George Washington Greene returned from France. Caty, anxious for his safety as the French Revolution gained momentum, had asked Lafayette to send George back to Georgia. (Lafayette later fled France for the Austrian Netherlands, where he was captured by Austrian soldiers and imprisoned for five years.) While on a river outing with a friend, George's canoe hit turbulent waters and overturned. His body was recovered not far from Mulberry Grove and entombed in the Savannah colonial cemetery vault next to his father.

French Attempt to Purchase Cumberland Island

Unbeknown to Caty and the Greene family at this time, an intrigue with international implications was in the works. In 1794, the French government briefly entertained a scheme to purchase Cumberland Island. A French interim consul stationed in Boston identified as "A.C.D." sent a letter dated September 30, 1794, from Philadelphia to a person with the initials "B.L." in Paris. The letter, destined for authorities in the French Navy, relays a conversation between A.C.D. and a U.S. senator from South Carolina regarding land and woods on America's southern coast, a subject of supreme interest to the French, who needed a reliable timber source for shipbuilding. "Glancing over the map of these regions," A.C.D. wrote, "he [the Senator] pointed out to me an island situated along the southern coast of Georgia at 30 degrees north latitude; which has some of the most beautiful live oak one can possibly find. Everyone knows that this is the wood which lasts the longest time in water. The island is called Cumberland; it is about 4 and a half leagues long by two wide; vessels of all sizes can unload there in the commodious harbors which lie between it and the mainland. One half of it belongs to General Greene['s heirs] & the other to Mr. Bowman. It would be possible to have it for a very modest price because those to whom it belongs, like nearly all Americans, have more land than capital to develop [it]."

A year earlier, President Thomas Jefferson had revoked the commission of French vice consul Antoine Charbonnet Duplaine ("A.C.D.") for exceeding his authority with "sundry encroachments and infractions on the laws of the land, and particularly having caused a vessel to be rescued with an armed force, out of the custody of an officer of justice." Duplaine relocated from Boston to Philadelphia and became president of the local Jacobin club, a pro-French Revolution society. The senator in question was Pierce Mease Butler, a rice planter and Founding Father described as "eccentric" and an "enigma" by his acquaintances. Butler's French-born wife might have had some influence on his pro–French Republican stance (the French Revolution was then in full swing) and his interactions with Duplaine. The "Mr. Bowman" mentioned in Duplaine's letter was John Bowman, whose wife had inherited half of the island from her father, Thomas Lynch.

Butler believed the island could be purchased for £20,000 and that the timber value, once harvested and cut to specification, could be worth three times that amount. Duplaine proposed to the French government that the island be purchased secretly through a third party, namely, Pierce Mease Butler. But the French navy rejected the idea for numerous reasons. In a letter to the powerful Committee of Public Safety, which provided oversight for much of revolutionary France's government agencies, naval authorities wrote that the nature of the proposals "for the purchase of Cumberland island gives rise to several reflections, which the Navy Commission believes should be submitted to the Committee of Public Safety so that it can judge their merit. By whatever manner General Greene and M. Bowman have acquired or obtained the ownership of this little island, one cannot doubt that they are the only owners, but that the sovereignty resides in the States, and that consequently they [Greene's heirs and Bowman] can dispose of it only with their [the United States] ratification."

The French navy's response raised other objections, such as the island's proximity to Amelia Island, part of Spanish Florida, and the reaction by Britain to this proposed

Eli Whitney by Samuel F. B. Morse,
1822. (Courtesy of the Yale University
Art Gallery, Yale University,
New Haven, Conn.)

purchase. But the main objection was that France could not have full sovereignty over Cumberland without first entering into a treaty with the United States. If that occurred, any secret purchase via a third party would be made public, which could spark unwanted controversies with Spain, Britain, and the United States. Apparently, Nathanael Greene's overtures to supply timber to the French navy ten years earlier had either been overlooked, or the principal players at the time were no longer in the service. Besides, the French navy had other sources for live oak, including Sapelo Island (owned by a consortium of Frenchmen), coastal Alabama, Mississippi, and Louisiana, still under French control prior to the Louisiana Purchase in 1803.

Meanwhile, Eli Whitney and Caty Greene suffered a series of setbacks, including the involvement of son-in-law John Nightingale (Martha's husband) in the Yazoo land fraud debacle, which thwarted their ability to adequately patent their cotton gin. Soon, pirated versions of their invention showed up on the market, and Caty's dreams of wealth and paying off debts vanished. In 1796, she and Phineas Miller married. Together they tried to sort out the complex finances still shadowing the Greene estate, but by the fall of 1798 they were forced to put Mulberry Grove on the market after selling twelve slaves to pay creditors and back taxes. It took two years to sell the plantation. In 1800, with an economic depression sweeping the South, Mulberry Grove sold at a "knocked down" price. Caty and Phineas moved the family to Nathanael's "investment"—Cumberland Island.

The Millers at Dungeness

Caty and Phineas were determined to clear up the issue of land ownership on Cumberland prior to removing there from Mulberry Grove. Their tenants-in-common title with Lynch's heirs meant neither party could do anything with the land without the other party's consent. Hardly a way to run a plantation. Their decision may have been prompted by a federal property tax on houses, land, and slaves that took effect in 1798. The Millers and the heirs of Lynch jointly sought to create a legal division, a "Writ of Partition," of the island, to determine which family owned which land tract outright. Two surveys were conducted, the first in 1798 and the second in 1802. Because the 1798 survey, executed by R. McGillis and two other surveyors, miscalculated part of Great Cumberland's northern land, a second survey by John McKinnon, the city surveyor of Savannah, was commissioned. McKinnon's 1802 map added considerably more details than the McGillis survey. When the surveys had been

Great Yazoo Land Fraud

The War of Independence had barely ended before the former colonies began speculating with their lands. Georgia's western boundary extended to the Mississippi River, and an unsuccessful attempt was made to sell its western lands in 1788. Some of the land was located in the Yazoo River (Rivière des Yazous) basin, named in 1682 by the French explorer La Salle for the Yazoo tribe who lived near the river's confluence with the Mississippi. In 1795 the state of Georgia renewed an earlier attempt to sell Yazoo land, transferring 35 million acres to four companies—the Georgia Company, the Georgia Mississippi Company, the Upper Mississippi Company, and the Tennessee Company—for 1½ cents per acre. One of the leading proponents of the deal was James Gunn, a U.S. senator, who had once challenged Nathanael Greene to a duel over a reprimand he received during the war with Britain. The four companies, and the political insiders associated with them, sold the land at a huge profit. To pass the legislation required for the sale, many state assembly members were bribed with shares in the companies. The resulting public outrage led to reform and a bill in 1796 nullifying the Yazoo Act.

Caty Greene's son-in-law, John Corliss Nightingale (married to Martha Greene), heir of a Providence mercantile family, was an original member of a group of New England industrialists involved in the Yazoo land speculation. Either unaware or choosing to ignore the shady nature of the deal, Nightingale convinced Caty and Phineas Miller to invest in the scheme. Though Eli Whitney cautioned them against it, his association with Nightingale and Miller hampered his ability to sell gins to cotton farmers or secure trade with firms in England.

Many of the bribed state legislators fled Georgia in the aftermath of the scandal, and the Yazoo Act was publicly burned on the grounds of the statehouse in Louisville, Georgia. The ramifications of the Great Yazoo Land Fraud resounded in Georgia politics for decades afterward.

Martha Washington Greene (Mrs. John Nightingale) by Edward Malbone. Gift of Josephine and Sarah Lazarus, in memory of their father, 1888–95. (Courtesy of the Moses Lazarus Collection, Metropolitan Museum of Art)

completed, General Greene's heirs acquired outright ownership of six tracts (1, 3, 5, 8, 9, 12, running south to north), and Lynch's heirs also received six tracts (2, 4, 6, 7, 10, 11). Caty and Phineas decided to settle on the south end (tract 1) where their mansion, Dungeness House, would be erected. Tract 12, their northernmost tract, was on Little Cumberland.

Dungeness as a place-name already had an almost mythical history on Cumberland Island—and an actual history elsewhere. In his 1880 *Lippincott* magazine article titled "Dungeness, General Greene's Sea-Island Plantation," naturalist Frederick Albion Ober repeats the unproven story that Dungeness received its name from the Duke of Cumberland, who, upon hearing the island had been named in his honor, "was so well pleased at this evidence of good-will that he caused a hunting-lodge to be erected there, and named it Dungeness, after his country-seat, Castle Dungeness, on the cape of Dungeness in the county of Kent." Other sources credit Oglethorpe for erecting a hunting lodge on the south end. Mary Bullard's research dispels those myths. For one thing, James Oglethorpe and his men were too busy establishing a colony, forming alliances with Natives, and preparing for battle with Spanish Florida to take time off for a hunt, especially on an island one river away from enemy territory. It is possible the Highlanders stationed on the south end of Cumberland stored meat and supplies there, which might have given rise to the lore of the hunting lodge. Neither Oglethorpe nor the men stationed on Cumberland under him mention Dungeness in their letters and reports, and the name doesn't appear on early maps of the island.

The first instance of the word "Dungeness" in association with Cumberland Island appears in a 1765 petition by Jonathan Bryan for eight hundred acres "near the South End of Cumberland at a place called Dungeness." In addition to the Dungeness in Kent and on Cumberland Island, Bullard found three other coastal promontories around the world with that name—in Australia, Chile, and the state of Washington at Puget Sound—all named by British sailors familiar with a prominent triangular headland named Dungeness in Kent on the English Channel; four of these five sites are spits. From the sea, Cumberland Island's spit appeared as a tall sand hill extending about two miles on the south end. A high sand dune remains there today.

The name "Dungeness" is derived from the Kentish name for reclaimed marshland, Denge Marsh or Denge Mersc, Old English for "manured marsh," meaning marshland manured with lime, and "naess," Old English for headland or promontory. One writer, C. J. Gilbert, wrote in 1933 that Dungeness "is of such distinctive character that British sailors have attached its name to similar formations in such distant localities as Paget [*sic*]

Detail of McKinnon map showing partitions. (Courtesy of the Georgia Archives, Carnegie Estate Records of Cumberland Island, acc. 1969-0501M)

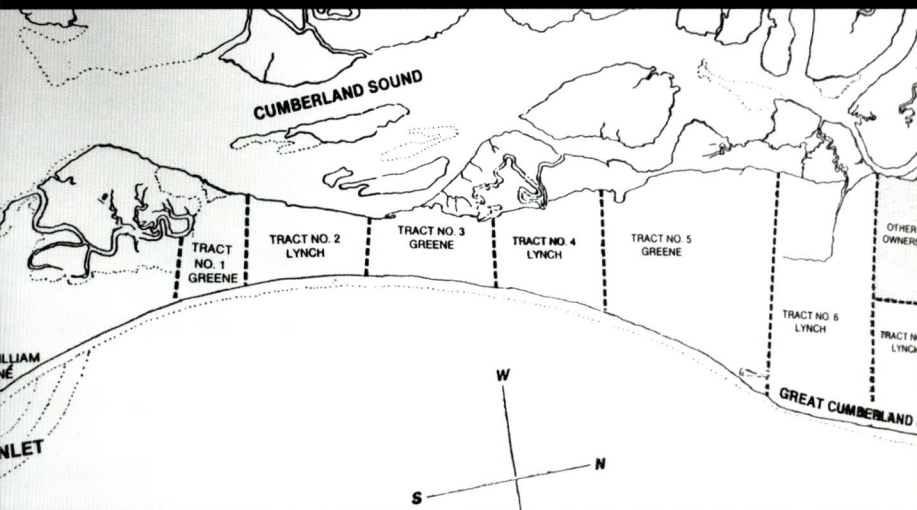

Detail of Greene-Lynch partitions on the south end of Cumberland Island. (Courtesy of the Cumberland Island National Seashore Museum NPS, Mary Bullard Collection)

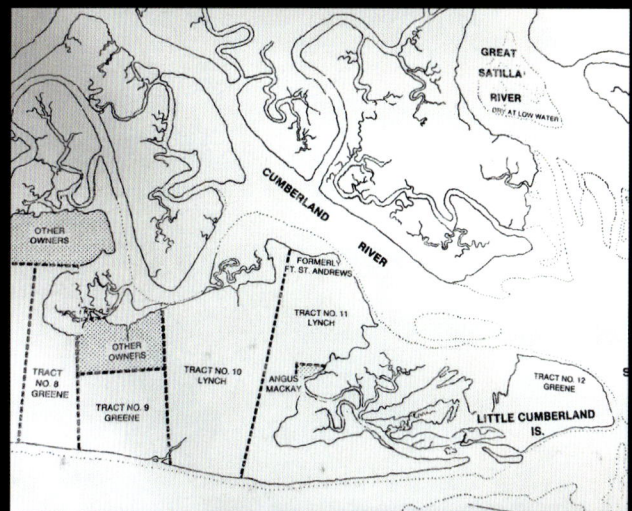

Detail of Greene-Lynch partitions on the north end of Cumberland Island. Angus Mackay owned a small tract at present-day High Point, possibly at what was known

Sound and the southern shore of Patagonia." An old chantey sung by British helmsmen aided their navigation of England's southern coast: "Now the first land we make it's called the Deadman / Then Ram's Head off Plymouth, Start, Portland and Wight / We sail then by Beachy, by Fairlee and Dung'ness / Then bear straight away for the South Foreland Light."

Bullard speculates that a British navy surveyor, James Cook, stationed at Port Royal in 1764, may have given Cumberland's Dungeness its name while inspecting coastal charts. She also writes that "the answer to the mystery of a Dungeness in Georgia may lie in the existence of an English ex-seaman, acting as an unlicensed pilot, who set up shop at Cumberland at the beginning of the 1760s to pilot Spanish and British ships through St. Marys Inlet." Indeed, the rounded profile of Cumberland Island's south end is similar to the contour of the Dungeness topography in Kent and would have naturally evoked comparisons to an English sailor. "It would not be surprising," Bullard continues, "to find in 1800 a handful of coastal frontiersmen who, ignorant of the reason, remembered only that the big sand spit at the south end used to be called Dungeness. This is what they told the Greene family, and the name has persisted ever since."

Nathanael Greene's earlier assessment of the island—"the place healthy and the prospects delightful"—proved to be prescient for Caty and her family. Having taken up residence on the south end of Cumberland, she and Phineas set about directing that the land be cleared, vegetable and flower gardens planted, and a mansion built on the foundations Nathanael had begun fourteen years earlier. Of course, slaves who had not been sold from Mulberry Grove did most of the work. The fields they cleared would be used to plant cotton and sugarcane.

Joining the Millers on Cumberland were Caty's son, Nathanael (Nat, twenty-one), her two unmarried daughters, Louisa (seventeen) and Cornelia (twenty-two), her married daughter, Martha (Patty, twenty-four), and Martha's husband, John, the son of Joseph Nightingale, a prosperous Rhode Island merchant who served as major general in the state militia during the American Revolution at Nathanael Greene's urging. Like her mother, Cornelia was full of life and spirit and did not relish moving to a place so remote from society. Writing from Mulberry Grove in an 1800 letter to a friend, she expressed her doubts about relocating to Cumberland, stating that Caty and other members of her family had gone "to Dungeness (a place so called at the South End of the Isle) to recover their health. Mama is building at Dungeness, where I fancy she will fix her residence for life if there does not come an English War & drives us away." Indeed, fifteen years later English war vessels would sail into Cumberland Harbor.

Dungeness

Cumberland Sound

Cumberland's south end.

Google Maps image of
Dungeness, Kent, England.
Imagery ©2019 Google,
Terrametrics, Data SIO, NOAA,
U.S Navy, NGA, GEBCO;
Imagery ©2019 CNES/Airbus,
Getmapping pic, Infoterra Ltd
& Bluesky, Landsat/Copernicus,
Maxar Technologies, Map data
©2019 United States.

Photograph of the General Nathanael Greene Cottage, a tabby structure built ca. 1800. (Courtesy of the Cumberland Island National Seashore Museum NPS)

What is now known as the Greene Cottage, constructed of tabby at about the same time as the Greene-Miller mansion, still stands at Dungeness and is the oldest intact structure on Cumberland. The first floor is divided into two rooms separated by back-to-back center fireplaces. It was used by the Millers while the mansion was being built and afterward housed two slave families. During the Carnegie period it became the estate superintendent's office.

Dungeness, the colossal tabby mansion, was likely designed by Phineas Miller with assistance from Caty's brother-in-law, Ray Sands, married to Caty's younger sister, Phebe. The exterior was constructed over three years, and the interior took another twelve years. The four-story structure was an imposing sight in its day, towering over the surrounding landscape. The house had two cellars, one above ground; the lower cellar had been built over the Timucuan shell mound, adding to the structure's overall height. The rectangular footprint of the house was sixty-three feet by forty-five feet, eight inches. Its walls were made of tabby, a mixture of shells, lime, sand, and water that dries to the consistency of concrete. The outer walls were probably protected by a layer of stucco or plaster. Sixteen of the twenty rooms were heated by fireplaces networked to four large chimneys. The

front of the mansion faced north. The upper stories afforded the family spectacular views of the ocean, harbor, mainland, and much of the island, while exposing them to breezes that abated the summer heat. The height offered protection from flooding but also made Dungeness susceptible to the ravages of hurricanes like the one in 1813 that blew away the roof, which was replaced with a costly copper one.

The imposing Miller home on Cumberland served as a landmark for pilots plying coastal waters. More modern estimates place its combined height, sitting atop a Native mound, at over ninety feet above sea level. By contrast, the lighthouse later built on Little Cumberland "with a revolving light, which can be seen at sea twenty miles," topped out at just sixty feet. One pilot's guide informed navigators that "vessels from the northward, after passing Jekyll Island ought to keep in 7, 6, or 5 fathoms water, as weather and size of the vessel may admit. As you proceed toward the southern part of Cumberland you will open [come into view of] Dungeness House, which is about 1 3/4 miles distant from the south point of said island, and is the only conspicuous large building on this coast."

A Dungeness visitor in 1818 from the Academy of Natural Sciences of Philadelphia observed that the mansion interior had not been plastered, creating an "incongruous, almost ludicrous" contrast between the elegant imported furnishings, a sumptuous dining table, and "oyster shells sticking out of the walls in every direction." Given that work on the interior continued over twelve years, a family tradition (or family joke) supposedly held that great tragedy would befall the Greene family or their descendants if the mansion were ever actually completed.

Although by 1879 and 1880, when naturalist Frederick Ober visited Cumberland, the Millers and the extended family had long since left Cumberland and Dungeness House was already a burnt-out shell, his 1880 article provides a clue about the views the family enjoyed from Dungeness: "From the walls of the second story—you can look across three thousand acres of salt marsh to Fernandina and St. Marys, along the river and beach, across miles of ocean." Ober describes the Greene mansion and its siting in some detail. "The summit of this shell-mound was leveled for the site of the house, and a terraced area of an acre or more constructed with the shells. Upon this base, raised above the general level of the island, its foundations were laid. The second story above the terrace contained the principal rooms: the room in the south-east corner was the drawing-room in the time of the Shaws [Louisa's married name] and the Nightingales. The room immediately back of the drawing-room, in the north-east corner, was the dining-room: a wide hall ran through the center, upon the opposite side of which were two rooms, used respectively as school- and sewing-room. Above these apartments, in the third story, were the chambers."

Ober goes on to describe a tract of twelve acres surrounded by a high wall made of tabby, "devoted to the cultivation of flowers and tropical fruits" that extended in a series of terraced gardens southward to the marsh at Beach Creek, formerly Lynch Creek. He mentions a variety of trees and bushes—"olive, fig, India-rubber, date-palm, tree of Paradise, crape-myrtle, guava, lime, orange, citron, golden date of Africa, coffee, Portuguese laurel, sago-palm, clove"—surrounding the house and filling the gardens. Another observer of the estate called the gardens "quite a paradise with hedges formed of lemon, groves of Orange trees, roses and other flowers in full bloom, though it was January."

To help pay for their new Cumberland enterprise, Caty and Phineas contracted with the government to provide timber for America's fledgling navy. Yet again, the impact of events occurring thousands of miles away (this time, the Barbary Wars) were felt on the island. Privateers from Tripoli, Tunis (now Tunisia), and Algiers attacked American vessels, demanding payments or tribute from the U.S. government to discontinue raiding merchant ships. President George Washington's response was to invest anew in America's naval force. The Naval Act of 1794 passed by Congress called for the construction of six seventy-four-gun warships. The U.S. Navy wanted the one thing found in abundance on the southeast coast and especially on Cumberland Island—live oak trees. Another act in 1799 called for additional naval construction. Phineas signed a contract with the government to provide live oak at a price of seventy-five cents per cubic foot.

The navy needed the durable live oak to construct parts of ships' frames: the "futtocks, knight heads, hawsepeices, bow timbers, stanchions, knees, transoms, and breasthooks." The big timber used in the hulls and compass pieces, curved parts used in frames, required trees with irregular shapes, and live oak fit the bill. The timber itself was cut on location to fit patterns or "moulds" provided by the War Department. Skilled carpenters who could shape the wood to fit the government's precise specifications ("good merchantable live oak, free from sap, or other defect & shall not exceed the Mould by more than one Inch in Breadth, Thickness or Length") were usually hired from northern states, where shipbuilding flourished. The navy provided inspectors to examine timber quality, ensure it fit the moulds, and was delivered to the proper landings in the quantities stipulated in contracts. At least one inspector was assigned to Miller's operation on Cumberland in January 1800, but by that November, Phineas wrote to the Secretary of the Navy requesting three more inspectors to ascertain the kind and number of pieces that remained to be cut to fulfill his obligations.

The challenges faced by live oak contractors, including Phineas Miller, were the labor-intensive nature of harvesting the wood, shaping it onsite, and transporting it to a landing. These stipulations were ruinous for many contractors who had to hire and transport axmen and shipwrights from the North, cut roads through forests, and acquire oxen "constantly fed with grain" to haul the heavy wood to boat landings where it could be loaded onto vessels. Most of these workers could not tolerate Georgia's summer heat, and the inevitable tick and mosquito-borne ailments made working in swampy areas miserable.

Miller ran an advertisement in a Savannah newspaper on April 4, 1800, offering to hire slaves from local plantations: "women would be employed in the culture of cotton, and the men in cutting timber," he wrote. He eventually hired over three hundred men and up to sixty oxen who delivered two thousand cuttings of live oak by the end of June to fifty landings in Florida, Georgia, and South Carolina. Inevitably, contractors like Miller underestimated the costs required to fulfill their obligations. That same month he wrote that "the further I advance in this purplexing contract for Timber, the greater do I find the difficulty the expense & the disappointment." He was convinced that the Secretary of Navy, Benjamin Stoddert, "has not the most distant idea of the trouble we meet with." Miller's monthly expenses were close to $5,000. He overspent the government's advance by July and was forced to borrow money to complete the terms of the contract.

Meanwhile, Caty employed a young St. Marys physician, Daniel Turner, to attend to the needs of her family and their slaves. Turner wrote that Dungeness slaves worked from sunup to noon, after which they could fish or work their own cornfields. Coastal plantation managers used the task system, which gave slaves a measure of control over their daily assignments and varied according to the slave's gender, age, and health. Those who finished their tasks early were permitted to use the rest of the day as they wished. So-called drivers, who assigned the tasks and meted out punishments, were usually Black. Each family, according to Turner, received meat and potatoes and were provided a suit of clothes twice a year. "The house servants live like the family," he wrote, "are generally well-dressed & much indulged." This view by whites that slaves were happy with their lot was a convenient rationalization for slavery. Turner described Caty's son Nat as "an eccentric, good-hearted soul," and her daughter Louisa as "agreeably charming." The doctor also spoke well of Patty (Martha), her husband (John Nightingale), and Cornelia.

In 1802, Cornelia had married Peyton Skipwith, a Virginian who moved further south to invest in the cotton business. Caty extended an open invitation to Turner to stay at Dungeness anytime he "[found himself] unwell or low spirited & at leisure."

Eli Whitney brought good news to Cumberland in 1802. Phineas and Caty met him at the Dungeness dock, where he informed them the South Carolina legislature had agreed to pay $50,000 for patent rights to their cotton gin. The three "danced a jig of happiness on the dock." By 1803, Dungeness was ready for habitation. The Millers (Caty, Phineas, Louisa, Nat) shared their new home with Caty's younger sister, Phebe, and her husband, Ray Sands, and their children. The two married daughters visited Dungeness frequently with their families; the Nightingales lived a few miles north of Dungeness, and the Skipwiths lived on the mainland.

Under management by Phineas and Ray, the cotton crops started to bring in much-needed cash. Twelve acres of gardens, "countless varieties of tropical and semi-tropical flowers, shrubs, and fruit trees, divided from the fields of cotton and cane by a high wall of masonry," surrounded the new mansion. It is said that sailors aboard ships approaching St. Simons Island could detect the wafting scents from the gardens of Retreat Plantation on its southern end long before sighting land. The same was likely said of Caty's gardens.

The Millers and other planters traversed the intracoastal waterways in a ten-oared barge capable of holding thirty passengers and powered by enslaved men. They used this mode of transit to visit families on St. Simons and for occasional excursions to Savannah. On a trip Phineas made to St. Augustine to purchase more tropical plants, a thorn punctured one of his fingers. He thought nothing of it until the finger became sore on his return to Cumberland. Despite the application of poultices, his hand began to swell, and a local doctor diagnosed blood poisoning, which at that time was almost always fatal. Caty tended to Phineas, who suffered chills and delirium before his death on December 7, 1803, at the age of thirty-nine. At the age of forty-eight herself, Caty was once again widowed.

The following year proved to be equally challenging, not just for Caty and her family but for the nation. On July 11, 1804, on the New Jersey side of the Hudson River at a place named Weehawken, Thomas Jefferson's vice president, Aaron Burr, and the former Secretary of the Treasury, Alexander Hamilton, stared at each other across loaded weapons. The duelists were facing off after years of enmity that exploded when Hamilton defamed Burr's character during a New York gubernatorial race that spring. Hamilton fired his gun into a tree over Burr's head, but Burr discharged his weapon

WHIPPING COTTON.

PICKING COTTON

PLANTING COTTON.

NOTING COTTON

HOEING COTTON.

SHIPPING COTTON

GINNING COTTON BY STEAM

FEGIN'S

PACKING COTTON

OUR COTTON CAMPAIGN IN SOUTH CAROLINA—GATHERING, GINNING, PACKING AND SHIPPING THE COTTON CROP OF THE SEA ISLAND ROYAL, BY THE FEDERAL ARMY, UNDER GENERAL SHERMAN.—FROM SKETCHES BY OUR SPECIAL ARTIST ACCOMPANYING THE EXPEDITION.—SEE PAGE 206.

Illustration of the cotton production process. (Courtesy of the Library of Congress)

into Hamilton, who died the next day. Caty was heartbroken when the news reached Cumberland. So was her daughter Cornelia, who had a teenage crush on Hamilton years earlier while in Philadelphia visiting George and Martha Washington.

After the duel, Burr fled to Butler Point on the north end of St. Simons, home to Pierce Mease Butler, the same senator who conspired with the Frenchman, Duplaine, to purchase Cumberland in 1794. Burr intended to lie low while the political storm caused by Hamilton's death raged in the new U.S. capital of Washington, D.C. The recently widowed Caty knew Burr and his reputation as a ladies' man and was in no mood to host him when word arrived that he intended to call on her at Dungeness. His arrival on St. Simons coincided with another tempest, the hurricane of 1804, which devastated coastal Georgia, blowing the roof off of Dungeness. The thick walls of the mansion provided shelter for many of the white and Black residents on Cumberland and was opened to the crews of ships whose vessels were driven aground on the island.

Within days of the hurricane's passing, Burr sent another note, this time from just across the river at St. Marys, requesting to see her. Adhering to the etiquette of the day, she replied that her home was open to him anytime he wished to visit. Meanwhile, she stationed a servant at the dock to warn her of Burr's approach and had a carriage at the ready so she and her family could decamp to the island's interior. "She could not receive as a guest one whose hands were crimsoned with Hamilton's blood," a friend of hers wrote. Burr arrived to an empty house and soon left, well aware that he had been snubbed by one of Hamilton's friends.

Although it wasn't possible to identify individual people at a distance, a platform on the roof at Dungeness—essentially a widow's walk—was outfitted with telescopes, allowing Caty and her family to identify craft entering or leaving the sound. From this vantage point they also had an unobstructed 360-degree view that took in the harbor, the ocean, Amelia Island, and the mainland. In the early 1800s they would have witnessed a constant flow of ships passing through St. Marys Inlet. At any time a hundred or more square-riggers—smugglers and privateers—lay anchored in the waters off Spanish-held Amelia Island. St. Marys likewise was a port of entry for the illegal slave trade conducted by Connecticut, Massachusetts, and Rhode Island adventurers. It was, at one time, a town of whites, free Blacks, enslaved artisans, and enslaved mechanics, with a growing timber industry, exporting wood products (shingles, planking, and spars to the Caribbean and Europe), and a budding shipyard, building gunboats for the U.S. Navy. With the Embargo Act of 1807, which banned trade with England and France, and the 1808 Act Prohibiting Slave Importation to the states, both Fernandina on Amelia Island

and St. Marys on the mainland became important distribution centers of illegal trade. Slaves brought here, often by U.S. ships flying the Spanish flag, were resold throughout the Southeast. The Millers, infuriated by the St. Marys merchants' complicity with the privateers, had a front-row seat on this activity.

But Caty's hands weren't entirely clean, either. Bullard notes that she and Louisa Greene allowed a family friend and Savannah merchant, Robert Mackay, to illegally smuggle slaves from Spanish Florida to Dungeness at night and to hold them there until they could be moved to the mainland. The enslaved had belonged to Mackay's father-in-law, John McQueen, whose interests in Cumberland Island had been acquired by Nathanael Greene. McQueen had relocated to St. Augustine in 1791 due to financial difficulties. After his death in 1807, his slaves legally belonged to Mackay's wife, Eliza Anne McQueen Mackay.

While protecting England's merchant fleet from pirates and privateers during the Napoleonic Wars, British men-of-war occasionally clashed with Spanish or French warships. One skirmish occurred in 1805 near Cumberland during the hazy days of summer. A Spanish privateer brought in two captured British merchant ships and anchored them near Amelia Island in the Cumberland Sound. They intended to unload the cargoes at St. Marys, where they could fetch higher prices than in Fernandina, but a British gunboat interrupted their plans. The gunboat, *Matilda*, fired on the privateer's vessel for an hour before its crew boarded and fought hand to hand until the Spaniards surrendered. Not long after that incident, another smuggler brought a captured 400-ton British vessel to Cumberland Sound. The captain promptly sold the British ship and its cargo to St. Marys buyers, then sailed away in search of a new victim. It was later learned that the forty British sailors on the captured ship had been massacred and their bodies thrown to the sharks.

On May 4, 1811, a detachment of forty-nine marines led by Capt. John Williams arrived in the Cumberland Sound aboard the warship *Enterprise* and came ashore. The island served as their base in an effort by the United States to take East Florida from the Spanish. Weakened by the Napoleonic conquest, Spain was vulnerable to British designs on Florida. The marines were placed on Cumberland for two reasons: to support Georgia volunteers preparing to seize Amelia Island, and, if they succeeded, to deter a British counterinvasion. The marines spent most of 1811 training and building defense works. Georgia militiamen, mostly from the area surrounding St. Marys, induced to join the cause with the promise of five hundred acres of Florida land, invaded Fernandina on Amelia's west coast on March 17, 1812. The outnumbered and outgunned Spanish

Portrait of Catharine Littlefield Greene at age fifty-four (1809), attributed to James Frothingham (1786–1864). (Courtesy of the Telfair Museums)

garrison quickly surrendered. The Cumberland Marines occupied Amelia Island along with army troops while the Georgia volunteers advanced on St. Augustine. Captain Williams died from eight wounds suffered in a skirmish with Natives in September 1812. Seven other marines were wounded; one was killed and scalped. The marines continued to make military excursions from Cumberland into Spanish territory until May 1813, when they were ordered to Washington to protect the capitol from the British.

By 1810, relations between two of the Greene children and their mother began to unravel. Her third child, Cornelia, shocked local society two years after her first husband (Peyton Skipwith) died by eloping in October 1810 with her much younger first cousin, Edwin (Ned) Brinley Littlefield (Caty's nephew), whom Caty labeled a fortune hunter. The elopement came as a grave disappointment to Caty. Her eldest daughter, Martha, also fell out of favor. Four years earlier (1806), John Nightingale had died suddenly at the Springs (now Greyfield) and was buried there. In 1810 Martha married Henry Turner of East Greenwich, Rhode Island. Henry and Ned convinced their wives that their shares of the Greene estate had been inequitable. The Greene family entered an agreement to divide the estate in 1810, with each sibling receiving about 30 of the 196 total number of slaves belonging to the Greene Estate. However, a proviso stated that "it is by the nature and meaning of this our voluntary agreement that the negro property be held by Catharine Miller until every debt against said Estate be paid," a restriction that led to turmoil. The family schism widened when discussions turned to dividing the general's library and medals. By 1812 Caty was no longer speaking to Martha and Cornelia and would not mention them by name in her correspondences. "I would not see them or permit them through my gate," she wrote Eli Whitney.

On a visit to Savannah in August 1813, Caty spotted Cornelia and Ned and their children passing in carriages on a side street. She realized they were moving to property in Tennessee that had been divided among Nathanael Greene's heirs. Accompanying them was a wagonload of Cumberland Island slaves who legally belonged to Caty. She quietly acquired a court order preventing the Littlefields and her slaves from leaving Savannah, then left for Dungeness. Cornelia and Ned were arrested and held for several days while bonds guaranteeing Caty payment for the slaves were processed and signed.

There are two sides to every conflict, and though Caty is often portrayed as the long-suffering matriarch who rises above adversity and ungrateful relatives through sheer willpower, it's possible her sensitivity to perceived slights combined with a contentious nature fueled unnecessary battles (she once threatened to sue Eli Whitney). Caty suffered periods of illnesses, especially during her pregnancies—constant stomach pain, bleeding

Catharine (Caty) Littlefield Greene's grave, Greene Cemetery, Dungeness.

at the mouth—and was prescribed daily doses of mercury, then a common treatment but one now known to induce mood swings, insomnia, and irritability. During the war she was often absent from Martha and Cornelia while visiting Nathanael and relations. On one occasion her daughters, Martha, age two and diagnosed with rickets, and Cornelia, less than ten months old, hadn't seen their mother for six months. Who can say what affect this had on their estrangement later in life? It is also possible her two eldest children perceived her to be an uncompromising *femme formidable* and wished to be free of her domineering influence. The siblings' loyalties split along order of birth with the two eldest living siblings disengaging from their mother and Nat and Louisa, the two youngest, remaining in her good graces.

Louisa married James Shaw in March 1814. A Scot, Shaw had originally been contracted by Caty in 1812 to complete the mansion's interior when funds became available. At the time of their wedding, many of the Dungeness rooms remained unfinished. James, who also helped Louisa manage the plantation, resided in the mansion for two years before their marriage. Caty wrote to Eli Whitney about James: "We all respect, honor, and love him. He is not only tender and affectionate to her [Louisa]—but to me the most dutiful son and excellent friend." However, other contemporaries described him as having "uncouth manners," "obstinate ignorance," or displaying "anti-scientific" and "anti-American" attitudes.

By 1814 the United States had been at war with Great Britain for two years—later termed the War of 1812—and the Georgia coast was under the threat of invasion. From the upper floors of Dungeness, the Millers and Shaws could see British warships and transports at anchor offshore. The *Savannah Republican* on May 7 reported, "a large British force was off St. Marys bar and that an attack was momentarily expected." This may have been a reconnaissance force. The actual invasion wouldn't come until January 1815. In late August 1814, Rear Adm. Sir George Cockburn set fire to the capitol in Washington, D.C. That same week, Caty fell victim to a fever. She struggled, her body wracked by violent chills, until September 2, 1814, when she drifted off to her reward. The family buried her in the Greene Cemetery, which lies between the beach dunes and Dungeness. Her marble slab bears the words "In memory of Catharine Miller (widow of the late Major-General Nathanael Greene, commander-in-chief of the American Revolutionary Army in the Southern Department in 1783), who died Sept. 2d, 1814, aged 59 years. She possessed great talents and exalted virtues."

Caty's youngest offspring, Louisa Shaw, was now mistress of Dungeness.

CHAPTER VI

The War of 1812 and British Invasion

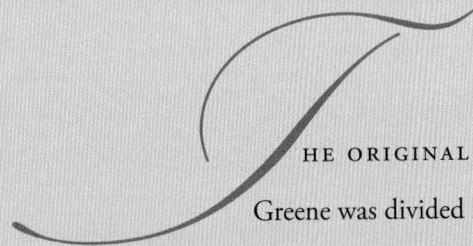

THE ORIGINAL CUMBERLAND TRACT acquired by Nathanael Greene was divided into plots for each of his and Caty's four surviving children. Louisa and James Shaw managed Dungeness, also called Dungeness Place, on which they raised lemons, oranges, peas, corn, potatoes, hogs, cattle, and Sea Island cotton that "took the prize at the World's Fair in London," according to Bernard Nightingale, a Greene descendant. The Shaws also managed two other plantations on Cumberland not in the original Greene tract. The Littlefield tract was located immediately north of Dungeness. Rayfield Plantation, named after the Greene's Ray relatives in Rhode Island, was originally intended for Louisa's older brother, Nathanael (Nat) Ray Greene. But, having no desire to be a slaveholder, Nat in 1813 signed over his share of the estate's chattel property (thirty-three enslaved men, women, and children) to his mother. Nat married in 1808 and lived at Dungeness, where his wife bore a son named Nathaniel, in 1809. In her will, Caty bequeathed Rayfield to Nat's children, but Louisa Shaw also managed that plantation. Meanwhile, Nat moved to the mainland to join the militia when the new war with Great Britain began.

Rear Admiral George Cockburn (1772–1853), by John James Halls ca. 1817. The portrait depicts Cockburn's burning of Washington (August 24, 1814). Soon after he burned the capitol, Cockburn sailed to Cumberland Island and made his headquarters at Dungeness. (Courtesy of National Maritime Museum, Greenwich, London)

In early January 1815, the British navy returned to Cumberland Island as part of a military operation devised by Vice Adm. Alexander Cochrane. His plan called for an attack on the Chesapeake region and a raid on the capitol of Washington, after which British ships were to harass coastal Georgia and South Carolina with a thousand soldiers. Half of these troops were Blacks belonging to the West India Regiment, an infantry unit primarily comprised of former slaves brought to British-held Caribbean islands. All of this was part of a larger diversionary effort against the southern states and New Orleans to draw U.S. resources away from Canada. Cochrane's second-in-command, forty-two-year-old Rear Adm. George Cockburn (*CO-burn*), led the attack on Washington before sailing south to rendezvous with other British ships at Cumberland Island.

Most of the British vessels that arrived ahead of Cockburn anchored less than half a mile off the Cumberland Island shore southwest of Dungeness. Cumberland Harbor, as it was sometimes called, provided up to forty-two feet of water depth and space for vessels to freely swing around their anchors with the shifting winds and tides. Entering the St. Marys Inlet meant winding through a maze of constantly changing underwater sandbars. The British might have brought pilots from Bermuda to negotiate these channels. Meanwhile, Admiral Cockburn lay anchored off of Charleston, South Carolina, for several days, mistaking it for the designated rendezvous point. In his absence, the senior officer, Capt. Philip Somerville ("Old Somerville"), decided to invade Cumberland. In his possession were these general orders: "It is the intention of the Admiral to take possession of Cumberland Island and make a hospital of Mrs. Miller's plantation home. It is stated they intend wintering on Cumberland Island." Somerville's decision may have been precipitated by illness among the troops and a shortage of drinking water aboard the ships.

On January 10, 1815, Royal Marines and West India Regiment soldiers, many of them newly freed Chesapeake slaves recruited into service, landed on the north end near Fort St. Andrews where William Clubb and his family lived (another source indicates the landing was at what is now Plum Orchard). A number of squadrons remained there while the rest marched south to Dungeness, arriving there on January 11. More troops and military equipment at High Point were transported to Dungeness by ship the following day, while two schooners and a shore detachment were left behind to guard the north end for the duration of the island occupation.

A witness traveling from Savannah to St. Marys reported meeting "a great number of men, women and children, on the road with wagons carts, loaded with furniture on their way to the interior of the country." He learned from them that "a large force was

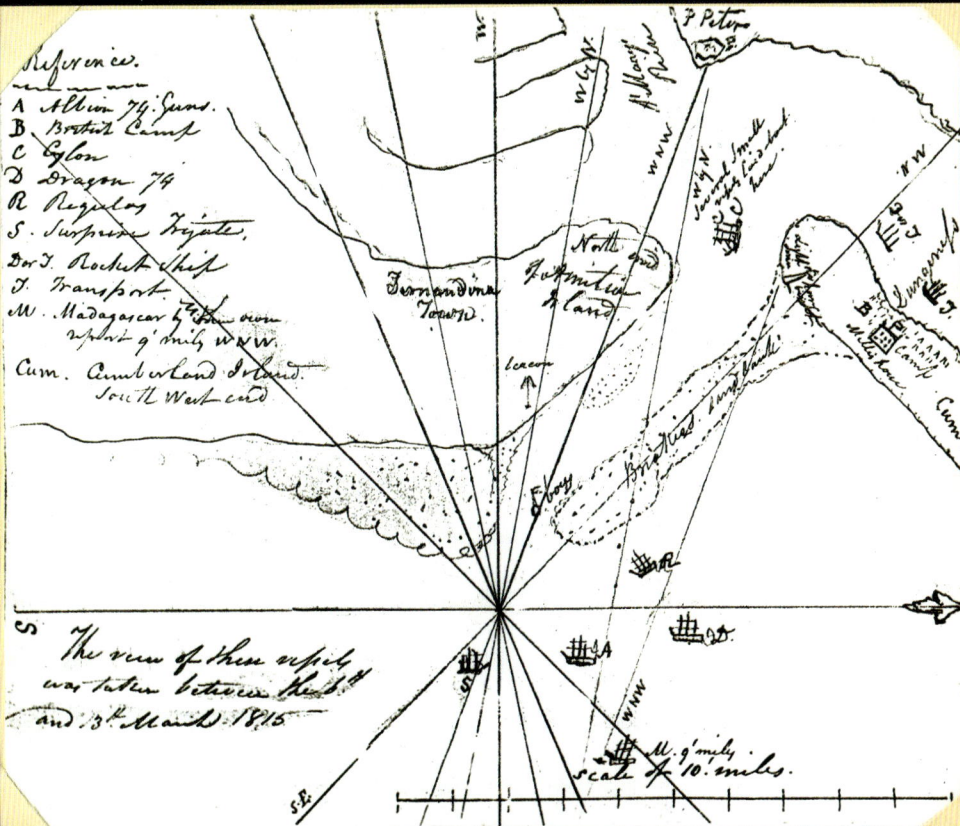

War of 1812 map of British ship locations on the
south end of Cumberland Island. (Courtesy of the
Cumberland Island National Seashore Museum NPS)

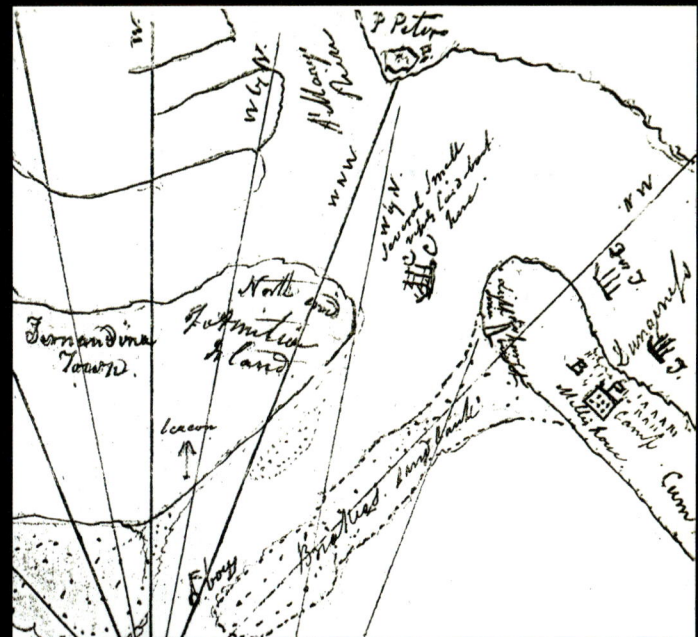

Detail from War of 1812 map indicating location
of Point Peter, Fernandina Town, and Dungeness.
A buoy marks the entrance to Cumberland Sound.
The harbor entrance was further marked by a
beacon on Amelia and a lighthouse on the south
end of Cumberland. The Miller House (Dungeness)
is depicted on the far right. (Courtesy of the

An aide probably wrote this letter from Admiral Cockburn. The top lines read: "Head Quarters Cumberland Island 11th Feb 1815." (Courtesy of the Library of Congress)

off Amelia, and that they had effected a landing on Cumberland Island who would no doubt pay a visit to St. Marys and that the town was nearly deserted."

The invaders had orders from their superiors to destroy shore batteries at St. Marys. These commands were carried out on January 13, when six hundred soldiers landed at Kings Bay (now home to a U.S. Navy submarine base) and marched southward toward the American battery at Fort Point Peter, located on a peninsula east of St. Marys. The Americans ambushed the British and put up a brisk fight but were quickly overwhelmed by the much larger enemy force. One British observer wrote, "part of the black regiment employed on this service acted with great gallantry. [They] had no idea of giving quarter; and it was with difficulty the officers prevented their putting the prisoners to death. The Yankee riflemen fired at our men in ambush. [The Black troops] on the impulse of the moment, left the ranks and pursued them in the woods, fighting like heroes. A poor Yankee, disarmed, begged for mercy; [a Black soldier] replied, 'he no come in bush for mercy,' and immediately shot him dead!"

The British next turned their attention to St. Marys, where they ransacked the town, taking away everything they could find, including "mahogany tables, chests of drawers, &c." Cockburn arrived the next day, happy to report to Admiral Cochrane that his men had seized "great quantities of Cotton and other goods" along with two merchant ships hidden thirty miles up the St. Marys River. The total prize money from the looting was estimated by the invaders to be £30,000. Though Cockburn had arrived too late to share in the booty, he quickly turned his attention to "begin further Depredations on the Enemy's Coast."

He sent men on a scouting mission up the Altamaha River to find Native allies who might be nearby. "Our operations in this Neighborhood," he reported, "have already created the greatest Consternation in Georgia. All Commerce is of course (as I have previously observed to you) completely at an end." Had his forces been large enough, Cockburn's next move would have been against Savannah. As it was he could only muster "a thousand bayonets" and contented himself by putting Cumberland Island in a state of defense.

One Savannah paper printed the following hurried dispatches about the invasion, dated January 18, 1815:

> SIR, The men of war lay in lines off our bar. The Spanish pilot refused to bring them in, but that lead to a greater evil. They discovered a new channel to the southward of the present one, and found water enough to bring in their heavy bomb ships and brigs, (now lying at St. Mary's) the *Devastation*, *Terror* and *Primrose*. The destruction is beyond what I can write; Mrs. Miller's house [Dungeness] is head quarters.

> DEAR SIR: In haste I drop a few lines to you. You will have heard, of course, of the possession of St. Mary's and Cumberland by the British. They still remain there, with about two thousand troops [and] marines. Admiral Cockburn is at St. Mary's, plundering. All the property has been shipped, such as cotton, tobacco, brandy, gin, dry goods. Stores have been broken open, and given up to plunder to the soldiers and sailors. Two 74's [74-gun warships] and eight frigates are at anchor off the bar, and four sloops were inside and at St. Mary's. I think they intend leaving St. Mary's in a few days, but will keep possession of Cumberland. No reinforcement has yet arrived. There are yet some troops on board the ships off this port. Their whole number is about three thousand. I think they are waiting the arrival of reinforcements; and your city is their object.

British Ships Anchored at St. Marys, by Martin Pate, Newnan, Georgia.
(Courtesy of Southeastern Archeological Center NPS)

Detail from *British Ships Anchored at St. Marys*, by Martin Pate, Newnan, Georgia. (Courtesy of Southeastern Archeological Center NPS)

Detail of St. Marys dock from *British Ships Anchored at St. Marys*, by Martin Pate, Newnan, Georgia. (Courtesy of Southeastern Archeological Center NPS)

Cockburn stationed troops at each plantation house on the island, placing able-bodied white males under house arrest. Not five months after Caty Miller's death, on January 25, 1815, Cockburn established his headquarters at Dungeness House, using the first floor as an infirmary for his sick and wounded. As head of the occupying military force on Cumberland, his word was absolute. He ordered the construction of a large wharf on the river near Dungeness, using expensive red cedar already brought to Cumberland for transportation elsewhere and possibly also had cedar trees felled on the island. He erected a breastwork extending from Dungeness to the marsh and an entrenchment to surround the well-sited mansion. Most of the British troops camped in the orange groves between the house and beach. During that eight-week occupation, his fleet raided coastal plantations, seizing almost fifteen hundred enslaved people. One white observer described the admiral as "a far greater scourge to mankind than the locusts of Africa."

Emancipation, and Alliances with the British

Within days of his establishing his Dungeness headquarters, Cockburn began carrying out the terms of an emancipation proclamation conceived by his superior officer, Alexander Cochrane, which read, in part, "all those who may be disposed to emigrate from the United States, will with their families be received on Board his Majesty's Ships or Vessels of War, or at the Military posts that may be established upon or near the Coast of the United States." In essence, Cochrane considered British ships and British military camps to be British soil and subject to English laws. The proclamation went to say freedom seekers could enter into "His Majesty's Sea or Land forces" or be sent as "Free Settlers" to British possessions. The enslaved people scooped up from Cumberland were transported first to Bermuda and eventually to the British Canadian provinces of New Brunswick and Nova Scotia and to the island of Trinidad, where they were freed. Cockburn had achieved some success with similar emancipation efforts in the Chesapeake Bay region after razing Washington. But, as Mary Bullard observed, "Cumberland Island almost surely must have been the scene of one of the most extraordinarily effective mass military emancipations seen in the United States."

In one respect, the safest place for the Shaws was on British-occupied Cumberland Island. Cockburn certainly wasn't going to torch Dungeness, the most convenient place on the coast to establish headquarters, encamp his men, and process freed men, women, and children for embarkation to British-held locations. As had happened to her mother, destiny now had placed a man with immense military authority in Louisa's orbit. After most of her slaves were later returned to Dungeness, wagging tongues attributed this inexplicable reversal to her having been intimate with Cockburn, though Cockburn's central role in burning the U.S. Capitol and other federal buildings in August 1814 were unlikely to endear the man to her.

The admiral's arrival at the Shaws' home coincided with a monthlong Christmas holiday party at Dungeness. Guests from neighboring plantations, including members of the Couper and Page families on St. Simons Island, were already on hand. The admiral banished Louisa, James, and their visitors to the upstairs rooms. Among the guests were young daughters of wealthy planters. Whether for the sake of morale or because of his officers' pleas, Cockburn allowed the Shaws and their houseguests to return to the lower floors and entertaining rooms. Much to the chagrin of the older girls and to the amusement of the British officers, the youngest and prettiest of the party, Anne Page, scalded her lips while sipping hot coffee from a silver cup. One of the young local men came to her defense and informed the officers that the "little girl" stood to inherit Retreat on St. Simons, one of the largest cotton plantations on the coast. Cockburn promised Anne that his forces would not molest the Page family property.

James Hamilton Couper, son of John Couper of Cannon's Point on St. Simons, then in school in Connecticut, wrote a friend about the British invasion: "I yesterday received a letter from Roswell King. He states that my mother, sister, the Misses Johnstons, and Miss Page were on Cumberland when the British landed. I think they must have been very much terrified when they [the British] approached and very glad to hear that my father had obtained a [undecipherable] and gone after them."

During the occupation, a young Royal Marine lieutenant named John Fraser fell in love with James Hamilton Couper's dark-eyed sister, Anne Sarah. Over the following weeks, in the course of his duties, Fraser had ample opportunities to visit the Couper home at Cannon's Point. She wrote to him on February 25, 1815:

> No one could be a fortnight in your society without feeling some spark of regret at separation. The time is not perhaps very distant, when if you are the amiable and noble being you appear to be, gratitude which we now feel may be changed into reciprocal affection, and rest assured that it will be the first time that passion of love has been a guest in this heart.

The two were married less than a year later. After the war they would settle on St. Simons at Lawrence, a plantation a mile south of Cannon's Point.

Susannah Stafford, the sister of Robert Stafford who would one day own most of Cumberland, met Lt. George Drew Hawkins during the British occupation. They, too, married in 1815. Their son, Thomas Drew Hawkins, an only child, was born in London the following year. Susannah and Thomas returned to Cumberland after George Hawkins's death in 1818.

On January 28 Adm. Cockburn issued orders for the captains of the ships *Canso*, *Manley*, and *Regulus* to take possession of Jekyll and St. Simons, which would suffer the same fate as Cumberland. The British were to plunder and bring back produce and livestock, make prisoners of white male Americans living there (likely placing them under house arrest as he did on Cumberland), and return to Cumberland with as many enslaved "as may be willing to join our standard." By February 4 he wrote Commodore Evans in Bermuda to request five hundred extra uniforms for West India Regiment troops and newly freed slaves recruited into his ranks as part of the Corps of Colonial Marines. In the same letter, penned at Dungeness, he wrote that "the Negroes inclined

Next page: Chimneys of former Stafford Plantation slave cabins.

to take advantage of the Commander-in-Chief's Proclamation appear to be even more numerous in this part of the country than in the Neighborhood of the Chesapeake. I therefore foresee that I will be obliged to send many into Port [Bermuda] by every opportunity. I trust however as the Season is so fast advancing you will have frequent opportunities of forwarding them on to Halifax [Nova Scotia] and thereby, prevent the increase of difficulty and inconvenience which would arise to you from an accumulation of them at Bermuda." Cockburn had created an emancipation pipeline through which former slaves on the Georgia coast would be relocated to Canada.

The coastal winter was particularly brutal that year. In a letter from "Head Quarters, Cumberland Island, 27 January 1815" to Major Ross of the Second West India in the Bahamas, Cockburn wrote, "I am sorry to have to state to you that many of your men have suffered excessively from the cold of this climate, and some few of them have been so frost bitten as to render amputation necessary to preserve their lives." James Shaw became ill during the occupation and was permitted to leave for Scotland. He evidently got no farther than St. Simons Island, where he stayed with the Couper family, who "feared such a voyage in his present state of health would be disastrous."

Soon after occupying Cumberland, the British realized the island lacked enough provisions to feed all of the troops stationed there as well as the island inhabitants and the influx of refugees brought there from the surrounding area. They relied on existing ships' stores and provisions sent from Bermuda to feed the island's burgeoning population. Cockburn's ship log records one transport brought 1,783 pounds of fresh beef and another delivered 1,645 pounds of potatoes. Even then, food shortages on Cumberland were widespread, affecting the invading forces, newly freed men and women, and white residents alike.

During the occupation, some "distressed inhabitants" sought shelter and sustenance aboard the frigate *Surprize*, anchored on the north end of the island. Among them were William Clubb Jr. and his wife, Alice; his three unmarried sisters, Rachel, Rebecca, and Martha; Nanny (Nan), a "Negro woman"; and Penny and Clarice Clubb, listed as white children. It is believed that Penny and Clarice were actually mulatto and that Nan was their mother. It is further speculated (without proof) that William Clubb Jr. was their father. William Clubb Sr. had sided with Britain during the American Revolution and sat out that war in East Florida, like many southern Loyalists. After Britain ceded Florida back to Spain, he returned to Georgia with his family and purchased lots on Cumberland in a planned town that never materialized. Carrying the speculation a bit further, perhaps William Jr., like his father, was a Loyalist who wished to emigrate with his family to another British possession for the sake of the mulatto Penny and Clarice, and then later changed his mind. Whatever the reason, the Clubbs were soon "discharged" from the *Surprize* back onto Cumberland.

Cockburn allowed Louisa Shaw to have a young enslaved female "house servant" wait on her, and he secured the services of an older enslaved female who cooked for him and his staff. The rest of the Rayfield, Littlefield, and Dungeness enslaved were transported to the *Devastation*, a bomb vessel anchored nearby.

A close friend described how Louisa dealt with the removal of the enslaved from Cumberland: "Mrs. Shaw has lost every negro she owned—they went on shipboard, & as Admiral Cockburn and Col. Williams, the Commander of the land forces occupy Mrs. Shaw's house as HQ on Cumberland Island, at Mrs. Shaw's request all her negroes [about 150] were brought on shore, & she gave them a long talk & told them how kind they had been treated by all the family—all this had no effect—I suppose the British had been tampering with them, & they all preferred to go on shipboard again." No evidence survives that the British under Cockburn's command were willing to transport the freed Blacks back to Cumberland for their white owners to make a plea for their return.

Local whites believed the British had been "tampering" with the enslaved population, telling them their masters would seek vengeance on them for ginning cotton and slaughtering cattle on behalf of the English and for abandoning their fieldwork. They were "seduced by the most absurd & fallacious tales," one contemporary wrote. "They were informed that the Queen of England was a Negro Woman—that in England, whither they were about to be carried, the Ladies preferred Negro Men as husbands, and the Gentlemen Negro Women as wives, & that, at the expense of the British Government, they would for the rest of their lives, be maintained in affluence, without labor, having servants, horses & carriages kept for their use. I have known them morning after morning to be at the Negroes houses, arguing with & soliciting them to go off." But the essential enticements to the Black population were real: freedom from slavery; clothing, food, and shelter until they could be transported to British soil; and for men the chance to enlist in the British military. Indeed, one of the Shaws' slaves, Ned Simmons (or Simons)—who had been with the Greene family since their time at Mulberry Grove—enlisted in the British military service as a Colonial Marine upon gaining his freedom. He was issued a used uniform and a weapon and drilled along with other newly freed men. The newly freed Blacks who enlisted or who boarded British ships, including women who served as laundresses (presumably for pay), were asked to provide a surname; notably, Ned's chosen surname had nothing to do with Mulberry Grove or Dungeness.

Some Blacks seeking freedom made their way by boat from elsewhere in the area, landing at the British encampment on the north end of Cumberland. One escaped slave named Ben fled with his wife and child from the Hardee plantation on the Little Satilla River. An American overseer still living on Cumberland wrote that "Ben was an excellent performer on the violin and often amused his comrades on that instrument." He was soon after relocated to the camp near Dungeness, where he joined the British West India Regiment as did other slaves brought there from plantations on Cumberland, Jekyll, St. Simons, and the surrounding area. Cockburn was more than willing to recruit freed slaves into his military ranks for several reasons. Since Parliament's 1807 ban on the slave trade, the British navy could no longer purchase them directly from slave ships en route from Africa to the Americas. Here, on Cumberland, he could recruit new men to the ranks by the hundreds. Black soldiers had also proven themselves against enemies in battle.

An unintended consequence of Cochrane's emancipation proclamation was the arrival of slaves fleeing their masters in Spanish Florida. One group escaped from nearby Amelia Island. More than sixty slaves fled to Cumberland from a plantation on the St. Johns owned by Jonathan Forbes, a wealthy British planter. When he contacted Cockburn at Dungeness to demand their return, the admiral replied by letter on February 26, 1815, that the boat they escaped in would be delivered to Forbes "upon your substantiating her to be actually your Property, but the People you refer to having of their own accord come from *the Sea* to this Island now under the Dominion of His Britannic Majesty, I do not conceive myself (even were you to substantiate that they formerly belonged to you) called upon or even authorized *to force* these Individuals to return to you, they have however full Permission so to do collectively or Individually whensoever they please."

When the Spanish governor of East Florida, Sebastián de Kindelán y Oregón, protested to Cockburn for giving Forbes's slaves sanctuary, the admiral replied on February 13, 1815, from Dungeness that "to prevent their Desertion from the Spanish Territory must I think remain with Your Excellency and those Acting under your Excellency's Orders." In other words, it was incumbent on the Spanish governor to prevent runaway slaves from leaving his territory. Cockburn also informed the governor that "as this Island now appertains to H. B. MJ [His Britannic Majesty] by rights of Conquest, and for the moment must of course be Governed by the Laws of Great Britain (which know not of Slavery) I do not conceive it to be within my Powers *forcibly* to send back any individuals should they after Effecting their Escape from other countries at the Risk of their lives." This, after more than two hundred years of heavy engagement in the transatlantic slave trade, was indicative of Great Britain's historic reversal on slavery. Cockburn was sincere and thwarted all attempts to have people seeking freedom on Cumberland returned to their former masters. He did allow slave owners, both Spanish and American, to come to Cumberland to try to persuade refugees to voluntarily return to slavery.

Not all slaves left their masters' estates, and not all of the British solicited them with fantastic promises. Lt. John Fraser discouraged slaves on St. Simons from leaving with him and informed them they were being misled by his fellow countrymen. The fact that he was in love with Anne Sarah Couper, the daughter of a wealthy island planter, John Couper, apparently influenced his actions. Couper's head driver, a Muslim, was born Suli-bul-Ali or Salih Belali in Macina (or Massina), Mali, and renamed Tom or Africa Tom. He convinced many Couper slaves to remain, telling them that he had known slavery under the English in the West Indies and considered them to be worse masters than the Americans. (Although Britain abolished the slave trade in 1807, slavery in the British West Indies remained in place until 1838.) The English may have used misleading tactics to entice the enslaved to leave their plantations, but the real catalyst for fleeing was a genuine thirst for freedom, a concept many slaveholders had trouble comprehending. Most slaveholders saw themselves in a benevolent light. But for the newly freed, it was an exodus that brought to mind the Israelites' flight from Egypt.

Treaty of Ghent

On Christmas Eve 1814, U.S. and British representatives signed a preliminary treaty in Ghent, Belgium—a full month before Admiral Cockburn settled into his headquarters at Dungeness. By February 9, 1815, he became aware of the treaty. "The day before yesterday," he wrote Admiral Cochrane on 11 February, "a schooner under Swedish colours arrived here, after a short passage from Portsmouth, having on board an English gentleman who provided to me a London Newspaper, the *Courier*, dated the 27th December containing Accounts (therein stated to be Official) that Peace between Great Britain and the United States had been concluded between the Plenipotentiaries at Ghent on the 24th Dec. last subject to the Ratification of the Prince Regent and the President of the United States, and that it had been ratified by the Prince Regent on the 27th."

The first article of the treaty stated that "all territory, places, and possessions whatsoever taken by either party from the other during the war, or which may be taken after the signing of this Treaty . . . shall be restored without delay," including "any slaves." However, Cockburn went on to write that he would continue to act as if he had not

Admiral Sir Alexander Inglis Cochrane (1758–1832), Governor of Guadeloupe, by Robert Field, dated 1809. (Courtesy of the National Galleries of Scotland)

received this news until "this is officially made known to me, with due notifications of the President having also ratified it." In a letter dated February 27 to the U.S. commander of the Southern Division, Maj. Gen. Thomas Pinckney, from "Head Quarters Cumberland Island," the admiral reiterated his stance. "An official Intimation of its [the treaty] having been actually ratified by the President, is required to authorize my Acting upon it in full conformity with your request."

Cockburn's plans to invade Savannah were interrupted by the treaty, but his men continued to ransack St. Marys and plantations along the coast under his watch while he delayed acknowledgment that the war had already ended. On February 26, 1815, the HMS *St. Lawrence*, a fourteen-gun Royal Navy schooner, was captured near Havana by Thomas Boyle, a U.S. privateer and captain of the clipper *Chasseur*. Aboard the British ship he confiscated letters from Admiral Cochrane and Admiral Cockburn, written at Dungeness, both of whom refer to the Treaty of Ghent. Cockburn wrote: "We are in daily expectation of a flag of truce to inform us of Mr. [President] Madison's having ratified the treaty, on his doing which, hostilities will immediately cease. I confess myself by no means sorry for this event. I think we have quite enough of war for some years to come, although [I] should have wished we had made the Yankees more sensible of our power to punish them, should they again provoke us. As it is, except the injury done to their trade, we have little to boast of." Regarding the British defeat at New Orleans, Cockburn wrote, "our loss seems to have been immense."

On March 5, Cockburn wrote from Cumberland acknowledging that "the Treaty of Peace between Great Britain and America" had been "duly ratified," but he continued to ignore the first article of the treaty, claiming that he had not received "Official Notification" from his superiors and therefore could take no steps to comply with the treaty. On March 6, two U.S. commissioners, Thomas Spalding and Thomas M. Newall, arrived at Dungeness. They were authorized by Maj. Gen. Thomas Pinckney (a former U.S. ambassador to Great Britain) and Brig. Gen. John Floyd to negotiate the return of slaves and property to their owners. Spalding owned a large plantation on Sapelo Island and had armed his slaves under the direction of his overseer, a Muslim slave named Bu Allah (or Bilali Mohammed, from present-day Sierra Leone), to defend the island from British attack. Newall was a member of the Sea Fencibles, a naval corps raised by an act of the U.S. Congress to defend East Coast ports and harbors.

Cockburn had already been in communication with Admiral Cochrane concerning the issue of returning slaves to Spanish Florida and cited precedence that allowed him to retain freed slaves who were on British soil or British navy vessels. Citing from

"Commentaries On The Laws Of England" by Sir William Blackstone, Cockburn wrote, "the Spirit of Liberty is so deeply implanted in our very Soul that *a Slave or a Negro* the Moment he lands in England, falls under the Protection of the Laws and so becomes a Freeman." This, and other precedents he quoted to Cochrane, formed the logic of his responses to those demanding restitution for slaves taken from them.

On March 7, 1815, he sent Spalding and Newall a letter from Dungeness replete with legal obfuscation and verbal gymnastics worthy of a seasoned barrister: "I must beg to decline venturing an Opinion as to whether the Treaty is properly worded according to the Intentions of the [American and British] Commissioners, but I apprehend had they wished to imply (as you conceive) that all private Property and Slaves in my possession *whether on Land or Water* were to be restored it might have been specified without Difficulty. . . . I must beg to be excused from entering into Discussion relative to Captures made *elsewhere* [other than on Cumberland Island] *on Land or Water* and which have been removed from the Places where Captured prior to the Exchange of the Ratifications of the Treaty." He further informed them that "I shall as quickly as possible evacuate it [Cumberland Island] without causing destruction, and I shall leave on it or deliver to you, whatever Public or private Property or Slaves (*originally captured here*) remained upon the Island at the date of the Ratification."

Three days later, still on Cumberland, Cockburn alerted Native allies that the war had ended. On March 10 he sent a short communication from Dungeness to "The Chief of any Indian Tribes on or near the Borders of Georgia," informing them of the treaty "in which the Indian Nations allies of His Britannic Majesty are included and it is agreed that they should be placed upon the same footing in respect as they were in the Year 1811 provided they cease all Hostilities against the United States." He went on to urge them to accept the terms of the treaty.

Cockburn delayed further communication with Spalding and Newall until he could consult with Admiral Cochrane, expected to arrive any day from Bermuda. The vice admiral's flagship, *Tonnant*, anchored at Cumberland on March 8. Spalding and Newall watched for two days from their vantage point, possibly a boat anchored in the harbor, as a flurry of activity surrounded Sir Alexander's ship. On March 10 their window to present their case closed when the *Tonnant* departed for Bermuda. On March 11 they received a letter from Cockburn, endorsed by Cochrane, restating their position. The upshot was that any slave or private property *not* onboard a British ship on the hour and date the United States ratified the Treaty of Ghent (11:00 p.m., February 17, 1815) would be returned to their owners. In this letter he included a "list of the Property and Slaves originally captured on Cumberland Island, and which appear to have remained on it at 11 PM of the 17th Ultimo [the previous month], the Period at which the Ratifications were exchanged."

The names of eighty slaves were on Cockburn's list, most of them belonging to Louisa Shaw and her cousin, Ray Sands. They were returned to the island along with "A few Bales of Cotton, some Horses and some Cattle." Unfortunately for Ned Simmons, the slave who joined the Colonial Marines, his name was also on the list. Ned's time as a free man had been brief, and he would remain a slave until his second emancipation by federal troops in 1863.

Cockburn allowed Spalding and Newall to board the British ship *Regulus*, where they convinced thirteen slaves to return with them to shore. Hundreds of others did not leave the ship. On March 13, 1815, the British flag at Dungeness was lowered. Cockburn's ship, the *Albion*, sailed away five days later after assisting another vessel that had floundered on the bar. Twenty-five U.S. Army soldiers led by Capt. Abraham Massias were ordered to Cumberland Island to capture remaining refugees still attempting to board British ships. One of Louisa's slaves, fifty-five-year-old Sancho Panza (apparently named for Don Quixote's traveling companion), boarded the *Albion* the day before its departure and sailed with Cockburn. Though there was a slave named Sancho on the list of eighty returned to Cumberland, Sancho Panza may have been a free Black man taken in raids by Georgia Patriots and sold into slavery, which would account for Cockburn's willingness to give him sanctuary.

Thomas Spalding, John Couper, and other local planters sailed to Bermuda, where they unsuccessfully petitioned for the return of their slaves, most of whom were sent to Nova Scotia. Accustomed as they were to thinking of slaves as their property, the planters were surprised by the cold reception given by their former slaves. Georgia's planters were more successful in submitting "spoliation claims" with Britain. The Shaws claimed more than $22,000 in losses for crops, cattle, equipment, planks, boards, and live oak timber. A British soldier smoking a cigar accidentally burned down their three-story cotton house, used as a barracks by the occupiers. Nat Greene, Louisa's brother, saw the blaze from his patrol on the Crooked River on the mainland. Their carpenter and blacksmith shops burned with their tools. The British had already carted off almost two entire cotton crops in bales marked "E.G.G." for "Estate of General Greene" and had axed valuable cedar trees and most of the lemon and orange tree orchard.

Other area planters claimed as much or more for their losses. St. Simons planters John Couper claimed $22,450, Pierce Butler $56,470, and James Hamilton $74,590. Louisa Shaw, like her mother before her, engaged in a long-term legal battle seeking

George Cockburn

George Cockburn was born in London April 22, 1772, the second son of Sir James Cockburn, a baronet, and Augusta Anne Ayscough. Because second sons could not inherit the father's estate, they were expected to pursue a military career. Cockburn joined the Royal British Navy in 1781 and quickly rose through the ranks, seeing action in the French Revolution and the Napoleonic War. He was promoted to rear admiral in 1812 and reassigned to the North American and West Indies Station, where he served under Admiral Sir Alexander Cochrane. Twelve months after participating in the burning of Washington, D.C., and then invading Georgia's coast, he transported Napoleon to the island of Saint Helena and remained as governor for several months. In 1818 Cockburn was elected to Parliament as a member of the Tory party. His promotions in the admiralty continued, eventually rising to First Naval Lord. On his brother's death he inherited the family baronetcy in 1852 and died the following year. Cockburn is buried in Kensel Green Cemetery, Chelsea, a London borough.

compensation, choosing Judge John McPherson Berrien to represent her. Whereas Caty Greene's quest for compensation from the U.S. government took twenty-five years, Louisa's case only took ten, by which time her husband James had already died. Like her mother, Louisa was also managing Dungeness on her own. The 1822 Convention for Indemnity, with Emperor Alexander I of Russia acting as arbiter, found in favor of the Americans. Britain was to compensate the slaveholders, and a joint British-U.S. commission would work out the details. Four years later, the indemnity amount was set at $1,204,960, which Britain paid to the United States in 1827.

The following year, local planters, including Louisa, were finally recompensed for property losses suffered during the War of 1812, including crops, cattle, live oak, and the freeing of slaves. She received $20,883 (less than her original claim) in compensation for her losses, or $450,000 in today's dollars. Her lawyer, John Berrien, known as the American Cicero, later became a U.S. senator and attorney general under Andrew Jackson. Berrien County, Georgia, is named for him.

Light-Horse Harry Lee

In February 1818 the schooner *Betsy* moored at the Dungeness dock, where several men carried a feeble passenger ashore. Revolutionary War hero Maj. Gen. "Light-Horse Harry" (Henry) Lee had been at Valley Forge with Nathanael and Caty Greene and had served under Nathanael in the southern theater. Lee had eulogized George Washington with the famous lines, "first in war, first in peace, and first in the hearts of his countrymen."

Henry Lee. This posthumous portrait of Henry "Light-Horse Harry" Lee, former governor of Virginia and father of Robert E. Lee, is by William Edward West, ca. 1838. West studied with Thomas Scully, whose portrait of Nathanael Greene appears in the previous chapter. (Wikimedia Commons)

Since then, however, the father of Robert E. Lee had fallen on hard times through unwise business dealings and investments and had fled the States for Barbados, in part to avoid creditors and in part to recuperate from wounds received while defending a newspaper editor who opposed the recent war of 1812. But now he was dying of cancer and had returned to the United States, making it as far Cumberland Island.

Louisa Shaw's nephew, Phineas Miller Nightingale (Martha Greene and John Nightingale's second son) was at the dock when the schooner arrived. Lee threw his arms around the boy when he learned Phineas was Caty and Nathanael's grandson, exclaiming "tell Mrs. Shaw I am come purposely to die in the house and in the arms of the daughter of my old friend and compatriot." The Shaws accommodated Lee in a room on the third floor. But he proved to be a headstrong patient. "Mrs. Shaw welcomed the old General and tried to make him comfortable in his last days," wrote Bernard Nightingale. "Terrific pain made him cross at times. It was hard to supply him with competent servants. At length an old negro woman, who had been Mrs. Greene's favorite maid, and who was then the privileged family servant, was selected to wait on him. The first thing General Lee did as she entered the room was to hurl his boot at her head and order her out. Entirely unused to such treatment, without saying a word she deliberately picked up the boot and threw it back at him. The effect produced by this strange and unexpected retort was marked and instantaneous. The features of the stern warrior relaxed. In the midst of his pain and anger a smile passed over his countenance, and from that moment until the day of his death, he would permit no one except 'Mom Sarah' to do his special service."

An incident later cited to demonstrate Lee's "veneration for Washington and his fondness for expressing it" recounts that a surgical operation was proposed by a doctor to prolong his life. Harry Lee "put an end to the discussion by saying: 'My dear sir, were the great Washington alive and here, and joining you in advocating it, I would still resist.'" Years later Frederick Ober wrote that the chamber "directly above the drawing-room [was] the most interesting of all, for it was occupied by General Harry Lee, who was confined there by sickness, and there died."

A witness to Lee's funeral expressed it more poetically: "Mr. Shaw and his family strove all in their power to keep the lamp of life burning, and although the oil was expended, they still blew the gentle breath of affection and attention, to preserve the wick alive." Despite Louisa's and Mom Sarah's ministrations, and the care of a nearby naval doctor, Lee passed away two months after arriving at Dungeness. Lee's only possessions were a "ramshackle" hair trunk and a cask of Madeira. The Shaws buried Lee in the Greene cemetery near Dungeness. The *Savannah Republican* described his funeral:

Dungeness Wharf, 1889. (Courtesy of the Georgia
Archives, Lucy Coleman and Thomas M. Carnegie

Commodore Henley superintended the last sad duties. Captains Elton, Finch, Madison, Lieutenants Fitzhugh and Richie, of the Navy, and Mr. Lyman, of the Army, were pallbearers. As the procession moved, the swords of the first two crossed the old man's breast—they were in their scabbards: for his heart beat no more, and I thought they said, "rest in peace." The other officers of the Navy, and Captain Payne of the Army, followed. The marines of the U. S. ship *John Adams* and the brig *Sarnac* formed the guard, and a band from our army assisted. A Mr. Taylor performed the last ceremonial duties. The sight of a long train of sailors, cleanly dressed, their respectful deportment, and rough but independent looks, interested my feelings. I was immediately absorbed in contemplation. They were marching over the field where once a fine orange orchard flourished. An invader of our country [Admiral Cockburn] destroyed it. A volley of musketry over the grave of General Lee aroused me while the howling of the minute-guns from the *John Adams* echoed through the woods.

Lee's son, "Black-Horse" Harry Lee—Robert E. Lee's half-brother—arranged from Paris to have a marker placed on their father's Cumberland grave in 1832. Phineas Nightingale personally placed the headstone over Lee's resting place. The marker still stands in the Greene family cemetery near Dungeness, though "Light-Horse Harry's" remains were disinterred in 1913 and placed next to Robert in the Lee Chapel at Washington and Lee University in Lexington, Virginia.

Ober's 1880 *Lippincott* article mentions "the Park, a little tongue of land [that] runs from the garden into the marsh, and here the inhabitants of this favored estate would resort for recreation in the afternoon and evening. Near this strip of land, beneath the shade of an immense live-oak, luxuriates a clump of West India bamboo, said to have originated from a single stalk brought here by General [Harry] Lee."

The End of an Era at Dungeness

Louisa made a name for herself as a horticulturist by overseeing the estate's extensive gardens and citrus orchards. Despite the devastation by the British in the War of 1812, by the mid-1820s Dungeness boasted an orange grove of two thousand trees. An advertisement in the March 23, 1830, edition of the *Daily Savannah Republican* crowed: "Sweet Oranges: 12,000 just received from Mr. Shaw's Grove on Cumberland Island in fine order and large sizes." In 1824 the aldermen of Savannah approached Louisa and other local planters "for the purpose of ascertaining by their science and experience the native trees best adapted for planting in the city, with the periods most favorable for setting them out." Perhaps the trees now seen in Savannah's parks and lining its streets—live oak

(*Quercus virginiana*), palmetto (*Sabal palmetto*), and magnolia (*Magnolia virginiana*)—are the end result of this inquiry.

An indication of the Shaws' financial standing may be deduced from an April 29, 1825, notice placed in the *Savannah Republican*. Under the heading "Liberal Donation," the editor wrote, "We understand that the Greene and Pulaski Monument Committee have received a donation of Five Hundred Dollars [over $10,000 in today's currency] to be appropriated to the erection of the monuments of this city from Mrs. Shaw, of Cumberland. Mrs. Shaw, it will be recollected, is the daughter of the former of these revolutionary heroes."

That same year, planning to be absent from Cumberland for a period, Louisa ran advertisements in Savannah, Charleston, and New York newspapers headlined "Dungeness, on Cumberland Island, to Rent." (Before James's death, Louisa and James Shaw had often spent their summers at Newport, Rhode Island, to avoid Georgia's sweltering heat.) The house, fully furnished, was available "for either one summer or eighteen months, as shall be preferred." The ad continued in a manner similar to future advertisements for hotels on the north end of the island. "The House is situated within half a mile of a very fine beach, and is quite open to the sea. There is an excellent spring of water, and a good garden, and peach orchard, attached to it. The post town of St. Marys is only eight miles distant, and vessels are running constantly between that place, Charleston and Savannah." Louisa also offered for rent, with or without Dungeness, "an Orangery, the usual crop of which is two hundred thousand." Interested parties were to contact Louisa's nephew, Phineas Nightingale (misspelled "Pheneas" in the ad), her authorized attorney. By this time, Phineas Nightingale was a full-time resident of Dungeness helping manage the estate, and like his aunt he had taken a serious interest in horticulture.

In 1828 Louisa offered $50—more than $1,000 in present value—for the capture and return of a slave named Johnny, "about five feet nine inches high, thick set, of a bright black complexion, had on clothes made of satinett [cotton and wool fabric], with a piece of the tooth next to the eye tooth broken out, has an intelligent countenance with a downcast look and can seldom look a person in the face when speaking." Apparently, Johnny had married "abroad," meaning he wedded a slave from another plantation. His wife lived on "Captain Stockton's plantation, on Turtle River," near Brunswick. Johnny was thought to "be lurking about that place or the neighborhood of Darien." The $50 reward would be paid to anyone who brought Johnny to a jail, and $100 was offered "if delivered at Mrs. Shaw's plantation on Cumberland Island."

Louisa died childless in 1831, leaving her estate, including Dungeness and Oakland, valued at $48,377, to her nephew and attorney, Phineas Nightingale. She was buried

Louisa Shaw placed this advertisement for 12,000 oranges in the March 23, 1830, edition of the *Daily Savannah Republican*. (Georgia Historic Newspapers, Digital Library of Georgia)

Charles Gibbs's Buried Pirate Treasure

The same year Louisa passed away, the notorious pirate Charles Gibbs (born James D. Jeffers in Newport, Rhode Island) was charged with mutiny and murder. The U.S. attorneys who prosecuted him were James Alexander Hamilton and Philip Hamilton, sons of Alexander Hamilton. Gibbs was hung at Ellis Island April 22, 1831. The *Atlanta Weekly Sun* mentioned him in an 1872 article: "At one part of the beach, the heaving, restless waters of Old Ocean are slowly wearing away a mound exposing fragments of pottery, together with the bones of its Aboriginal builders. Near this spot the celebrated pirate Gibbs is said to have hidden an immense treasure of golden coin. Prior to his execution—so goes the story— touched by the kindness of his jailor, he described to him the spot on the Southern end of Cumberland Island, stating that he [Gibbs] had taken ten men ashore to bury the treasure; and to preserve his secret, he had murdered these ten men and thrown them overboard so soon as he got to sea. The treasure has often been searched for. We did not take time to search for so small a sum—only $170,000 in gold! Indeed, had we found it, the weight would have been inconvenient to carry."

Image from "Dungeness, on Cumberland Island, to Rent" advertisement placed by Louisa Shaw in the *Savannah Republican*, April 29, 1825. (Georgia Historic Newspapers, Digital Library of Georgia)

beside her husband, James Shaw, who had died in 1820, and her mother, Caty. Her marble slab reads "Louisa C. Shaw, relict of James Shaw, Esq., and youngest daughter of Major-General Nathanael Greene of the Army of the Revolution. Died at Dungeness, Georgia, April 24th, 1831, aged 45 years."

The majority of the estate's value rested in the 151 slaves, each worth about $275. Following Louisa's death, Nightingale posted probate notices in a number of Georgia newspapers: "All persons having demands against the Estate of Mrs. Louisa C. Shaw, of Dungeness, Cumberland Island, deceased, are required to render in their accounts, properly attested; and all persons indebted to said Estate will make payment without delay to P. M. Nightingale or Henry R. Sadler, executors."

A month after Louisa's death, her nephew took out a mortgage and put down $13,500 to purchase property on Great Cumberland that still belonged to the heirs of Thomas Lynch. The sale put Nightingale, already in debt, further in arrears, a problem exacerbated by another economic depression that began with the Panic of 1837. Nightingale had also inherited the enslaved people at Oakland. This did not sit well with his wife, Mary Ray King Nightingale, a northerner and daughter of John Alsop King, a U.S. congressman and future governor of New York, whose political and moral leanings aligned with those of the abolitionists.

On June 14, 1838, Mary Nightingale, her daughter, Louisa, and a "Negro nurse Rhynah" were traveling north on the 687-ton ss *Pulaski* with several of Georgia's most

Greene Cemetery.

prominent citizens on board when its boiler exploded off the North Carolina coast. James Hamilton Couper rescued Mary and Louisa from the sinking ship and got them safely ashore after a harrowing encounter with breakers near the beach. The ship sank forty-five minutes after the explosion, causing the deaths of 128 passengers and crew. Rhynah and a number of other passengers survived the ordeal by "clinging to fragments from the wrecked ship for several days without food or water."

Several killing frosts drove Nightingale to the point of bankruptcy, and by 1841 Dungeness was no longer a working plantation, though the house became a refuge for the Nightingale family to escape the summer heat on the mainland. In January 1842 Phineas advertised the sale of Dungeness, "2000 acres of which 200 are cleared and 300 covered with valuable live oak timber, which has never been culled. The house is large and convenient, built of tabby, and never infested with sand-flies or mosquitoes. The Garden is well laid out and contains many rare and valuable plants. There are on the place 1200 Orange Trees, most of them bearing, and about 200 Olive Trees, which with Limes, Lemons, Citrons and other tropical fruits, do well without protection."

The sale also included Oakland, "in the middle of the island, a Sea Island Cotton Plantation with the facilities for producing Corn, Rice, and Sugar Cane," and "50 prime Negroes and families." He offered the property "to pay the debts of the estate of the late Mrs. Shaw, and will be sold low and on easy terms." Two tracts of land and slaves were auctioned off by the county. A sheriff's sale advertisement appeared in Georgia newspapers in June 1843. The eventual beneficiary of the land sale was Robert Stafford, a former worker on the Shaw estate and now the island's major landholder.

Island Shipwrecks

Ships have run aground on Cumberland Island's shores and surrounding bars since the arrival of the Europeans. Two shipwrecks occurred in 1873. The bark *Monarch*, improperly loaded with timber at Doboy Sound and bound for Newcastle, England, ran aground on the St. Andrews Bar in severe weather. "The puny arm of man and all his ingenious contrivances for such emergencies were powerless to contend against the wild and wrathful elements of nature," one paper reported. Seven sailors died attempting to escape the wreck by boat. Eight survived. Captain Thomas, seeing his wife drown, chose to go down with her despite the crew's efforts to rescue him. "My wife is gone, and I will go with her," he said, refusing a rope that had been cast by his crewmen.

In September 1873, the Spanish brig *Guanche*, en route from Havana to the Satilla River, experienced rough weather and struck shore on the south end of Cumberland in a blinding rain and "perfect darkness," though it was during the day. Captain Pedro Revis de la Freente and his crew escaped by lifeboats after three hours of futile attempts to save the ship.

The *Athens Banner* reported on May 3, 1881, that "the steamship *City of Austin*, of the Mallory Line, was wrecked off Cumberland Island last Sunday afternoon. It is said the pilot was color blind and mistook one buoy for another. The passengers, 60 in number, have been landed in Savannah, but the vessel and cargo are a total loss."

The *New York Times* carried a dispatch from Savannah dated March 31, 1893: the "tug *Mascotte* of Brunswick [Georgia] went ashore at Cumberland Island, ten miles south of the Hotel Cumberland in a heavy gale which raged on Wednesday evening. She was towing a schooner bound for Satilla River. The hawser parted and wound around the tug's propeller, rendering her helpless." After their lifeboat overturned, most of the crew swam ashore with the aid of life preservers. The ship steward drowned, and "Capt. Potter is thought to be dying from exposure."

The schooner *John H. Tingue*, bound from Philadelphia to Jacksonville with a cargo of coal, ran aground on Cumberland in October 1899. Captain Taylor and his crew escaped unharmed, but the vessel and cargo were a total loss.

Numerous wrecks have occurred since then, including the *Rambler*, a small vessel that became stranded on a sandbar opposite the Little Cumberland lighthouse by stormy seas that battered the boat to pieces. Four crewmen perished, with only one body being recovered. In 1909, a launch manned by Atlanta fire chief W. B. Cummings, hotel proprietor Walter Miller, Dr. Henry Carnes, and an African American porter ran aground half a mile from shore and began to break up under a barrage of battering waves. They escaped in a small boat with only one oar.

CHAPTER VII

The Monarch of Cumberland Island

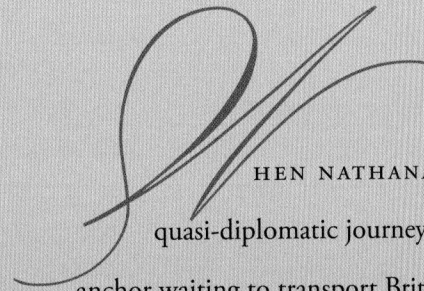

WHEN NATHANAEL GREENE entered St. Marys Harbor after his quasi-diplomatic journey to St. Augustine in 1785, a number of vessels lay at anchor waiting to transport British Loyalists from East Florida to Jamaica, Bermuda, and other British possessions. Many of these evacuees had set up temporary camps on the south end of Cumberland. Among this group were two English natives, brothers Robert and Thomas Stafford, who had migrated from Barbados to British East Florida and were now seeking new lives in Camden County. Robert, a tenant farmer, owned a male slave and a horse and had been employed as an overseer on a St. Johns River plantation. Thomas, a carpenter on First Lord of the Admiralty, Lord Hawke's, plantation seventy miles from the mouth of the St. Johns, was unmarried. He, too, owned a horse and one slave. He also owned a boat, likely the brothers' means of transportation to St. Marys.

About the same time as their arrival to Georgia, a Bahamian planter (Colonel Roger Kelsall) sent his former business partner, James Spalding, then living on St. Simons Island, a sack of Anguilla cottonseed (*Gossypium barbadense*), named for the Caribbean island where it flourished. It took two growing seasons for Spalding to produce a

Remains of trolley path leading to the north end pier where hotel guests arrived by boat.

crop of this long-staple variety, but the result was superior, silky, long-staple cotton that commanded high prices. Other planters received similar seed shipments from expatriates living in the Bahamas, and a cotton belt soon developed along the coast among the sea islands from South Carolina to Cumberland Island. Sea island cotton thrived in the salt air environment up to thirty miles inland. These two events—the arrival of the Stafford brothers and sea island cotton—set in motion a new era of expansion on Cumberland Island.

Thomas and Robert Stafford initially found employment from 1788 to 1813 under Phineas and Caty Miller on Cumberland, overseeing workers harvesting timber on the island. Thomas may have even been involved with the construction of Dungeness mansion. In 1789 he attended the state convention in Augusta as an elected delegate from St. Marys to ratify the U.S. Constitution; Georgia was the fourth state to do so. A map of Cumberland drawn up about that same time indicates the location of a settlement named Staffords near Dungeness where one or both of the brothers lived. Together the brothers owned the *Camden Packet*, a sloop that transported cotton from Spanish East Florida to Savannah and rice from Charleston back to Florida.

Thomas Stafford married Lucy Thomas, who gave birth on December 8, 1790, at their home near Dungeness; that son, Robert Thomas Stafford, would one day own most of the island. Lucy bore six other children: Elizabeth, Susannah, Clarissa, Mary, Thomas, and Harriet. Young Robert grew up in a culture deeply immersed in the use of slave labor. When he turned two years old, his uncle Robert gave him a slave companion named Peter (or Petter), about the same age. Thomas Stafford died in 1800 when Robert was ten, bequeathing to his family eight slaves worth $2,670, twenty cows, a number of hogs, and five hundred acres on the mainland near White Oak. In addition, his estate was owed $1,200 for loans he had made. On August 8, 1800, Lucy Stafford purchased 125 acres belonging to the estate of General Greene, the first recorded purchase of land by a Stafford on Cumberland. Between 1800 and 1802, she married a friend of her husband's, Virginia native Isham Spalding. Sometime after Robert's twelfth birthday, Phineas Miller sent him to a school in New London, Connecticut, where he received a "right smart" Yankee education. By his eighteenth birthday he was finished with schooling and was permanently settled in Camden County.

During the British occupation of Cumberland Island in 1815, Robert, then aged twenty-five, was placed under house arrest at the Springs Plantation, where he and other detainees observed Admiral Cockburn's men drilling their former slaves and transforming

Robert Stafford wearing spectacles, 1790–1877. (Photograph courtesy of Bill King and the Cumberland Island National Seashore Museum NPS)

them "into regular soldiers, of good discipline and appearance," as Zephaniah Kingsley, who owned a plantation on Fort George Island, wrote. The Staffords-Spaldings did not sue the British government for the loss of slaves, suggesting they either rented them from the Greene estate or had kept them on the mainland, away from the British liberators.

A month after the occupiers left Cumberland, Robert purchased five slaves from his father-in-law for one dollar. The following year (1816) he bought seven slaves for $2,000. Shortly after his uncle Robert's death in 1818, Robert assumed the management of his family's financial affairs. A year later, the Stafford-Spalding family purchased the Littlefield tract (tract 5) for $3,000 from Cornelia Greene Littlefield. Robert, Susannah, Mary, and Lucy and Isham divided the six-hundred-acre tract in equal quarters. From that point on, Littlefield became known as Stafford Plantation. Robert continued to purchase property until the Civil War, accumulating almost a third of Great Cumberland from Dungeness to Table Point, including Rayfield, which he bought from Greene's descendants. He managed Stafford and Rayfield separately, creating a rivalry between the properties to see which one could obtain the highest yield and profit.

A good portion of Stafford's wealth came from loans he made to farmers and planters who put up land and enslaved men and women as security. He foreclosed when they could not repay the loans. The 1820 federal census shows that at the age of thirty he owned 50 enslaved people: 10 males under the age of fourteen, 10 males between the ages of fourteen and twenty-five, 10 males between twenty-six and forty-four, 10 males over forty-five, and 10 females under fourteen. Ten years later (1830), that number had more than doubled to 112, 33 of whom were males and 79 females. Approximately half of the females were of childbearing age. By 1850 he owned 125 enslaved males and 223 females, but by 1860 owned fewer people (110). He sold a large number of his enslaved in 1857, possibly in anticipation of spending more time in New England. His estate value in 1860 totaled $99,534 (over $2 million in today's dollars), a considerable accumulation of wealth at that time in an era of few millionaires. It appears he sold most of the enslaved before the Civil War or, like Phineas Nightingale, leased them out to construct canals and railroads on the mainland when cotton prices slumped.

James R. Silva, a contemporary St. Marys resident, described slave quarters on Cumberland as "small cabins, each with sufficient ground for a garden, hen house, and a pig pen. Married couples and their children were quartered together and the unmarried males and females were located separately in different sections. Rations of corn or grits, meal, bacon, salt and articles of food grown on the plantation were issued weekly. They

A riding stirrup recovered at Rayfield Plantation. (Courtesy of Southeast Archeological Center NPS)

Remains of cabins where Stafford Plantation enslaved families lived. (Courtesy of the Cumberland Island National Seashore Museum NPS, Mary Bullard Collection)

A brass thimble excavated at the Rayfield Plantation slave cabins in 2006. (Courtesy of Southeast Archeological Center NPS)

Wound beads excavated at Rayfield Plantation slave cabins in 2006. A small number of drawn beads were also excavated. (Courtesy of Southeast Archeological Center NPS)

Lead buckle, possibly for a belt or harness. Excavated at Rayfield Plantation slave cabins in 2006. Robert Stafford leased Rayfield from Nathanael Ray Greene by 1829 and purchased the 600-acre tract in April 1934. The slave village consisted of eighteen cabins in two rows. (Courtesy of Southeast Archeological Center NPS)

A gunflint (gun spall). Its dark gray–black color suggests it is from an English flint source (French flints tend to be honey colored). Recovered at Brickhill Bluff in 2007. (Courtesy of Southeast Archeological Center NPS)

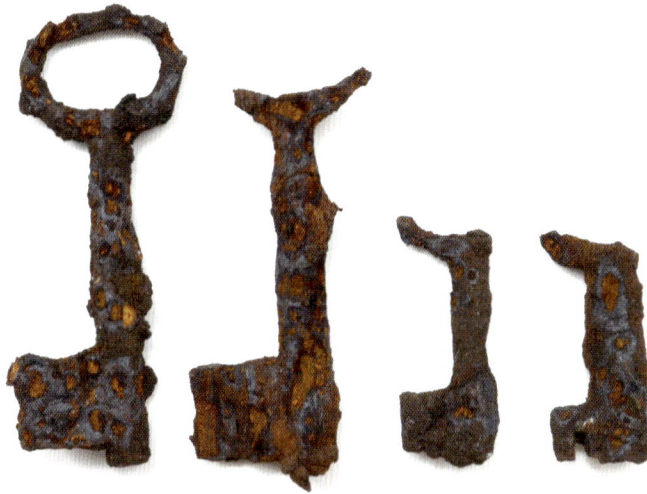

Short lead keys used by the enslaved to lock interior doors and cabinets. (Courtesy of Southeast Archeological Center NPS)

A lead key possibly used to lock slave cabin door. (Courtesy of Southeast Archeological Center NPS)

planted little patches of sugar cane, pumpkins, melons, or whatever they cared for and raised chickens and hogs." Although he wasn't writing specifically about the Stafford-Spalding holdings, it's reasonable to infer that these were the general conditions on the island.

Descriptions by Frederick Law Olmsted of a slave settlement (comparable to Stafford's) on the mainland might shed more light on the Stafford slave quarters: "Each cabin was a frame building, the walls boarded and whitewashed on the outside, lathed and plastered within, the roof shingled; forty-two feet long, twenty-one feet wide, divided into two family tenements; each tenement divided into three rooms—one, the common household apartment, twenty-one by ten; each of the others, (bedrooms), ten by ten. There was a brick fireplace in the middle. Besides these rooms, each tenement had a cock-loft, occupied on an average by five persons. There were in them closets, with locks and keys, and a varying quantity of rude furniture. Each cabin had a front and back door, and each room a window, closed by a wooden shutter, swinging outward, on hinges. Between each tenement and the next house, is a small piece of ground, enclosed with palings, in which are coops of fowl, with chickens, hovels for nests and for sows with pig. The negroes' swine are allowed to run in the woods, each owner having his own distinguished by a peculiar mark. In the rear of the yards were gardens—a half acre to each family."

The Quarters, by Martin Pate, Newnan, Georgia. (Courtesy of
Southeastern Archeological Center NPS)

Detail of slave cabins from *The Quarters*, by Martin Pate, Newnan, Georgia. (Courtesy of Southeastern Archeological Center NPS)

Detail of Stafford house from *The Quarters*, by Martin Pate, Newnan, Georgia. (Courtesy of Southeastern Archeological Center NPS)

Stafford built a three-story home, which he named Planters House (ca. 1823), south of Plum Orchard, the Bernardey property. The house was erected on an elevated foundation that provided a measure of flood protection as well as exposure to cool summer breezes. His rise in prominence on the island coincided with the steady decline of Phineas Nightingale's inherited Cumberland holdings. By 1841, Nightingale was not raising crops at Dungeness, though he left eight slaves to keep the house and cultivate the garden. He was no longer a full-time resident of Dungeness by 1850 and moved to Baker County in southwestern Georgia. In 1855 Nightingale purchased Cambers Island (near Darien), a rice crop island, using Dungeness as collateral before losing the estate to creditors.

Workers picking cotton, 1898.
(Courtesy of the Library of Congress)

In 1839, at the age of forty-nine, Robert fathered a daughter named Mary. At the time of Mary's birth, Stafford's mother and sisters were deceased. The woman who bore their daughter was a twenty-year-old mulatto named Elizabeth (or Elisabeth) Bernardey, also known as Zabette (perhaps a French form of Elizabeth, a term of endearment). Elizabeth's mother, a mulatto from Martinique named Marie-Jeanne, had been a servant of Pierre Bernardey, a French plantation owner, and perhaps Elizabeth's father. In 1841, Elizabeth's owner, Marguerite Bernardey, sent the mother and child to live with Stafford with the understanding that Elizabeth, Mary, and any other children Elizabeth conceived would remain her property. Bernardey, a neighbor at Plum Orchard (the name is derived from an orchard that once flourished there), had relocated to Cumberland from Jekyll, where her husband, then deceased, once worked for Christopher DuBignon. Even though Bernardey had unsuccessfully tried to pass Elizabeth off as white, and it is not clear that Elizabeth was born into slavery, she was considered Bernardey's chattel.

Tabby ruins of the Bernardey Plantation home.(Courtesy of the Cumberland Island National Seashore Museum NPS)

Picking cotton, 1917. (Courtesy of the Library of Congress)

This former cotton field now serves as an airstrip and a grazing ground for feral horses. The Carnegie family turned this field into a nine-hole golf course.

As a skilled nurse, and one who could read, Elizabeth played an important role in the daily affairs of plantation life, caring for the slave population and the master's family alike. It is probable that Stafford met her in that capacity when she came to his home to care for his mother and sister prior to their deaths. Over the next fifteen years, she bore Stafford five more children: Robert (1842), Armand (1843), Ellen (1849), Adelaide "Addie" Clarice (1851), and Medora (1853). Unlike plantation owners who approved of forced sex with slaves to increase their population, Stafford considered his children by Elizabeth as his wards. For a precedent, Stafford could look no farther than a few islands south of Cumberland, where the planter Zephaniah Kingsley married an African princess and left his estate to their offspring. Similarly, when Stafford later sent his children to New England for schooling, he followed in the steps of another slave owner: in 1836, Patrick Gibson of Darien, Georgia, sent three daughters born to him by a female slave (who lived with him as "man and wife") to New Bedford, Massachusetts, where they received an education.

Stafford began purchasing buildings and land in and around Groton and New London, Connecticut, beginning in 1843 as part of a plan to remove Elizabeth and her children from Georgia in the event of Margaret Bernardey's death. He was familiar with Bernardey's financial situation and believed her heirs would be tempted to pay down her debts by selling off slaves, including his children. One of Stafford's early northern property purchases was a brick store he acquired for $10,000 in New London, followed by a second property there for $15,500 in 1850. Three years later he purchased the City Hotel in New London for just over $7,000, leasing it to a third party for ten years at an annual rent of $1,000. He arranged for guardians to care for his children and established a trust using income from the properties he purchased to support them.

One New Englander described Stafford as a "tall, commanding figure, erect, spare, gentlemanly, haughty, evidently used to deference—a man of great firmness and decision, dressed in the most elegant broadcloth and linen, gold-bowed spectacles and heavy gold chain. He moved in a lordly way, was accustomed to lavish expenditures, was exquisitely neat and orderly, and was liberal with all who served him in any way. Nearly everyone who served him in any capacity while here [Connecticut] got double pay, and so the arrival of Mr. Stafford was looked forward to by the hotel and liverymen."

Stafford sent his eldest child, Mary, to Bacon Academy in Colchester, Connecticut, in 1846. The academy (now a public high school) opened its doors in 1800 and counted among its alumni Stephen F. Austin, the "Father of Texas." Four years later, her brothers Robert and Armand were residing in Groton and attending school there. That same year,

State Street, New London, Connecticut, ca. 1875. Robert Stafford purchased downtown property here. He established a trust, using income from leased property to support his children. (Courtesy of the Cumberland Island National Seashore Museum NPS)

1850, Stafford purchased the Buswell Building in Norwich, Connecticut, for $20,000 and used the profits from renting office and store space to support his children. (All four Stafford daughters became co-owners of that building upon reaching adulthood.) In 1851 Stafford acquired a seventy-seven-acre farm on the Thames River, followed by the purchase of a thirty-three-acre Groton farm in 1853, where he constructed a home for his family, including Elizabeth, who had moved to Connecticut in 1852 with daughters Ellen and Ada; the youngest, Medora, was born in Groton. The Connecticut Stafford home was a well-built, two-story structure that remained standing until 1979.

Stafford spent most of his time managing his Cumberland Island plantations but made annual journeys to Connecticut during the hot summer months of July and August, residing at his City Hotel property instead of the home he built. By moving his children to Connecticut for their education, he was able to protect them from the vicissitudes of slave life until the end of the Civil War removed that danger.

The Wanderer

An incident connected to Cumberland Island occurred in 1858 that still resonates today. On November 28 the slave ship *Wanderer*, carrying illegal cargo—more than four hundred slaves from Angola—steered toward the lighthouse beacon on Little Cumberland Island and anchored in the St. Andrews Sound. Conditions on the *Wanderer* had deteriorated during its forty-two days at sea. Provisions were almost gone, and cockroaches infested the ship. Eighty Africans had perished (another source puts the death toll at two hundred) on the Atlantic crossing. That November evening, the owner and captain, William C. Corrie, and co-owner of the vessel, John Egbert Farnum, feared a storm might be brewing in the Atlantic and rowed ashore to find the harbor pilot. The assistant lighthouse keeper, Horatio Harris, informed them the pilot, James Clubb, was on Jekyll Island. Farnum returned to the ship while Corrie and Harris rowed across the sound to Jekyll. They found Clubb, described as "in his sixties, a burly man with deep-set blue eyes and lock of white hair that fell over his forehead," on Jekyll's north end tending the light there.

"A damned slaver!" Clubb replied when Corrie told him the name of the vessel. "Don't pull the wool over my eyes." He initially refused to guide the ship in, but Corrie prevailed, citing the conditions onboard: further delay could cost more lives. Clubb finally relented but charged $500 for the service, ten times the normal rate for piloting a ship across the bar. In the predawn light the following morning, Clubb rowed out to the ship and could see for the first time the slaves, mostly young males, many of them emaciated. He watched as the crew threw a dead African overboard.

The man spearheading the scheme to smuggle slaves into Georgia was Charles Augustus Lafayette Lamar, a Savannah businessman and a silent partner of the expedition. At the age of fourteen, he, along with his father, had survived the sinking of the *Pulaski* (1838), the same vessel Phineas Nightingale's wife (Mary) and daughter (Louisa) were on. Lamar's mother (Jane Cresswell Lamar), three sisters, and two brothers, and a niece died in the aftermath of the *Pulaski*'s explosion.

Lamar had arranged with John DuBignon of Jekyll Island to bring the slaves ashore there. Word got out about the ship's arrival, and Lamar, Corrie, and Farnum were apprehended and brought to trial. The federal prosecutor was Hamilton Couper, son of James Hamilton Couper (the man who rescued Mary Nightingale from the *Pulaski*). However, key witnesses either refused to testify or claimed poor memory of events, and Lamar walked away a free man. Separate trials were held for Corrie and Farnum. Though James Clubb identified them as the men aboard the *Wanderer*, neither were convicted. Clubb was not prosecuted for abetting a crime, but a prosecutor asked him if he understood that transporting African slaves violated federal and state statutes. He replied, "No. . . . Two or three days later, I heard that bringing in the *Wanderer* was a violation of the law."

The *Wanderer* was one of the last ships to transport African slaves to the United States (the *Clotilda* brought 110 slaves into Mobile in 1860). Lamar considered the *Wanderer* a success for fomenting disunion in the state of Georgia and emboldening other southern fire-eaters to pursue secession from the United States. News of the illegal importation made national headlines and stoked antebellum sectional tensions. During the Civil War, Farnum served on the Union side and was nominated brevet brigadier general by President Andrew Johnson for meritorious service. Seven days after Lee surrendered at Appomattox, Lamar died leading a charge against Union soldiers in the Battle of Columbus. He is thought to be the last Confederate officer killed in the war.

The Civil War

Phineas Nightingale's elder son, John Alsop King Nightingale, joined the Confederate war effort and served under cavalry general Fitzhugh Lee, nephew of Robert E. Lee, for the duration. His other son, William, was ten at the time and too young for military service. In November 1861, Robert E. Lee took command of the Confederate Department of South Carolina, Georgia, and Florida. He immediately set about establishing defenses along the Florida, Georgia, and South Carolina coasts in anticipation of a Union naval blockade and invasion. Lee made his headquarters at Coosawhatchie, South Carolina (named for the Coosaw Natives who inhabited the area and their word for river, "hatchie"), now a small community along I-95. At the time, it was far enough inland to defend against bombardment by Union gunboats. Lee was already familiar with parts of the Southern Atlantic coast. As an engineer fresh out of West Point, he had already served two tours of duty in Savannah in the winters of 1829–30 and 1830–31, where he oversaw the drainage and earthen buildup of Cockspur Island so it could support the large fortification, Fort Pulaski, later built on the site.

Lee visited Cumberland Island twice in his life: once during his time bolstering coastal defenses during the Civil War, and again in 1870 shortly before his death. The reason for

Island Lighthouses

Congress appropriated money to erect a lighthouse on the south end of Cumberland Island in 1802. The State of Georgia ceded 6 acres of land for this purpose, but a dispute over ownership of the land delayed construction until 1820. Winslow Lewis of Boston contracted with the government to erect the lighthouse, a keeper's dwelling, and to provide a lantern. The lighthouse was to be a round structure with a lime mortar foundation on a 25-foot-diameter base rising 65 feet to a 12-foot-diameter platform that would hold the lantern. The lantern was a revolving light that rotated once every four minutes. The tower and lantern topped out at 74 feet above sea level. It became operational on July 4, 1820, at a cost of $17,000. The keeper's house was a 20-by-34-foot brick home with two rooms divided by a chimney. Part of the contract required Lewis to construct a nearby well.

The first two keepers, Robert Church and Amos Latham, served a combined total of eighteen years before it became apparent that a lighthouse on the north end of Amelia would be better suited to guide ships to the entrance of Cumberland Sound. In 1838 the lighthouse was dismantled and reassembled on Amelia. The keeper's dwelling remained on Cumberland. At the same time, Congress funded $8,000 to construct a new lighthouse on Little Cumberland Island to mark the entrance to the St. Andrews Sound. Gen. John Floyd (a distinguished officer in the War of 1812), who had purchased Little Cumberland for $1,000 from Nathanael Greene's heirs with his brother, Charles, sold 6 acres to the government for $500. Another Bostonian, Joseph Hastings, contracted to erect a round 50-foot tower supporting an iron, 11-foot-tall octagonal lantern, and a 20-by-30-foot keeper's dwelling. The lantern would be a stationary light "containing fourteen lamps, a type that distinguished it from the revolving light at the south end of Great Cumberland Island." The contract was obviously written before the south-end lighthouse had been relocated to Amelia Island.

The new lighthouse, called the St. Andrews Lighthouse, became operational on June 26, 1838, under its first keeper, David Thompson, who earned $400 a year. William F. Kelley replaced Thompson in 1849. The St. Simons, Little Cumberland, and Amelia Island lighthouses were fitted with new Fresnel lenses in 1857, which allowed the light to be seen from greater distances. James A. Clubb, who served as the Little Cumberland lighthouse keeper during the Civil War, removed the lens to Brunswick for safekeeping by the Confederates. Damage to the lighthouse by "the rebels" required a new lantern room and lens. The lighthouse became operational again on September 2, 1867, and remained in use until 1915, when the U.S. Lighthouse Service (now part of the Coast Guard) deactivated it. Though it no longer serves as a guiding light to captains plying coastal waters by night, the lighthouse was placed on the National Historic Register in 1989, a reminder of its role in the island's historic past.

St. Andrews Lighthouse, Little Cumberland.

Robert E. Lee, 1838. Portrait of Lee as a U.S. Army Lieutenant of Engineers, by William Edward West (1788–1857). West painted the "Light-Horse Harry" Lee portrait in chapter 6. (Wikimedia Commons)

his visit on both occasions was to see the grave of his father, Gen. "Light-Horse Harry" Lee. Curiously, he did not attempt to visit Cumberland while stationed in Savannah in 1829. His father, a war hero of the American Revolution, abandoned the family when Robert was six years old, returning only to die at Dungeness. Robert E. Lee visited the island for the first time in January 1862 while inspecting coastal fortifications. He wrote to his wife of this experience.

"While at Fernandina I went over to Cumberland Island & walked up to Dungeness, the former residence of Genl Green. It was my first visit to the house & I had the gratification at length of visiting my father's grave. He died there you may recollect on his way from the West Indies & was interred in one corner of the family cemetery. The spot is marked by a plain marble slab, with his name, age, & date of his death. Mrs. Green is also buried there, & her daughter Mrs. Shaw and her husband. The place is at present owned by Mr. Nightingale, nephew of Mrs. Shaw, who married a daughter of Mr. James King." In fact, James King was Mary Nightingale's uncle; her father was John Alsop King. Lee might not have been aware that it was Phineas Nightingale who, as a lad, had greeted "Light-Horse Harry" Lee at the Dungeness dock. "The family have moved into the interior of Georgia, leaving only a few servants & a white gardener on the place. The garden is beautiful, enclosed by the finest hedge I have ever seen. It was of the wild olive. The orange trees were small, & the orange grove, which in Mrs. Shaw's lifetime, my tour of duty in Savannah in early life, was so productive, had been destroyed by an insect that had proved fatal to the orange on the coast of Georgia & Florida" (Thomson and Santos). Lee references his early days stationed in Savannah, when Louisa Shaw was still routinely shipping oranges by the thousands to that port city.

"There was a fine grove of olives," the letter continues, "from which, I learned, Mr. N procures oil. The garden was filled with roses & beautiful vines, the names of which I do not know. Among them was the tomato vine in full bearing with the ripe fruit on it. There has as yet been no frost in that region of country this winter. I went into the dining room & parlour, in which the furniture still remained. In the latter room hung the portraits of Mr. John & James King, father & uncle of Mrs. N, rabid abolitionists, with a bad likeness of Genl Green, & a handsome print of Florence Nightingale & some landscapes. There also hung over the mantle a representation of Genl Green & Mrs. Slute, presenting him the purse. The house has never been finished, but it is a fine, large one & beautifully located. A magnificent grove of live oaks envelops the road from the landing to the house" (Thomson and Santos).

March 1864 photograph of Robert E. Lee by Julian Vannerson. (Courtesy of the Library of Congress)

Maj. Armistead L. Long accompanied Lee to Cumberland Island that day in January 1862. His memoir adds a few more details to Lee's graveside visit. "We came to a dilapidated wall enclosing a neglected cemetery," Long recalls. "The general then, in a voice of emotion, informed me that he was visiting the grave of his father. He went alone to the tomb, and after a few moments of silence plucked a flower and slowly retraced his steps, leaving the lonely grave to the guardianship of the crumbling stones and the spirit of the restless waves that perpetually beat against the neighboring shore."

Years earlier in a letter to his brother, Charles Carter Lee, from Savannah dated January 4, 1831, Robert E. Lee mentioned Louisa Shaw, suggesting that he met her or perhaps even knew her. "Mrs. Shaw and the Miss Turners [Martha Greene Turner and likely her stepdaughters] were in Savannah a few days ago," he informed Charles. "They took their passage a N. Port [perhaps Newport, Rhode Island] in a schooner bound to N. Orleans, expecting to be landed at Cumberland Island, Geo and after 34 days put into Sav. in distress. Their suits were all in rags, and they had been allowanced [rationed] in their water for two weeks. Three times they were in sight of Cumberland & each time they were blown off. The old lady has a great deal to talk about now."

At the outbreak of the Civil War, however, Camden County was offering up its men to the cause. At age twenty-four, Nathan (Nate) Atkinson Brown (born 1836) of White Oak, Georgia, formed the Camden Rifles, rising quickly from first lieutenant to the rank of captain. The Camden Rifles were attached to the Fourth Georgia Cavalry under Colonel William Henry Stiles, part of Brig. Gen. Hugh W. Mercer's brigade. (Mercer's great-grandson was the celebrated lyricist and composer Johnny Mercer of "Moon River" fame.) In 1861 Brown served at both Fort Atkinson on Little Cumberland Island and Camp Bartow on Cumberland's south end. Nate bore a sword his family members had taken to war against the British in 1775 and again in 1812.

His cousin, twenty-six-year-old Col. Edmund Nathan Atkinson, commanded the fort on Little Cumberland. Colonel Atkinson graduated from the Georgia Military Institute in 1856 at the age of twenty-one, making him "one of the few people in this part of the state who knew how to drill raw troops or move a military unit from one point to another." That, and a distinguished family pedigree—his grandfather, Moses Waddell, was president of the University of Georgia from 1819 to 1829—contributed to the advanced military appointment despite his youth.

Nate Brown served a second tour at Fort Atkinson in October 1862. His role, and that of his comrades, was to prevent Union troops from landing there. Memories handed

Nathan Atkinson Brown. (Courtesy of Brown family descendants)

The Brown sword. (Courtesy of Brown family descendants)

The Brown sword hilt. (Courtesy of Brown family descendants)

down of Admiral Cockburn's raids on coastal plantations in 1815 had not been forgotten by Confederate authorities who feared Federal invaders would destroy property, incite slaves to rebel, and enlist them into their ranks just as the British had done. St. Marys's mayor in 1861 wrote to Jefferson Davis at the Confederate capital (then Montgomery, Alabama), reminding him of Cockburn's occupation during the War of 1812 when they made St. Marys and Cumberland "a place of attack and a basis of operations." The mayor requested that the governor place garrisons at Fort Clinch on Amelia and on the north end of Cumberland. He cited the number of voters in the county at about 250 while the slave population stood at four thousand, giving alarm to fears of an uprising "should the enemy land and arouse them to hostilities."

Nathan and his wife, the former Louisa Tupper Nicholes, exchanged letters that provide insight into the life of a planter-turned-soldier stationed on Cumberland Island

Colonel Edmund Nathan Atkinson, a Georgia Military Institute graduate and commanding officer on Cumberland Island during the Civil War. (Courtesy of Richard Atkinson)

during the Civil War and into Confederate plans to defend the coast. The two were newlyweds, having married on March 12, 1861, a month before Confederate forces fired on Fort Sumter. Their anguish over being separated so early in their marriage is evident in the letters. The writing at times sounds excessively sentimental to the modern ear and overwrought with metaphors, but the sincerity of their devotion to one another remains genuine. Brown was twenty-five and Louise twenty-one when they began their war correspondence. Following are excerpts from a few of these letters. The first, from Louisa, is simply dated "Sunday night."

My own, my *dearest*,

You cannot imagine how my heart *yearns* to see you *now* in this quiet hour, when a holy hush has fallen on all nature and twilight wraps its soft, purple veil around her. I am seated in my own little room all alone, musing on the changes time bears on its swift chariot. The gorgeous dreamings of my girlhood have faded like the Winter clouds above me, to the somber hue of reality. In my sky, even the star of hope is shrouded. For I have recently heard of War beginning in our noble little state, and know not at what time, honor will prompt the *dearest* objects of my heart (my *precious* Lover) to fly to her rescue. I will try not to count sorrow by indulging forebodings. But somehow this evening I feel like a lonely mariner, tempest tossed on some pathless ocean, without chart or compass. I could write much more but Morpheus is waiting for his nights embrace, but not until I entreat *my darling* to visit me as *soon* and as *often* as he can, for while you are away a cloud seems to rest on the landscape. Your own true, Loulie

Fort Atkinson, Cumberland Island, Sept. 8th [1861]

My *own precious* Wife,

Your letter was brought to me on yesterday from Brunswick by Col. Styles (Stiles); who paid us a flying visit of only half an hour to see if we were prepared to meet the enemy. He is exceedingly indignant with Gen. [Alexander] Lawton for his gross neglect of duty in not sending us our cannon and says if Lawton does not have them here in three days, he will take us from this place and put us on Big Cumberland Island. We are expecting an attack daily and every man is on the alert to see who will see the "*Fleet*" first; Col. Styles says he thinks we will have a fight in less than ten days unless some providential interference prevents them from landing. We are very much opposed to leaving this place; for we can from this point cooperate with both St. Simons and Big Cumberland Batteries in a fight; and then at the same time defend our own homes. Col. S. thinks we hold the most important post on the coast. "You see" if we are removed from this point the enemy can land at Brunswick or St. Marys without going in gunshot of the batteries on the Islands.

Louisa Tupper Nicholes Brown, Nathan Brown's wife.
(Courtesy of Brown family descendants)

Gov. Brown will pay us a visit on Monday or Tuesday when we will have a shower of all the big officers on the coast. They are going around inspecting our batteries and reviewing the companies. You must tell her [Eula] to be a good little girl and not bother *Mamma* while *Papa* is off from home. . . . I have just returned from prayer meeting. Mr. Patterson gave us a splendid prayer and oh darling! I did with *all* my heart ask the Kind Ruler (that looks over the destinies of all) to keep watch over, be with, and guard my darling wife from all danger. I don't know when we will meet again as Col. S. won't consent to let you come on the Island and has issued orders not to let *any* one go home till he finds out where "Lincoln's fleet" is bound for. So my pet "you see" it was very well that your Father stopped you. It is almost time for me to go the grand rounds and inspect the sentinels so I will have to close. I am quite well, in fact camp life agrees with me so well that I am *actually getting fat*. You may tell them [the family] if I should get into a fight with the enemy they will hear a good report from their boy. Goodbye my sweet-loved one; may Heaven's sweetest blessings ever attend you is the fond prayer of your own darling boy. Nate

Fort Atkinson, Sept 12th 1861

My *dearest little Wife*

You must not think strange or hard of me for not writing more often to you, for my chances of sending letters are "like angels' visits, few and far between." I am in much better spirits than I was in when I wrote you my last about our company. We now muster *sixty-nine* men, and hope to have over an hundred in a few days. Recruits are coming in daily, and I have just heard that "Dufores" company is about to disband and that 35 or 40 of his men are coming to join us. I hope that will not be the case. However badly I might want men I should hate to get them from an unfortunate company that could not fill its ranks.

You appear to be somewhat alarmed about us being taken "prisoners." Now *little darling* don't fear about that; we have fifty of as *trusty* rifles as ever were fired; and the strongest natural fortification in the Confederate States to shield us from the enemy. So you see we neither intend to abandon our post; nor do we expect to be taken prisoners; for just as sure as the sun rises and sets, if the Yankees land at this point they will get themselves into a fight. We made 900 cartridges yesterday and expect to make five or 600 more as fast as we can, we now have 2000 made and ready for use.

Camp Atkinson, Oct. 3d 1861

My precious darling pet.

I expect you think that I will never write you again, but you *see* it has been blowing a storm ever since my return to the Island. I hope it has blown all of Lincoln's ships ashore. If it has, I would be satisfied to lose my crop. The sea is now very rough, so much so, that no steamboat can pass between here and Brunswick. One of our men "Jones" shot one of Capt. Dasher's men while I was home. He did it accidentally, but the wound is not dangerous as he was shot through the thigh. Col. Styles has ordered Jones to be sent to Brunswick to be court martialed for the offense. Col. Styles has ordered that Capt. Stockwell shall vacate the premises of the Light House because he sold whiskey to the men. I am very glad that he did it. I hope now that the infernal practice of getting drunk will now be stopped.

Your own dear Nate.

Now dearest wife for a private talk with you and Miss Eula. You know when I left you in such a good humor at the end of the avenue? Well I had to drop a tear for you before I got out of sight. None save you in this world shall ever know how hard it is for me to leave my precious wife. I am willing that the public should think us cold and indifferent to each other, but dearest, we know how warmly our hearts beat in unison with the other's. You must take good care of yourself and *don't get my little baby hurt*. If it were not for you and *her* I would not care a straw if I were dead.

[Letter from Louisa]

White Oak. Oct. 19, 1861

Darling love sweet boy,

The last letter I wrote was to inform you that K had carried a box of eatables (and a long letter was in that, to you), a bundle of blankets, and ten pairs of socks for the Camden Rifles, for you to divide among them, keeping of course the best for your dear self, and one bag of peas, but as the [railroad] cars left a little while before I got to the depot, I wrote to Capt. H. T. Hall and asked him please to forward the afore said things to Lieut. N. A. Brown of the Camden Rifles as soon as possible, but I heard since then that the things did not go down the next night in consequence of the cars being so very full of soldiers, so precious love I am afraid the things will spoil before you get them.

Your own, Loulie

Brunswick, Oct. 28th

    My dearest Wife,

    I arrived here safely at 12 o'clock last night. The cars had no one on board except myself. Oh! How I did wish you had been with [me]. The ride was so long and lonely. I leave here in a few minutes on board the Steamer Chatham. She will take our Company to the south end of Cumberland Island. You must be sure to come down to St. Marys on Sat.—I will meet you there. Well darling please excuse this short letter as I have not time to write another word. Give love to all, and believe me ever your affectionate boy.

    Nate. A Brown

Camp Bartow, Nov. 1st, 1861 [south end of Cumberland]

    My dear little wife,

    We arrived here on Tuesday evening last, and since that time have been continually engaged in making out pay rolls for the company, pitching tents and clearing our camp ground. It has been raining all day long accompanied with high winds, which of course makes it very disagreeable, but you know darling it is the duty of a poor soldier to bear with patience every trial and not murmur at hardships. When you see Mrs. Mumford please give her my kindest regards, and tell her I do not think I have coughed more than a half a dozen times since she gave me that dose of Turlington's Balsom. We have just received a telegraphic dispatch from Richmond to Fernandina that sixty steamer and warships had left New York and Philadelphia on the 26th of last month for southern parts, and to be on the lookout for them. I guess if they come we will give them a warm salute before retreating.

    Nate

The "sixty steamer and warships" Captain Brown mentioned were part of Samuel Francis Du Pont's South Atlantic Blockading Squadron. Admiral Du Pont, aboard the frigate *Wabash*, was maneuvering his fifty-ship fleet, among which were transports carrying ground forces under Gen. Thomas W. Sherman (no relation to William Tecumseh Sherman), down the coast. Nate wrote to Louisa from Camp Styles on St. Simons Island on November 10, 1861, informing her that "the reverses our forces have received at Port Royal [South Carolina] have thrown a gloom over the whole encampment." He refers here to the November 7 capture of Port Royal fortifications, Forts Walker and Beauregard, by Du Pont's forces.

Nate believed his unit would soon be sent to assist Confederate forces at Port Royal and wrote his wife on November 14, 1861: "I think it is General Lawton's intent to evacuate the Island and move us to some point on the main, but I hope it is not the case. If we are going to run every time we hear of a superior force coming against us it will stimulate

Admiral Du Pont

Samuel Francis (Frank) Du Pont was born at Bergen Point (Bayonne), New Jersey, on September 27, 1803, to Victor Marie du Pont (in adulthood Francis spelled his surname with a capital D) and Gabrielle Josephine de la Fite de Pelleport. Due to his father's financial straits, he pursued a military career. After study at Mount Airy College (the U.S. Naval Academy, which Du Pont helped establish, did not open until 1845), he received his commission as a midshipman in the U.S. Navy in 1815. His naval apprenticeship began at age fourteen with Mediterranean Sea cruises aboard the USS *Franklin*, a seventy-nine-gun warship, and the USS *Constitution*, constructed with live oak from Georgia's barrier islands, followed by duty in the Caribbean aboard the USS *Congress* hunting pirates. He steadily rose in the ranks but did not shy away from criticizing incompetent naval and civil superiors. Du Pont participated in a naval blockade of the California coast during the Mexican-American War. He achieved the rank of captain in 1855 and two years later transported the U.S. minister to Beijing aboard the steam frigate USS *Minnesota*. His blockade of the southeast coast during the Civil War proved successful, but he was unduly blamed for a failed attack on Charleston using ironclads in April 1863. His career spanned the transition from wooden sailing vessels to iron steam ships. While serving on a navy board in Washington in March 1865, Du Pont developed a cold that turned into bronchial attacks. He died as the result of that illness in a Philadelphia hotel room on June 23, 1865, two months after Lee's surrender. Seventeen years after his death, on February 25, 1882, Congress renamed a traffic circle and park in Washington, D.C., in his honor. Now known as Dupont Circle, it is surrounded by a historic district.

our enemies and cast a shadow of fear over the brave hearts of our own people, and besides what would be said of me in after years: that I ran when I heard the enemy were coming merely because I heard their forces were a little greater than ours." He added that if "the Yankees should come down here you must not let them catch you, and tell Pa if they should come he had better get the Negroes out of the way." He also advised his family to gin the cotton crop quickly and ship it farther inland for storage.

Robert E. Lee telegrammed General Lawton on November 11 for a reassessment of Confederate coastal defenses, but he still maintained the "entrance to Cumberland [Island] and Brunswick must be secured" and that "every measure must be taken to prevent the enemy using the inland navigation and to oppose his approach from points where he might land." In a November 21 telegram to Gen. Samuel Cooper (who reported directly to Confederate president, Jefferson Davis), Lee wrote, "The entrance to Cumberland Sound and Brunswick and the water approaches to Savannah and Charleston are the only points which it is proposed to defend," but added that "the greatest difficulty to be contended with is the want of artillerists and proper officers as instructors."

Nate Brown wrote his wife on February 15, 1862: "judging from what I see and hear, our head men have come to the conclusion to abandon the logic of holding the Islands and will abandon all of them." He was right. Admiral Du Point had already demonstrated the superior firepower of Union vessels at Port Royal, and a few months later, on April 11, 1862, Du Pont's heavy thirty-pound Parrott Rifle field guns would breach the massive brick walls of Fort Pulaski on Cockspur Island from a distance of sixteen hundred to two thousand yards. Lee's confidence in his coastal defensive positions was tempered by the knowledge that the batteries were only as effective as the personnel manning them. He telegraphed Gen. James Heyward Trapier at Fernandina on January 2, 1862: "I have not yet been informed whether you have determined to remove the guns from the south end of Cumberland Island. The battery at that point, in conjunction with the fire of Fort Clinch would add greatly in my opinion to the defense of the harbor. Its fire would reach a ship after it had passed beyond the range of the guns of the fort." This echoed Oglethorpe's strategy of placing a gunboat in Cumberland Sound to assist fire from Fort William 120 years earlier.

Trapier evidently lacked confidence in the manpower and firepower on Amelia. Lee's message to him on February 24, 1862, read "I had hoped that guns could be obtained in time to defend these rear approaches, but as I now see no possibility of doing so, and as the men on the island are incompetent in your opinion for its defense, you are authorized to retire both from Cumberland and Amelia Islands to the mainland, taking such positions as will best defend the interests of the State, and using the guns and troops for that purpose." Lee ordered the evacuation of island coastal defenses, including St. Simons, to protect vital interior rail lines and towns. Thirteen hundred men stationed on the two Cumberland Island batteries and three more on Amelia, including the unfinished Fort Clinch, prepared to leave. The big guns on Cumberland were dismounted and relocated to the mainland. In their place, the Confederates erected log imitations made to resemble cannons from a distance.

With the rest of his fleet blockading Charleston and the nearby coast, Du Pont's flotilla sailed into St. Andrews Sound on March 1, 1862, with twenty men-of-war and eight transport ships carrying a marine battalion commanded by Maj. John G. Reynolds and an army brigade under Brig. Gen. Horatio Wright. The admiral's next objective, after Port Royal, was Fernandina, an important Confederate supply link on the eastern terminus of the Florida Railroad, which extended to Cedar Keys on the Gulf of Mexico. Confederate blockade-runners used Fernandina's deepwater harbor as a port, but Du

Samuel Francis du Pont (1867–68). National Portrait Gallery, Washington. Posthumous oil on canvas portrait by Daniel Huntington (1816–1906). (Wikipedia, public domain, https://en.wikipedia.org /wiki/Samuel_Francis_Du_Pont)

Pont intended to base Federal ships on blockade duty there. Possessing Port Royal and Fernandina was key to the Union's overall plan to seize Savannah and Charleston, thereby controlling the Florida, Georgia, and South Carolina coasts.

The admiral met no resistance from shore batteries on Little Cumberland and received word through two local escaped slaves, Isaac and Louis Napoleon, that all the Confederate batteries in the area had been abandoned. Louis had escaped from a fort on Amelia only the night before, and rowed out to sea beyond the sight of land hoping to meet a Union blockading vessel. Luckily for him, he was spotted and brought aboard Du Pont's flagship. James A. Clubb, the lighthouse keeper and "a Union man" on Little Cumberland, confirmed that Confederate troops had evacuated the area. Clubb boarded the *Wabash* and "impressed me very favorably by his spirit and loyalty," Du Pont wrote.

The admiral had originally planned to approach Fernandina by way of the inland passage based on coastal charts that showed the Cumberland River's average depth at sixteen to eighteen feet. Isaac, the "Negro contraband" who had an intimate knowledge of the local waters, doubted the river was that deep anywhere along its entire length. As with Georgia's other barrier islands, shoals form along Cumberland's inland river where seawater from the incoming and outgoing tides meet and divide each day—the dividings. Sand deposits there create ever-shifting sandbars and mud banks that can ground larger vessels. Isaac may have had this in mind when he voiced his concerns.

Du Pont apparently took Isaac's advice. He wrote to his wife, Sophie, of a fellow officer's opinion that slaves "had the knowledge of locality, of the forests, of the waters; for no white man in the South can handle a skiff, are stupid and awkward on the water, while Negroes are skillful and daring." Du Pont ordered gunboats and steamers drawing eleven feet or less down the river while he, aboard the *Mohican*, and the larger ships retraced their route out of St. Andrews Sound to the south end of Cumberland by way of the ocean. "The weather was threatening," he wrote, "and there had been eastings in the wind sufficient to knock up a sea and oh, the rolling of this ship! It is beyond description."

The following day, March 4, 1862, several Union vessels ran aground attempting to enter the inlet between Amelia and Cumberland (the same inlet where one of Cockburn's ships ran aground in 1815). However, the USS *Ottawa*, a two-masted, steam-powered schooner, entered Cumberland Sound that afternoon after negotiating the intricate river route from St. Andrews Sound, possibly eased over the dividings by a high tide. The *Ottawa* proceeded to Fernandina just in time to bombard a train leaving the island.

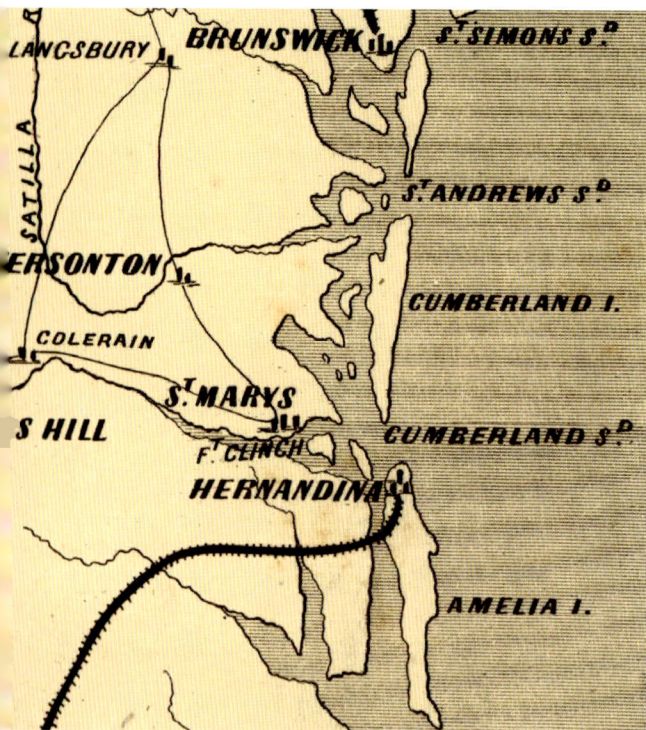

Civil War U.S. Army map of rail terminus at Fernandina. (Courtesy of the Library of Congress)

"They could have destroyed the cars," Du Pont wrote Sophie, "but not being certain whether they were troops in them, they fired ahead." It turned out the train carried only civilians, many of whom dashed out of the railcars for shelter when the shelling began. The last Confederate soldiers marched off the island ahead of the train and burned the railroad bridges to the mainland after the final railcar safely passed.

Du Pont described the Confederate forts to Sophie as "perfect wonders of scientific engineering skill. They faced every angle of the channel and, I believe, could have stood shelling a whole day without a shell dropping in. If they had stood to their guns and we had entered the main channel, they could have destroyed every vessel." In his official report he wrote that "it is impossible to look at these preparations for a vigorous defence without being surprised that they should have been voluntarily deserted." He described two batteries on the north and northeast shore of Amelia as perfectly camouflaged from view: "A battery of six guns, though larger and affording a better mark, is equally sheltered and masked. These batteries and the heavy guns mounted on Fort Clinch command all the turnings of the main ship channel, and rake an approaching enemy. Besides them was another battery of four guns on the south end of Cumberland Island, the fire of which would cross the channel inside of the bar. The difficulties arising from the indirectness of the channel and from the shoalness of the bar would have added to the defences by keeping the approaching vessels a long time exposed to fire under great disadvantage." Even if Union ships made it through the gauntlet of fire, "they would have to encounter a well-constructed and naturally masked battery at the town [Fernandina], which commands access to the inner anchorage." This was perhaps a nod to Lee's engineering acumen. Lee certainly thought the batteries were tenable but relied on Trapier's judgment regarding the gunners' ability to hit enemy targets. Du Pont's follow-up comment was anything but complimentary: "We captured Port Royal, but Fernandina had been given to us."

Over the next several days, Union men occupied Amelia Island, Cumberland Island, and St. Marys. In their haste to leave, and with little notice, the Confederates saved eighteen large caliber guns but left fourteen spiked cannons behind. But Trapier praised his Confederate soldiers in a follow-up report. With "very limited means of transportation," he wrote, "and the extreme difficulty of removing heavy ordnance over sand hills, reflects, in my judgment, high credit upon the officers to whom was assigned this arduous duty; all this was accomplished in four days and nights under the most adverse circumstances." He and Du Pont would meet again in 1863 when Trapier commanded the garrison on Sullivan's Island during Du Pont's unsuccessful assault on Charleston.

Du Pont always took time out of a demanding schedule to write his wife (who was also his first cousin), Sophie Madeleine du Pont, the daughter of his uncle, Eleuthère Irénée du Pont, who in 1802 founded a gunpowder firm, E. I. du Pont de Nemours and Company (today its successor, DowDuPont, is among the world's largest chemical companies). The admiral and his wife had read about Nathanael Greene in Washington Irving's five-volume *Life of George Washington* the previous winter, and Du Pont was eager to see Dungeness House. On March 9 1862, he wrote Sophie to describe a brief visit he made there while inspecting the abandoned Confederate south-end battery. He, like Robert E. Lee on his own visit two months earlier, was effusive in his admiration. His description of the premises might be the most detailed account penned by anyone before its destruction by fire in 1866.

"You approach it by the noblest avenue a mile in length through the finest live-oak grove I have yet seen," he wrote, "loaded down with the hanging moss. The house is a great quadrangle three stories high—all the evergreen forest trees and gigantic magnolias with their glossy leaves surround the premises. I was at once struck with an air of order pervading the place. A magnificent hedge surrounded the garden of several acres, beautifully trimmed like boxwood. Open archways in this high natural enclosure opened into the kitchen gardens. The house had never been finished inside—that is, the walls of concrete, shell, pebbles, and lime had never been wainscoted; the pine rafters had never been covered and the whole woodwork of the building had never known paint; the floors are uncarpeted and yet the whole aspect was different from anything I had ever seen in the *South*. Every particle of furniture was in the house—the Carcel lamp [which used a clockwork mechanism to pump oil to the burner] on the center table; handsome bookcases filled with nice books, French and English; pictures, large and small; on the walls. Upstairs in the same way—immense airy chambers, clean nice bedding carefully piled up. A large well-used family Bible and a prayer book were on the lady's toilet table. The garrets as cleanly swept at the chambers—the *Wabash* [Du Pont's flagship] was not nicer in all her appointments; the keys were in the doors. I said, 'What is the meaning of this? No Southern house was ever kept this way'—when several officers exclaimed, 'Why, Sir, the lady is a Northern woman.' Mrs. Nightingale is the daughter of Governor King of New York, and soon after I saw the portrait of her father, which I immediately recognized, and that of Mrs. James King. I did not [see] the one of my friend President King of Columbia College, another uncle."

His letter concludes with comments about Dungeness's horticulture. "The gardens bore the same impress, and my table is loaded before me at this moment with the most

"Dungeness, Cumberland Island," wood block engraving printed in *Harper's* magazine (vol. 57, 1878) and captioned "Ivy-colored ruins of stone plantation house, Georgia." (Courtesy of the Library of Congress)

magnificent tea roses and buds, which I am afraid to tell you how large. Verbenas, geraniums, extraordinary fringed hyacinths; all the extraordinary bulbs, gladiolas, irises, and tiger lilies; all the creepers, heliotropes, reseda-like weeds, all in the open air. Steedman, a rose fancier, Dr. Gunnell of the *Pawnee*, a botanist, were transported, and I myself could not move a foot without saying to myself, 'Oh my, if Sophie could only see these plants and shrubbery!' Mr. Nightingale, whose portrait was on the walls, is the grandson of General Greene; they were both, he and his wife, here until lately when [Confederate] General Lawton told them they would be in danger from the bombardment—which was not true. Two old women darkies were there and an old white man in charge." The two men Du Pont mentioned were well known to the admiral: Commander Charles Steedman (1811–1890), USN, was a native of South Carolina who returned to the United States in December 1860 from duty in Paraguay; Francis MacKall Gunnell (1827–1890), USN, later served as surgeon general of the navy (1884–88).

In another letter to Sophie, the admiral informs her of island Blacks' industrious work ethic, as long as it doesn't involve tasks they performed when they were enslaved. "That seems to make their condition the same as before. They will sit up all night and fish and catch crabs and go and catch horses and wild cattle and cross to the main [mainland] in sculls and get corn and so on, but [laboring in] the cornfield they do not like."

On March 24, 1862, a message from the U.S. president was recorded in the Congressional Records, 37th Congress, 2nd Session. It reads in part "I cordially recommend that Captain Samuel F. Du Pont receive a vote of thanks of Congress for his services and gallantry displayed in the capture, since the 21st December 1861, of various points on the coasts of Georgia and Florida, particularly Brunswick, Cumberland Island and Sound, Amelia island, the towns of St. Mary's, St. Augustine and Jacksonville, and Fernandina." The document was signed, "Abraham Lincoln, Washington City"—now Washington, D.C.

Despite Du Pont's orders to prevent troops from trespassing on the property of "the revolutionary hero and patriot, Gen. Greene," some pilfering occurred. After returning from a brief tour of the St. Johns River, he wrote on May 22 that "Dungeness was not so much injured as we heard. Some pictures are gone; one of General Greene in relief and a woman presenting him with a purse, was stolen and is said to be in possession of the major of the regiment. The picket guard was removed, being loafers who plundered the house instead of protecting it."

The War Winds Down on Cumberland

Nate Brown, still stationed in the vicinity of St. Marys, wrote Louisa in June 1862 that "it seems that we will never have a fight down here, and if we should have one it would be to contend with those miserable gunboats where there is no chance of doing anything." He reported seeing several Union vessels cruising near Fernandina, one of which fired a cannon in their direction, "but the ball fell so far short they did not shoot any more." He wrote again on September 15, 1862, about a federal raid on a Confederate picket, a forward guard unit, housed on the mainland across the river from Cumberland. "They [the Federal forces] came up in their boats from Fernandina and surrounded the house the picket were in. All the picket, fifteen in number, were asleep but one. The Yankees landed at an unexpected point and took them in the rear. They took Malcolm Crawford and Mat Thomas prisoners. The rest of them made their escape good to the camp, but they had to run twenty miles in their shirt-tails, bare headed and footed. Quite a ridiculous sight. One poor fellow got cut off escaping by land, so he being a good swimmer plunged into the river and swam a mile across to my picket on this side. He said he preferred the sharks to the Yankees. They fired thirteen times at him as he ran, but fortunately did not succeed in hitting him."

Nate's final letter during his service on Cumberland is dated October 16, 1862. He and his company were back on Little Cumberland, where he wrote "We are looking for the steamboat to take us down to the 'south-end battery' every minute. I don't know when we will leave." Brown took part in the Battle of Olustee some fifty miles west of Jacksonville in 1864, temporarily assuming command when Gen. Duncan Lamont Clinch Jr. (Fort Clinch on Amelia was named after his father) left the field of battle with an injury. Nate's regiment eventually joined the Army of Tennessee in Jonesboro, Georgia, and participated in the Battle of Atlanta against William T. Sherman's advancing army, fulfilling his desire to "lend a hand in driving back the invader from our homes."

Nate Brown's military career ended near Nashville, Tennessee. He survived the war without serious injury and returned to Louisa but died on February 23, 1866, three days after contracting smallpox from a former member of his company who passed through White Oak. He is buried in the Atkinson family cemetery in Camden County. During the war, Nate had visited Louisa on furlough several times, and she bore two more children: Lilly and Nathan Atkinson Brown Jr. Louisa relocated to Marietta years after the war and lived with Lilly, who was by then Mrs. R. G. Dunwoody. Louisa died on October 6, 1929, at the age of eighty-nine. Nathan Brown Jr. became an attorney and a deputy clerk serving on the U.S. District Court in Columbus, Georgia. His son, Nathan Atkinson Brown III (born 1901), continued the military tradition and retired with the rank of army colonel. He married Lucile Bruce, whose family developed East Beach on St. Simons Island. The brick home they had built on the northwest corner of Bruce Drive and Tenth Street still stands.

In 1862, Robert Stafford's second son, Armand, at the age of fifteen, enlisted in Company K of the Connecticut 26th Infantry Regiment. He was among the eight hundred men sworn into service on September 25, 1862, for a nine-month stint. On November 12 of that year they sailed to Long Island and stayed for a month before sailing by steamship to Louisiana. They camped near a swamp eight miles north of New Orleans, using the muddy Mississippi as their source of drinking water. The object of their expedition was the Confederate stronghold at Port Hudson. Armand was wounded in the initial assault on the fortification, and after two failed attacks, their commander, Gen. Nathaniel Banks, began the longest siege (at that time, forty-eight days) in U.S. military history. After the Confederates surrendered Port Hudson, Armand returned to Norwich by rail and steamer, arriving on August 7, 1863. He mustered out with the rest of the regiment on August 17. However, his postservice life was short lived: he died of consumption at age twenty-one on February 25, 1864, and was buried at the Starr Burying Ground Cemetery in Groton, where an ornate headstone marks his grave. Robert, Stafford's eldest son, "somewhat shiftless in his method of living," according to one legal document, died on August 6, 1872, and is buried next to him.

Only two local whites are known to have remained on Cumberland Island during the Union occupation: Robert Stafford at Planters House and Rachel (Clubb) Church, wife of Robert Church, at High Point. By remaining on the island, Stafford could watch over his property and prove he had not left his estate should the U.S. government attempt to seize his land on the premise that it been abandoned—a prescient move, as it turned out. The Federals relocated his slaves to Amelia "for their own safety." Some were granted permission to return to Cumberland armed with guns and ammunition to hunt and butcher deer and cattle for Union troops and sailors. A number of Stafford's slaves returned to Stafford and Rayfield Plantations along with several Blacks unknown to him, who slaughtered his cattle and kept him under house arrest. Stafford, fearing for his life, summoned help from the Federals at Fernandina.

"I at once proceeded with the steamer up Brickhill River," the officer sent to Cumberland wrote in his report, "and dispatched an armed party under command of Acting Masters West and Stimpson. At sunset Mr. West returned by my orders, bringing with him the nine negroes belonging to Mr. Stafford, and said to be dangerous. I placed them in irons, but have since, at their own request and at the desire of their master (who gives up all claim to them), released them and placed them on the ship's books as a portion of her crew."

Stafford sold to the Union forces over $56,000 in timber, horses, cattle, hogs, corn, and potatoes, though no evidence survives that he sold them his plantations' most abundant

Robert Stafford's house. (Courtesy of the Cumberland Island National Seashore Museum NPS, Mary Bullard Collection)

commodity—cotton. A news account indicated before the war he "once sent North as many as one hundred [horses] at a single shipment." The horses may have been Marsh Tackies, a breed of small feral ponies descended from horses the Spanish introduced to the barrier islands, or horses remaining from Oglethorpe's day. Stafford used local whites and slaves to round up wild horses, occasionally herding them into the river to swim to the mainland, where they were corralled and fed before being sold. Much of his cotton had gone up in flames, burned "either by Confederates to keep the Yankees from getting at it, or by the Federals for the same reason: to keep it away from the Confederates." Stafford later claimed the Federals forced him to torch his own cotton. It took two days for the bales to burn, blanketing the island in smoke. After peace was declared, Stafford sought compensation from the federal government, claiming to have been "loyally adherent to the cause and the Government of the United States during the war."

Frederick Ober wrote in *Harper's Weekly* (1880) that "at the close of the war, it is related, Mr. Stafford, proprietor of the central portion of the island burned his negro

Stafford slave cabin chimneys (2019).

houses to the ground, telling his people to go, as he had no more use for them nor they for him." However, an archaeological dig at Rayfield (reported in a 1971 issue of *Historical Archaeology*) as well as subsequent archaeological excavations of the chimneys—the only surviving parts of the slave quarters—conducted by the National Park Service in 1999 and 2014 failed to find evidence that Stafford's slave cabins had been burned. "Instead," Park Service archaeologists wrote, "the lack of structural remains [besides slave cabin chimneys] has now been attributed to scavenging of material over the years."

Sometime in 1864, during the Union occupation of Amelia Island, a northern correspondent submitted this dispatch from Fernandina: "Ned Simons [Simmons], an old negro belonging to the Dungeness estate of Gen. Nathan Greene, on Cumberland Island, and who was left by the rebel inheritor, Nightingale, on his evacuation of the place, died here last week at the house of the lady teachers, who have kindly cared for him since his arrival here [in Fernandina]. Ned was over one hundred years old, and remembered Gen. Washington well, and was one of the number who assisted in carrying him through the streets of Savannah on his last visit to that place. Though partially blind with age, he desired himself to learn to read. On being asked why, he replied, 'As the tree falls, so it will lay;' his attainments on earth would contribute to higher attainments on high; and during the last months of his life, he, with much labor and effort, acquired a knowledge of his letters and syllables. Poor old Ned!"

Ned, born about 1775, had been the property of Gen. Nathanael Greene while living at Mulberry Grove and participated in the celebrations honoring George Washington during his visit to Savannah and Mulberry Grove in 1790. Having relocated in 1798 or 1800 with the family to Cumberland Island, he was there during the British occupation in 1815. As we've seen, he was on the list of slaves who Admiral Cockburn returned to the Shaws at Dungeness House. He eventually became the property of Robert Stafford. His second freedom from bondage, whatever form that took in the last year of his life, had been almost as brief as his first emancipation. "Poor old Ned," indeed. Free at last.

After Union general William Tecumseh Sherman's successful march through Georgia to Savannah, he issued Special Field Order 15 on January 15, 1865, which seized all the property from Charleston, South Carolina, to the St. Johns River, taking in the coastal islands and extending thirty miles inland. The order, approved by Abraham Lincoln, called for about four hundred thousand acres to be distributed among the freedmen in forty-acre increments. The land redistribution, and the promise of a mule for each family, not only served to punish white planters but provided settlements and work for former slaves, especially the forty thousand newly emancipated refugees who had been following in the wake of Sherman's advance on Savannah. Lincoln's assassination and President Andrew Johnson's Amnesty Proclamation on May 29, 1865, which pardoned southerners and restored property rights, cast uncertainty on Sherman's order.

Maj. Gen. Oliver Otis Howard, commissioner of the Bureau of Refugees, Freedmen, and Abandoned Lands (BRFAL, also Freedmen's Bureau), issued circular 13 on July 28, 1865, to "establish a definite and uniform policy relative to confiscated and Abandoned Lands" for all confiscated properties in the southern states, not just the area specified in Sherman's field order. Circular 13 assigned these properties "to every male citizen whether refugee or freedman . . . not more than forty acres . . . for the term of three years at an annual rent not exceeding six per centum upon the value of such land." The occupants of each forty-acre parcel could purchase the land, based on its value, during the three-year term or at the end of three years.

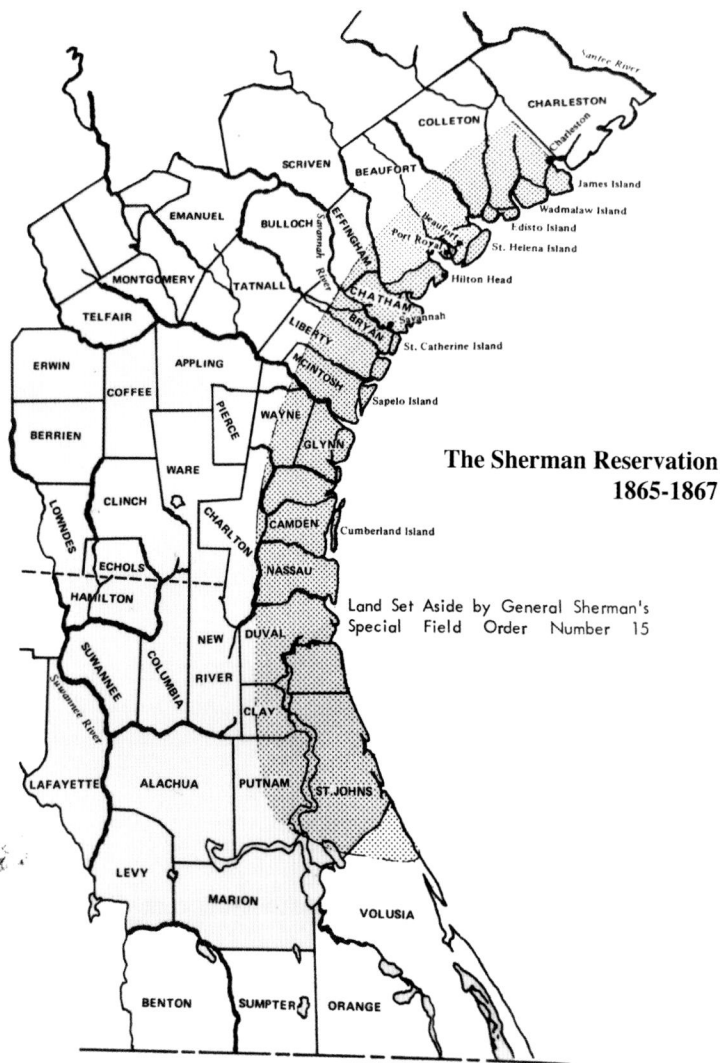

**The Sherman Reservation
1865-1867**

Land Set Aside by General Sherman's
Special Field Order Number 15

Coastal region comprising the Sherman Reservation
Area. (Cumberland Island National Seashore image,
from *Forty Acres and a Mule*, Claude F. Oubre, Baton
Rouge: Louisiana State University Press, 1978)

But Sherman's order and the subsequent circulars were short lived. Stafford was able to prove he had not abandoned his property. William F. Eaton, the Freedman's Bureau agent on St. Simons, reported on July 31, 1865: "On Cumberland Id. I believe there are thirteen plantations, all of which have been abandoned except Robert Stafford's and Mrs. Church's. Very few persons live upon this island, probably not a hundred black and white." In the end, confiscated properties, including Stafford's and Nightingale's, were restored to their former owners, and the Freedman's Bureau concentrated on enforcing wage labor for freedmen who became tenant farmers on former plantations. Congress disbanded the Bureau in 1872.

In 1863, a small garrison of Union troops were stationed at Dungeness, ostensibly to protect the house and property. The following year, a number of Black men and women were sent by the Freedman's Bureau from overcrowded Fernandina to settle in Dungeness's former slave quarters. By 1865 that number had grown to sixty freedmen. A suspect fire in April 1866 destroyed Dungeness House, leaving behind a shell of the mansion's tabby walls and brick chimneys. Years later, one of Robert Stafford's maidservants, Tecumsah "Cumsie" Commodore, recounted to Carnegie family member Lucy R. Ferguson what happened: "I vas livin at Dungeness wen e burn. Oh my! Yankee sojers station in de Big House. All kine of bad tings goin on. Drinkin, carousing, whorin. No place for a young gal. Day and night. Yes mam. I saw de Big House on fiah."

Admiral Du Pont died on June 23, 1865, the year before Dungeness House, the home of Revolutionary War hero Nathanael Greene, burned to the ground. Given what he had seen of Union troops' behavior elsewhere in the South, Du Pont might not have been surprised. He once lamented in a letter to Sophie the actions of Federal troops after they plundered slaves' possessions on Hilton Head and destroyed homes. "I can't tell you the disgust I feel for our soldiers—there is a moral degradation about them which haunts me. To think that I should have every instinct of a gentleman and officer outraged by any association takes away half the satisfaction of our success."

"Cumsie" Commodore. Taken on Cumberland Island by John H. Ricketson, ca. 1940. (Courtesy of the Cumberland Island National Seashore Museum NPS)

A northern reporter visiting Robert Stafford at his home shortly after the Civil War ended described him as "tall as a chimney and has a voice like a trip-hammer. He fairly made the chairs move when he spoke. His only companions are an aged negress, a decanter of choice brandy, the *Journal of Commerce*, and thirty-four dogs. It is said he is worth one million dollars in hard cash."

Not long afterward, two of his daughters by Elizabeth Bernardey arrived unannounced at his home on Cumberland, wanting to know if they were his heirs. Stafford, incensed over their unexpected visit and their questions, sent them away. Apparently they were unaware that their mother had been born a slave. Under Connecticut law, if Stafford legally acknowledged them as his children, as he once did informally, Elizabeth, his common-law wife and a freedwoman, could claim one-half of his estate.

Sometime in the postbellum period, Elizabeth returned to Cumberland Island from Connecticut, though she apparently did not return to Stafford's house. Stafford's four daughters, described as tall, handsome women, studied French, Italian, music, and painting and enjoyed active social lives, entertaining their upper-class friends in the North with amateur theatricals and private parties. All of them married white men. Mary Elizabeth was wedded first to Frederick Palmer, a mortgage broker, whom she divorced. Her second husband, Charles Gaylord, graduated from Yale Theological Seminary and Yale Medical School. Mary died of tuberculosis on May 22, 1879, at the age of forty-one. Having married and then divorced a New York calligrapher, Benjamin Brady, Ellen later married Frederick Engels, a New York artist. Adelaide, described as tall, lithe, graceful, with olive-tinted skin and lustrous eyes, moved to France, where she met and married, at the age of thirty-one, a Polish member of the Russian diplomatic corps, Count Charles Dieudonné Cybulski (Zivulki). Their marriage took place in London on July 8, 1882, though an August 30, 1882, *New York Sun* article states they exchanged vows in the Notre-Dame de Paris. Medora (Dora), the only Stafford child born in Groton, married Francis Vosburgh. She died in New York City on March 10, 1891.

Stafford offered to purchase Dungeness for $6,000 from Phineas Nightingale in 1868. At the time, Nightingale was in debt to Stafford for at least

Mary Elizabeth Stafford. (Courtesy of Bryan-Lang Archives)

$10,000. Stafford reminded him that trespassers, Black and white, had been using Dungeness as a staging ground to "[steal] my cattle, hogs, and everything else they can lay their hands on, even my dogs, for the last five or six years." Stafford also undiplomatically—but characteristically—wrote Phineas that "you never ever said friendly to me." He was probably right: because the social hierarchy was as rigid as the tabby walls of Dungeness House, despite Stafford's accumulated wealth, his unconventional lifestyle prevented his ascent into elite southern society—perhaps accounting for his many trips to the North. Maybe Stafford hadn't expected Nightingale to sell to him, and in any case Nightingale had no intention of turning over his family home to the son of his family's former overseer. He instead hoped to sell the estate for $80,000 to Rhode Island senator William Sprague Jr., but the deal never materialized. In 1870, Eliza H. Molyneux, a Georgia native then living in England, acquired Dungeness for $25,000. Nightingale died at his Brunswick home on April 21, 1873, at the age of sixty-nine and is buried at Oak Grove Cemetery. His great-grandson, Bernard Nicolau Nightingale, established a Brunswick law firm, now (2020) under the name Nightingale, Liles, Dennard & Carmical, still in business. Another descendant, William N. Nightingale, resides in Jacksonville.

Robert E. Lee made his final journey to Cumberland Island in April 1870 in the company of one of his daughters. The *Weekly Atlanta Intelligencer* reported that "this distinguished visitor sailed on the steamer *Nick King* last Tuesday to visit the grave of his father, General Harry Lee ('Light-Horse Harry') situated at Dungeness, Cumberland Island, on the coast of Georgia. Dungeness is now the property of William Nightingale, a grand-son of General Greene [actually a great-grandson], and whose guest Gen. Lee is at the present time." Lee wrote of his visit, "The cemetery is unharmed and the graves in good condition, but the house at Dungeness has been burned and the island devastated." Lee died that October following a stroke.

On May 1, 1877, three months to the day before Stafford's death, a Georgia newspaper printed a travelogue submitted by an anonymous writer who visited Cumberland with several companions. "Proceeding on our way through one continuous avenue of noble oaks," the article begins, "we finally reached the elegant grounds and mansion of Mr. Stafford, which are surrounded by a massive tabby wall, the barns and out-buildings forming quite an imposing group in the shape of a parallelogram. Boldly opening the gate, and, leaving the vehicles outside, we push on to the verandah of the dwelling and are met at the steps by a venerable gray-haired personage who says, with a shrewd look and twinkle of the eye, that he is *not* Mr. Stafford, but the old man is within.

"A committee of one [the writer], with gingerly foot-steps advances forthwith into the presence of the old Island Monarch, and finds him stretched upon a lounge in a handsome parlor, paneled and finished in the old style. He is received courteously when his mission is made known, albeit the old man, being quite deaf, roars rather than talks and *does* resemble a superannuated lion. Our companions are invited in and introduced, and then little interviewing ensues with the following results: Mr. Stafford was born at Dungeness [the south end of the island, not the mansion] on Cumberland Island and is nearly *ninety* years of age, though his erect figure and unshrunken frame show him to be still possessed of considerable vigor. His has been an eventful life, owing to early family differences, improper to be mentioned, but which cast a glamour over the future, and perhaps had no little to do with the comparatively reckless life he had led and utter disregard for the customs, proprieties and conventionalities of society.

"But we do not intend to lift the veil upon the sins and eccentrics of our almost centenarian host but prefer to cast over them the mantle of charity, only regretting that he should still continue to 'swear like a pirate.' The old gentleman accumulated a vast fortune in the cultivation of a fine grade of Sea Island cotton and was once the owner of about 500 slaves, 2,000 head of cattle and *nine hundred* horses. The latter ranged in a perfectly wild condition over his immense estate of twenty thousand acres, with no attention save the introduction of imported stallions from time to time. They subsisted wholly upon the rank salt marsh which exists in limitless fields all around the island, except seaward, and were possessed of great beauty and endurance. When wanted they were driven into strong enclosures and lassoed. Whole ship loads were frequently caught and sent North, bringing an average price each of about one hundred dollars. We saw grouped close together in one field forty of these animals, some of them exceedingly handsome and well-grown.

"The old man informed us that the Yankees had destroyed 200 bales of Sea Island cotton worth $1.25 per pound, killed all his cattle, and carried off nearly every one of the horses. When casually asked who fired [set fire to] his cotton, he yelled out, 'Damn 'em, they made Robert Stafford do it!'

"In the midst of our colloquy suddenly he shouted to his alter ego, Mr. McHardy, the old Scotchman we first met, 'bring out the jug.' The old man fumbled over a bunch of keys as though he did not know the right one and was again saluted with a thunderous oath and ordered to hurry up. During the serving of the refreshments, a funny little by-scene was enacted. The 'canny Scot' at a moment when the host was not observing,

Robert Stafford's headstone in Stafford Cemetery. His mother and sisters are buried next to his grave.

turned his back to him, and pouring out a tumbler of the poteen [alcohol] with a comical leer of the eye exclaimed, 'now I'll get even with him' and downed it at a gulp. These old men have been living together for a quarter of a century, and Mac is himself well off. Mr. Stafford is still immensely wealthy, owning large amounts of real estate in Brooklyn, New York [unsubstantiated] and New London. His grounds and gardens are models of taste and beauty, and all admitted that they had never seen anything handsomer in the most cultivated portions of the North. Of all his vast landed estate, not five acres are now under cultivation. Soon he will be gathered to his fathers and then, what next? Ah, let us look no further."

The federal 1870 census lists Stafford's occupation as farmer (he reported himself as a planter in the 1850 census). Just five years after the Civil War, his personal estate remained substantial, valued at $250,000, and his real estate value was $100,000. By then the only listed household members were a sixty-five-year-old Black female housekeeper, Catherine Williams, born in San Domingo (now the Dominican Republic), and two female servants, one sixteen, the other fifteen. He also retained a young gardener and stable hand, Henry Commodore, and Tecumsah "Cumsie" Cooper, a young maidservant who later married Henry.

Robert Stafford was eighty-seven when he passed away on August 1, 1877, at Planters House, his Cumberland Island home. His personal wealth included real estate north and south of the Mason-Dixon Line, stocks, bonds, shares of railroads and banks, and hard currency. He had assigned Thomas D. Hawkins, a nephew by his sister, Susannah, to execute the provisions of his will. Stafford left his Cumberland Island estate, totaling $108,756, to a niece and two nephews and his New England holdings, totaling $345,600, to his four surviving children by Elizabeth. He left nothing to Elizabeth, who died about 1891. Mary Bullard, the indefatigable chronicler of Cumberland Island history, wrote the libretto for a Curtis Bryant opera about Elizabeth, *Zabette*; the Georgia State University School of Music produced the opera, which premiered April 29, 1999, at the Rialto Theatre in Atlanta.

CHAPTER VIII   The Hotel Era and the Settlement on the North End

THE ECONOMIC AND political shockwaves that washed over the South in the wake of the Civil War forced Black and white residents on Cumberland Island to reinvent themselves and the way of life they previously knew, ushering in a new era of settlement and industry. Northerners seeking investment opportunities and warmer climes set their sights on the Florida and Georgia coasts. Newly freed island Blacks established several settlements, including one at Brickhill Bluff (Downes' Landing), one near Greyfield Landing, and another on Robert Stafford's land. Before his death, Stafford hired freedmen to clear land, raise stock, repair boats, and tend vegetable gardens. However, the days of free labor tending plantation crops were gone. For their part, island Blacks learned to subsist off the land and surrounding waters.

One freedman, Uncle Quash, recounted: "We lib on fish and grit and der run of de crik, and some time we catch a hawg. Dere plenty berries in de woods, and de grape he thick all 'round here. Don tek much wuk raise little corn. De chillum ketch de crawb, and de oyster, he all over de bank." Quash's name is perhaps derived from the African *kwasi* (*quashee*).

Christmas Creek

Cumberland Hotel / High Point

Whitney Lake

The Settlement
& First African Baptist Church

Half Moon Bluff

Airstrip

The approximate
locations of the
Settlement and First
African Baptist Church
are visible in this
photograph of the
north end. An airstrip
was built in 1948–49 by
Olaf Olsen Sr. for the
Candler family.

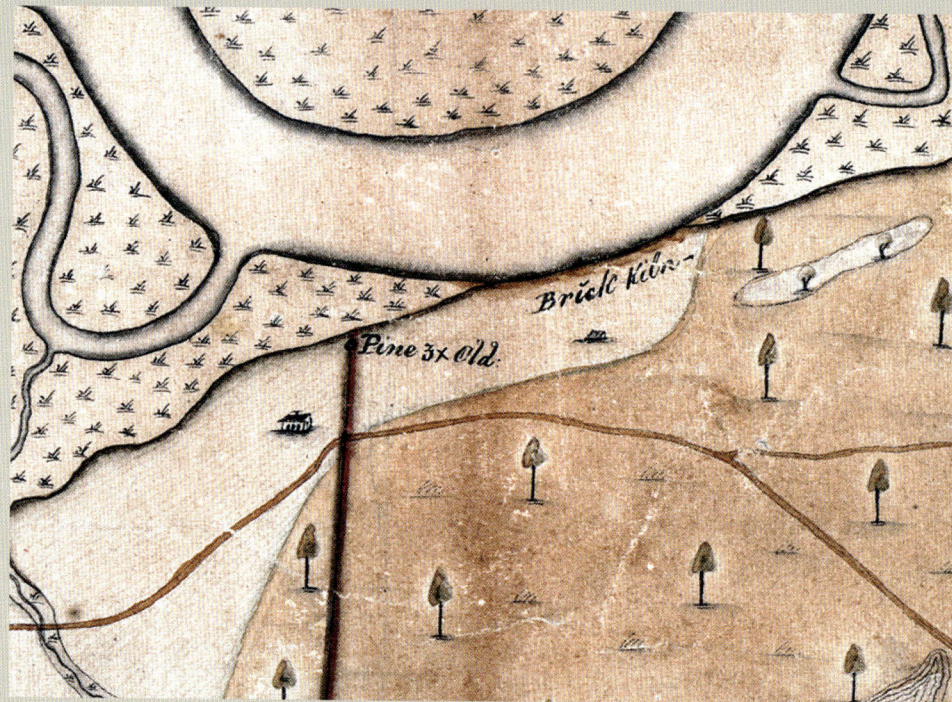

Brick kiln

Pine 3× Old.

Detail of McKinnon Map
showing Brickhill and kiln
location. (Courtesy of Georgia
Archives, Carnegie Estate
Records of Cumberland Island,
acc. 1969-0501M)

Large basket made from pine straw and caning. Made in the Gullah-Geechee tradition and used to toss rice in the air so the husks blow off. (Courtesy of National Park Service Photo/Darryl Herring)

The term "Gullah-Geechee" refers to African Americans living on the South Carolina and Georgia coasts whose customs, beliefs, speech patterns, and ways of life are unique to that region, especially on the barrier islands where isolated communities retained their African-influenced dialects well into the twentieth century. Many members of Gullah and Saltwater Geechee communities practiced the art of basket weaving, a skill passed down from their African ancestors. Tales of the wily Br'er (Brother) Rabbit popularized by Joel Chandler Harris are largely the retelling of the folktale character, Anansi (or Aunt Nancy). Stories of this trickster spider, who used his wits to outsmart larger opponents, crossed the Atlantic on slave ships. These tales, their dialects, and music were all the enslaved people brought with them. On this side of the ocean they remade their cultural image into a unique blend of Euro-African languages and customs. However, some African American islanders believed in the supernatural, which included sorcery and witches or root doctors.

The Brickhill tract belonged to William and Winifred Downes, who willed it to their sons, James and Robert Downes. Brickhill may have been the location of a kiln used to

Primus Mitchell, ca. 1917. (Courtesy of the Cumberland Island National Seashore Museum NPS)

make brick or lime for tabby, hence the name. The 1802 McKinnon map designates the location as "Brick Kiln." The freedmen living at Brickhill raised corn crops and gardens on its rich soil. One of them, Primus Mitchell, cast a long shadow on the island's history.

Primus was born on Cumberland Island in January 1825 to a female slave, Bettie, and a male slave named Stepney (born about 1797). At least one historian contends Primus's father was Robert Stafford. Primus grew up on Rayfield Plantation when it was owned by Nathanael Ray Greene, the son of Gen. Nathanael Greene. Greene, who renounced slavery and moved his family to Rhode Island, sold Rayfield and fifty-three slaves to Robert Stafford for $11,000 in 1834. Primus initially worked as a field hand at Rayfield. He attended a biracial Baptist mission church, the Cumberland African Church, established in 1837. With the support of Stafford and Phineas Nightingale, Primus and other freedmen erected a place of worship a few miles north of Planters House, Stafford's home. Religion took hold of young Primus. He became a Baptist preacher, holding meetings and religious services in praise houses made of grass and palmetto fronds.

Thatched dwellings on Cumberland date back to the Timucua. Spanish missionaries, Edmund Gray's settlers, Oglethorpe's men, and squatters illegally harvesting oak in Nathanael Greene's day also constructed thatched buildings. Primus and the freedmen settlers made use of palmetto trees and sedge to build their homes or to use as roofing material. In 1861, at the age of thirty-six, Primus married Amanda, another Cumberland slave, born about 1830. A white preacher conducted the ceremony.

Primus died on July 27, 1917, in Nassau County, Florida. He is buried on Cumberland Island at High Point. Though he died at Fernandina, his marker reads, "Uncle Primus Mitchell And wife Amanda, Born Slaves At Stafford, Faithful Field Hands On Cumberland Island Until Death."

Primus would have been in his mid- to late thirties when he enlisted in the U.S. Navy during the Union's Civil War occupation of the island. Confederate raiders swept through Stafford's plantations in 1862 and 1863 looking for food and slaves to capture. Stafford sent seventeen of his enslaved people to Union-held Fernandina for their protection and may have urged Primus to enlist. Primus joined with the rank of landsman, the navy's lowest rate, assigned to new recruits with no experience on seagoing vessels. Records show he served aboard the USS *Perry* and other ships before his discharge in 1865. Before the war he went by the name Primus Stafford but was thereafter known as Primus Mitchell. He returned to Amelia Island, where his friend, Rogers

Thatched cabin on Cumberland Island, Camden County, Georgia. Detail from stereograph, New-York Historical Society

Primus and Amanda Mitchell, ca. 1888. Their granddaughter, Beulah Alberty, was one of the last Settlement residents. Primus died on July 27, 1917, at Fernandina and is buried on Cumberland Island at High Point. His marker reads, "Uncle Primus Mitchell And wife Amanda, Born Slaves At Stafford, Faithful Field Hands On Cumberland Island Until

Freedman's cabin. Margaret Downes set up a sharecropping community at Brickhill (formerly Brick Kiln). Between thirty and forty people lived at Brickhill during Reconstruction until 1890. (Courtesy of the Cumberland Island National Seashore Museum NPS)

Alberty (or Alberti, who married Ellen, a Bunkley slave) lived with his family along with other freedmen, including the Webber and Price families.

Article 3 of General Sherman's Special Field Order 15 stipulated that "Whenever three respectable negroes, heads of families, shall desire to settle on land, and shall have selected for that purpose an island, or a locality . . . the inspector of settlements and plantations will himself, or by such sub-ordinate officer as he may appoint, give them a license to settle such island or district, and afford them such assistance as he can to enable them to establish a peaceable agricultural settlement." Sherman's order further allowed the "three parties named" to subdivide the settlement into forty-acre plots of tillable ground.

While the lands on Sherman's Reservation were eventually returned to the previous owners, the freedmen at Brickhill were allowed to remain at their settlement. Two "Yankee carpetbaggers," Silas Fordham (from upstate New York) and his brother-in-law, Colonel Joseph Shepard (originally from Pennsylvania), bought three thousand acres of island property from James Downes's widow, Margaret Bernardey Downes, and her children in 1870. Fordham, who came to Georgia in 1869 for relief from rheumatism, charged a nominal rental fee—a small quantity of their crops—to Mitchell and the other Brickhill settlers. He resided at St. Marys in Orange Hall, an antebellum Greek Revival home, now a museum. Both he and Shepard served as Collector of Customs for the port of St. Marys for a number of years, and Joseph was elected mayor of St. Marys

Cumberland Island's north end facing southwest.

in 1871. They purchased two other tracts on Cumberland, including land at High Point, one of the highest points on the Atlantic coast south of New York. Shepard transferred his interest to a sister who sold her interests to J. M. Hunter, a childhood friend of Fordham's. One of Fordham's and Hunter's schemes that didn't pan out included building an "all seasons seaside sanitarium" located on the island's mineral springs (artesian wells) and a hotel with "drives, walks and electric railways to the beach." The two advertised lots for sale on Cumberland in 1891. They also intended to develop a brickyard at Brick Hill due to the high-quality clay found there.

The pair planned to build a hotel at High Point encircled by a subdivision of 125 lots with a hunting preserve extending south to Brickhill. The sale did not go through as planned due to objections raised by heirs of Winifred Downes and William R. Bunkley, who claimed ownership of acreage at High Point. But the scheme exposed the precarious position of Primus Mitchell and others living at Brickhill. The 1880 census lists Primus as a "farm laborer" and Amanda (born 1830) as "Wife, Keep House." The census indicates they had one son and six daughters: Douta (age twenty, could read, "work on farm"), Catherine (eighteen, could read, "work on farm"), Laura (thirteen, attended school, could read), Irene (twelve), James (six), Hester (six), and Elizabeth (five). Twenty-five years after the Civil War ended, the Mitchells and other freedmen and women still had no legal claim to the land they lived and worked on. However, their deliverance came in the form of a new industry taking hold on the island.

Amanda Mitchell on Cumberland Island, about 1895. (Courtesy of the Cumberland Island National Seashore Museum NPS)

One of the first serious attempts to establish a hotel on Cumberland occurred in 1869 when Phineas Nightingale, deep in debt, joined with a Manhattan banker, James Gore King (his wife's uncle), to draw up plans for the Dungeness Hotel. The brochure they created to attract investors highlighted the fact that steamers routinely ran between Fernandina and Savannah, stopping at Dungeness, and the soon-to-be-completed Brunswick Railway would shuttle passengers between Savannah and Brunswick. Though their plans came to nothing, the recipe for success—the steamers and rail service—played significant roles in the future establishment of hotels on the island's north end.

An April 3, 1872, editorial in the *Atlanta Weekly Sun* opined, "Were a sea-bathing establishment opened here [on Cumberland] it would eclipse in many respects such resorts in the Northern States. The climate throughout the heats of summer is never oppressive, and in the winter the cold is seldom disagreeably felt."

Two years later, the *Georgia Weekly Telegraph* published an account of a visit to perhaps the first Cumberland hotel on the north end in April 1874. A party of ten men and women from Macon arrived at dusk near High Point aboard the *Lizzie Baker* and rowed a hundred yards to shore. After becoming mired in mud, they were rescued by wagons that took them "through dense thickets, dark as Erebus, to Bunkley's Hotel." The correspondent described a later encounter with a wild horse. "This island is noted for its breed of sturdy ponies called marsh tackeys, which are as plentiful as rabbits and as easily reared. They subsist by feeding upon the salt marsh, and when wanted are run down and lassoed in Western style. They are exceedingly hardy and ofttimes very beautiful." The next part of the story reveals just how wild Cumberland's horses were and continue to be. (Tourists today are warned not to get too close to the horses; encounters have resulted in serious injury to visitors who got too close.) "Some two weeks ago Mr. Bunkley succeeded in capturing thus a splendid mare, about six years old, which has been tied up closely ever since. His son, a strong and active young man, at the request of the crowd essayed to mount his prize, assisted by one of the amateur horse-trainers present. In a second, however, he was sent flying through the air. Again was the attempt made, his volunteer stoutly affirming that he could hold the fiery beast by the rope attached to her head. Seizing it, therefore with a firm grasp, once more young Bunkley sprang upon her back. But the furious creature, with glaring eye-balls, reared

Antique photograph labeled "Sand Hills Cumberland Island Beach." (Author's collection)

upon her hind legs and lashed at him with her fore feet, narrowly missing his person. In an instant down came Bunkley again, and our Maconian found that in his efforts to restrain the animal his hand had been lacerated to the bone by a turn of the rope around it. Mrs. Butts, who is the Sister of Mercy of the expedition, came promptly to his relief with arnica and bandages, and the wounded member was deftly cared for. That wild horse is still untamed."

As early as 1875, another proprietor, Elias Clubb, ran newspaper ads for the "Oriental House." A typical ad described the property and amenities: "The above house, pleasantly situated on the north end of Cumberland Island, is open for the accommodation of the Public. Parties from the Interior will find it a pleasant place for a maroon." A popular leisure activity of the day involved camping on a barrier island, as if marooned on a deserted isle. The Oriental House was actually the Clubb home, where his family and mother, Rebecca, widow of James A. Clubb, lived. Turning one's home into a boardinghouse or hotel was not uncommon. Long before the rise of AirBnB, local residents opened their homes to paying guests. A number of "tourist homes" lined Brunswick's Glynn Avenue overlooking the marsh in the early 1900s.

Elias Clubb

In 1880 Elias Clubb permanently moved his family to Brunswick, where he became pilot of the Brunswick Bar. In 1882 he announced in the local Georgia papers a notice of intention to change his last name and the last name of his wife and five children from Clubb to Peerson. Glynn County Court documents researched by local historian Amy Hedrick shed some light on his decision. Superior Court minutes of his petition show that Clubb stated his family's name, "known and respected since the County's earliest history, has become the subject of the idle talker, the hinting and surmising professional gossip, until a story, enlarged at every repetition has passed to the full grown; yet irresponsible scandalmonger and the Repeater of scandal who, true to their instincts, have made the name odious, a barrier to social intercourse, and a burden to bear." The motive for the slander is not stated, though possible reasons include his father, harbor pilot James Clubb, bringing the slave ship *Wanderer* across the bar to Jekyll Island twenty-five years earlier, or James Clubb's cooperation as a "Union man" during Du Pont's occupation of Cumberland during the Civil War. In 1875, William T. DuBignon, whose father, Henry, allowed *Wanderer* slaves to disembark on Jekyll, had legally changed his surname to Turner due to the ensuing scandal. Clubb's petition to change his surname was granted by the court.

ORIENTAL HOUSE,

CUMBERLAND ISLAND,

ELIAS CLUBB, — — Proprietor.

THE ABOVE HOUSE, pleasantly situated on the north end of Cumberland Island, is open for the accommodation of the Public. Parties from the Interior will find it a pleasant place for a maroon For further particulars address the Proprietor at Brunswick, Ga.

·····:0:·····

Terms Very Low.

Newspaper advertisement for the Oriental House on Cumberland, placed by Elias Clubb, proprietor, in 1876. "Terms Very Low." *Brunswick Advertiser*, August 9, 1876. (Georgia Historic Newspapers, Digital Library of Georgia)

Regional railroad companies worked hand in hand with hotel owners to pack their railcars with more passengers. The Macon & Brunswick Railroad ran ads in 1878 offering reduced excursion rates, as in this one: "Parties of 4 $11, parties of 5 to 9 $8, parties of 10 to 14 $6.50, parties of 15 or more, Macon to Brunswick and return $5. Baggage, tents, dogs, outfit, etc, free. Roundtrip tickets between Brunswick and Cumberland Island $1.75 each. The first class passenger steamer, FLORENCE, runs daily between Brunswick and Fernandina, touching at Cumberland Island coming and returning."

Another northerner, Mason T. Burbank of Vermont, moved to Fernandina for health reasons, namely asthma. A builder (the 1880 census lists him as a carpenter), he erected a number of houses in Fernandina, including the Fairbanks House, now an inn. After one of his daughters died during an epidemic on Amelia Island, he purchased Clubb's property at High Point, renaming it High Point House. He was appointed postmaster on Cumberland in 1882 and opened a small store and post office on the north end. His eldest daughter, Catherine (Katie), taught island children at the family home.

Burbank bought five acres of land near Half Moon Bluff in 1890 from Luther Martin and divided them into 50-by-100-foot lots. He sold the lots to Primus Mitchell and other Brickhill residents. The list of purchasers represents a who's-who of Cumberland Island African American families: Stiles, Alberty, Trimmings (also Trimings or Trimmins; a surname perhaps adopted from what slaves called "outside" or "trimmings," names given to

A steamer approaching Cumberland Island. (Courtesy of the Cumberland Island National Seashore Museum NPS, Mary Bullard Collection)

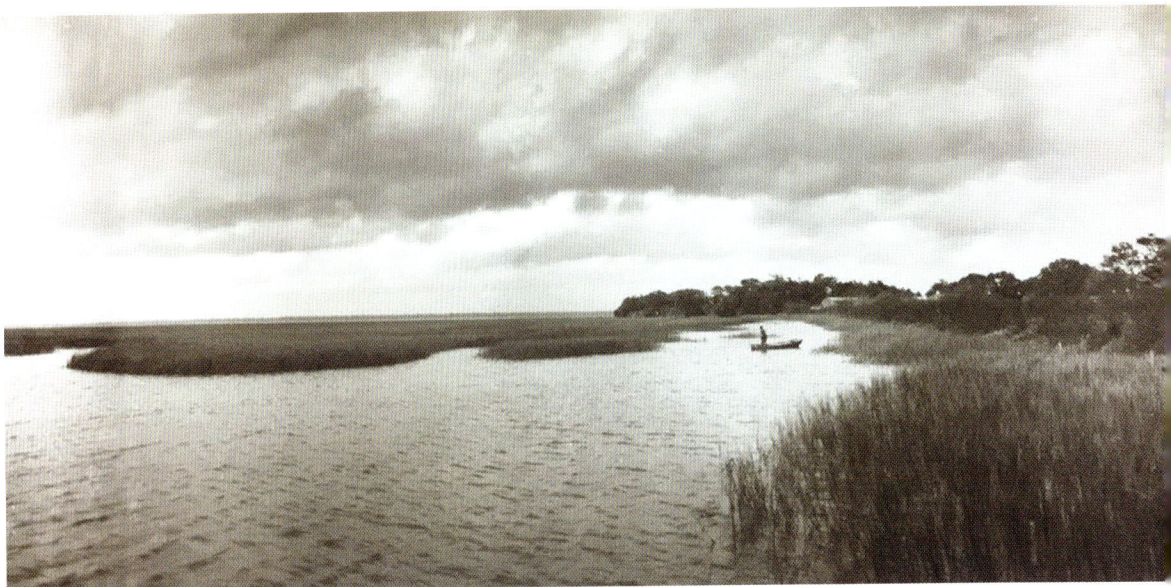

African American fisherman. (Courtesy of Bryan-Lang Historical Archives)

them by masters), Holzendorf, and Merrow (also Mayo or Merrou). African Americans who relocated from Brickhill to the Settlement on the north end found employment at island hotels as kitchen and restaurant staff, tram drivers, and hunting and fishing guides. They also kept hotel cooks supplied with oysters, clams, shrimp, fish, venison, and other game.

In 1893, Deacons Primus Mitchell, William M. Alberty, Thomas Alberty, and Charles Trimmings, trustees of the Old Baptist Church, along with Rev. T. Lockett, constructed a one-room log cabin—the First African Baptist Church—in their new settlement. The former slaves now had a home, known as the Settlement, to call their own and a church to serve their spiritual needs. The church doubled as a schoolhouse.

In 1937 the African American residents built a new place of worship several yards away from the 1893 cabin using lumber from an abandoned house donated by Charles Howard Candler. Weatherboard siding and a tin roof covered the new 28-by-16-foot one-story structure. Two windows (six-over-six panes) on each side and a window at the rear (north end) let in light and a cross breeze. Several steps led up to a double door on the south end of the church. Up to a dozen wooden pews in two rows face a

FADER'S TRACT						
						LOT 27. CHAS. TRIMINGS
LOT 36. DOCK TISON	LOT 37. DOCK TISON	LOT 38. DOCK TISON	LOT 39. DOCK TISON	LOT 40. ?	LOT 41. ?	LOT 16. CHURCH LOT / ... ALBERTY
LOT 35. GEO. ALBERTY	LOT 34. GEO. ALBERTY	LOT 33. GEO. ALBERTY	LOT 32. GEO. ALBERTY	LOT 31. PRIMUS MITCHELL	LOT 30. NELSON	LOT 29. NELSON
LOT 22. NELSON MERRO	LOT 23. NELSON MERRO	LOT 24. NELSON MERRO	LOT 25. NELSON MERRO	LOT 26. PRIMUS MITCHELL	LOT 27. CHAS. TRIMINGS	LOT 28. CHAS. TRIMINGS
LOT 21. ELIZABETH MITCHELL STILES	LOT 20. ELIZABETH MITCHELL STILES	LOT 19. CAROLINE STILES	LOT 18. ?	LOT 17. ROGERS ALBERTY BY CHAS. TRIMINGS	LOT 16. CHURCH LOT	LOT 15. CHURCH LOT
LOT 8. MORGAN HOGENDOF	LOT 9. MORGAN HOGENDOF	LOT 10. CAROLINE STILES	LOT 11. CHAS. TRIMINGS	LOT 12. CHAS. TRIMINGS	LOT 13. WM. ALBERTY	LOT 14. WM. ALBERTY
LOT 7. SAM ALBERTY	LOT 6. EILLEN ALBERTY	LOT 5. QUASH MERROU	LOT 4. CHAS. TRIMINGS	LOT 3. CHAS. TRIMINGS	LOT 2. WM. ALBERTY	LOT 1. WM. ALBERTY

MILLER'S TRACT

ACCESS ROAD

MACON TRACT SOUTH 213

Mason Bunkley divided 5 acres of his land into 50-by-100-foot plots and sold them to Brickhill residents and other tenant farmers on Cumberland. The fifty-two plots became known as the Settlement. (Courtesy of the Cumberland Island National Seashore Museum NPS)

Rogers Alberty home on tract, adjacent to the First African Baptist Church. (Courtesy of the Cumberland Island National Seashore Museum NPS)

Liz Trimmings, wife of Charles Trimmings, holding a family Bible. Liz was one of Primus Mitchell's daughters. Photo, titled "The Book of Ruth," was taken by C. Graves Sr. (Lexington, Ky.) about 1939. (Courtesy of the Cumberland Island National Seashore Museum NPS)

Charles (Charlie) Trimmings was a north-end resident, a landowner, and one of the founders of the First African Baptist Church in 1893. His mother, Sally, was born a Bunkley slave. Photo by Joseph C. Graves Sr., ca. 1940. (Courtesy of the Cumberland Island National Seashore Museum NPS)

Nelson Merrow, February 1981. (Courtesy of the Cumberland Island National Seashore Museum NPS)

The altar, First African Baptist Church. (Courtesy of Sonja Olsen Kinard)

Founder's plaque, First African Baptist Church, the Settlement.

Photograph of the First African Baptist
Church and the Rogers Alberty home.
(Courtesy of Sonja Olsen Kinard)

First African Baptist Church
interior, 2019.

Colorized photograph titled "Scene Along Lake Road, Cumberland Island, Ga." (Author's collection)

wooden altar in the sparse interior. The church officers were Charles Alberty, Beulah G. Alberty (clerk), P. Trimmings, and Nelson Merrow. Reverend L. Morrison of Amelia Island presided over the congregation. Nelson Merrow's son, George, helped construct the new church. The structure still stands and is open to public visitation.

In 1890 Burbank transferred his remaining property to William R. Bunkley and Bunkley's newly formed Cumberland Island Company. The purpose of the company was to establish a permanent hotel business at High Point. Mason Burbank and his son, George, assisted Bunkley with this new enterprise by shuttling guests to and from the mainland by boat. An 1887 advertisement Bunkley ran in Georgia newspapers promised that "George Johnson will furnish you with a nice horse and buggy to ride on the beach. Tommie Miller will take you out in his handsome street car and land you on the rolling surf. Mr. Pratt will give you a delightful sail down the bay, and George Burbank will show you how and where to catch fish."

Whereas Nightingale's proposed Dungeness Hotel targeted more upscale families looking to escape northern winters, the north-end hotels attracted a middle-class clientele as well as civic groups and professional organizations. Early attempts to establish hotels on Cumberland were hampered by a lack of money and convenient access to the island. However, a growing fleet of steamboats—called by locals the "steamboat navy"—like the *Hildegarde* and the *Atlantic*, routinely plied the Cumberland Route between Jacksonville and Brunswick, transporting mail, consumable goods, and passengers. The steamboats maintained well-established routes that brought tourists to Cumberland's shores. To remain profitable, though, hotels needed a steady flow of guests, more than the surrounding populations in St. Marys, Brunswick, and other nearby towns could sustain. The second factor, improved rail service, gave residents of Atlanta, Macon, Savannah, and other inland cities easy access to Cumberland's hunting grounds, natural fisheries, and miles of wide, open beach.

The *City of Brunswick* carried passengers from Brunswick to Fernandina for $2, to Jacksonville for $3, and soon made regular stops at Cumberland's north end. Other steamers bringing hotel guests to the island included the *Florence*, the *Pope Cotlin*, and a slow-moving wood-burning steamer named the *Emmeline* that took two hours to make the sixteen-mile jaunt from the Brunswick docks to Cumberland's north-end landing, near the site of Oglethorpe's Fort St. Andrews. In the early days of the hotels, the *Emmeline* and other steamers unloaded passengers into rowboats midriver to be brought ashore. To avoid this time-consuming and potentially hazardous procedure, the hotel proprietors erected a pier extending into the river where steamboats docked.

William Hunter Burbank Sr.

In 1915, William Hunter Burbank Sr. moved to Fernandina and started a net-making business. It's likely he learned the craft from Black and white fishermen on Cumberland who made casting nets for use in tidal creeks and seining nets to corral schools of fish along the beach shoreline. He and his sons developed superior, turtle-friendly trawling nets for the fishing industry. Their enterprise evolved into Burbank Sport Nets, a producer of sport-related products, including backstop netting used by college sports programs and found in many Major League Baseball stadiums across the country.

Local fishermen seining on Cumberland Island beach, 1898. (Courtesy of Georgia Archives, Lucy Coleman and Thomas M. Carnegie Family Papers, acc. 1994-0003m, 94-3m_VII_27)

North-end church and school for white children, ca. 1900. (Courtesy of the Cumberland Island National Seashore Museum NPS)

Passengers could now easily disembark into waiting carriages and later horse and mule-drawn trolleys that carried them on rails two miles through pine forest to the hotel. An additional mile of trolley tracks took guests from the hotel to the beach.

Another inn, a three-story edifice, opened on north-end property overlooking the Cumberland River. The proprietor, Marietta resident George W. Benson, intended it to be a religious colony. The colony never took root, but the house became a well-used hunting lodge from 1896 to about 1902. Local historian Mary Miller recounts that over time the house became dilapidated and "known as the haunted house of the island. The only evidence remaining today is a still flowing artesian well."

The 1860 census lists William R. Bunkley, born 1825, as a farmer. By 1870 he had become a lighthouse keeper, and by 1880 the census recorded his occupation as a hotel keeper. Like other islanders, Bunkley assumed many roles to support his family. His father, Thomas Pitt Bunkley, had married Rebecca Clubb, and William married Isabella Miller, a Downes family descendant. As a result, many of the north-end properties belonged to a small number of families. William Bunkley located his inn, Sea-Side House, on inherited land overlooking Christmas Creek midway between the river and the beach. The following excerpt praising Bunkley's hotel and Cumberland Island appeared in the April 20, 1877, edition of the *Macon Telegraph and Messenger*:

Undated photo of Cumberland Island's beach and dune system. (Courtesy of the Cumberland Island National Seashore Museum NPS)

The *Atlantic* was part of the "steamboat navy" that routinely plied the "Cumberland Route" between Jacksonville and Brunswick. (Courtesy of Bryan-Lang Archives)

Brunswick & Forida Steamboat Co.
Cumberland Route
Brunswick, Cumberland Island & Fernandina SCHEDULE

Leave Brunswick	8:30 a. m
Arrive Cumberland	10:45 a.m
Arrive Fernandina	1:15 p.m
Returning	
Leave Fernandina	2:45 p.m
Arrive Cumberland	5:15 p.m
Arrive Brunswick	7:30 p.m

J. B. WRIGHT, Mgr.

The Brunswick & Florida Steamboat Company regularly promoted the Cumberland Route, connecting Brunswick, Cumberland Island, and Fernandina on a daily basis. *Brunswick News*, November 18, 1910, p. 5. (Georgia Historic Newspapers, Digital Library of Georgia)

The steamer *Emmeline* transported passengers and goods daily between Brunswick, Cumberland Island, and Fernandina, about a two-hour journey between each stop. (Courtesy of the Cumberland Island National Seashore Museum NPS)

LANDING AT CUMBERLAND, GA.

Passengers disembarked from the *Emmeline* and other steamers onto this north-end pier. Note the trolley tracks used to transport passengers to the Cumberland Hotel. (Author's collection)

"Mr. Bunkley, resolved to do everything in his power for the entertainment and amusement of his [50] boarders, has also provided an ample billiard room, numerous sail and row boats, a ten pin [bowling] alley (not quite completed), saddle horses and buggies, [hunting] dogs, fishing tackle, guides and all other essentials to their comfort and happiness. His table is well supplied with choice fish, oysters, clams, venison, birds, honey, sweet milk, fresh butter, green peas, celery, beets, new Irish potatoes and other delicacies. Georgians cannot do better than come hither for rest and recreation from the consuming cares of business. From personal experience we can assure them that Cumberland Island is a panacea for a very large number of the ills of frail mortality."

In 1881 Bunkley leased the Sea-Side House for five years to Edgar Alfred Ross, a Macon native. Ross moved his family to Cumberland in 1881 to run the hotel. Years later, his daughter, Mary Hermione, recalled that the inn consisted of an eight-room house with a new wing "over the big dining room" and cottages that slept four in each room, though

The Cumberland Island Hotel, Cumberland, Ga.

Horse- and mule-pulled trolleys carried passengers from the boat landing to the hotel and from the Cumberland Island Hotel to the beach. (Courtesy of Bryan-Lang Archives)

The Cumberland Hotel. (Author's collection)

Cumberland Island Hotel, Cumberland Island, Ga.

This colorized image of the Cumberland Hotel displays men with fishing gear and the day's catch. A mule stands nearby ready to pull a baggage trolley. (Author's collection)

"PAVILION" CUMBERLAND ISL. GA.

One reporter for the *Macon Telegraph* (July 14, 1894) wrote that "the pavilion overlooking the water at night is a scene of beauty, filled with beautiful women and handsome men, dancing to the sweet strains of music." (Author's collection)

The pavilion as seen from the Cumberland Hotel. Macon Row is visible on the left. (Courtesy of the Cumberland Island National Seashore Museum NPS)

"men put cots out and slept under the trees." Ross added bathhouses, a wooden tram railroad to the beach, and a pavilion with a dance floor covered by a palmetto thatch roof, inspired by the thatched roofs his wife, Ann, saw at the Brickhill settlement.

Ross posted advertisements for Sea-Side House in Georgia papers, including one in the July 15, 1881, *Georgia Weekly Telegraph* (Macon) that stated his hotel rates were "$1.50 per day, $9 per week, $30 per month. Children and servants half price. Train leaves Macon 7:30 p.m. and arrives in Brunswick about 6 o'clock a.m.; breakfast at Oglethorpe Hotel, thirty yards from wharf; boat leaves at 7 o'clock a.m.; arrives at Cumberland Island at 9 o'clock a.m. Cheap rates from Macon to the Island and return. Free transportation from

Grant Visits Cumberland

In early January 1880, a distinguished visitor made a brief visit to Cumberland Island. Former president Ulysses S. Grant stopped there during a successful tour of Florida, accompanied by Gen. Philip Sheridan. *Harper's Weekly* informed readers in its February 7 issue that one of Grant's first stops in the state had been Fernandina, where he was well received by Blacks and whites alike. "After the reception," the magazine reported, "the party, with a large company of invited guests, visited the ruined Dungeness estate on Cumberland Island—a place once famous for its cotton staple and the baronial splendor of its hospitality. An hour or so was spent in wandering among the avenues cut through the moss-draped forest of live oaks. An incident of the occasion was the visit of the General to the little woodland [cemetery], a short distance from the ruin, where General Henry Lee ('Light-horse Harry Lee,' of Revolutionary fame), the father of the great Confederate chieftain, lies buried."

Harper's Weekly image of Grant coming ashore on Cumberland. (Courtesy of the Cumberland Island National Seashore Museum NPS)

In January 1880, former President Ulysses S. Grant visited Dungeness, "where he was well received by Blacks and whites alike," according to *Harper's Weekly*.

At Dungeness, near Fernandina.
visited with Gen U. S. Grant. Gen Sheridan
and party in 1880
Frank H. Taylor

"Ruin of home
of Light-Horse Harry Lee,"

Taylor

"Dungeness" Grave of "Light Horse Harry Lee"
Cumberland Isld. ga.

visited, Dec. 1880 with Gen U. S. Grant and Gen P H Sheridan.

F H Taylor

A wash titled "Dungeness, Grave of 'Light Horse Harry' Lee,
Cumberland Isld. ga." by Frank H. Taylor, artist and publisher who
accompanied President Grant (and Gen. Philip Henry Sheridan) on
his December 1880 tour, which included a visit to Fernandina and
Dungeness on Cumberland Island. (Courtesy of the Cumberland
Island National Seashore Museum NPS)

Beachgoers on Cumberland Island, early 1900s. (Courtesy of the Cumberland Island National Seashore Museum NPS)

the landing to the [Sea-Side] House. Tramway from hotel to the beach." The tram ride to the beach cost a small fee, which paid for its construction cost. Hermione Ross described the tram as a "rural street car pulled by a gray mule whose name is 'Whoa Emma.' Suspended from a cross piece is a hunter's horn. About five o'clock in the morning this horn is sounded and everyone hurries to the car. After it is loaded to full capacity, old Emma starts for the beach."

This description of the hotel appeared in an 1882 newspaper: "The hotel is an old-fashioned rambling building with little cottages built all about to accommodate the summer guests. In the front yard are gray old olive trees, and near the house is a grove of bananas larger than any others in the United States."

Repeated storm damage to the pavilion and the boat landing, along with nonpaying guests and relatives invited by Ross, put him in too much debt to continue. After he and his family returned to Macon in 1883, William Bunkley turned over management of Sea-Side House to his son, William H. Bunkley. The younger Bunkley made improvements to the hotel, including a "two-story building with 12 to 15 large rooms, and a double colonnade on all sides, and a dining hall 40 x 60 feet with a seating capacity for 300 guests."

The "new and improved" Sea-Side House opened for its 1884 summer season on April 20. Boarding rates had increased to "$2 per day, $10 per week," with special rates for families. The "safe, commodious and fast sailing Steam Yacht Egmont" shuttled guests to and from Brunswick. Like Ross, Bunkley negotiated special excursion rates with the East Tennessee, Virginia, and Georgia (ETV&G) and Brunswick & Western Railroads.

One traveler aboard the *Egmont* marveled at the abundance of fish as the boat steamed through St. Andrews Sound: "There were two shoal of mullet—one half a mile long and 200 yards wide, and the other a quarter of a mile long and 100 yards wide. The steamer passed right through them, and the fireman killed several with his boat hook. Scores of porpoises were on hand, having a high carnival and making the water fairly boil. There must have been fish enough in those two shoals to have given every man, woman and child in Georgia a square meal." Arriving at Sea-Side House, the writer met guests from Macon, Atlanta, LaGrange, Albany, Perry, Milledgeville, and Brunswick.

Bunkley displayed his marketing acumen in an 1884 Georgia newspaper ad that extolled the virtues of Cumberland Island, "The Gem Of The Atlantic." He wrote: "To the business man whose mind and brain needs rest, and to the invalid, dyspeptic, asthmatic and nervous sufferers there is no place like Cumberland with the bracing salt air, surf bathing, boating, fishing, shooting and all out-door sports. We have here the finest beach in the world, extending to the grand old Dungeness 22 miles and lined with beautiful shells of every description and forming the handsomest drive on the American coast. A tram railway takes visitors from the hotel to the bath houses on the beach for one nickel. Ample conveyances with good drivers meet the boats daily at the landing. Mr. A. T. Putnam, of Brunswick, has moved over his hacks, buggies, and spring wagons for this purpose. P.S.—Bunkley post-office is a new office just established in the hotel." About this time the hotel name changed to the Hotel Cumberland or Cumberland Island Hotel.

Bunkley continued to upgrade hotel facilities, adding cottages and a new pavilion and, in agreement with the Bensons, laying a rail track for horse-drawn trolleys from the boat landing, across Benson property, to the hotel and on to the beach. He hired an "Italian band" to play for guests during the 1885 season, replacing his fiddle player, W. W. Wallace, a hotel carpenter who had previously played the dance tunes. And he kept the hotel operating during the winter to attract hunters and fishing parties. He ran an ad in 1890 announcing "30 New Rooms Added since last season. Artesian Well, Shower Baths and everything that is necessary for the ease and comfort of guests." Despite the improvements and year-round service, the hotel continued to lose money. Guests still paid the same $2 per day as they had in 1884. The weekly rate of $10.50 had increased only fifty cents over six years. The stagnant rates perhaps reflect increasing competition from beach hotels on St. Simons, Tybee, and other barrier islands. The St. Simons Hotel in 1892 advertised competitive rooms for $10 per week, "Everything First-Class, Satisfaction Guaranteed. Special rates $2.50 from Saturday Night till Monday Morning, including Two Lodgings and Three meals."

In 1890 William R. Bunkley sold the hotel and outbuildings along with a thousand acres of land and six hundred acres of marsh to a Middle Georgia firm, the Macon Company, for $75,000. He reserved thirty acres of the Bunkley property for his family's use. The company paid half of the purchase price in cash and agreed to pay the balance in $2,500 annual installments. The Macon Company poured more money into renovating the boat landing and expanding the hotel's capacity to five hundred patrons. The company hired Lee Shackleford to manage the hotel, a position he held for years. But within four years, when the Macon Company was unable to pay creditors in 1894, another group of Macon investors, who formed the Cumberland Company, purchased the hotel for $12,000.

Local state militias, including the Albany Guards, the Fifth Regiment of the National Guard of Georgia, and the Macon Volunteers, made annual trips to the island. The Macon militia (formed in 1825, now a National Guard unit) enjoyed a long-standing tradition of making camp twice a year on Cumberland long before the advent of hotels there, "one for instruction and the other for fun." In early July 1879 they camped on the island for the seventy-second time, taking with them "a large cooking range, thirty-five bags of tents, barrel after barrel of crockery, ropes and cooking utensils, boxing gloves and other gymnasium apparatus, washstands, mirrors, tubs, a small chest with heavy hinges and locks, well-stocked with medicine. You see," said Captain Hunter, one of the Volunteers, "Cumberland Island is somewhat infested with venomous reptiles." The *Macon Telegraph* reported, "At least one hundred Maconites will accompany the Volunteers, including, of course, a great many young ladies as brass buttons are said to be irresistible attractions for the fair sex."

A tragedy marred one of their outings four years earlier when lightning killed John W. Burke Jr., a Macon Volunteer corporal. The *Athens Weekly Banner* informed readers that "he was standing in his tent dressing for a dinner that was to be given by the ladies at the hotel today complimentary to the Volunteers, when lightning struck the pole at

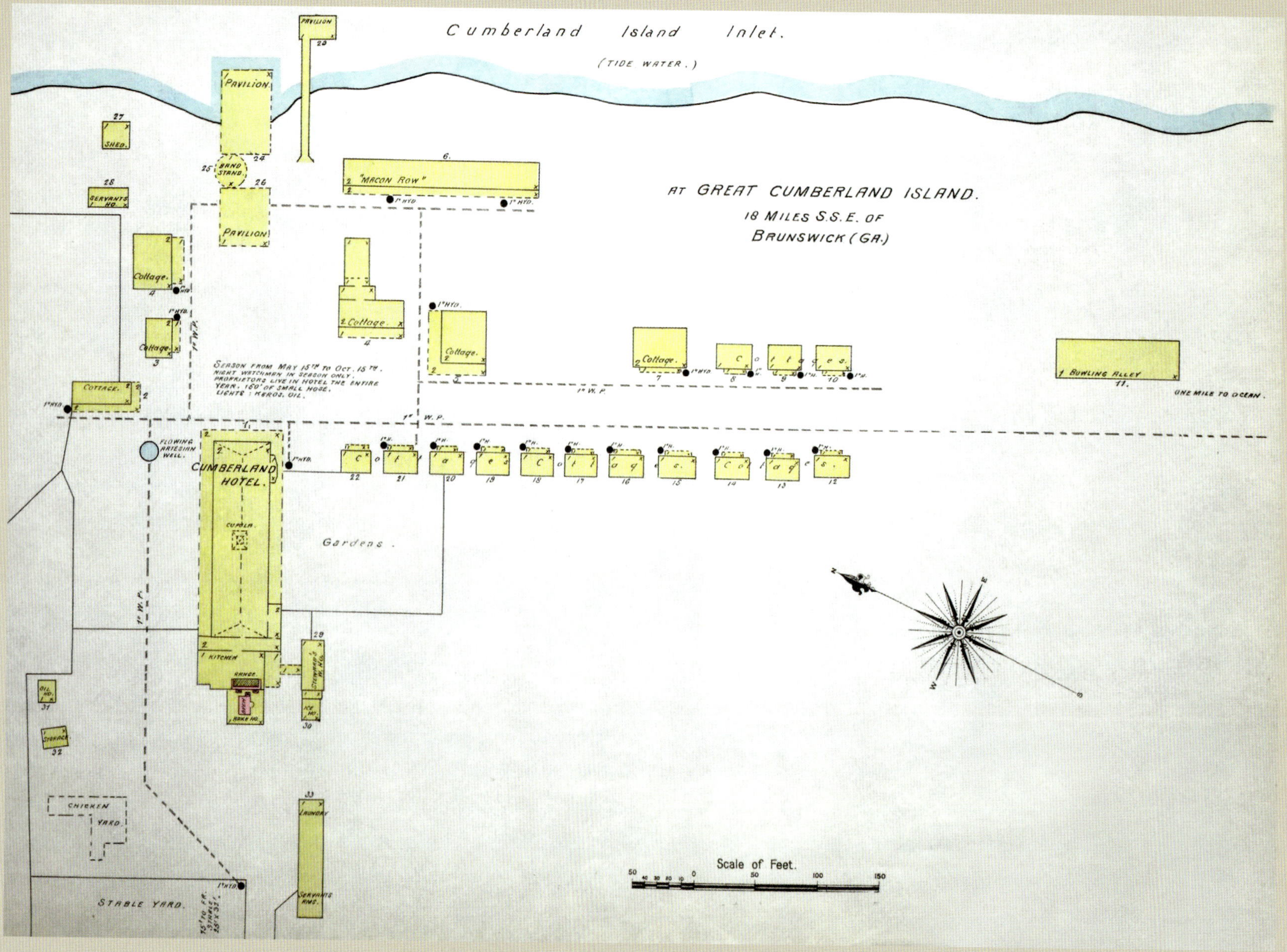

Cumberland Island Inlet.

(TIDE WATER.)

AT GREAT CUMBERLAND ISLAND.
18 MILES S.S.E. OF
BRUNSWICK (GA.)

PAVILION
23

PAVILION

27
SHED.

25
BAND
STAND
24
26

PAVILION

28
SERVANTS
HO.

6.
"MACON ROW"

2
Cottage.
2

1"HYD.
1"HYD.

1 Cottage. X
Cottage.
3

Cottage.

2
Cottage. X
2

1 Cottage. X

Cottage.
7

C o t t a g e s.
8   9   10

1 Bowling Alley X
11.

ONE MILE TO OCEAN.

SEASON FROM MAY 15TH TO OCT. 15TH.
NIGHT WATCHMEN IN SEASON ONLY.
PROPRIETORS LIVE IN HOTEL THE ENTIRE
YEAR. 150' OF SMALL HOSE.
LIGHTS: KEROS. OIL.

1"HYD.

Cottage.
2

1" W.P.

1" W.P.

1" W.P.

1
FLOWING
ARTESIAN
WELL.

1"HYD.

CUMBERLAND
HOTEL.

C o t t a g e s.   C o t t a g e s.   C o t t a g e s.
22   21   20   19   18   17   16   15   14   13   12

CUPOLA.

Gardens.

N
S
E
W

OIL
HO.
31

STORAGE
32

1 KITCHEN X
RANGE
1 BAKE HO.

28
Cistern
W.H.O.

ICE
HO.
30

33
LAUNDRY

CHICKEN
YARD

Scale of Feet.
50 40 30 20 10   0   50   100   150

STABLE YARD.

SERVANTS
RMS.

This montage of Sanborn Fire Insurance maps displays the layout of
the Cumberland Hotel structures in 1893. The bowling alley lies to the
right (east) of the cottages. (Courtesy of the University of Georgia,
Digital Library of Georgia)

the opening of the tent, tore off his shoes and threw him rolling out of the tent. His companions rushed to him at once but found his heart still in death. The ladies were to give the company a special dinner. The table had been decorated for the occasion, but the flowers were transferred to the body of the young officer whose death is so deeply mourned by every one who knew him."

By the mid-1890s, Cumberland's north end had become a leading destination in Georgia, the "It" place to be during summer months. A series of cottages referred to as Atlanta Row and a two-story building dubbed Macon Row housed the many regulars from Atlanta and Macon. The *Macon Telegraph* reported on July 14, 1894, that four hundred people were staying at the Cumberland Island Hotel, "The Leading Southern Resort." The article stated, "Cumberland is quite the rage now. Larger crowds are going to this delightful resort than ever before. Parties from Macon, Forsyth, Griffin, and Chattanooga are expected the first of next week. The pavilion overlooking the water at night is a scene of beauty, filled with beautiful women and handsome men, dancing to the sweet strains of music. Many society belles and beaux from all parts of Georgia and other states are among the guests now. If you want a real jolly time, come to Cumberland."

The *Brunswick Times* reported on June 15, 1897, that "Loveland's orchestra gave an elegant concert" at the Cumberland Island Hotel. "The clarinet solo, rendered by Mr. Dan Mack, was one of the finest numbers on the program and was applauded to the echo." The paper went on to describe highly anticipated races scheduled for July 3, a Saturday. "The principal trotting event will be in three heats, one-half mile each, best two of three, for a purse of $50. The running race will be under the same conditions and for the same amount." Bicycle races were arranged by J. A. Montgomery of the Brunswick Cycle Company, with "handsome prizes" for the winners. The final race featured one hundred potatoes "placed at equidistant intervals in a straight line, with a basket at the end." Six African American youngsters were to participate in the race, with the grand prize, a suit of clothes, "awarded the one who puts the largest number of potatoes in the basket." Advertisements in the same paper the following month let readers know that a boat would "stay over until 10 o'clock" on Sunday night for those remaining late to see a military dress parade and "sacred" concert.

Civic groups representing firemen, physicians, dentists, textile producers, agriculturalists, and various fishing and hunting clubs held annual meetings on the island. Among their number were the Great Council of Georgia Improved Order of Red Men, the Americus Fishing Club, the Georgia Agricultural Society, the County Ordinaries'

Hotel Guests

The hotels on Cumberland's north end attracted honeymooners, invalids, and return visitors for years, many of whom announced their pending or just-completed excursions to the island in local papers. Announcements like the following were common.

"August 16, 1887. Messrs F. H. Kroner and Tobe Clark, who have been spending July on Cumberland, have returned. They report a most delightful trip beyond description. Mr. Kroner is much improved in health, while Mr. Clark, making a very hasty calculation, gained 12 pounds."—*Weekly Banner-Watchman*

"August 18, 1895. Mr. George H. Slappey, one of Fort Valley's society young men, is spending a while at Cumberland Island. Mr. Slappey has been suffering with brown fever, and his many friends in the city hope that the trip may benefit him."—*Macon Telegraph*

"July 20, 1909. Mrs. H. D. Capers, who has been absent for ten days at Cumberland Island, had returned to her home, 234 Peachtree-st."—*Atlanta Georgian and News*

Association, the Rome Fire Department, the Georgia Medical Association, the Georgia State Dental Association, and the Georgia Industrial Association. The civic organization that most consistently held meetings on Cumberland Island may have been the Georgia Teachers' Association (now the Georgia Association of Educators). They met at the Oglethorpe Hotel in Brunswick April 29 through May 1, 1891, to select a permanent location for their annual meetings. The two sites under consideration were Cumberland Island and St. Simons Island. Companies representing hotels on both islands submitted proposals. The Cumberland Island Hotel won, and the teachers gathered there annually over the next twenty years. They even constructed a large auditorium near the hotel for their use. The business was good for the island and for the railroads that transported the teachers to the yearly assembly. An 1895 railroad circular promised a "one fare rate" good for "one limited first-class fare for the round trip from all points in the state." It advised attendees to reach Brunswick the morning of June 25, as "all trains running into Brunswick reach there early in the morning or late in the afternoon. There is no boat which runs from Brunswick to Cumberland Island in the afternoon, hence it is desirable to reach Brunswick in the morning."

The *Macon Telegraph* reported over six hundred "Pedagogues" converged on Cumberland on June 26, 1895. "The hotel and cottages are crowded to the utmost limit. Its accommodations are strained, cots and mattresses being luxuries" with some "occupying cots in the corridors," but "everybody is in good humor and the hotel manager is praised for the way he is taking care of the unprecedented rush." The Georgia Teachers' Association even brought an orchestra from the Georgia Female Conservatory of Music to entertain them.

The years 1897–98 provide a snapshot of the vicissitudes the Cumberland Island Hotel Company faced maintaining its barrier island operation over the years. In January 1897 a new steamboat, the *Governor Safford* (named for Florida resident and former Arizona Governor Anson P. K. Safford) capable of carrying "600 passengers with ease and comfort," began to ply the waters on the Cumberland Route between Brunswick, Jekyll, Cumberland, and Fernandina, which drew some guests to other locales. For the first time in years, the inn's biggest and most dependable customer, the Georgia Teachers' Association, shifted its annual meeting to Warm Springs in an effort to attract more rural schoolteachers. The hotel company then reported having to "build an immense dam across the inlet in order to preserve our property." The company fell behind on a mortgage payment, and the Bunkley family took them to court over the matter. The *Athens Daily Banner* reported on September 25 that the Cumberland Island Hotel had been destroyed by fire due to a lightning strike but provided no further details. The following September, one of the strongest hurricanes on record made landfall on Cumberland Island, packing winds estimated at 135 mph. Brunswick recorded a sixteen-foot storm surge (high-water marks from that 1898 flood are still visible on some downtown buildings), and Fernandina reported a twelve-foot tidal surge. Most of the docks between Amelia and Darien were either damaged or destroyed. Newspapers reported 120 area lives lost, 108 of which were African Americans. Eight people died on a vessel that wrecked off the St. Andrews bar. The *Vienna Progress* newspaper reported that "Mrs. Lucy Carnegie's steam yacht Dungeness was washed upon the bluff and badly damaged. The Carnegie mansion at Dungeness apparently had been under water some feet." Total estimated property loss—rice fields, stock, cattle, and structures—from Darien to Cumberland Island was estimated at $1 million.

"The Hotel Cumberland property was damaged $5,000," one paper reported. "Macon row was completely ruined. The seas washed the underpinning away and wrecked it all. The pavilion was washed up on the railroad [trolley] track. Atlanta row was unroofed and undermined. The main hotel building's cupola is gone and portions of the roof. The steamboat dock had nothing left but the piling. The main bluff at High Point, Cumberland, is washed away from one hundred to one hundred and fifty feet back into the mainland." Forty workers on Cumberland made repairs to the hotel, cottages, the bathhouse, and built a new wharf. The hotel reopened in 1890 with thirty new rooms. Despite the outflow of money to repair the hotel, the going rate remained at $2 per day, $10.50 per week, and $30 per month for guests. The hurricane's destruction forced the *Governor Safford* to relocate farther north, where it could service customers at wharves that hadn't been damaged by the storm. As a fitting bookend to this topsy-turvy two-year period, the Georgia Teachers' Association resumed its annual meeting on Cumberland.

Travelogues about Cumberland, as in this quotation from an 1895 guide, touted the island's climate: "During the summer months the heat is always tempered by a delightful sea breeze, which keeps the atmosphere as delightfully cool as at any mountain resort, at the same time driving away disagreeable insects. It has been truthfully said that the ozone [agreeable, fresh air] of mountaintop, the balsam of the fir trees and the healing of the sea are all combined in the superb climate of Cumberland. Here is the finest beach in the world, and the guests of Hotel Cumberland thoroughly enjoy the surf and take a dip in the old ocean twice a day." Living in less ecologically minded times, the writer lists the many amusements awaiting guests, chief among them turtle hunting at night, when the turtles were on the beach to dig nests or lay eggs. Turning the creatures on their backs to

Lee Interment

The Georgia Society of the City of New York, a club for Georgia expatriates (male and female) living in or around New York City, met at the Fifth Avenue Hotel on April 26, 1907. One member, T. Smith Cuyler, put forth a resolution to "co-operate with the Southern Society of New York City and other Southern societies to have the body of General ['Light-Horse Harry'] Lee removed from the grave at Dungeness on Cumberland Island to some place in Virginia." The resolution was unanimously adopted. Six years later, Lee's remains were disinterred from the Greene Cemetery at Dungeness and reburied next to the grave of his son, Robert E. Lee, at Washington and Lee University in Lexington, Kentucky.

immobilize them was considered great fun. One group of zealous state militiamen overturned seven turtles in one evening. Another party raided eighteen turtle nests between Dungeness and the bathhouse of the Cumberland Island Hotel, taking 628 eggs. "It was best to leave some eggs for a similar sport next summer," they concluded.

William Alberty and Charles Trimmings, who lived at the Settlement, were experienced fishing guides, frequently taking hotel guests to Christmas Creek. Guests could use sailboats, rowboats, or "a commodious nap[h]tha launch," a long boat usually covered with a canvas and powered by naphtha. Many anglers headed for the hotel's ark, "a boat-shaped floating platform covered with canvas to keep off the sun, and situated in the inlet where gamey fish are most abundant and bite best. Beautiful specimens of trout, sheephead, bass, and croakers were pulled in almost as fast as the hooks were baited and thrown in." Anglers brought the day's catch, including crabs, to the hotel kitchen for the guests to enjoy.

Other favored pastimes included shooting sea gulls, blue heron, white crane, and alligators. "A fresh water lake about a mile and a half from the hotel abounds in alligators," the article read, "some of them quite large. A few days ago a party visited this lake and returned in triumphal procession bearing an alligator nearly seven feet long."

The African Americans living in the Settlement were an integral part of the hotel machinery on Cumberland's north end, tending to the white guests' every need. An October 23, 1907, article in the *Atlanta Georgian* about the two fishing guides mentioned earlier sheds light on the important roles Blacks played in attracting and keeping customers. "Two Fishermen Guest Of Mayor," reads the headline. "Charles Trimmings and William Alberty, two distinguished residents of Cumberland Island, well known and universally popular over the state, are the guests for several days of Mayor W. R. Joyner and of Chief W. B. Cummings, of the Atlanta Fire Department." The mayor stated that Alberty and Trimmings "have been fishermen at Cumberland Island since three years after the [Civil] war. They have never left the island except once or twice, when they came to Atlanta. Were it not for them, I would not go to Cumberland Island, and I have been going nearly every year since I can remember. I told them whenever they came to Atlanta I would be ready to receive them. Here they are in my office and I don't mind telling anybody I am proud to have them." The mayor gave both men passes to a fair and sent them to his home, "where they may enjoy city cooking." Their visit took place during the Jim Crow era, so, while both men dined at the mayor's Atlanta residence, they did so with his servants. Their sleeping quarters were "apartments at the fire department, Chief Cummings having provided them suitable places to spend the nights."

A 1908 newspaper advertisement placed by L. A. Miller, a Bunkley cousin who leased the Cumberland Hotel from 1902 to 1910, touted Cumberland's "miles upon miles of delightful roads for driving." Miller's ad continued the tradition of promoting the facility as a health resort, "a veritable sanitarium in effect. The invigorating tonic salt sea breeze, the cool delightful weather and the wonderful mineral qualities of the artesian water are remarkably effective in the restoration of perfect, lasting health." Whereas Bunkley had dubbed Cumberland "The Gem Of The Atlantic," Miller called it the "pearl of the Atlantic coast. Here you will enjoy the finest surf bathing in America, a splendid beach 22 miles long, where there is no danger from undertow. The opportunities for the boatman are unequalled, and there are streams threading the island which constitute a veritable angler's paradise. The sea breezes here are a medicine in themselves, which never fail to make one wake to a day wherein the sheer glory of life throbs through every fiber of the being." Miller outdid himself in another ad a year later, claiming Cumberland's mineral waters were "famous throughout the country for the effectiveness of its cures in cases of dyspepsia and indigestion."

Despite Miller's assurance of "no danger from undertow," drownings and near-drownings did occur due to the undertow. J. L. McNinch of Atlanta almost drowned on Cumberland in June 1907, "caught by the undertow and carried out to sea," according to the *Atlanta Georgian and News*. Another vacationer, W. R. Sassnett, also of Atlanta, "noticed a dark object floating on the surface. He swam out to it and discovered that it was McNinch. The drowning man was unconscious and almost dead. Sassnett's cries for help were heard and McNinch was carried ashore where he was revived after an hour of hard work."Another Atlantan, William Sims, rescued three sea bathers on June 24, 1911, while he and friends from Brunswick and Atlanta picnicked on Cumberland's north-end beach. The *Atlanta Georgian and News* recounted that Sims made "three trips into a choppy sea off the beach at Cumberland Island and each time bringing to the shore an exhausted bather who had been borne into deep water by the swiftly running tide." One of the victims was Fay Petty, the thirteen-year-old daughter of an Atlanta realtor. The other two were "Miss Margaret Bridge of Brunswick, and a Mr. McCaray of Brunswick [who] were caught in the tow and carried beyond their depth. Their shouts for help attracted Sims's attention and while not an expert swimmer, he gallantly went to their rescue. His rescue of Miss Petty was the most daring of the three. Spent from

his previous exertions, Sims's battle with the sea and tide to reach the little girl, who had gone down twice, and drag her thru the combers to a place of safety, was a bit of stubborn courage such as is seldom seen." Several members of Sims's party "are making an effort to have the exploit brought before the Carnegie medal commission."

Andrew Carnegie established the Carnegie Hero Fund in 1904 to "recognize persons who perform acts of heroism in civilian life in the United States and Canada, and to provide financial assistance for those disabled and the dependents of those killed helping others." Since its inception, more than ten thousand Carnegie medals have been awarded from eighty-nine thousand nominees. However, Sims's daring-do did not rise to the level of heroism worthy of a Carnegie Medal that year.

The hotel changed hands several times during the final two decades of its existence as various owners tried to keep it solvent. However, a new railroad line began to carry passengers directly from Brunswick to Florida, doing away with the need for boat transportation between the two points. Steamers on the Cumberland Route found it increasingly difficult to remain profitable with freight and passenger service moving to rail, spelling the demise of hotel activity on the island. New Florida resorts promising exotic attractions beckoned tourists farther south by rail. Some coastal vacation spots, like Tybee Island and St. Simons, laid causeways that connected them to the mainland, ensuring a continued flow of customers by automobile.

The Bunkley family acquired the hotel once again in 1901 and held it until 1918, when it was purchased by Walter T. Johnstone, a Bibb County resident. Johnstone died in 1919, and a year later the hotel was back in R. L. Bunkley's possession. He sold it in 1920 to the Cumberland Island Club, a group of Brunswick residents who turned it into a private lodge offering hunting, golfing, and fishing for members. The charter's by-laws restricted hunters to one deer and one turkey per season and duck hunting to "two days of each week on Club property." A number of Atlantans joined the club, including Charles Howard Candler, president of the Coca-Cola Company, son of Coca-Cola founder Asa Candler. Candler purchased multiple memberships, and when the club faced financial difficulties in the late 1920s, exacerbated by the Great Depression, he offered to sell his membership shares to the remaining stockholders or purchase their shares. The other members agreed to sell. By the late 1930s, Candler had acquired all of the hotel property and much of the High Point acreage once owned by the Benson, Burbank, Fader, and Stockwell families.

At the same time that hotels took hold on Cumberland's north end, events were unfolding on the island's south end that continue to impact the island's history to this day.

CHAPTER IX   The Carnegies and the National Seashore

BOUT THE SAME TIME Ulysses S. Grant visited Cumberland Island in 1880 (see chapter 8 sidebar), Confederate general William George Mackay Davis purchased Dungeness from Molyneux family heirs, who had acquired the property from Phineas Nightingale. Davis planned to build an inn at Dungeness or lease the land to investors interested in building a hotel on the site. But he was not the first to consider doing so at that location. There was Phineas Nightingale's unfulfilled plan to make Dungeness a hotel in 1869, and in addition the *Savannah Morning News* reported on January 22, 1877, that an A. W. J. Warrenton purchased land near Dungeness House to "erect a fine hotel at or near the old site known as Dungeness on that beautiful island."

Davis, a cousin of Confederate president Jefferson Davis, had retired from a successful law practice in Washington, D.C., and returned to his home state of Florida. In early March 1880, the day after Davis moved from Fernandina to Cumberland to oversee his new purchase, his son, Bernard M. Davis, accidentally shot his own five-year-old son while loading a gun at his island home. The *Savannah Morning News* reported the younger Davis "got down his breech loader and standing in the door

Confederate Brigadier-General William George Mackay Davis (1812–98). Davis practiced law in Washington, D.C., after the Civil War. (Wikimedia Commons)

proceeded to put in a couple of cartridges when, in adjusting the barrel, by some means the charge of one barrel was exploded, the load striking the little boy in the right arm and penetrating the lung." After this tragedy, General Davis contemplated selling Dungeness. A buyer stood in the wings.

The interested party wasn't just anyone. As a young woman, Lucy Ackerman Coleman Carnegie had attended a boarding school in Fernandina and no doubt had heard about Dungeness then. Her curiosity about Cumberland Island is thought to have been piqued many years later by naturalist Frederick Albion Ober's 1880 article titled "Dungeness, General Greene's Sea-Island Plantation." The author had visited Cumberland in November 1879 and again the following April and August. The Carnegies and Ober may have even met as hotel guests at Fernandina. Now the wife of Thomas Carnegie, Lucy was so taken by Ober's description of the island that she encouraged her husband to purchase Dungeness and a large part of Cumberland.

Like many wealthy northerners, the Carnegies were seeking a seasonal home to escape harsh northern winters, a place to get away from the smoke and grime of industrialized Pittsburgh, dubbed at various times Smoke City and Hell with the Lid Off. Ober's article praised Cumberland's climate as "temperate and healthy: many of the former slaves live to a great age." Gallea Pollakov "Polly" Stein Carnegie, who married one of Lucy's grandsons, Carter Carnegie, recounted in a 1979 National Park Service interview that Lucy, an accomplished sailor, had stopped at Fernandina for supplies while sailing down the coast to Florida. "While the boat was being serviced she had her small launch take her over to Cumberland Island. Some of the natives took her over, she went through the island, came back home to Pittsburgh and told her husband about it, and talked about it so incessantly that he bought if for her for a birthday present."

Books abound about Lucy's brother-in-law, Andrew Carnegie, the founder of Carnegie Steel Company, but relatively little has been written about his younger brother, Thomas. Both were born in Dunfermline, Scotland, just north of Edinburgh. Their father, a master hand weaver, lost his livelihood to a new technology, automated weaving looms, and relocated the family to the Pittsburgh area in 1848. Thomas's older brother, Andrew, made enough money investing in stocks to buy a new home for the family, but smog and soot from the nearby forges and factories forced the family to move to a suburb. The brothers entered the iron business, founding the Carnegie Brothers Ironworks, and were well positioned to meet the burgeoning demand for iron and steel during the Civil War. They made their fortunes in the postwar years supplying the nation's booming cities and

Fernandina dock and Center Street, 1888.
(Courtesy of the Cumberland Island National
Seashore Museum NPS)

Lucy Carnegie and Frederick Albion Ober may
have met as guests at a hotel similar to this one
in Fernandina. (Courtesy of the Cumberland
Island National Seashore Museum NPS)

Brothers Thomas and Andrew Carnegie in 1851. (Courtesy of Project Gutenberg)

expanding railroad networks with iron and steel. As one newspaper editor wrote, "their fortune is immense, and it is so disposed that is grows with the growth of the country." Andrew relied on Thomas's business acumen to manage the conglomeration of iron and steel plants and related financial operations.

Thomas Carnegie courted Lucy in 1864 while the Civil War raged. They married in 1866 when she was twenty. Andrew Carnegie presented the newlyweds with his former home as a wedding gift. Lucy's father, William Coleman, an iron manufacturer, mentored Thomas, offering advice for improving mill production and entering emerging markets such as railroads. Thomas oversaw the construction and operation of a new seventy-five-foot-tall blast furnace, named the Lucy Furnace after his wife, capable of producing almost three hundred tons of pig iron a day. Lucy was productive in her own right, giving birth to nine children between 1867 and 1881: William Coleman, Frank Morrison, Andrew II, Margaret, Thomas Morrison, George Lauder, Florence (Flossie) Nightingale, Coleman, and Nancy Trovillo.

William Davis replied to Thomas Carnegie's offer to purchase Dungeness for $25,000: "I have not the remotest idea of selling at any such price." Claiming that he had received "many enquiries" for the property, he counter-offered $40,000. Davis also had reservations about selling the property to a "Yankee." A few months after that exchange, Bernard Davis died and was buried next to his son in the Greene Cemetery. With the deaths of his son and grandson, the grief-stricken old general was ready to sell his 1,891-acre tract and move off the island. He lowered the asking price in 1881 to $35,000, which Carnegie accepted, instructing Davis to "Please make deed to my wife, Mrs. Lucy C. Carnegie." Thomas graciously agreed to allow Davis to visit his son and grandson's graves at any time. "I hope to have the pleasure of seeing you frequently at Dungeness after the old house has been rebuilt," he wrote. "Should anyone of your family wish to occupy the premises, I would be glad to have them do so."

At that time, the fire-damaged ruins of the Greene-Miller Dungeness home still loomed over the south end of Cumberland like a regal specter from a bygone era. *Harper's New Monthly Magazine* provided its readers with a romanticized perspective of the mansion and island in 1878, more than twelve years after the fire: "The exterior was stuccoed above the first story, the façade was adorned with six stone pilasters rising to the eaves, and the entrance faced with hewn granite, was approached by a flight of massive steps, which are now gone. The four towering chimneys suggest the comfort and good cheer for which Dungeness was celebrated when Mr. and Mrs. Miller there dispensed a

Lucy Carnegie, ca. 1882. (Courtesy of the Cumberland Island National Seashore Museum NPS, Mary Bullard Collection)

Thomas Carnegie at age thirty-one, 1875. (Courtesy of the Cumberland Island National Seashore Museum NPS, Mary Bullard Collection)

liberal hospitality. The place is so full of sentiment, of old-world romance and beauty, that one can hardly believe that what he is gazing on can be in the United States. Enough has been said to indicate the manifold attractions of Cumberland Island. It is destined to become before long a resort for artists, sportsmen, and tourists. Few spots as interesting are to be found in our country. But when the day shall come when the solitude of its forests and its ruins is broken by the inroad of visitors, it is to be hoped that they will respect the beauty, the picturesqueness, and the associations of Dungeness, and that the venerable pile may remain for ages untouched and unchanged by man. The curse of generations yet to be should fall on the head of him who first dares to desecrate and despoil Dungeness."

In 1882, along with his cousin, Leander Morris, Thomas Carnegie paid Robert Stafford's heirs $40,000 for the 8,240-acre Stafford property and Planters House. Overtaxed by stress—and, it was said, the burdens of working for his older brother, who was overly critical and a dogged micromanager—Thomas intended to retire and enjoy a tranquil life on Cumberland where he could restore Dungeness to its former glory. Instead of rebuilding the Greene mansion as some locals had hoped, they had the burned-out edifice pulled down. The Carnegies laid the cornerstone on February 26, 1884, for a two-story home on the site of General Greene's Dungeness. Some local residents and historians lamented the loss of the Greene ruins for years afterward. But there was not much of the old home to resurrect. One newspaper described "Dunginess" as "dismantled and despoiled by vandal treatment during the war, it is no longer tenantable; and its former lofty walls seem to have lost half their altitude."

Thomas hired Pittsburgh architect Andrew Peebles to design their Queen Anne Gothic winter home. Bullard writes the family might have sold blocks of tabby from the Greene mansion to the U.S. Army Corps of Engineers then working on the north and south jetties at the St. Marys River inlet. Much of the remaining crumbled tabby from the Greene's Dungeness House served as fill for island roads under construction. The new mansion went up in less than a year for $285,000 (more than $7 million in today's dollars).

One Georgia newspaper mistakenly reported in 1883 that Andrew—rather than Thomas—Carnegie had purchased "Dungeness Island." It went on to inform readers that "the new proprietor has spent much of this winter near Dungeness in his yacht [the *Wissoe*], and a force of architects and gardeners are already at work. The walls of the old Greene mansion are being destroyed, and a superb house will be built on its site. Every flower and fruit of the tropics will be planted, and thousands of acres will be

Greene-Miller Dungeness mansion ruins. (Courtesy of the Cumberland Island National Seashore Museum NPS)

Visitors on the south side (rear entrance) of the Greene-Miller mansion ruins. (Courtesy of the Cumberland Island National Seashore Museum NPS, Mary Bullard Collection)

Pierre Haven's photograph, south-side view of the first Carnegie Dungeness House built by Lucy and Thomas Carnegie, with the fountain in full force. (Courtesy of Bryan-Lang Archives)

Another view from the south side of the first Carnegie Dungeness House before the fountain was installed. (Courtesy of the Cumberland Island National Seashore Museum NPS)

Thomas and Lucy Carnegie's yacht, *Wissoe*, 1888. (Courtesy of Georgia Archives, Lucy Coleman and Thomas M. Carnegie Family Papers, acc. 1994-0003m, 94-3m_v32_23)

Rowing on Beach Creek at Dungeness. (Courtesy of Georgia Archives, Lucy Coleman and Thomas M. Carnegie Family Papers, acc. 1994-0003m, 94-3m_v32_20)

devoted to gardens and groves. The deer and game, already abundant on the estate, will be protected, and will in a few years furnish a preserve that a winter's shooting will make no impression on. The island will be largely devoted to stock raising. Mr. Carnegie having already purchased four or five hundred cattle and droves of marsh tackeys [horses] having been brought with the place." The "game" the paper mentioned included black bears, known to swim over to Cumberland from the mainland. Lucy's second son, Frank, killed a four-hundred-pound black bear near Dungeness in February 1887.

In the fall of 1886, while still working in Pittsburgh, Thomas Carnegie fell ill with a cold that developed into pneumonia. He died on October 19, one day shy of his forty-fourth birthday, and was buried in Pittsburgh. His mother, Margaret Carnegie, passed away a month later. One obituary read that "her end was hastened by the death of her son, Thomas." Thomas left everything to Lucy, including his shares of Carnegie Steel

Company. That same year, Lucy acquired Morris's interest in the Stafford property for $38,000. When Andrew Carnegie sold out to J. P. Morgan's syndicate in 1901, forming U.S. Steel Corporation, Lucy's payout totaled $6.2 million (more than $181 million in today's dollars). She continued to purchase Cumberland acreage until 90 percent of the south end of the island belonged to her.

From 1890 to 1905 Lucy hired Boston architects Peabody and Stearns to more than double the footprint of the family's winter home from 120 by 56 feet to 250 by 150 feet. The mansion took on enormous proportions, featuring wide, wraparound verandas, numerous turrets, and a hundred-foot tower. The August 11, 1897, morning edition of the *Brunswick Times* reported Lucy's improvements since 1890 totaled $100,000 (almost $3 million in today's dollars). A $5,000 veranda had been torn down and carted away, and most of the interior flooring was replaced with parquet, "various fine woods matched in a mosaic effect." The Fernandina contractor, James McGiffin (born in Ireland), reached out to local communities, including Brunswick, to secure construction workers to expedite the work. "The whims of the wealthy are most peculiar," the *Times* editor wrote. "Those who have been watching the transformation at Dungeness would not be at all surprised to hear that Mrs. Carnegie has ordered the monumental manor house with its towers and great pillars, entirely demolished and a new structure erected in its place." Building supplies, like granite for the exterior, Carrara marble from Tuscany used for bathroom washstands, and silver-plated fixtures, were "rafted" from Pittsburgh and from northern ports to the Dungeness wharf.

The May 7, 1904, *Town and Country* magazine informed its readers that "every year from the first of November to the first of May the Carnegie mansion, Dungeness, is astir with guests; for Mrs. Carnegie, who has an international reputation as a hostess, is fond of company. Her house parties are continuous from the time of her arrival at the island until the day of her departure. They average from thirty to one hundred persons at a time, and to those who are fortunate enough to be included in Mrs. Carnegie's visiting list to Cumberland Island, the days are made memorable."

The Carnegie children and grandchildren had the run of the island: swimming, boating, hiking, hunting, fishing, horseback riding. "Roping sea turtles to small wagons for races, dragging alligators out of the water, and baiting rattlesnakes were less approved excitements" (Dilsaver). "The island was a young boy's paradise," Thomas Carnegie IV recalled. "It welcomed everybody and rejected nobody. It was a private world, running on a timetable all its own. Though I was often alone on Cumberland Island, I was never lonely."

South-side view of the first Carnegie Dungeness House being remodeled and expanded, ca. 1896. (Courtesy of the Cumberland Island National Seashore Museum NPS)

From 1890 to 1905 Lucy paid Boston architects Peabody and Stearns to more than

Statue of the fleet-footed Roman god Mercury (messenger of the gods, god of financial gain, commerce, communication, and guide of souls to the underworld) in the Dungeness rose garden. (Courtesy of the Cumberland Island National Seashore Museum NPS, Mary Bullard Collection)

The original Dungeness statue of Mercury, sounding his salpinx, a trumpetlike instrument of the ancient Greeks. A replica now stands at Dungeness, while the original is in the Cumberland Island National Seashore Museum.

Lucy spared no expense building a large greenhouse and establishing vast, elaborate flower and vegetable gardens where Caty Greene's had once flourished. In her 1979 interview, Polly Carnegie recalls thinking that the house was surrounded by "a beautifully mown lawn, like an English garden."

Only white women, including those from European countries, served on Lucy's staff inside the new Dungeness House. She relied on New York agencies to supply house servants, and she paid for their travel to Georgia. Her staff in 1913 consisted of "three laundresses, one seamstress, one butler, three cooks, three chambermaids, and two waitresses" (Bullard). To help manage her Cumberland estate, Lucy Carnegie turned to her youngest son's tutor, twenty-nine-year-old William E. Page. "The first person that she brought on that I remember hearing about was a Mr. Page," Polly Carnegie recalled.

Lucy Carnegie and Graham Blandy. (Courtesy of Georgia Archives, Lucy Coleman and Thomas M. Carnegie Family Papers, acc. 1994-0003m, 94-3m_v31_11)

The visitors who made these footprints on this Cumberland sand dune are long gone. This undated and unattributed photograph inspired the title of this book. (Courtesy of Bryan-Lang Historical Archives)

"Now, the small house across from the remains of Dungeness is called the Grange, and that originally, I understand, was built as the home for Mr. and Mrs. Page. Mr. Page was a Harvard graduate, a very elegant gentleman, and he came and dined with her [Lucy] every night. I imagine that was when the business was talked about at Cumberland Island. He loved the place very much. In fact, he's buried in the family cemetery."

Page assumed management of Dungeness in 1891, overseeing more than two hundred employees (Black and white, men and women) and the estate's operations—lumber, cattle, cotton crops—designed to make the Carnegies' holdings on Cumberland self-sufficient and income producing. Thirty structures, each with a specific function, dotted the landscape. An combined ice house and boat house and a home for the Carnegie

The Main Road, also known as Grand Avenue, on Cumberland, undated. (Courtesy of Georgia Archives, Lucy Coleman and Thomas M. Carnegie Family Papers, acc. 1994-0003m, 94-3m_v10_21)

yacht skipper went up near Dungeness dock. Both still stand. The Recreation House near Dungeness contained a heated swimming pool, a squash court, a steam room, and guest rooms. Other structures included a dairy barn, carpentry shop, ice plant, steam laundry, carriage house and stables, an electrical power plant, separate dormitories and dining facilities for Black and white employees, a commissary, recreation hall, kennel, chicken houses, bakery, and separate houses for the gardener, the poultry manager, and the dairy manager. Page was, in effect, the city manager of a small town spread over 250 acres. Because of his position with the Carnegie family, Page's influence in the county was such that a request from him to relieve a key employee from jury duty would usually be granted.

The approach, facing south, to Dungeness Mansion. (Courtesy of the Cumberland Island National Seashore Museum NPS)

The Grange, 1906. Home of estate manager William E. Page and his wife. (Courtesy of the Cumberland Island National Seashore Museum NPS, Mary Bullard Collection)

Dungeness as seen from the water tower facing west, 1905. (Courtesy of the Cumberland Island National Seashore Museum NPS)

"Uncle Sam Green," coachman at Dungeness, ca. 1900. (Courtesy of the Cumberland Island National Seashore Museum NPS)

This carriage, stored for decades on the second floor of the Dungeness Carriage House, was restored in 2010. It is marked with the monogram of Louise Whitfield Carnegie, Andrew Carnegie's wife. Andrew spent the early part of 1906 at Dungeness working on his autobiography. The carriage is housed in the Cumberland Island National Seashore Museum, St. Marys. (Author photo)

This four-seater carriage sat high off the ground, appropriate for excursions around the island. (Author photo)

This two-seater "Piano Box" carriage was a popular model in the early 1900s. (Author photo)

The Dungeness recreation house, built ca. 1900, enclosed a heated swimming pool, a squash court, and a steam room, and had guest rooms. (Courtesy of the Cumberland Island National Seashore Museum NPS)

Indoor swimming pool at the recreation house, Dungeness. (Courtesy of the Cumberland Island National Seashore Museum NPS)

Carnegie employees pose with estate cattle. Revenue from island timber, cattle, and cotton sales helped defray operating

Dungeness's massive stables, ca. 1930. (Courtesy of Bryan-Lang Historical Archives)

Seventy Carnegie African American employees pose for the camera. Wearing his signature
top hat, coachman Sam Green is seated in the middle. (Courtesy of the Cumberland Island
National Seashore Museum NPS)

Stafford Lawsuits

In early January 1890, a "New York lawyer" came to Brunswick to represent Stafford children in a lawsuit against the Carnegies. "The original owner of this island was Robert Stafford, who married a mulatto woman and left six children," the *Athens Banner* reported. "They are claimants to the property." The attorney represented Robert Stafford's four living daughters, Mrs. Mary Palmer (London), Countess Ada Zivulki (Paris), Mrs. Medora Vosburgh (New York), and Mrs. Frederick P. Engels (Lynbrook, Long Island). The daughters claimed that the deed of sale for Stafford property acquired by the Carnegies "is clearly defective" and sought $2 million in damages. In 1907 two other plaintiffs filed a separate suit that sent a Savannah U.S. deputy marshall to subpoena Lucy Carnegie. Cornelia Stafford Williams and Nancy (Nanette) Stafford Gassman claimed to be daughters of Robert Stafford by another mistress of his (not Elizabeth [Zabette] Bernardey). Nancy Gassman, an accomplished woman in her own right, graduated in 1878 with a medical degree from Howard University Medical College in Washington, D.C., and joined the University of Zurich medical department. She and her sister hoped to prove that as Stafford's daughters they were eligible to inherit part of his wealth even though they were not named in his will. Neither this suit nor the one brought against Lucy Carnegie in 1890 bore fruit for the plaintiffs.

Dungeness employees relax in the Dungeness workmen's quarters. (Courtesy of the Cumberland Island National Seashore Museum NPS, Mary Bullard Collection)

Hog racing on Cumberland Island, ca. 1903. (Courtesy of the Cumberland Island National Seashore Museum NPS)

GAME RULES

The Estate of
Lucy C. Carnegie
Cumberland Island
Georgia

1 No game is to be hunted or shot from an automobile.
2 Only Turkey Gobblers shall be shot.
3 No shore birds, plover or any bird not classed as a game bird, or bear or alligators shall be shot.
4 Open season on duck is governed by the Federal Game Laws. (Closed season on wood or summer duck all year.)
5 Ashley Pond is a sanctuary for all game the year around.
6 No game is to be hunted at night with lights.
7 Guests will please observe the above rules and the following Federal and State bag limits.

Duck	15	daily limit
Turkey Gobblers	2	season limit
Deer	2	season limit

8 Guests will please not hunt with a rifle without special permission.
9 Employees of the families and employees of guests are not to hunt without permission of a trustee, and then only in company with their employer or a member of the family.
10 Fishing in Whitney Lake is closed until further notice.
11 No turtle eggs shall be dug or their nests disturbed.
12 Persons smoking will please take every precaution to prevent fire, especially when riding in automobiles. Put butts out on floor of car.

Rules for hunting on Cumberland were codified in this *Game Rules* handbook printed by Lucy Carnegie. (Courtesy of the Cumberland Island National Seashore Museum NPS)

V. IT IS FORBIDDEN—

1. To abuse alcoholic liquors.
2. To play games for money.
3. To smoke in or near any building except boarding houses and quarters.
4. To use firearms or other weapons.
5. To kill or disturb any living creature, excepting snakes and rats, and other small vermin.
6. To pluck or gather any shrub, plant, blossom, fruit or vegetable.
7. To enter or approach any dwelling house, stable, shop, boathouse or garden, except on business.
8. To make a thoroughfare of any building or lawn, or cultivated tract where paths are not laid.
9. To leave open any gate or door intended to be closed.
10. To meddle with valves, pumps, hose, or heating and lighting apparatus not intended for general use.
11. To drink water from surface wells near the stables.
12. To receive visitors without permission.
13. To receive messengers without reporting at Office.
14. To encourage or deal with any agent, peddler, beggar or collector.

8

15. To suggest to any applicant for work that he make other than a written application.
16. To disturb persons in their proper quarters by social or other meetings at improper places or times.
17. To abuse domestic animals in any manner whatever.
18. To keep bicycles, except by permission, and on specified conditions.
19. To make litter or trash.
20. To do anything whatever contrary to the interests of the owner, more particularly by shirking duty, by encouraging jealousies, or by mischief-making.

9

Excerpts from *Rules and Regulations Governing Employment on the Property of Mrs. Lucy C. Carnegie on Cumberland Island*, a twelve-page pamphlet printed by the H. & W. B. Drew Company, Jacksonville, Fla., 1901. (Courtesy of the Cumberland Island National Seashore Museum NPS)

A small sample of books from William Page's personal library, housed in the Cumberland Island National Seashore Museum NPS, St. Marys. (Author photo)

Sam Bealey served as head superintendent of Dungeness, a position his English-born father, Richard Bealey, had held until his death. Sam oversaw poultry and dairy production, managed the estate's vegetable gardens, and kept the commissary supplied. His brother, Will, supervised the power plant. After 1916 Sam left the island to work at the Jekyll Island Club, and Will took a position managing a new power plant in St. Marys.

Page developed an accounting system whereby Lucy's nine children could contribute to maintenance expenses on the island and build their own homes. As each child married, Lucy presented them with $10,000 as a wedding gift. Georgia newspapers, reflecting the public's interest in the lives of this celebrity family in their midst, followed the Carnegies' every move. The *Americus-Times Recorder* informed its readers in March 1900 that "Carnegies Are Building Palatial Residences at Cumberland. While Andrew Carnegie is busy endowing libraries and settling troubles with his old partners, the [Thomas Carnegie] family, headed by Mrs. Lucy Carnegie, is busy building winter palaces on Cumberland island. Morris Carnegie is building near his mother, while toward the north end of the island, at Plum Orchard, George Carnegie is erecting a beautiful home, and at the old Stafford place Will Carnegie has a handsome new place. Andrew Carnegie [II], now in New Orleans on his wedding tour, will commence to build shortly, and Mr. Rickston [Ricketson]; Mrs. Carnegie's son-in-law, will build [Greyfield] this coming summer." Peabody and Stearns of Boston was again chosen as the architects for Plum Orchard, Stafford Place, and Greyfield. The Pittsburgh family's move to Georgia began a wave of land purchases by other wealthy northerners who purchased large tracts in southern Georgia for hunting and fishing during their vacation periods.

William (Will) Coleman Carnegie married Martha Gertrude Ely, described as "the petite blond order of pretty and attractive women, graceful, with an abundance of golden hair and sweet blue eyes." Their wedding took place in December 1890 at Trinity Cathedral in her hometown of Cleveland, Ohio. It was "One of the Most Brilliant Weddings in the History of the City," the *Cleveland Plain Dealer* proclaimed. Will's youngest sister, Nancy, was a flower girl. Lucy gave her son Robert Stafford's mansion along with funds to modernize it. (After fire destroyed the old Stafford home on January 5, 1901, Will built another mansion at that location.)

He purchased a steamroller in 1901 to convert one of Stafford's cotton fields into a nine-hole golf course, hiring Thomas Hutchinson, a touring pro hailing from St. Andrews, Scotland, to design the course. But shortly after his arrival, Hutchinson fell

Head superintendent of Dungeness Sam Bealey poses with his workers. He oversaw poultry and dairy production, managed the vegetable gardens, and kept the commissary supplied. (Courtesy of Bryan-Lang Historical Archives)

Carnegie dairy barn and herd on Cumberland. (Courtesy of Bryan-Lang Historical Archives)

Dungeness as seen from the gardens south of the mansion. (Courtesy of the Cumberland Island National Seashore Museum NPS)

Dungeness Gardens, by Martin Pate, Newnan, Georgia. (Courtesy of Southeastern Archeological Center NPS)

Detail of hothouse from *Dungeness Gardens* by Martin Pate, Newnan, Georgia. (Courtesy of Southeastern Archeological Center NPS)

Dungeness gardens hothouse. (Courtesy of Georgia Archives, Lucy Coleman and Thomas M. Carnegie Family Papers, acc. 1994-0003m, 94-3m_V10_26)

Detail of pump house from *Dungeness Gardens*. (Courtesy of Georgia Archives, Lucy Coleman and Thomas M. Carnegie Family Papers, acc. 1994-0003m, 94-3m_V10_26)

Plum Orchard, home of George Carnegie. (Author's collection)

Stafford Place, home of William "Bill" and Martha Gertrude Ely Carnegie. (Author's collection)

headlong from a horse into a tree stump, killing him. His younger brother, Jack Falls "Jock" Hutchinson, oversaw completion of the nine holes and stayed on as an instructor long enough to marry a Carnegie employee. (Jock later won the 1920 PGA Championship and the 1921 British Open Championship at St. Andrews.) Andrew Carnegie routinely played the course on his visits to the island, usually pairing with his sister-in-law, Lucy. One of the par-three holes, a mere sixty yards from tee to green, was described as "so beset with hazards that a three was welcome and a four was not unusual." The course is now an airstrip where feral horses also graze. Near the golf course, Will erected a clubhouse and had an indoor pool and tennis courts installed.

Andrew Carnegie's numerous trips to Dungeness were more than perfunctory family visits. He spent months at a time there recuperating from overwork and escaping northern winters. "Have got rid of that half suffocated feeling which troubled me in the city," he wrote a relative on one such visit, "and am much stronger than I was. I

Iconic photograph of Lucy Carnegie and her children at Dungeness, February 1900. Left to right: George Lauder Carnegie (back left), Nancy Carnegie (Johnston), Frank Morrison Carnegie (front left), Margaret Carnegie Ricketson, William Coleman Carnegie (standing), Andrew Carnegie II (sitting), Lucy Coleman Carnegie (standing), Thomas Morrison Carnegie, Coleman Carnegie (standing), Florence Carnegie (Perkins). (Courtesy of the Cumberland Island National Seashore Museum NPS)

Florence Nightingale Carnegie's wedding ceremony, Dungeness, 1901. (Courtesy of the Cumberland Island National Seashore Museum NPS)

Lucy Carnegie and family on the Dungeness veranda, February 1900. Left to right: Florence Carnegie (Perkins), William Coleman Carnegie, Gertrude Ely Carnegie, George Lauder Carnegie, Frank Morrison Carnegie (standing), Lucy Coleman Carnegie (standing), Oliver Garrison Ricketson, Lucy Carnegie Ricketson (infant), Margaret Carnegie Ricketson, Andrew Carnegie II, Oliver G. Ricketson Jr., Virginia Beggs Carnegie, Nancy Carnegie (Johnston), Margaret Thaw Carnegie, Bertha Sherlock Carnegie (standing), Thomas Morrison Carnegie, and Coleman Carnegie. Two women watch from an open window (top left). (Courtesy of the Cumberland Island National Seashore Museum NPS, Mary Bullard Collection).

Stafford Place Burned

"W. C. Carnegie's Beautiful Winter Home on Cumberland Destroyed by Fire," read the *Savannah Morning News* headline. "Stafford Place was almost totally destroyed by fire yesterday about 2 o'clock. Mr. Carnegie, with his party of guests, were out on the golf links when the fire occurred. Although eighteen wagonloads of help responded quickly from Dungeness, the home of his mother, Mrs. T. M. Carnegie, in less than two hours the ruin was complete. Very little of the furniture was saved. The estimated loss is $50,000. The origin of the fire is unknown."

Stafford Ruins, 1900. (Courtesy of Georgia Archives, Lucy Coleman and Thomas M. Carnegie Family Papers, acc. 1994-0003m, 94-3m_v10_15)

Jock Hutchinson, ca. 1914. (Georgia Archives, Lucy Coleman and Thomas M. Carnegie Family Papers, acc. 1994-000CM, 94-3m_v06_12)

Stafford golf course steamroller near Dungeness. It was used to smooth over the shell roads. (Courtesy of the Cumberland Island National Seashore Museum NPS, Mary Bullard Collection)

African American caddies at Stafford Links. (Courtesy of Georgia Archives, Lucy Coleman and Thomas M. Carnegie Family Papers, acc. 1994-0003m, 94-3m_VII_09)

Four caddies for Carnegies at golf links (Stafford "Big Field"): Nervous, Pervous, Jasper, and Lemon Green. (Courtesy of the Cumberland Island National Seashore Museum NPS, Mary Bullard Collection)

Andrew Carnegie at Stafford Links, ca. 1900. (Courtesy of Georgia Archives, Lucy Coleman and Thomas M. Carnegie Family Papers, acc. 1994-0003m, 94-3m_V10_10)

Stafford airfield (once a cotton field and later a nine-hole golf course) and location of Stafford home and slave cabin chimneys.

Maids at Stafford in front of Planter's House in 1895; they likely worked for William and Gertrude Carnegie. (Courtesy of the Cumberland Island National Seashore Museum NPS)

Two women play tennis on the southeast side of Dungeness, undated. (Courtesy of the Cumberland Island National Seashore Museum NPS)

Andrew Carnegie's Buick. (Courtesy of Georgia Archives, Lucy Coleman and Thomas M. Carnegie Family Papers, acc. 1994-0003m, 94-3m_VII_06)

Andrew Carnegie with wife, Louise Whitfield Carnegie, and daughter, Margaret, at Dungeness, ca. 1900. (Courtesy of Georgia Archives, Lucy Coleman and Thomas M. Carnegie Family Papers, acc. 1994-0003m, 94-3m_VI9_34)

Left to right: Margaret (Retta) Coleman Carnegie, Andrew Carnegie, Lucy Carnegie, two unidentified (ca. 1904). (Courtesy of Georgia Archives, Lucy Coleman and Thomas M. Carnegie Family Papers, acc. 1994-0003m, 94-3m_VI9_35)

walk a great deal, a little at a time. The yacht is my delight." He adored Lucy Carnegie, who doted on him, taking him on fishing excursions, walks, and playing whist in the evenings. When it came time to write his memoirs, he "exiled [himself] from New York to Cumberland Island" to complete the task.

Thomas Morrison Carnegie Jr. married Virginia Beggs of Pittsburgh and built what came to be called the Cottage (designed by Peabody and Stearns) several hundred feet west of Dungeness. Thomas and his mother, Lucy, were great readers, and he was a favored child of hers. It is said he built the Cottage so that his bedroom faced her bedroom at the Big House. Most mornings she raised her bedroom window shade, signaling she was ready for him to come over. The two would talk and read in her library. A fire accidentally started by Thomas III gutted the Cottage in the late 1940s and has since been replaced with a smaller home, more recently used by National Park Service personnel.

Thomas and Virginia's daughter-in-law, Polly Carnegie, later recalled her initial visit to Cumberland Island: "When I first came on the boat, it was late at night. We went on one of the boats called the *Maskee*, which was a frightening thing. It was top-heavy, and we were crossing [the Cumberland Sound] at night, and that channel was about as rough as I've ever seen it [since that first visit]. After we crossed the channel and came up to the big dock, I could see just a few lights on the rest of the island—only one house showing, and that was The Cottage, through the trees. Well, I knew nothing at all. Couldn't see anything. We got to the house. It was warm, friendly—The Cottage. The next morning I woke up, and I did not believe my eyes. I saw such sheer beauty. I cry when I think of what that island was. I woke up at The Cottage facing up towards the big house [Dungeness]."

A new mansion was built in 1898 at Plum Orchard (land once owned by Peter and Marguerite Bernardey and later Robert Stafford) for Lucy's sixth child, George Lauder Carnegie, on his marriage to Margaret Copley Thaw. Peabody and Stearns designed the home in the Italian Renaissance style, then popular among the nation's leading families. The couple enlarged the mansion in 1906 to thirty principal rooms, twelve bathrooms, and many smaller rooms. After George's death in 1921, Margaret moved to Europe and remarried, and Nancy Trovillo Carnegie, the youngest Carnegie sibling, took up residence at Plum Orchard. Like a plotline from *Downton Abbey*, she married her father's coachman, George Hever. The marriage took place after Thomas died, but Nancy's uncle, Andrew Carnegie, who had risen from humble beginnings, approved of the match.

The Cottage, built ca. 1900 for Thomas Morrison Carnegie Jr. and his wife, Virginia Beggs. (Courtesy of the Cumberland Island National Seashore Museum NPS)

The Cottage as seen from the duck pond. (Courtesy of the Cumberland Island National Seashore Museum NPS)

Plum Orchard, erected 1898, was home to George Lauder Carnegie and his wife, Margaret Copley Thaw, and later by Nancy Carnegie and her husband, Marius Early Johnston. (Courtesy of the Cumberland Island National Seashore Museum NPS)

George Lauder Carnegie and Margaret Thaw Carnegie at Plum Orchard. (Courtesy of the Cumberland Island National Seashore Museum NPS)

Lucy's oldest daughter, Margaret (Retta) Coleman Carnegie, married Oliver Garrison Ricketson. They built a two-story home several miles north of Dungeness in 1901. The home passed on to their daughter, Lucy Carnegie Ricketson Ferguson, who turned Greyfield into an inn in 1962. It is now a luxury inn owned and operated by Ferguson family members.

Lucy Carnegie succumbed to complications from cerebral arteriosclerosis on January 16, 1916, at the age of sixty-eight. She died at McLean Hospital near Boston, but her remains were transported to her beloved Cumberland Island on a special train accompanied by her son-in-law, Dr. Johnston, and five family members. She was buried in the Carnegie family cemetery on Cumberland beside her husband, Thomas, whose remains were disinterred in Pittsburgh and removed to the island (Thomas died in 1886, well before the private burial ground was laid out in 1912). She left behind "a complex trust arrangement designed to keep the island available for her heirs' enjoyment. The trust made it difficult to sell or subdivide before the death[s] of all nine of her children"

Bridge over the pond behind Plum Orchard. (Courtesy of the Cumberland Island National Seashore Museum NPS)

Plum Orchard Great Hall. (Courtesy of the Cumberland Island National Seashore Museum NPS)

In 1901 Lucy's oldest daughter, Margaret (Retta) Coleman Carnegie, and Oliver Garrison Ricketson built Greyfield, a two-story home several miles north of Dungeness. (Courtesy of Bryan-Lang Historical Archives)

Opposite: Greyfield Inn

Greyfield is now a luxury inn operated by Lucy Ricketson's grandchildren. (Courtesy of the Cumberland Island National Seashore Museum NPS)

The *Lucy R. Ferguson* docked at Fernandina to pick up passengers staying at Greyfield. (Author photo)

The *Lucy R. Ferguson* on the Cumberland River bound for Greyfield. (Author photo)

Lucy Carnegie on the Cumberland beach. (Courtesy of the Cumberland Island National Seashore Museum NPS, Mary Bullard Collection)

Lucy Coleman Carnegie at Dungeness. (Courtesy of the Cumberland Island National Seashore Museum NPS)

(Dilsaver). A Pittsburgh bank had been the designated trustee, but the National Bank of Brunswick became the successor trustee after a Georgia law prohibited out-of-state trusts from owning Georgia property. At the death of Lucy's last child, the Carnegie heirs would become the trustees. In 1962, Florence (Flossie) Nightingale Carnegie Perkins was the last child to die.

Termites, humidity, and storms soon take their toll on barrier island structures. The Carnegie homes, outbuildings, and fencing required constant maintenance. Though Lucy had established a separate trust that generated rent income from an office building in downtown Pittsburgh, the money proved insufficient to maintain Carnegie lifestyles and properties on the island. Neither could revenue from island timber, cattle, and cotton sales cover all of the operating expenses. In a saltwater environment where even total renovations last only a generation or two, the financial cost became too burdensome. By April 1916, William Page had reduced the Dungeness payroll to five men and one employee at Stafford. Thomas Carnegie II exchanged letters with New York land agent

A. A. Ainsworth in 1923 and 1924 to discuss plans to buy all of Cumberland Island and develop it into a Coral Gables–like resort.

It is easy to see similarities between the Carnegie and Greene families beyond the fact that both Nathanael Greene and Thomas Carnegie died soon after acquiring Cumberland property, that they built mansions named Dungeness on the same spot, and that—spoiler alert—both mansions were eventually destroyed by fire (see later in this chapter). Both the Greene and Carnegie families were confounded by the difficulty of making their Cumberland holdings a self-sustaining enterprise. In the eighteenth century, Nathanael Greene hoped selling parcels of land on Cumberland's south end and harvesting timber would relieve his staggering financial debt. The death of Lucy Carnegie brought the problem of what to do with Cumberland's resources front and center in the twentieth century—a problem delayed until the death of her last child nearly fifty years later and exacerbated by the fact that, instead of one person managing the estate, the terms of the trust decreed that nine families would now be involved in the decision making. Meanwhile, the land under their feet had become an increasing tax liability. For some family members, placing the island in the hands of a well-funded, tax-exempt conservation group or government agency seemed a viable solution.

The National Park Service began surveying Atlantic and Gulf coast shorelines for preservation purposes in the 1930s, designating Cape Hatteras as the first Atlantic coast National Seashore in 1953. Philanthropist Paul Mellon—son of Andrew Mellon, of another famous Pittsburgh family—bought and donated most of the land in that effort. However, any government plans to acquire Cumberland Island or Carnegie family endeavors to generate profits from it were interrupted by the Second World War.

World War II

Four Carnegie men—Tom Carnegie, Coleman Johnston, Marius Johnston, and Coleman Perkins—served honorably and in some instances with distinction in Europe and the Pacific. George Merrow, a resident of the Settlement, joined the army and served in Europe. Olaf Olsen Jr., whose father managed the Candler property, joined the merchant marines, transporting ammunition and supplies across the Atlantic. The U.S. Coast Guard patrolled Cumberland's shoreline. The Carnegie's Duck House, a hunting lodge, became a radio relay station. More soldiers were stationed at the lighthouse on Little Cumberland.

The coast guard erected observation towers along the beachfront and maintained a small camp in the north-end sand dunes. Guards at this camp took their laundry for cleaning to Beulah Alberty (Primus and Amanda Mitchell's granddaughter) at the Settlement every two weeks. Occasionally, they were able to get wine. The dune barracks had a walk-in cooler to store meat, dairy products, and bread. Food came by boat from Fernandina. Guardsmen stationed on the island were allowed to visit Amelia Island on weekends. As a young man still in his teens, Billy Spivey, originally from Appling County, served during World War II riding mounted beach patrols on Cumberland for the U.S. Coast Guard.

"I went to take my training up in New York," Spivey recounted in a 1995 interview with Joyce Seward. "They needed some guys for mounted beach patrol. I was a farm boy, so I was picked to come back to Hilton Head for my training. We had three different posts [with] about seven of us on each post. I don't remember how many guys they had over there on Little Cumberland. We had a tower on farther up north there. One guy manned that tower during the day hours. It'd only take one guy, so they had two guys ready to ride at night. We had a horse stable right behind the barracks. They brought them [horses] over on barges. I believe they got them from the Army. After the Coast Guard left, they got them off. They gave them away or sold them. If we didn't have watch during the day, we'd either go hunting, fishing, most anything you want until dark. Then you'd make the night patrol. At night we'd ride the beach on horses and carry a trail dog with us. Every time you ride, you'd have to clean them [horses] up and feed them." Spivey spent the rest of his time in the service at sea, first on an icebreaker in the Aleutians, then on escort vessels for troopships.

Residents on the island, as in all coastal communities, observed blackout requirements by painting the top half of automobile headlights black and by covering windows with black curtains. These efforts, however, didn't stop U-boat captain Reinhard Hardegen from sinking two tankers, the ss *Oklahoma* and ss *Esso Baton Rouge*, in the early morning hours of April 8, 1942. Hardegen waited near channel buoys, whose lights gave away the positions of passing ships, and launched torpedoes. Twenty-four seamen died in the attacks. Olaf Olsen, a member of the Georgia State Guard, was at his home on the north end of Cumberland Island when Robert Ferguson (Lucy Carnegie Ferguson's husband), a member of the Civil Air Patrol, buzzed Olsen's house on the north end. Olsen's daughter and son, Sonja Olsen Kinard and Olaf Olsen Jr., recall what happened next in interviews conducted by Joyce Seward (1995).

Sonja Kinard. Olaf Olsen was her father.
(Photo by Karol Kimmell)

"They always circled the house," Sonja recounted. "Every time a plane would circle low, we'd know there was a message somewhere or another, and everybody would run out of the house. Daddy was in the Georgia State Guard. His main job was to carry supplies back and forth. He could come to Cumberland, whereas Mr. Candler could not. He could watch the property and keep up with that. I think they [the coast guard] may have had an office or a headquarters in one of the Candlers' houses. During the war people could not come down to Cumberland because of the threat of submarines and so forth. Daddy was dropped a note, I think with a wrench tied onto it. My understanding is that the note said, 'Two ships have been torpedoed off the coast,' and gave the longitude and latitude [and] for Daddy immediately to go, fuel up. The boat that Daddy always had was called the *Lourine*. It stood for Louisa and Catherine, Mr. Candler's children. The *Lourine II* was a forty-two-foot Fairform Flyer built by the Huckins Yacht Corporation in Jacksonville. They were fast boats. So Daddy got in the [Candler] boat. When he got in the middle of St. Andrews Sound, he read the rest of the note, which said, 'Sit down in the field if you can go.' Well, Daddy was already in the sound. He went on in to St. Simons Sea Island Yacht Club [at Gascoigne Bluff], which was later Olsen's Yacht Yard, and picked up a crewmember [Brunswick physician John Byron Avera] and gassed up, and then went out. Whereas the coast guard had to follow the buoys in the channel, he knew a cut-through."

Olaf Olsen Jr. picks up the story here. "He went out what we call Portuguese Slough, which is right out in front of the King and Prince Hotel. He had a twenty-knot boat against a six-knot coast guard boat [that] had to go all the way to the STS sea buoy, about seventeen miles offshore. He had about half the distance that they went, so he got there first. He picked up the [tanker] lifeboats and had them in tow. The ones [crewmen] in bad shape they put on his boat, and Dr. Avera tried to take care of them. I think a couple of them died on the way."

"He brought in fifty-four survivors," says Sonja, "which is about all them, because there were about thirty-five on each ship. He met the coast guard boats on the way back in and did some transferring. Then he came on up to what we call the Weesecot, a kind of sailboat dock, which is right next to the coast guard docks on Frederica River. I remember seeing them, merchant marines, on the ramp of the coast guard station wrapped in blankets."

"They wanted to confiscate [Candler's] boat to go back out there," Olaf Jr., continues, "but Daddy said, 'Ain't nobody going to run this boat but me!' They put Daddy in the National Guard so that he could run the boat. He went back out there that evening."

For the next three days, before going to school, Olaf Jr. picked up the *Baton Rouge* captain and engineer at 4:30 in the morning at the Brunswick docks and transported them to the bouy off St. Simons, where another boat took them to the wreck.

The following day, April 9, 1942, another unarmed merchant ship, *Esparta*, sank off the coast of Cumberland Island after being torpedoed. One man drowned when fumes forced him and others overboard. The rest of the crew were rescued by an American patrol boat after drifting for seven hours at sea in lifeboats and a raft.

Strip Mining, Development, and the National Seashore

The first of two new potential revenue streams using Cumberland's natural resources was presented to the Carnegie heirs in 1955. Their Georgia trustee, the National Bank of Brunswick, informed them that several companies had expressed interest in mining Cumberland soil for ilmenite, used to make paint and other products. The Glidden Company's proposal, favored by a number of Carnegie heirs (now numbering fifteen), called for strip mining seven thousand acres of Cumberland land in exchange for minimum royalties of $2.25 million with the possibility of doubling that amount over a twenty-year period. The company planned to employ a hundred workers and erect a 150-acre settlement at Brickhill Bluff, with fencing to prevent employees from trespassing on Carnegie land. They would transport the ilmenite by barge via the intracoastal waterway to Glidden plants in Maryland, where it could be made into titanium dioxide. In all, Glidden proposed to invest $9 million in the mining operation. For some of the heirs, including Lucy's last living child, Florence, and Lucy Ferguson, the only Carnegie living full-time on Cumberland, it seemed like a godsend. And why not? Titanium mining in Florida was booming. Thomas and Andrew Carnegie had made their fortunes turning iron ore into products that benefitted the country. Besides, Amelia Island had sustained two paper mills since the late 1930s. Why not introduce new industry to Cumberland? To sweeten the deal, Glidden offered to bring free electricity to Cumberland in support of its operations and provide free boat service to and from the mainland. The company also agreed to contour the landscape into "lakes or terraces as desired" and reforest the mined area once operations ceased.

Despite the potential income and Glidden's promises and the fact that some Carnegies approved of the deal, other Carnegie heirs strongly objected, going to court to prevent it from proceeding. Three of Lucy and Thomas's grandchildren—Nancy Rockefeller, her sister, Lucy Rice, and their first cousin, Margaret Wright—blocked the deal in court after several appeals. The final decision in their favor relied on the fact that Florence Carnegie Perkins, then age seventy-eight and in declining health, would not likely live another twenty years, the term of the lease. With her death, the trust, "a party to the contract," would cease to exist, thus making the contract invalid. While the Carnegie heirs slugged it out in Georgia's courts, the price of titanium nosedived on the worldwide market, making Glidden's investment in Cumberland uneconomical. Glidden executives very likely breathed a collective sigh of relief that the deal failed to materialize.

The other opportunity to generate income for the Carnegie heirs coincided with a movement to permanently protect the island from commercial and residential development. Larry Dilsaver's book, *Cumberland Island National Seashore: A History of Conservation Conflict*, provides a detailed account of these events. Prior to Florence Perkins's death in 1962, Carnegie family heirs formed the Cumberland Island Company to manage island affairs. They divided the island into ten tracts, with each of the five family branches receiving two segments—one north tract and one south tract. All members were allowed to use the main road, Dungeness dock, and the Carnegie cemetery. The partition allowed some family members to sell their property to outsiders and others to donate their land to the National Park Foundation or sell it to the foundation at a minimum price.

One heir, Oliver G. Ricketson III, a New Mexico resident, sold his southern tract (2S) (just north of Greyfield) to Robert Davis for $60,000. Davis, a cowhand and close friend of the Fergusons (some Carnegies referred to him as Lucy Ferguson's adopted son), quickly sold off sixty-seven lots on the west side of the Main Road, in what became known as the Davisville subdivision. Some of the buyers were Atlanta investors hoping to build a hotel there. Ricketson formed an eponymous corporation, OGR, and sold more lots in his northern (2N) segment. Those lots were further divided and resold. Lucy Ferguson sold twenty-eight acres to two friends, Wilbur Readdick and J. B. Peeples, who then subdivided their portions. Lucy turned Greyfield into an inn and retained the surrounding property for her family's use. She was adamantly opposed to selling to a private owner or turning the property over to the state or federal agencies. The Miller family, who owned a hundred acres near the Settlement, began another subdivision.

Disturbed by the rapid sell-offs and construction, the remaining Cumberland Island landowners, including the Candlers and branches of the Carnegie family, formed the Cumberland Island Conservation Association in 1969. The Carnegies and Candlers turned to two attorneys, Georgia native Thornton Morris and Stewart Udall, to help in their search for a "trustworthy, interim buyer" who would hold island property until it could be acquired by the National Park Service. Udall, a decorated World War II B-24 gunner, former member of the U.S. Congress, and former Secretary of the Interior, was devoted to land and water conservation. He had published *The Quiet Crisis* in 1963, in which he wrote, "Each generation has its own rendezvous with the land, for despite our fee titles and claims of ownership, we are all brief tenants on this planet. By choice, or by default, we will carve out a land legacy for our heirs." Morris, Udall, and other influential friends were needed to derail the aggressive development plans of a new perceived threat, Charles Fraser, who was at that time turning Hilton Head, a South Carolina barrier island, into a residential resort.

Fraser traced his South Carolina and Georgia ancestors back to colonial days. He viewed the Carnegies as interlopers who took advantage of the South's post–Civil War misfortunes by acquiring southern lands at bargain prices. "We fought the war against those people," he said in a 1995 interview with Joyce Seward. "They had bought up our prized islands from impoverished planters who had lost ninety-eight percent of their wealth." His own interest in land management began at Yale Law School, and he put that knowledge into use by developing Sea Pines Plantation on Hilton Head. He was approached through an intermediary whose clients (Thomas Carnegie IV, Andrew Carnegie III, and Henry Carter Carnegie) wanted to sell their two Cumberland tracts: one just south of High Point on the north end, and one just north of Dungeness on the south end. Fraser purchased their property, one-fifth of the Carnegie island holdings, for $1.5 million in 1968. His planned development, Cumberland Oaks, depended on Carnegie and Candler cooperation. Fraser's proposal in 1969 was met with disdain in large part due to what they perceived as his brash manner and belief that he wanted "the whole island to develop and make a fortune off of."

Fraser turned to Camden County's state representative to introduce a bill in the Georgia legislature that would create the Camden County Recreational Authority, a county-run agency empowered to condemn undeveloped coastal areas for recreational purposes, thus, preempting the National Park Service's acquisition of Cumberland property. Another bill sought to give the North Georgia Mountains Authority (a recreation and hospitality company) power of eminent domain across the entire state. Fraser's publicist served as the director of that authority. But the Carnegies and Candlers were not without influence. Lucy's husband, Robert Ferguson, a former Georgia state legislator, remained on good terms with his former colleagues. Though Lucy was not a strong

Massive live oak tree on Cumberland Island. (Courtesy of the Cumberland Island National Seashore Museum NPS)

proponent of turning over island land to the federal government to create a national seashore, the pending bills backed by Fraser could force her family to vacate Cumberland after eighty-four years of stewardship, which gave the national seashore effort more appeal to her. Nancy Rockefeller's scathing letter to Fraser noted that "everyone should thank the Carnegies for real conservation of Cumberland at their own expense." She ended the letter by extending an olive branch: "hoping you will reconsider and retract your present plans for Cumberland and be my good neighbor." The Carnegies and Candlers, along with allies in the state house and senate, defeated the pending state legislation and passed a competing bill authorizing a Cumberland Island study commission, on which Carnegies and Candlers would serve. If nothing else, Charles Fraser's efforts to develop Cumberland became the catalyst that turned the island into a National Seashore.

The National Park Service's interest in Cumberland was nothing new. In 1955, NPS director Conrad Wirth visited the island with Paul Mellon. That same year, with Old Dominion funding (a predecessor of the Andrew W. Mellon Foundation, formed in

1969), the NPS published *A Report on Our Vanishing Shoreline*, a survey of the Gulf and Atlantic coasts that called for preserving undeveloped areas. The booklet identifies several places suitable for public use. The first mentioned is Cumberland Island, "considered by the survey to be the best of its type. Brilliant sands lined with palmettos, moss-draped live oaks, and white shell roads help make Georgia's Cumberland Island one of the most attractive of the 16 prime areas. The possibilities of developing Cumberland Island for public recreation and cultural enjoyment are considered to be exceptional."

However, the NPS would need approval from the Candlers and the four Carnegie branches—Ferguson, Perkins, Johnston, Rockefeller/Rice—who still owned land on Cumberland. They would need the support of Camden County government officials and the State of Georgia. And a bill turning Cumberland into a national seashore would have to pass in the U.S. Congress before being signed into law by the president. In 1958 only nine people or entities owned land on Cumberland Island, including the Trust for Lucy C. Carnegie, which held 91 percent of the island, and the Candler family on the north end. But the dissolution of the trust after Florence Perkins's death left twenty-five stakeholders for the NPS to negotiate with. After some of those stakeholders sold their tracts to Davis, Fraser, and others, the number increased to 140.

After helping defeat the eminent domain bills in the Georgia legislature, Morris and Udall drafted legislation to make Cumberland Island a national seashore. U.S. Representative W. S. (Bill) Stuckey Jr. of Georgia would be the one to introduce the legislation. He had won his seat in part by attacking former Rep. Russell Tuten on a contentious Cumberland Island transportation issue——building a causeway versus ferrying people to the island. Tuten favored extending a roadway from the mainland to the island but reversed his stance after meeting with the NPS and environmentalists. Stuckey opposed ferry travel to Cumberland long enough to win the election, then made an about-face, siding with proponents of water transportation. Ferry transportation proved to be a good choice for Camden County. The Kings Bay Naval Submarine Base might not have located there had a nearby bridge spanned the Intracoastal Waterway.

Stuckey recounted in a 1996 interview with Joyce Seward that the Cumberland Island Parkway at first "was to come from I-95 to the Crooked River" and "kick off to the Crooked River Ferry," the main embarkation point. Brunswick Pulp and Paper offered to donate the land, and ferries to the island would have docked at Brickhill Bluff. The Camden County Commission agreed "a roadway to Cumberland was not vital as long as a ferry service to the island had its starting point in the county and not from nearby islands," such as Amelia or Jekyll. Another plan called for a visitor center to be located across the river from Cumberland at Point Peter. In the end, Camden County officials ensured that ferry access to the island would originate at St. Marys.

Representative Stuckey introduced HR 15686 to establish the Cumberland Island National Seashore on February 3, 1970. He had been visiting the island since his twenties. "We used to fly over there and land on the beaches," he recalled, "just fish and surf, and if the fish weren't biting we'd take off, fly to another beach. If you don't fall in love with it [Cumberland] then something's wrong with you. I was determined to preserve it." The proposed legislation excluded Little Cumberland Island.

Stuckey explained why he worded the bill so that the larger island would remain open for agricultural development: "It was the horses. It wasn't the cattle," he said. "Miss Lucy [Ferguson] said they were hers. She was a lovable person and a character on top of it. She would bring people over from Waycross and break those horses, and she would sell those horses, and that was income to her. She wanted to make sure that she kept those horses. We put that in there [the legislation]." Stuckey noted that Lucy Carnegie's will divided the island among her children into noncontiguous sections, which prevented would-be developers from acquiring large tracts next to each other. Charles Fraser had acquired two noncontiguous tracks, which frustrated his efforts. "When Charlie tried to put it all together," Stuckey said, "you didn't have anybody that had a big tract. One [tract] was a very attractive piece and the other wasn't worth a darn. That little quirk kept somebody from putting together a pretty good tract. They couldn't get contiguous property."

That April, undaunted by the patchwork problem, encouraged by the prospect of Stuckey's pending legislation and the potential for developing the island, Fraser hired bulldozers to carve two roads out of the forest leading to the beach. The bulldozers also made a 500-foot runway on his northern tract adjacent to Candler property. Sam Candler flew a cameraman to film Fraser's crews at work clearing the land and even got one of the workmen to speculate on camera that Fraser had in mind to build a jetport. Fraser called it "an extremely clever, very brilliant public relations campaign. An absolutely brilliant strategy on their part because their objective was to stop me from doing anything here." Public outcry and financial setbacks at Sea Pines brought Fraser's plans to develop his Cumberland tracts to a halt. He claimed the runway would only accommodate his De Havilland plane and said opening Cumberland to tourists was a way to reduce overcrowding on other Georgia islands like Tybee, St. Simons, and Jekyll. Fraser thought development would also be a way to generate jobs and tax revenue for Camden County.

Loggerhead sea turtle nest.

Meanwhile, Alfred W. (Bill) Jones had been orchestrating a merger of interests between the Carnegies, the National Park Foundation, and Charles Fraser. Jones and his cousin Howard Coffin, dubbed the auto industry's Father of Standardization, cofounded the Sea Island Company and the Cloister hotel, making Sea Island, once the only large resort between Pinehurst and Miami, an upscale destination and residential area. Jones had previously used his influence and negotiating skills to make Jekyll Island a state park and was active in other land preservation efforts. He now played a pivotal role in bringing together constituencies with competing interests to make Cumberland a national seashore. "A lot of people have said he [Jones] did it so Charlie Fraser would not have it [Cumberland] as competition to Sea Island," Stuckey recalled. "But don't for a minute believe that. Bill Jones, Sr. believed in the beauty of these islands."

By June 1970, Fraser and several Carnegie families were ready to sell three tracts to the National Park Foundation (NPF). The foundation, created by the National Park Service in 1967, was empowered to purchase and hold land until a new national park could be established, after which the NPF could either donate or sell the land to the National Park Service. The acquisition of these three tracts met the Andrew W. Mellon Foundation's requirements to allocate money for more Cumberland property with the goal of making the island a national seashore. "There would have been no bill had we not had the Mellon money," Stuckey said.

After eighteen months in committee, Stuckey's bill died. But by then the National Park Foundation had acquired three-quarters of Cumberland Island, and all signs pointed to success in acquiring more land. Stuckey introduced another bill, HR 9859, on July 15, 1971. Georgia's senators, Herman Talmadge and David Gambrell, introduced the same bill in the Senate. The new proposed legislation placed Little Cumberland Island in a conservation trust (it is now owned by a homeowners association). After much debate and revision, both bills were passed. President Nixon signed Public Law 92-536 on October 23, 1972, creating the Cumberland Island National Seashore. The final act prohibited building a causeway to the island and called for Cumberland to be maintained "in its primitive state." The NPF continued to acquire land, expanding the boundaries, with help from Congress. Jimmy Carter, a frequent visitor to Cumberland, urged Congress both as governor and president to increase the spending limit to purchase land there. The National Parks Omnibus Bill of 1978 raised the ceiling of money allocated to acquire more island property to $28.5 million.

After the bill became law, no visitors were allowed on Cumberland for two years while the NPS built facilities to handle the expected influx of visitors, negotiated retained rights with families (who sold or donated property), and finalized its acquisition of 140 tracts through purchases and eminent domain. The government's acquisition of private land ended with the purchase of George Merrow's Settlement plot in 1984. For its efforts, the NPS acquired 18,687 acres through donations, purchases, and condemnation at a price tag of $23,843,700. Twenty-one parties who gave up or sold their land retained rights to their property with terms ranging from twenty-five years to the lifespan of their children and grandchildren. Since the NPS ran out of funds to purchase more acreage, some owners kept (and still retain) fee simple deeds to island property and own their land outright. The negotiations for rights devolved into a byzantine patchwork of rules and regulations that varied by party, granting access to specified roadways, trails, docks, and beach entry points. The deeds also prescribed who could add to existing structures or build new ones. More legislation in 1982 by Congress created wilderness areas on Cumberland, further complicating how the land and structures should be maintained.

Three government entities declined to sell their Cumberland property to the NPS. The Department of the Navy owned Drum Point Island, 139 acres of mostly dredge spoil west of Stafford. The U.S. Army Corps of Engineers kept its 518-acre tract at Raccoon Keys on the southwest end of the island, also for the purpose of depositing dredge sediment. And the state of Georgia retained 13,820 acres of beach and tidal waters, "all land below the mean high-tide line, all saltwater creeks, and extensive marshes west of the northern half of Cumberland Island" (Dilsaver).

The push by the Georgia Conservancy and the Sierra Club to designate wilderness areas on Cumberland arose from initial NPS plans to develop the island and later, the U.S. Navy's selection of Kings Bay as a submarine base. The Park Service anticipated 10,000 visitors a day to the island and made plans to purchase twelve 100-passenger ferries that would shuttle visitors to the island where they would have access to 150 camping areas and 300 picnic sites. A University of Georgia study projected 225,000 visitors to Cumberland in the first year of operation and as many as a million by year fifteen.

Two local utility companies, Georgia Power and the Okefenokee Rural Electrification Membership Corporation (OREMC), anticipated a huge spike in revenue and vied to bring electricity to the island. Having won the contract, OREMC erected single-pole transmission lines across the marshes and Cumberland River to Table Point, then laid 34.5 miles of underground cable along the main road from one end of the island to the other. Another cable beneath Christmas Creek at High Point provides power to residents on Little Cumberland. The NPS ultimately limited island access to three hundred people at a time, restricting campers to a maximum of seven nights per visit, and built just one camping area with running water and bathroom facilities. The U.S. government compensated OREMC "for loss of the development sales base" and for the expense of installing transmission lines, transformers, and meters.

Charles Fraser took issue with the original intent of the NPS to establish a National Seashore and the virtual wilderness park it has become: "Every other National Seashore gets as many as one hundred and fifty times more people per square mile as Cumberland," he said. Instead, "It provides sanctuary for several very wealthy families to have their forty acre enclaves for forty years. [The] management plan permits only fifteen people per mile, and we're protecting it for the Carnegie, Rockefellers and Candlers. They've transferred security costs to the government. The government keeps the American public away from the government lands."

Miss Lucy

After Lucy Coleman Carnegie's time, no other person had an impact on island life as much as her granddaughter, also named Lucy. Margaret (Retta) Carnegie Ricketson, Lucy Carnegie's fourth child and eldest daughter, gave birth to Lucy Carnegie Ricketson

Portrait of Lucy Ferguson wearing a bandana and buck knife on her belt. (Photograph by Richard McBride)

in New York City on September 14, 1899. She arrived on Cumberland for the first time six weeks after her birth. She and her parents stayed at Dungeness while Greyfield was being built for them (a wedding gift from Lucy Carnegie). A childhood bout with scarlet fever affected her hearing, which troubled her, especially in crowds, for the rest of her life. Visits to the island were usually in the winter, when the family traveled south for warmer weather. "We did not go up to Jekyll much as we were self-sufficient on Cumberland," she recalled. "Lots of children and cousins and plenty of guests. We on Cumberland were a world of our own." Life on an isolated island, unencumbered by societal norms, allowed Lucy to skinny-dip or lie on the beach in her natural state, a habit she practiced well into her later years. A rumor that Thomas Carnegie purchased Cumberland Island because Jekyll Island Club members blackballed him is easily disproved by the fact that the Jekyll Island Club was founded five years after Lucy and Thomas Carnegie acquired Dungeness.

Even as an adult, "Miss Lucy," as she was known to locals, stood about five feet tall and weighed less than ninety pounds. She attended a private school in Washington, D.C., and in 1920 married Robert W. (Bob) Ferguson, a New Englander with a background in the lumber business. Robert, too, fell for Cumberland's charms, and the two took up a lifelong residence at Greyfield. Both became pilots and learned the island's hidden secrets by air, land, and water. They kept a small airplane at Stafford, transforming William Coleman Carnegie's nine-hole golf course into an airstrip. Lester Morris, an African American "bull gang" employee, in an interview with Joyce Seward, had vivid memories of Lucy's flying days: "She had plenty of nerve. She'll just do anything whatever she [wanted to] do. She bought this airplane, and Osbie Jackson used to crank it for her. You have to get down and take it by the blade and pull that thing. You got to step back out the way. She used to get in that thing and by herself go over to Fernandina and come on in to St. Marys and land. Right in St. Marys!" St. Marys Street parallels the river in downtown St. Marys, just wide enough and long enough to land a small plane on.

Lucy was also a proficient horseback rider. Billy Spivey, a coast guardsman on Cumberland during World War II, recounted to Joyce Seward an incident that occurred there in 1943. "One of the fellows got to talking with this lady [who] owned the island. She was a real friendly, nice lady. There was an old boy from Billings, Montana. He's the one that was doing all the big talk. They got up a horse race, so she goes out and catches one [a horse] off the beach. It was running loose, and [she] put the saddle on him and a bridle. The race was on. He took that horse I rode all the time, and they had a race on the beach. I can't remember who won."

Margaret Carnegie and Lucy Ricketson, ca. 1901. (Courtesy of Georgia Archives, Lucy Coleman and Thomas M. Carnegie Family Papers, acc. 1994-0003m, 94-3m_v19_04)

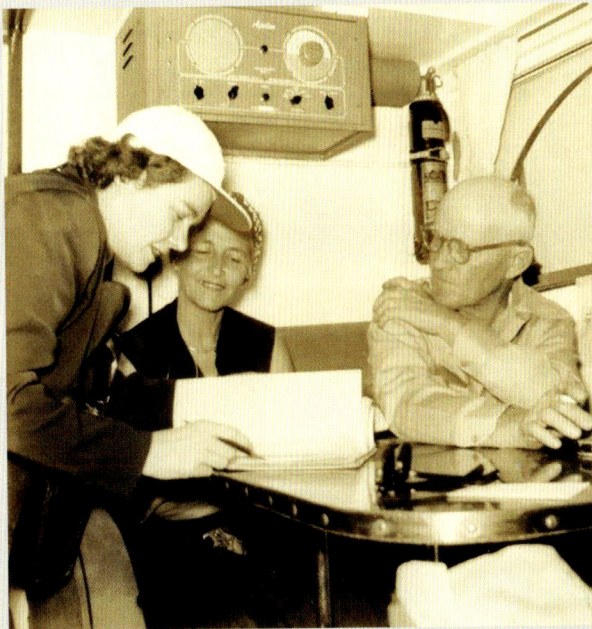

Lucy Ricketson Ferguson (center) on a boat. (Courtesy of Bryan-Lang Historical Archives)

Lucy Carnegie holding Lucy Ricketson. (Courtesy of Georgia Archives, Lucy Coleman and Thomas M. Carnegie Family Papers, acc. 1994-0003m, 94-3m_v18_04)

Lucy Ferguson learned to ride at an early age. (Courtesy of Georgia Archives, Lucy Coleman and Thomas M. Carnegie Family Papers, acc. 1994-0003m, 94-3m_v19_23)

She and Robert started raising cattle in the mid-1940s and by the early 1950s had a herd of a hundred cows and two bulls. By the late 1950s their herd of up to four hundred head had free range of Cumberland Island. Lucy put her horseback prowess to practical uses, leading cattle round-ups (to sell them) and herding cows through pesticide plunge dips. She also introduced new breeds of pigs to the island.

While Lucy didn't mind friends and locals hunting on Cumberland with permission, she spent many nights patrolling the island for poachers, often catching them in the act. One night she and a cousin, Carter Carnegie, and his wife, Polly, corralled several hunters. They soon discovered the men were Brooklyn Dodgers teammates who had paid a local on the mainland a fee to hunt on Cumberland. Carter, a baseball fan, took the entourage to the Cottage for breakfast and invited the players back to hunt another time as his guest. Lucy sent the sheriff to the local man's home, and his scheme came to an end.

The Fergusons employed a young teen, J. B. Peeples, soon after moving to Cumberland. Peeples won their trust and eventually oversaw much of their island operations. He lost the fingers on one hand to a saw while running their lumber business. He and Robert Ferguson dabbled in moonshining during 1930s and 1940s, mostly for personal consumption, or so they claimed.

J.B. was under Lucy's strict orders to keep poachers off the island. One night in 1959 he shot a trespasser in the leg, but the man and his accomplice escaped by boat. The injured man visited a doctor on the mainland, claiming he accidentally shot himself. The doctor later identified him as a poacher Lucy had the sheriff arrest not long before. A few weeks later the coast guard found the Carnegie's bullet-riddled yacht, *Dungeness*, adrift at sea. Several weeks after that, Dungeness mansion burned to the ground. No one was ever charged for either crime.

After inheriting Greyfield and its outbuildings from her parents, Lucy built more structures on the property (named Serendipity) she received after the extended family divided their island holdings. Though she resisted turning "her" island over to the National Park Service, Lucy in due course consented partly to appease her relatives. Once the park was established, her relationship with most park employees remained strained. She often butted heads with superintendents when her hogs and cows strayed onto park property. By law they belonged to the U.S. National Park Service. "We don't do it that way on Cumberland," she protested and invariably got her way. In the end she saw the benefits of opening the island to visitors. "I think the national parks are

Cattle going through a dip or "plunge" on Cumberland for tick treatment. (Courtesy of the Cumberland Island National Seashore Museum NPS, Mary Bullard Collection)

Homer Hail photographed Dungeness going up in flames in 1959. (Courtesy of the Cumberland Island National Seashore Museum NPS, Mary Bullard Collection)

necessary, especially for the poor city man," she once said. "When you see them enjoying the island, I feel good about the park being here." One perk of having a national park was the extension of electricity from the mainland to the island. Lucy wrote a friend in May 1965 that "we are fixing up our old house, Greyfield, and hope by next year to have power from the main[land]. It will be great to be able to run washing machines, electric irons, fans, and the 1001 things everyone takes completely for granted."

Lucy Ferguson died September 11, 1989, and is buried on Cumberland in the Carnegie family cemetery.

Carol Ruckdeschel

Another rugged individual, Carol Ruckdeschel, has called Cumberland Island her home since 1973. She moved there with John Pennington, a journalist, to work as caretakers of the Candler property. But she had visited the island before as a biology student at Georgia State: "One of my professors, Helen B. Jordan, studied malaria in lizards, and set up a trip to Cumberland in 1968. We camped at Serendipity, which was being fixed up for Lucy R. Ferguson. Trips continued." Carol's relationship with Pennington ended after a few years of their move to the island, and her next romantic interest, Louis McKee, helped her purchase Charles Trimmings's three-bedroom home in the Settlement. Trimmings got the land in 1893 when he was in his early thirties. He built the house a stone's throw from the First African Baptist Church, which he also helped erect. "The present [First African Baptist] church was built to the east of the old church," Carol says. "You once could see the footers or posts of the old one immediately to the west. It was between the present building and the 'Red Barn,' as the last owners called the rotting structure to the west. George Merrow, who belonged to the church, used to keep it painted, following the owner of the Red Barn's lead and painted the doors red. The Park took paint samples and supposedly returned it to its original colors." A deal with the National Park Service, which bought the house from her, allows Carol to occupy it for the rest of her life. "When I die, my cabin will be torn down and plowed under."

Carol doesn't leave the island when hurricanes blow through. She wants to study firsthand the impact of storms on the island's ecosystems. Even before her arrival on Cumberland, Carol was interested in the scientific study of animals, including reptiles, and had a well-earned reputation for her wild and free lifestyle. One park ranger recounted hearing the thunder of hooves coming toward him in the woods. A herd of feral horses soon emerged with Carol riding bareback in their midst, gripping a horse's mane in one hand and a bottle of Tennessee whiskey in the other. Her reputation took on new dimensions in 1980, when she killed McKee with a shotgun as he tried to attack her in a jealous rage. A jury ruled that she acted in self-defense.

Carol married a University of Rhode Island herpetologist, Robert Shoop. Next to her home the two created a research museum, which they filled with shells, animal bones, skeletons, and tissue from dissected animals. Though Carol lives at the Settlement, few African Americans remained on the north end. "By the time I got to the island," she said, "there was only one original black inhabitant here: George Merrow. He was born in The Settlement, and except for his time in the military during World War II, lived on the

Carol Ruckdeschel near her home on Cumberland Island, 2018.

George Merrow and his wife, Audrey Holzendorf Merrow, at High Point, 1980s. (Courtesy of the Cumberland Island National Seashore Museum NPS)

Charles and Liz Trimmings in front of their home, 1940s. (Courtesy of the Cumberland Island National Seashore Museum NPS, Mary Bullard Collection)

Crime on the Island

Murders committed on Cumberland are rare but not unheard of. Eighteen-year-old Richard "Dick" Fader, the son of harbor pilot Capt. George Fader, was shot in the back with a Winchester rifle in November 1884. Before he died he told his father he had been bird hunting to feed a cat and a pet raccoon he kept on the pilot boat. A witness fingered the hotel carpenter, W. W. Wallace, a "quiet and inoffensive man," whom the younger Fader "loved to tease because he thought Wallace was afraid of him." Though Wallace was not arrested, he demanded a trial. Apparently, the younger Fader's story did not hold up in court, and Wallace was acquitted.

In July 1906, George Fader's youngest son, Edgar, shot and killed Robert Mayo [possibly Merrow] while acting as a "special constable." The *Atlanta Georgian* depicted Mayo as "the bully of the section of Cumberland where he resided for several years and has been mixed up in several scrapes. The negro, who has always been regarded as a bad man, made for Fader with an ax, and the latter shot him, the negro dying about forty hours later." Mayo's version of the fatal encounter (not surprising for the Jim Crow Era) was not reported.

The same paper reported another murder in February 1909. "Body Is Identified by Tattoo on Arm," read the headline. "Jim Olsen, a Swede [no relation to the Olaf Olsen family] who has been a resident of Brunswick for ten or fifteen years, is in jail on a charge of murder, which it is alleged was committed on February 1, but which came to light a few days ago when the body of the man who, it is charged he murdered, [washed] up on Cumberland Island near the house of Mrs. Carnegie."

Edgar Fader made news again in 1911 when he was accused of dynamiting the Settlement home of William Alberty, an African American. This led to a later altercation when Edgar, carrying a shotgun, and his wife rode by the Albertys' home in their buggy. Alberty, armed with a rifle, and his wife, Renda, inside their home with a gun, exchanged fire with Fader. No one was arrested, and a preliminary trial went nowhere.

During Prohibition, Edgar operated a still on Pine Island, part of Little Cumberland. When someone asked, "What is Captain Ed doing on Pine Island?," the usual reply was "hush your mouth." To this day, residents refer to Pine Island as Hush Your Mouth or simply Hush-a-Mouth.

island working for Carnegies and Candlers until health problems made that impossible. The Blacks that resided on the island when I first came were, except for George, all caretakers. Jesse Bailey [Candler] was born on Sapelo Island. George Merrow's wife Audrey [Candler] was born on the mainland, and Nate Lane [Fosters] was from St. Marys. I interviewed all I could, but most are now dead. I have tried to communicate with the children, but only through emails, and that is NOT a productive way. I met a great grandson or great-great grandson of the Trimmings, and he was interested, but knew little."

Carol's passion for Cumberland is best seen in her life's work—the study of island plants and animals. She has written several books on the subject, cataloging hundreds of plant, animal, and insect species. In the 1970s, about the time Carol moved to Cumberland, feral

Jesse Bailey. "River Man." (Courtesy of Sonja Olsen Kinard)

hogs then in abundance on the island devastated loggerhead sea turtle nests. Interested in their recovery, she has conducted an invaluable longitudinal study of dead sea turtles that washed up on Cumberland's shores, the result of run-ins with shrimp trawler nets. The ones that escape turtle-friendly nets can subsequently die of trauma or injuries sustained trying to free themselves. Her studies have earned Carol the moniker the Jane Goodall of Sea Turtles. Her book, *Sea Turtles of the Atlantic and Gulf Coasts of the United States*, includes a chapter on loggerheads (*Caretta caretta*) belonging to the family Cheloniidae. These sea turtles are characterized by their wide, rounded shells and paddle-like flippers. Unlike tortoises, loggerheads cannot retract their heads into their shells.

Loggerheads migrate as far north as Canada and appear from May through October on the U.S. East Coast, where they dwell about twelve miles offshore from Florida to North Carolina. Adult loggerheads feed primarily on mollusks (sea snails) and crabs but also diet on invertebrates like jellyfish and barnacles. East Coast loggerheads mate during the spring followed by egg laying from April to September. Hatching on the Georgia coast might continue through November. Female loggerheads come ashore at night to deposit an average of 110 eggs near the sand dunes using their hind limbs to dig a chamber in the soft sand where their eggs are deposited, then covered with sand. The procedure takes forty-five to ninety minutes and might be repeated three times each nesting season.

Hatchlings emerge from nests at night after about four days. Juvenile loggerheads rely on wave action and Earth's magnetic field to find their way to the brown *Sargassum* seaweed and calm waters of the Sargasso Sea. They return to U.S. coastal waters after seven to twelve years to inhabit warm waters up to 160 feet deep. Most of their time is spent underwater foraging or resting. They sleep on the bottom at night and surface intermittently to breathe. Adult loggerheads grow up to thirty-four inches in length, reach sexual maturity between seventeen and thirty-three years, and live up to sixty-seven years.

Unlike the thousands of tourists who come to the island to photograph Cumberland's feral horses, Carol does not favor their presence on the island and has lobbied for their removal to a more hospitable environment. "In the 1920s," she says, "the Carnegies brought a trainload of horses from Arizona to Fernandina and then to the island for release. The horses have been genetically tested, and they are *not* descendent of Spanish stock, as is sometimes reported. Horses are not native to this continent, nor is this habitat conducive to their good health. In fact, it is the contrary." The horses are preyed on by alligators, suffer from snake bites, and are prone to parasitic diseases. Horses can become trapped in marsh bogs and then drowned by incoming tides. Some become entangled in dense foliage and vines, leaving them to starve and exposed to predators. Carol also

Loggerhead hatchling. (Courtesy of the Jekyll Island Authority)

Loggerhead sea turtle. Photograph by Upendra Kanda. Figure reproduced under the Creative Commons Attribution 2.0 Generic License. https://bit.ly/2XyQF5E

objects to the damage wild horses can wreak on the dune systems and marshes: "Horses also have a detrimental impact on the island ecology. Because of that, the NPS wishes to get rid of them but fears public outcry based on [public] ignorance of the situation. In other parks they have begun doing vasectomies, which would be an acceptable solution to most, I assume."

Over the years, the National Park Service has attempted to control white-tailed deer, feral hogs, and other animal populations. Deer and hogs have been implicated in the reduction of native vegetation, including young live oak trees. In an effort to control the deer population and other herbivores (rabbits, squirrels, raccoons, rats) on Cumberland, the National Park Service and the Georgia Department of Natural Resources, in cooperation with the University of Georgia's Wildlife Department, reintroduced in 1988 thirty-two bobcats fitted with radio collars to track their movements. The university monitored their activity for three years. One female bobcat swam to the mainland almost immediately after her release onto Cumberland. Ultimately, the bobcats' impact on deer and hog populations proved to be limited, as they went after easy prey such as rabbits and rats. As one local hunter put it, "bobcats are in the Okefenokee, and they have a deer problem there." A 2012 study estimated that fourteen descendants of the original thirty-two bobcats were on the island, evidence that they have adapted to the island environment.

Kennedy Wedding

Cumberland Island made national and international headlines in 1996. On September 21 of that year, John Kennedy Jr. and Carolyn Bessette were married in the First African Baptist Church in the Settlement. Thirty-three years earlier, Beulah Alberty and her neighbors held a memorial service and candlelight vigil in that same church to mourn the death of John F. Kennedy. Now his son was exchanging vows there in one of the most anticipated weddings of the decade, an event many members of the press eagerly sought to cover. Somehow, they were kept in the dark until the newlyweds had left on their honeymoon.

John Jr. and Janet "Gogo" Ferguson (Miss Lucy's granddaughter) had known each other for years. He had been a frequent guest on Cumberland and an ardent supporter who helped raise $10 million to renovate Plum Orchard. He developed a keen sense of Cumberland's history and an appreciation for its beauty, having spent many hours exploring the island on horseback, hiking its trails alone, and taking long swims in the river and the ocean. Bessette made trips to the island to plan the wedding, occasionally lying on a car floorboard to avoid being seen by locals. Speculation ran high about who John, one of the most eligible bachelors of his day, would marry and where the wedding would take place. As one gossip columnist wrote, "on the celebrity safari, Kennedy was the lion of the big game hunter."

Gogo, an accomplished jeweler, is no stranger to hosting A-list celebrities. She orchestrated this highly secretive affair, keeping all but a handful of people in the dark, a feat that "required the skill of James Bond and the whole CIA," Jacqueline Kennedy's former social secretary later commented. Most wedding guests weren't invited until five days before the event. Kennedy family members and other wedding guests stayed at Greyfield Inn, managed by Gogo's brother, Mitty, and his wife, Mary Jo. From the county clerk to the catering staff, locals at St. Marys and on Cumberland drawn into the new Kennedy conspiracy all conducted themselves with professional dignity, honoring the couples' wish for privacy throughout the affair. To ensure that stray journalists and curious onlookers were kept away, the staff on Cumberland were required to carry at all times a small card on which was attached an Indian-head buffalo nickel and an old penny—an ID badge that would be hard to duplicate. Guests arrived the day before the wedding and enjoyed a rehearsal dinner on the veranda of Greyfield Inn, followed by a bonfire on the beach.

John Kennedy Jr. and Carolyn Bessette Kennedy leaving the First African Baptist Church moments after exchanging wedding vows. (Photo by Denis Reggie)

David R. Davis, a gospel singer from nearby Yulee, Florida, was engaged to sing a capella at the wedding service. John Jr. and Carolyn requested "Amazing Grace" and "Will the Circle Be Unbroken?," songs that no doubt reverberated throughout the tiny sanctuary during Sunday services in years past. Guests were shuttled the seven miles to the church in Jeeps and pickup trucks. John wore one of his father's shirts and cuff links. By the time the bride and groom arrived at the Settlement from the Greyfield Inn, two hours late, guests were wandering through Carol Ruckdeschel's museum admiring her specimens. In the darkening evening, Carol and the National Park Service employees provided guests with flashlights. Candles and gas lanterns lit the church interior, providing a warm glow for the intimate setting.

Sitting on a milk crate, Carol watched the proceedings from her horse barn, enjoying a beer and a bowl of popcorn. "A couple of mix-ups occurred," Carol recalls, "so it took place after dark. It was low key and very nice, with people were eager to get back to Greyfield Inn to party. So eager, that they departed without Carolyn and John." After the ceremony, while Carolyn smoothed her dress for the photographer, she felt a tug on the bouquet in her left hand. It was Ruckdeschel's horse, enjoying an evening snack. Following an evening of celebration at Greyfield Inn, the newlyweds sailed away the next morning on the Kennedy family yacht, *Honey Fitz*.

Their marriage lasted just over a thousand days, about the length of John F. Kennedy's presidency. On a hazy day, July 16, 1999, the couple and Carolyn's sister, Lauren, departed in a Piper Saratoga aircraft from Fairfield, New Jersey, bound for Martha's Vineyard. They were flying to attend his cousin's (Rory Kennedy's) wedding. A massive search and rescue operation ensued when their plane failed to arrive as scheduled. Five days later, the two sisters' bodies were recovered on the seafloor near the wreckage. Divers found John Jr. still strapped in his seat. Their wedding bands, designed by Gogo, went down with them.

Afterword

The history of Cumberland Island is the history of change. Sometimes it arrives slowly, like an incoming tide on a lazy summer day. Other times it arrives as part of a great wave. A local resident, Thora Olsen Kimsey, once said of Cumberland, "It's a constant movement. The island is never still if you take time to look. Sometimes you're not aware of it until all of a sudden something happens to make you stop and take notice, and then you realize that things have changed."

In 2018 the U.S. Mint issued a new Cumberland Island Georgia quarter designed by Donna Weaver and sculpted by Don Everhart. On it, a snowy egret prominently perches on a tree branch overlooking a salt marsh, its wings spread wide as if soaking up the sun. Or is it about to take flight? Either way, it is an apt metaphor for events unfolding on the island and across the river on the mainland. Amid the tranquility of island life stir new undertones of change, including (of all things) space travel.

The National Aeronautics and Space Administration (NASA) considered establishing its space program on Cumberland Island in the 1960s and even tested large solid-rocket motors in Camden County opposite the island. But the U.S. Air Force already had an air base near Cape Canaveral and convinced NASA to locate its program there. Now, another rocket program is back in Camden.

On August 3, 2017, the rocket launch company Vector Launch conducted a suborbital test spaceflight. The rocket blasted off from Spaceport Camden, a newly created launch site located on the mainland opposite Cumberland Island's north end. The spaceport sits on eleven thousand acres once occupied by Thiokol, a rocket and missile propulsion systems company, and Bayer Crop Science, a plant biotechnology company. Camden County officials hope the site will become a "premier spaceport," attracting commercial

The Cumberland Island quarter was minted in 2018.

Loggerhead hatchling. (Courtesy of the Jekyll Island Authority)

companies needing to launch payloads and people into space. Spaceport Camden officials hope to conduct twelve launches and twelve landings each year. A Georgia Southern University study placed the spaceport's annual economic impact at over $22 million in revenue.

The Georgia Conservancy and other conservation organizations want to know what the environmental impact will be. Each launch might require Greater Cumberland and Little Cumberland residents to evacuate. Burning debris could ignite fires during drought periods. What catastrophic events are possible, or even likely? What would be the results of such catastrophes? How might Cumberland's wildlife be affected? What will happen if manned spaceflights requiring larger rockets are allowed at the spaceport? The National Park Service is concerned about these issues and about the potential loss of revenue due to closures and visitor restrictions during rocket launches.

More recently, island watchers have sounded alarms over the construction of a new private dock along with Candler and Carnegie family members' rezoning efforts to build new homes on property they own. Eight hundred acres on Greater Cumberland, most of which belongs to Carnegie heirs, remain in fee simple—without limits or conditions. Several Carnegie descendants took to Facebook to make their case: "Our group's purpose is to gain government approval for a reasonable use of our property while still protecting Cumberland Island. . . . With the [Camden County] commissions [*sic*] help we hope to be able to restore our rights to continue as we have for over 100 years, quietly live our lives on Cumberland and occasionally build a home for family use." The family members point out that the zoning proposal would only affect two percent of the island, all on private property. Wilderness and National Seashore zones would not be affected.

They also tout their 130-year tradition of island stewardship, stating "we don't want a large-scale development and never will."

Skeptics point out there is no guarantee that descendants will continue the stewardship of this generation. They point to the 1950s strip-mining proposal by the Glidden Company, which some Carnegies favored. And they point to the 1968 sale of two Carnegie tracts to Charles Fraser, who planned to develop as much island property as he could acquire. Other Carnegies and Candlers stood firm and blocked both deals, but who is to say whether their progeny will be able to respond similarly to future development efforts?

What does the future hold for Cumberland Island? Today's crystal ball is as cloudy as the ones used by Chief Tacatacuru, Pedro Menéndez de Avilés, Jonathan Bryan, James Oglethorpe, Nathanael Greene, Lucy Carnegie, Lucy Ferguson, and others attempting to foresee what lies ahead. Their visions always turned out differently than anticipated. If the island could speak, what would it say? Does it care who is riding on it? Would the island laugh at their plans as it continues its slow but inexorable journey along the continental shelf?

Humans measure long stretches of time in eras. Cumberland Island measures time in eons. It has seen many peoples come and go—the nameless first arrivals, the Timucua, the Spanish, the English, the land barons, and, yes, even today's tourists and conservationists—each perhaps presuming to be the final word in the island's history. Men and women still leave their mark on the island. But as with footprints in the sand, all evidence they were ever here eventually washes away with the next tide or the next rain. In the end, Cumberland Island, the Gem of the Atlantic, the Jewel of the Golden Isles, has the last word. But like everyone who has come before, new generations will fall under the island's spell, and however briefly, leave their footprints on Cumberland's sandy shores.

Selected Bibliography

The following sources were particularly useful in researching this book.

Some sources spanned chapters. In chapters 5 through 9, Mary R. Bullard's *Cumberland Island: A History* (Athens: University of Georgia Press, 2003) was indispensable.

In chapters 6 through 9, I relied on the Georgia Historic Newspapers database, Digital Library of Georgia; this is part of the GALILEO Initiative, https://gahistoricnewspapers.galileo.usg.edu.

In chapters 8 and 9, I utilized the collection at the Bryan-Lang Historical Library and Archives (Woodbine, Georgia) of oral histories of Cumberland Island residents and workers conducted by Joyce Seward (1995–96) and an unidentified interviewer (1971). U.S. Department of the Interior, National Park Service, Cumberland Island National Seashore, St. Marys, Georgia.

CHAPTER I

John E. Ehrenhard, "Cumberland Island National Seashore, Archeological Mitigation of NPS 9 CAM 5 and 9 CAM 6," Southeast Archeological Center, National Park Service, U.S. Department of the Interior, Tallahassee, Fla., 1981.

W. W. Ehrmann, "The Timucua Indians of Sixteenth Century Florida," *Florida Historical Quarterly* 18, no. 3 (January 1940): 168–191.

Albert S. Gatschet, "The Timucua Language," *Proceedings of the American Philosophical Society* 18, no. 105 (January–March 1880).

Georgia Conservancy, *A Guide to the Georgia Coast*, edited by Gwendolyn McKee and Carol Johnson (Savannah: Georgia Conservancy, 1984).

Count D. Gibson, *Sea Islands of Georgia: Their Geologic History* (Athens: University of Georgia Press, 1948).

Martha M. Griffin, *Geologic Guide to Cumberland Island National Seashore* (Atlanta: Georgia Geologic Survey, Department of Natural Resources, Environmental Protection Division, 1991).

John H. Hann, *A History of the Timucua Indians and Missions* (Gainesville: University Press of Florida, 1996).

Jerald T. Milanich, "Tacatacuru and the San Pedro de Mocamo Mission," *Florida Historical Society Quarterly* 50, no. 3 (January 1972): 283–91.

————, *The Timucua* (Oxford: Blackwell, 1996).

Carol Ruckdeschel, *A Natural History of Cumberland Island Georgia* (Macon, Ga.: Mercer University Press, 2017).

Fred Whitehead, *The Seasons of Cumberland Island* (Athens: University of Georgia Press, 2004).

John E. Worth, *The Struggle for the Georgia Coast: An Eighteenth-Century Spanish Retrospective on Guale and Mocoma* (Anthropological Papers of the American Museum of Natural History, no. 75, distributed by the University of Georgia Press, Athens, 1995).

————, *The Timucuan Chiefdoms of Spanish Florida*, vol. 2, *Resistance and Destruction* (Gainesville: University Press of Florida, 1998).

CHAPTER 2

Denise I. Bossy, ed., *The Yamasee Indians: From Florida to South Carolina* (Lincoln: University of Nebraska Press, 2018).

Larry Richard Clark, *Spanish Attempts to Colonize Southeast North America, 1513–1587* (Jefferson, N.C.: McFarland, 2010).

Jonathan Dickinson, *Jonathan Dickinson's Journal, Or God's Protecting Providence: Being the Narratives of a Journey from Port Royal In Jamaica to Philadelphia between August 23, 1696 and April 1, 1697*, edited by Evangeline Walker Andrews and Charles McLean Andrews (New Haven, Conn.: Yale University Press, 1945).

Rev. Maynard Geiger, O.F.M., *The Franciscan Conquest of Florida (1573–1618)* (Washington, D.C.: Catholic University of America, 1937).

Jerald T. Milanich, *Laboring in the Fields of the Lord: Spanish Missions and Southeastern Indians* (Washington, D.C.: Smithsonian Institution Press, 1999).

Fray Andrés de San Miguel, *An Early Florida Adventure Story*, translated by John H. Hann (Gainesville: University of Florida Press, 2001).

John R. Swanton, *The Early History of the Creek Indians and Their Neighbors* (Smithsonian Institution Bureau of American Ethnology, Bulletin 73, Government Printing Office, Washington, D.C., 1922).

John E. Worth, "A History of Southeastern Indians in Cuba, 1513–1823," presented at the 61st Annual Meeting of the Southeastern Archaeological Conference, St. Louis, Mo., October 21–23, 2004.

CHAPTER 3

Herbert E. Bolton, *Arredondo's Historical Proof of Spain's Title to Georgia* (Berkeley: University of California Press, 1925).

Herbert E. Bolton and Mary Ross, *The Debatable Land; A Sketch of the Anglo-Spanish Contest for the Georgia Country* (New York: Russell & Russell, 1968).

Allen D. Candler, comp., *The Colonial Records of the State of Georgia*, vols. 7, 8, 18, 19, and 26 (Atlanta: Franklin-Turner Company, 1909–11).

Edward J. Cashin, "James Oglethorpe's Account of the 1745 Escape of the Scots at Shap," *Georgia Historical Quarterly* 76, no. 1 (spring 1992): 87–99.

Kenneth Coleman and Milton Ready, eds., *Colonial Records of the State of Georgia*, vol. 28, *Original Papers of Governors Reynolds, Ellis, Wright, and Others, 1757–1763*, part 1 (Athens: University of Georgia Press, 1976).

Harold E. Davis, *The Fledgling Province, Social and Cultural Life in Colonial Georgia, 1733–1776* (Chapel Hill: University of North Carolina Press, 1976).

Jingle Davis, *Island Time: An Illustrated History of St. Simons Island, Georgia* (Athens: University of Georgia Press, 2013).

John C. Inscoe, *James Edward Oglethorpe: New Perspectives on His Life and Legacy* (Georgia Historical Society, Savannah, and the James Edward Oglethorpe Tercentenary Commission, Oglethorpe University, 1997).

James Edward Oglethorpe, *General Oglethorpe's Georgia, Colonial Letters, 1733–1737*, edited by Mills Lane (Savannah: Beehive Press, 1975).

———, *General Oglethorpe's Georgia, Colonial Letters, 1738–1743*, edited by Mills Lane (Savannah: Beehive Press, 1975).

Phinizy Spalding and Harvey H. Jackson, *Oglethorpe in Perspective: Georgia's Founder after Two Hundred Years* (Tuscaloosa: University of Alabama Press, 1989).

CHAPTER 4

Jonathan Bryan, *Life and Times of Jonathan Bryan, 1708–1788*, https://archive.org/stream /lifetimesofjonatooreddi/lifetimesofjonatooreddi_djvu.txt.

Mary Ricketson Bullard, *Black Liberation on Cumberland Island in 1815* (DeLeon Springs, Fla.: E. O. Painter Printing, 1983).

E. Merton Coulter, *Georgia, A Short History* (Chapel Hill: University of North Carolina Press, 1947).

Alan Gallay, *The Formation of a Planter Elite: Jonathan Bryan and the Southern Colonial Frontier* (Athens: University of Georgia Press, 1989).

————, "The Search for an Alternate Source of Trade: The Creek Indians and Jonathan Bryan," *Georgia Historical Quarterly* 73, no. 2 (summer 1989): 209–30.

Georgia Historical Society, *Collections of the Georgia Historical Society*, vol. 4, *The Dead Towns of Georgia* (Savannah: Georgia Historical Society, 1878).

Marguerite Bartlett Hamer, "Edmund Gray and His Settlement at New Hanover," *Georgia Historical Quarterly* 13, no. 1 (March 1929): 1–12.

William J. Northen, ed., *Men of Mark In Georgia, a Complete and Elaborate History of the State from Its Settlement to the Present Time*, vol. 1 (Atlanta: A. B. Caldwell, 1907).

William Ramsey, "The Final Contest for 'Debatable Land': Fort William and the Frontier Defenses of Colonial Georgia," *Georgia Historical Quarterly* 77, no. 3 (fall 1993): 497–524.

Rev. George White, *Historical Collections of Georgia* (New York: Pudney & Russell, 1854).

Virginia Steele Wood, *Live Oaking: Southern Timber for Tall Ships* (Boston: Northeastern University Press, 1981).

Virginia Steele Wood and Mary R. Bullard, *Journal of a Visit to the Georgia Islands* (Macon: Mercer University Press, in association with the Georgia Historical Society, Savannah, 1996).

CHAPTER 5

Mary R. Bullard, "In Search of Cumberland Island's Dungeness: Its Origins and English Antecedents," *Georgia Historical Quarterly* 76, no. 1 (spring 1992): 67–86.

————, "The Lynch-Greene Partition on Cumberland Island, 1798–1802," *Georgia Historical Quarterly* 77, no. 4 (winter 1993): 757–88.

Wesley Frank Craven, *A History of the South*, vol. 1, *The Southern Colonies in the Seventeenth Century, 1607–1689* (Baton Rouge: Louisiana State University Press, 1949).

General Nathanael Greene, *The Papers of General Nathanael Greene*, 13 vols., edited by Richard K. Showman (Chapel Hill: Published for the Rhode Island Historical Society by the University of North Carolina Press, 1976–2005).

Paul E. Hoffman, *The New Andalucia and a Way to the Orient: The American Southeast During the Sixteenth Century* (Baton Rouge: Louisiana State University Press, 1990).

Theodore Lyman Jr., *The Diplomacy of the United States: Being An Account of The Foreign Relations of the Country from the First Treaty with France, in 1778, to the Present Time*, 2nd ed., vol. 1 (Boston: Wells & Lilly, 1828).

Frederick A. Ober, *Dungeness: General Greene's Sea-Island Plantation* ([Philadelphia:] J. B. Lippincott, 1880).

John F. Stegeman and Janet A. Stegeman, *Caty: A Biography of Catharine Littlefield Greene* (Athens: University of Georgia Press, 1977).

CHAPTER 6

Allan D. Austin, *African Muslims in Antebellum America: Transatlantic Stories and Spiritual Struggles* (New York: Routledge, 1997).

Sir George Cockburn Papers, 1788–1847 (bulk 1800–1820), Library of Congress, reels 4, 5, 6, 7, 9, 10.

Caroline Couper Lovell, *The Golden Isles of Georgia* (Boston: Little, Brown, 1933). Map by Helene Carter.

Burnett Vanstory, *Georgia's Land of the Golden Isles* (Athens: Brown Thrasher Books, University of Georgia Press, 1981).

Harvey A. Whitfield, "We Can Do As We Like Here: An Analysis of Self Assertion and Agency among Black Refugees in Halifax, Nova Scotia, 1813–1821," *Acadiensis: Journal of the History of the Atlantic Region* 32, no. 1 (autumn 2002): 29–49.

CHAPTER 7

James Bagwell, *Rice Gold: James Hamilton Couper and Plantation Life on the Georgia Coast* (Macon: Mercer University Press, 2000).

Mary Bullard, *Robert Stafford of Cumberland Island: Growth of a Planter* (Athens: University of Georgia Press, 1995).

Erik Calonius, *The Wanderer: The Last American Slave Ship and the Conspiracy that Set Its Sails* (New York: St. Martin's, 2006).

Samuel Francis Du Pont, *Samuel Francis Du Pont: A Selection from His Civil War Letters*, 3 vols., edited by John D. Hayes (Ithaca, N.Y.: Cornell University Press, 1969).

June Hall McCash, *Jekyll Island's Early Years from Prehistory through Reconstruction* (Athens: University of Georgia Press, 2005).

James M. Merrill, *Du Pont, The Making of an Admiral: A Biography of Samuel Francis Du Pont* (New York: Dodd, Mead, 1986).

Charles R. Stark, *Groton, Conn, 1705–1905* (Stonington, Conn.: Palmer Press, 1922).

J. Anderson Thomson Jr. and Carlos Michael Santos, "The Mystery in the Coffin: Another View of Lee's Visit to His Father's Grave," in "They Were Men of Our Shape: Image and Ego in Civil War Biography," special issue, *Virginia Magazine of History and Biography* 103, no. 1 (January 1995): 75–94.

CHAPTER 8

Nathan Atkinson Brown Papers, 1850–1936 (bulk 1861–1864), MS808, Letters Written by Family Members, box 1, folders 1–3, Hargrett Rare Book and Manuscript Library, University of Georgia.

Mary R. Bullard, *An Abandoned Black Settlement on Cumberland Island, Georgia* (DeLeon Springs, Fla.: E. O. Painter Printing, 1982).

Margaret Davis Cate, *Our Todays and Yesterdays: A Story of Brunswick and the Coastal Islands* (Brunswick, Ga.: Glover Bros., 1930).

Stephen Doster, *Voices from St. Simons: Personal Narratives of an Island's Past* (Winston-Salem, N.C.: John F. Blair, 2008).

John E. Johns, *Florida during the Civil War* (Gainesville: University of Florida Press, 1963).

Mary Miller, *Cumberland Island: The Unsung Northend* (Darien, Ga.: Darien News, 1990).

———, *I Remember Cumberland* ([Cumberland Island, Ga.], 1993).

———, *On Christmas Creek: Life on Cumberland Island* (Darien, Ga.: Darien News, 1995).

CHAPTER 9

Larry F. Andrews, Joanne Werwie, and Rice H. Grant, *Cumberland Island: A Treasure of Memories* (Tampa, Fla.: World-Wide, 1986).

Patricia Barefoot, *Cumberland Island (GA), Images of America* (New York: Arcade, 2004).

Larry M. Dilsaver, *Cumberland Island National Seashore: A History of Conservation Conflict* (Charlottesville: University of Virginia Press, 2004).

Joe Graves, Mary Lloyd Ireland, and Sally Dodd, *Cumberland Island Saved: How the Carnegies Helped Preserve a National Treasure* (Lexington, Ky.: Gravesend, 2014).

Will Harlan, *Untamed: The Wildest Woman in America and the Fight for Cumberland Island* (New York: Grove, 2014).

Harold H. Martin, *This Happy Isle: The Story of Sea Island and the Cloister* (Sea Island, Ga.: Sea Island Company, 1978).

Thornton W. Morris, *Cumberland Island: A Place Apart* (Atlanta: Cumberland Island Conservancy, 2008).

Carol Ruckdeschel and C. Robert Shoop, *Sea Turtles of the Atlantic and Gulf Coasts of the United States* (Athens: University of Georgia Press, 2006).

Charles Seabrook, *Cumberland Island: Strong Women, Wild Horses* (Winston-Salem, N.C.: J. F. Blair, 2002).

Stewart Udall, *The Quiet Crisis* (New York: Holt, Rinehart & Winston, 1963).

U.S. National Park Service, *A Report on Our Vanishing Shoreline* ([Washington, D.C.:] U.S. National Park Service, Department of the Interior, [1955?]).

Index

Adams-Onís Treaty, 120
African American settlements, 245–260
Agustín, Domingo, 63
Ainsworth, A. A., 322
Ais (Native tribe), 78, 82, 90
Albany Guards, 271
Alberty, Beulah G., 260, 323, 346
Alberty, Charles, 260
Alberty, Renda, 341
Alberty, Rogers, 250, 254
Alberty, Thomas, 255
Alberty, William M., 255, 276, 341
Alexander, Ephraim, 129, 130, 135
Altamaha, Chief, 93
Altamaha Project, 124, 141
Altamaha River: as Timucua territory boundary, 9, 11; Father Andrés mention of, 86; disputed territory, 95–105 passim; fortifications south of, 106, 113; new border, 119, 120; Bryan land acquisition (Altamaha Project), 124; Gray's Gang, 128–134 passim; South Carolina claim to, 137, 138; Bryan's lease south of, 141; War of 1812, 179
Altamirano, Juan de las Cabezas, 84, 85
Amelia, Princess Sophia Eleanor, 103
Amelia Island, 17, 65; Dickinson party, 90–91; mission San Phelipe III, 93; naming of, 102–103; horse stud, 112; Highlander murders, 113; Spanish 1742 attack, 116; Gray's Gang, 131, 135; proposed East Florida capitol site, 147; French navy at, 155; illicit trade, 169; British gunboat

skirmish, 170; U.S. marines landing, 170–171; War of 1812, 178; enslaved escapees, 187; lighthouse on, 217; Civil War, 220, 226–228, 232–234; Primus Mitchell on, 248; epidemic, 254; 1898 hurricane, 275; paper mills, 325
Anansi, 247
Andrés de San Miguel, Father, shipwreck account of, 85–89
Andrew W. Mellon Foundation, 328, 331, 332
Anglo-French War, 149
Anne (ship), 98
Apalachee, Bay of, 130
Apalachi (Apalachee), 9, 19, 93, 141
Archivo General de Indias, 19
Arredondo, Antonio de, 106
Asao, 69, 70, 71, 76, 81; Father Andrés time on, 86, 87
Asencio, 82
Atkinson, Col. Edmund Nathan, 219
Atlanta Row, 273, 275
Atuluteca, 11
Aucilla River, 3, 9
Augusta, Ga., 94, 123, 124, 128, 204
Avendaño, Domingo Martínez de, 66, 75
Avera, John Byron, 324
Ávila, Father, 73
Ayllón, Lucas Vazquez de, 56

Bailey, Jesse, 341
Banks, John, 143, 144, 150, 152
Barriemackie, 106, 108, 109, 113

Battle of Culloden, 121
Bayer Crop Science, 349
Beach Creek, 4, 165
Bealey, Richard, 302
Bealey, Sam, 302
Bealey, Will, 302
Beggs, Virginia (Carnegie), 313
Bejessi, 70, 71
Benson, George W., 262, 270, 279
Beringia, 2
Bering Strait, 2
Bermuda, 176, 182, 183, 185, 190, 191, 203
Bernardey, Adelaide "Addie" or "Ada" (Zivulki), 213, 239, 300
Bernardey, Armand, 213, 233, 234
Bernardey, Clarice, 213
Bernardey, Elizabeth "Zabette," 210, 213, 214, 239, 243, 300
Bernardey, Ellen (Brady; Engels), 213, 214, 239, 300
Bernardey, Marguerite, 210, 313
Bernardey, Mary Elizabeth (Palmer; Gaylord), 210, 213, 239, 300
Bernardey, Medora "Dora" (Vosburgh), 213, 214, 239, 300
Bernardey, Pierre, 210
Bernardey, Robert, 213, 234
Berrien, John McPherson, 192
Bessette, Carolyn, 346, 347
Bessette, Lauren, 347
Bettie (enslaved mother of Primus Mitchell), 248

bird species, 6
bison (buffalo), 2, 22, 101, 126
Blackstone, Sir William, 190
Board of Trade (English), 128, 129, 132, 134, 137
Bolton, Herbert, 19, 63, 132
Boone, Gov. Thomas, 137
Boswell, James, 121
Bowman, John, 146, 155
Bowman, Sabina Lynch, 146
Boyle, Thomas, 189
Brady, Benjamin, 239
Br'er Rabbit, 247
Brickhill Bluff, 14, 70, 93; Gray's Gang
    settlement, 132–133; freedmen settlement,
    245, 248, 250, 254; in hotel era, 247, 251, 266;
    proposed Glidden Company settlement, 325;
    proposed NPS ferry dock site, 329
Brickhill River, 234
Bridge, Margaret, 277
Brooklyn Dodgers, 336
Brown, Eula, 222, 223
Brown, Lilly (Dunwoody), 233
Brown, Louisa Tupper (Nicholes), 220, 221, 223,
    232, 233
Brown, Lucile (Bruce), 233
Brown, Nathan Atkinson, Jr., 233
Brown, Capt. Nathan "Nate" Atkinson, 219–
    226, 232–233
Brown, Nathan Atkinson, III, 233
Brunswick Cycle Company, 273
Brunswick Pulp and Paper, 329
Bryan, Jonathan, 99, 113, 158; expedition to
    Florida, 124–127; Royal Council appointment,
    127; acquisition of Cumberland property, 138;
    opposition to British tax acts, 139; suspension
    from council, 140; sale of Cumberland
    property, 140; lease of Creek land, 141;
    dismissal from Georgia legislature, 141; escape
    to Cumberland, 142
Bryant, Curtis, 243
Bryant, Goodbe, 130
Bu Allah (Bilali Mohammed), 189
Bullard, Mary, 127, 170, 182, 243, 285, 291;
    Dungeness naming, 158, 160; *Zabette* libretto,
    243
Bullard, William, 67
Bulloch, Rev. James, 138

Bunkley, Isabella (Miller), 262
Bunkley, R. L., 279
Bunkley, Thomas Pitt, 262
Bunkley, William H., 269, 270
Bunkley, William R., 251, 260, 262, 264, 269;
    hotel owner, 252; sale of Sea-Side House, 271
Burbank, Catherine "Katie," 254
Burbank, George, 260
Burbank, Mason T., 254, 260, 279
Burbank, William Hunter, Sr., 261
Burbank Sport Nets, 261
Bureau of Refugees, Freedmen, and Abandoned
    Lands, 237, 238
Burke, John W., Jr., 271
Burnet, Ichabod, 144
Burr, Aaron, 143, 167, 169
Butler, Pierce, 191
Butler, Pierce Mease, 155, 169

Cabale, Juan Alfonso, 93
cacica, 74, 79, 81–82, 84
cacina, 10; use in war, 40; preparation of, and
    health benefits, 86
cacique, definition of, 19; interviews with, 19;
    social organization of Timucua and,
    25; Spanish missions and, 66–85.
    See also *mico*
Camden County, 6, 121, 126, 144, 352; Robert
    Stafford and, 203, 204; Civil War, 219, 233;
    National Park, 327, 329, 330; rocket launch
    site, 349
Camden County Recreational Authority, 327
Camden Rifles, 219, 223
Camp Bartow, 219, 224
Candler, Asa, 279
Candler, Catherine, 324
Candler, Charles Howard, 255, 279, 324
Candler, Louisa, 324
Candler, Sam, 330
Candler family, 326, 327, 328, 341, 353; National
    Seashore, 329, 333
Candler property, 322, 330, 339, 352
Canzo, Gonzalo Méndez de, 66, 67, 71, 77, 78,
    82; Guale revolt, 71, 73, 74; denounced by
    friars, 75, 78; Cumberland mission rebuild,
    79, 81
Capilla, Juan Baptista de, 84

Carlyle, Thomas, 112
Carnegie, Andrew, 278, 282, 284, 289, 302, 325;
    visits to Cumberland Island, 306, 313
Carnegie, Andrew, II, 284, 302
Carnegie, Andrew, III, 327
Carnegie, Carter, 282, 336
Carnegie, Coleman, 284
Carnegie, Florence "Flossie" Nightingale
    (Perkins), 284, 321, 325, 326, 329
Carnegie, Frank Morrison, 284, 288
Carnegie, Gallea Pollakov "Polly" Stein, 282, 291,
    313, 336
Carnegie, George Lauder, 284, 302, 313
Carnegie, Henry Carter, 327
Carnegie, Lucy Ackerman Coleman: yacht
    damage, 275; Dungeness purchase, 282;
    marriage, 284; inheritance, 288; Stafford
    property purchase, 289; Dungeness
    improvements, 289–291; Stafford lawsuits,
    300; cottages, 302, 313, 315, 334; Andrew
    Carnegie visits, 306, 313; death of, and trust,
    315, 321, 329; heirs, 325; will, 330
Carnegie, Margaret Morrison, 288
Carnegie, Margaret "Retta" Coleman
    (Ricketson), 284, 315, 333
Carnegie, Nancy Trovillo (Hever), 284, 302
Carnegie, Thomas Morrison, 282, 322, 325, 334;
    Dungeness purchase, 284; Stafford property
    purchase, 285; death of, 288; burial on
    Cumberland, 315
Carnegie, Thomas Morrison, II, 284, 313, 321
Carnegie, Thomas, III, 313
Carnegie, Thomas, IV, 289, 327
Carnegie, William "Will" Coleman, 284, 302,
    306, 334
Carnegie Brothers Ironworks, 282
Carnegie heirs, 321, 325, 326, 352
Carnegie Hero Fund, 278
Carnes, Henry, 200
Carter, James Earl, Jr., "Jimmy," 332
Casa de Contratacíon (Spanish Board of Trade), 57
Cascangue, 79
Castillo de San Marcos (Fort San Marcos), 113,
    134, 147
Castries, Marquis de, 146
ceramics, Native, 14, 16, 67
Charlesfort, 29

Charleston (Charles Town), 85, 94, 97, 100, 196; Oglethorpe's arrival, 98; American Revolution, 143; John McQueen in, 145; War of 1812, 176; Civil War, 225–228; Sherman's Special Field Order 15, 237

Chichimeco, 93, 94

Chozas, Pedro Fernández de, 69, 70, 71, 73, 76, 91

Christmas Creek, 4

Church, Robert, 217

Civil Air Patrol, 323

Civil War, 216–238

clans, Native, 25

Clinch, Gen. Duncan Lamont, Jr., 233

Clothogotheo, 103

Clovis culture, 3

Clubb, Alice, 185

Clubb, Clarice, 185, 186

Clubb, Elias (Peerson), 253, 254

Clubb, James A., 215, 216, 217, 227, 253, 254

Clubb, Nancy, 185

Clubb, Penny, 185, 186

Clubb, Rachel (Church), 185, 234

Clubb, Rebecca, 253, 262

Clubb, William, Jr., 176, 185, 186

Clubb, William, Sr., 185

Coastal Plain aquifer, 6

Coast Guard, U.S., 217, 334, 336; World War II deployment on Cumberland, 322–325

Cob, Don Ignatio, 105, 106

Cochran, Lt. Col., 110, 111

Cochran, Janet, 124

Cochrane, Vice Adm. Alexander Inglis, 176, 179, 188, 189, 192; emancipation of enslaved, 182, 187, 188; arrival on Cumberland, 190; Treaty of Ghent, 188

Cockburn, Rear Adm. Sir George, 173, 176, 183, 192, 195, 220, 227; headquartered at Dungeness, 179, 181; emancipation of enslaved, 182, 185, 187–189; conditions on Cumberland, 185, 186; enslaved recruitment into military, 187, 204; local planters' claims, 190, 191

Cockburn, Sir James, 192

Cockspur Island, 216, 226

Coleman, William, 284

Collett, E. John, 151

Colonial Marines, 183, 186, 191

Commodore, Henry, 243

Commodore, Tecumsah "Cumsie" (Cooper), 238, 243

Consejo de Indias (Council of the Indies), 57, 66, 81, 82

Cook, James, 160

Cook, Col. William, 112, 113, 119, 121

Cooper, Gen. Samuel, 225

Cooper, Tecumsah "Cumsie," 243

Coosawhatchie, S.C., 216

Corpa, Pedro de, 67, 69

Corrie, Capt. William C., 215, 216

Cottage, the, 313, 336

cotton, 6, 124, 153, 154, 157, 203; Bryan plantation, 140, 142; Miller plantation, 160, 166, 167, 175; War of 1812 seizures, 179, 183, 186, 191; Nightingale estate sale, 198; Anguilla cottonseed, 203; Stafford plantation, 204, 205; Civil War, 225, 235, 241; Grant visit, 267; Carnegie era, 294, 302, 321

cotton gin, 153, 154, 156, 157, 167

council house, Native, 10, 86, 87, 88

Couper, Anne Sarah, 183, 188

Couper, Hamilton, 215

Couper, James Hamilton, 154, 183, 198, 215

Couper, John, 182, 183, 188, 191

Creek Indians and Nation, 9, 95, 104, 129; Mary Musgrove, 99; land ceded to English, 102, 144; Gray's Gang, 130, 132, 134, 135; Bryan land lease, 141, 142; McQueen expedition, 145

Cumberland, Prince William Augustus, Duke of, 100, 113, 121; naming of Cumberland Island, 102, 104

Cumberland African Church, 248

Cumberland Company, 271

Cumberland Harbor, 160, 176

Cumberland Island Club, 279

Cumberland Island Company (I), 260

Cumberland Island Company (II), 326

Cumberland Island Conservation Association, 326

Cumberland Island Hotel, 270–279

Cumberland Island National Seashore, creation of, 326–333

Cumberland Route, 260, 274, 279

Cumberland Sound, 11, 67, 116, 170, 217, 313; Civil War, 225, 226, 227, 232

Cummings, W. B., 200, 276, 277

Cuthbert, James, 138

Cuthbert, John, 138

Cuyler, T. Smith, 276

Cybulski, Charles Dieudonné (Zivulki), 239

Darien, Ga., 69, 74, 78, 86, 209, 213; colonial period, 100, 101, 105, 113, 124, 126; Bryan land purchases, 138; advertisement for runaway slave, 196; 1898 hurricane damage, 275

Davis, Bernard M., 281, 284

Davis, David R., 347

Davis, Jefferson, 220, 225, 281

Davis, Robert, 326, 329

Davis, Brig. Gen. William George Mackay, 281, 282, 284

Davisville, 326

de Barbé-Marbois, Marquis, 149

De Brahm, William Gerard, 124, 125, 126, 127

de Bry, Theodore, 19, 29, 87

de Casinas, Marquess, 118

de Gourge, Dominique, 63

de Heredia, Alonso Fernández, 130

de la Freente, Capt. Pedro Revis, 200

de Lamberto, Don Pedro, 105

de Laudonnière, René. See Laudonnière, René de

Delegal's fort, 105

Demere, Capt. Raymond, 125

Demetre, Capt. Daniel, 125, 126

Deptford period, 14, 16

de Quevedo, Juan, 81

Desbrisay, Lt., 108, 109, 110

de Segura, Andrés (Father Andrés de San Miguel), shipwreck account, 85–89

de Soto, Hernando, 28–30, 46, 48, 56, 59–60

Dickinson, Jonathan, shipwreck account, 90–92

Dilsaver, Larry, 289, 321, 326, 333

dividings, 4, 118, 227

Doña Ana, 79, 81, 82

Doña María Meléndez, 82, 84

Don Francisco, 74

Don Juan: San Pedro cacique, 66, 67; 1597 Guale raid, 69–72; relocation to Fort George Island, 73; return to Cumberland, 75; 1598 Guale raid, 77; death of, 79; Father Andrés's description of, 88

Don Juanillo, 67, 74
Downes, James, 247, 250
Downes, Margaret (Bernardey), 250
Downes, Robert, 247
Downes, William, 247
Downes, Winifred, 247, 251
Downes' Landing, 245
Drum Point Island, 332
DuBignon, Christopher, 210
DuBignon, John, 215
DuBignon, William T., 254
Dunbar, George, 116
Dungeness: location of Native village, 11;
    location of Spanish mission, 62, 67; Miller
    mansion location, 158; naming of, 158–159;
    Dungeness I construction, 162; as landmark,
    164; Ober description of, 164; plantation life,
    166–167; Burr visit, 169; smuggling enslaved,
    170; Caty Greene's death, 173; Louisa Shaw's
    management of, 175; War of 1812, 176, 179,
    181–183, 186–191; "Light-Horse Harry" Lee at,
    192–193, 195; orange crop, 195–196; transfer
    to Phineas Nightingale, 196–197; sale of, 198,
    204, 209; ruins, Robert E. Lee description
    of, 218; ruins, Samuel Francis Du Pont
    description of, 230–231, 232; Ned Simmons
    emancipation, 236–237; Dungeness I burning,
    238; Stafford purchase offer, 239–240;
    Molyneux acquisition, 240; Robert E. Lee's
    second visit to, 240, 241; hotel plans for, 252,
    260; Grant visit to, 267, 270; well drilling,
    6; 1898 flood, 275; "Light-Horse Harry" Lee
    disinterment, 276; purchase by William Davis,
    281; Lucy Carnegie interest in, 282; purchase
    by Thomas Carnegie, 284; Dungeness II
    construction, 285, 288, 289, 291; management
    of, 294–302, 306, 313, 315, 321, 322, 334;
    Dungeness II burning, 336
Dungeness Hotel, 252, 260
Dungeness Wharf, 11, 67, 181, 289
Dungeness yacht, 275, 336
Duplaine, Antoine Charbonnet, 155, 169
du Pont, Eleuthère Iréne, 230
du Pont, Gabrielle Josephine de la Fite de
    Pelleport, 225
Du Pont, Adm. Samuel Francis, 224, 226, 254;
    biosketch, 225; occupation of Cumberland,

227, 229; description of Dungeness, 230;
    Lincoln commendation, 232; death of, 238
Du Pont, Sophie Madeleine, 227, 228, 230, 231,
    232, 238
du Pont, Victor Marie, 225

Eaton, William F., 238
Edisto River, 105
Ehrenhard, John, 14
Ehrmann, W. W., 9, 19
El Camino Real, 60, 79
Ellis, Gov. Henry, 130, 131, 132, 133, 134, 135
Ely, Martha Gertrude (Carnegie), 302
emancipation: Spanish era, 74; War of 1812, 182,
    185, 187; Ned Simmons, 191, 237
Engels, Frederick, 239
Eugene, Prince of Savoy, 97, 105, 106
Evans, Cdre., 183
Eve, Joseph, 154
Everhart, Don, 349
Eve's Horse Gin, 154
Eyre, Benjamin, 148
Eyre, Thomas, 112, 116

Fader, Edgar, 341
Fader, Capt. George, 341
Fader, Richard "Dick," 341
Fader family, 279
Farnum, John Egbert, 215, 216
Fatio, Francis Phillip, 148, 149
Ferguson, Janet "Gogo," 346, 347
Ferguson, Lucy. See Ricketson, Lucy "Miss
    Lucy" Carnegie
Ferguson, Mary Jo, 346
Ferguson, Oliver "Mitty," 346
Ferguson, Robert "Bob" W., 323, 327, 334, 336
Fernández, Col. Antonio, 148
Fernandina, 164, 169, 170, 248, 267; during Civil
    War, 218, 224, 226, 227, 228, 232, 233, 234, 236,
    238; during hotel era, 252, 254, 260, 261, 274,
    275; during Carnegie era, 281, 282, 289, 334,
    342; during World War II, 323
First African Baptist Church, 255, 339, 346
Fleming, George, 147
flora and fauna, 6, 7
Florida, Ice Age land mass of, 3
Floridan aquifer, 6

Floyd, Gen. John, 189, 217
Forbes, Jonathan, 187
Fordham, Silas, 250, 251
Fort Atkinson, 219, 221, 222
Fort Caroline, 31, 36, 63, 89; construction, 57;
    Menéndez raid, 59–60
Fort Clinch, 220, 226, 228, 233
Fort Frederica. See Frederica
Fort George Island, 19, 66, 73, 205
Fort King George, 100, 137
Fort Picolata, 113
Fort Point Peter, 178
Fort Pulaski, 216, 226
Fort San Marcos (Castillo de San Marcos), 113,
    134, 147
Fort St. Andrews, 19, 105, 106, 112–113, 126, 140;
    establishment of, 101–104; mutiny at, 108, 111;
    Spanish invasion, 117–118; War of 1812 British
    landing, 176; hotel-era landing, 260
Fort St. Francis de Pupa, 113
Fort St. George, 105
Fort William, 120, 121, 131, 140, 142, 226;
    construction and naming of, 112; Spanish
    invasion, 113, 116, 117, 118; Bryan expedition,
    126–127; Gray's Gang, 132
Forty-Second Regiment of Foot, 106, 108, 117
Franciscans, 19, 45, 66, 75, 78; Guale revolt, 67,
    69, 70; mission restoration, 79, 93
Fraser, Charles, attempt to develop Cumberland,
    327–353
Fraser, Lt. John, 183, 188
Frederica, 104, 105, 106, 111, 113, 135; naming of
    fort, 100; Oglethorpe's name for St. Simons,
    102; Spanish invasion, 111, 117, 118; Bryan
    expedition, 125, 127; Gray's Gang, 129, 130, 132
Frederica River, 324
Frederick, Prince of Wales, 100
Freedmen's Bureau, 237, 238
French and Indian War, 119, 132, 135, 137

Gambrell, David, 332
Gassman, Nancy "Nanette" Stafford, 300
Gatschet, Albert, 19, 20, 23, 39
Gaylord, Charles, 239
Geiger, Rev. Maynard, 19, 69, 81, 82
George II (king of England), 98, 100, 102;
    Oglethorpe military appointments, 106, 121;

Bryan appointment to Royal Council, 127; Gray's Gang, 129

George III (king of England), 100, 119

Georgia Commons House of Assembly (general assembly), 127, 128, 138, 140, 152, 157

Georgia Conservancy, 333, 350

Georgia-Florida border: Timucua boundary, 9; 1783 Treaty of Paris boundary, 120; Gray's Gang, 129

Georgia Power, 333

Georgia Society of the City of New York, 276

Georgia Southern University, 350

Georgia State Guard, 323, 324

Georgia Teachers' Association (Georgia Association of Educators), 274, 275

Gibbons, William, 152

Gibbs, Charles (James D. Jeffers), 197

Gibraltar, 108, 109, 110, 111

Gibson, Patrick, 213

Gilbert, C. J., 158

Glidden Company, 325, 326, 353

Goldsmith, Capt., 135

Goldsmith, Oliver, 121

Graham, Lt. Gov. John, 145

Graham, Patrick, 125

Grange, the, 294

Grant, Ulysses S., 267, 281

Gray, Edmund (Gray's Gang), 128–135

Greene, Catherine, 143

Greene, Catharine "Caty" Littlefield, 142–150; war debt appeal, 152; cotton gin, 154, 156; marriage to Phineas Miller, 156; Dungeness I, 156–164; Yazoo land fraud, 157; timber business, 165; Burr visit, 167, 169; slave smuggling, 170; conflict with children, 171; death of, 173

Greene, Cornelia, 142, 160, 166, 169, 172, 205; marriages, 167, 171

Greene, George Washington, 142, 152, 154

Greene, Griffin, 151

Greene, Louisa Catharine Shaw, 142, 160, 166, 167, 170, 175; marriage to James Shaw, 172, 173; War of 1812, 182, 186, 191; compensation for losses, 192; "Light-Horse Harry" Lee and, 193; as horticulturist, 195; death of, 196, 197

Greene, Martha (Patty), 142, 160, 166, 172, 193; marriages, 157, 171; Robert E. Lee mention, 219

Greene, Gen. Nathanael, 156, 157, 160, 170, 197, 203, 322, 353; Revolutionary War, 142, 143; "Light-Horse Harry" Lee's service under, 192, 193; land acquisition on Cumberland, 144, 146; Spanish Florida excursion, 147, 148; plans for Cumberland, 149–151; Ned Simmons enslaved by, 237; death of, 152; heirs, 171, 175, 217, 248; Samuel Francis Du Pont admiration of, 230, 238; Carnegies compared with, 322

Greene, Nathanael "Nat" Ray, 142, 160, 167, 172, 191; description of, 166; marriage, 175

Greene Cemetery, 173, 193, 276, 284

Greene County, 152

Greensborough (Greensboro), Ga., 152

Greyfield, 150, 171, 245, 334, 337; construction of, 302; Greyfield Inn, 326; Kennedy-Bessette wedding, 346, 347

Groton, Conn., 213, 214, 234, 239

Guale, 19, 63, 93; 1597 revolt, 67, 69–71; Spain's response to rebellion, 73–76; proposed relocation of St. Augustine, 78; reinstatement of, 79, 81; Ybarra tour of, 82; Cuban bishop tour of, 84–85; Father Andrés shipwreck, 86–89; Westo raids, 94

Guanabacoa (Havana), 93, 94

Gullah-Geechee, 247

Gunn, Sen. James, 157

Gunnell, Francis MacKall, 231, 232

Habersham, James, 139

Habersham, Joseph, 139

Half Moon Bluff, 254

Halifax. See Nova Scotia

Hamilton, Alexander, 143, 152, 167, 169, 197

Hamilton, James, 191

Hamilton, James Alexander, 197

Hamilton, Philip, 197

Hann, John, 19, 29, 30, 44, 63, 69, 71, 85, 87, 89

Hardegen, Capt. Reinhard, 323

Harris, Horatio, 215

Harris, Joel Chandler, 247

Hastings, Joseph, 217

Havana, 21, 57, 62, 63, 81, 84, 106, 189; removal of Timucua to, 93–94

Hawkins, Benjamin, 147, 148

Hawkins, Lt. George Drew, 183

Hawkins, Dr. Thomas, 106

Hawkins, Thomas Drew, 183, 243

Hedrick, Amy, 254

Hever, George, 313

Highlanders, 100, 101, 103, 121, 158; Fort St. Andrews munity, 109, 110; Spanish invasion, 113

High Point, 108, 176, 234, 252, 333; Guale revolt, 70; African American settlement, 251; Primus Mitchell burial place, 248; hotel era, 254, 260, 275; Candler purchase of, 279; Fraser development, 327

High Point House, 254

Hobe Sound (Fla.), 90

Holocene, 3, 4

Holzendorf, 255

horses: Don Juan's, 69, 70; gifts from Spanish, 74; Oglethorpe's stud farm, 112; English slaughter of, 113; Spanish slaughter of, 117, 118; Nathanael Greene mention, 149; returned to Cumberland by George Cockburn, 191; Samuel Francis Du Pont mention, 232; Stafford sale to Union forces, 234; Stafford antebellum sale of, 235; Stafford loss of, 241; 1874 travelogue account, 252, 253; trolleys, 262, 270; Lucy Carnegie herd, 288; airstrip grazing locale, 306; World War II patrols, 323; Lucy Ferguson herd, 330; horse race, 334; Carol Ruckdeschel riding with, 339; overgrazing, 6; proposed removal of, 342, 343

Horton, Capt. William, 117

Hotel Cumberland, 270–279

Houstoun, Gov. John, 146

Howard, Maj. Gen. Oliver Otis, 237

Huguenots, 29, 43, 125

Hunter, J. M., 251

Hunter, Banks & Company, 143, 144

Hush-a-Mouth (island), 341

Hutchinson, Jack Falls "Jock," 306

Hutchinson, Thomas, 302, 306

Hyrne, Maj. Henry, 134, 135

Ice Age, 3

Ile de la Seine, 11

Indian Springs, 150

indigenous language, 19, 25, 26

Iracana, 30
Irving, Washington, 230
Isaac (enslaved escapee), 227
Isle of Whales, 103

Jackson, Osbie, 334
Jefferson, Thomas, 145, 155, 167
Jekyll Island, 69, 84, 125, 164; colonial era, 103,
    105, 117; Spanish invasion, 118; War of 1812,
    183, 187; Bernardey relocation from, 210;
    Wanderer landing at, 215, 254; Cumberland
    Route, 274; National Seashore, 329, 330, 331
Jekyll Island Club, 302, 334
Jenkins' Ear, War of, 112, 119, 129
Jesuits, 63, 65, 66
Jim Crow, 276, 341
Jobe (Natives), 90
Johnny (enslaved runaway), 196
Johnson, George, 260
Johnson, Samuel, 121
Johnston, Coleman, 322
Johnston, Marius, 322
Johnstone, Walter T., 279
Jones, Alfred W. "Bill," 331
Jordan, Helen B., 339
Joseph's Town, 145
Joyner, W. R., 276
Juan del Puerto (Port of the St. John's River), 66,
    73, 84
Jusepe, 69, 70, 73

Kelly, William F., 217
Kelp Highway, 3
Kennedy, Jacqueline, 346
Kennedy, John Fitzgerald, 346, 347
Kennedy, John Fitzgerald, Jr., 346, 347
Kennedy, Rory, 347
Kennedy-Bessette wedding, 346–347
Kindelán y Oregón, Gov. Sebastián de, 187
King, James, 218
King, James Gore, 252
King, John Alsop, 197, 216, 218
King, Roswell, 183
Kings Bay, 6, 178; Naval Submarine Base, 329,
    333
Kingsley, Zephaniah, 205, 213
Knox, Henry, 143, 152

La Challeux, Nicolas, 17, 23, 54
Lafayette, Gilbert du Motier, Marquis de, 143,
    145, 146, 152, 154
Lake Whitney, 4
Lamar, Charles Augustus Lafayette, 215, 216
Lamar, Jane Creswell, 215
Land Tuesday, 138
Lane, Nat, 341
Lanning, John Tate, 19
Late Mississippi Period, 14
Latham, Amos, 217
Laudonnière, René de, 17, 19; Timucua customs,
    25–65; 1564 expedition, 29–31; Fort Caroline
    construction, 57; Fort Caroline attack by
    Spanish, 59
Laurens, John, 124
Lawless Crew, 128, 129, 146
Lawton, Gen. Alexander, 221, 224, 225, 231
Lee, "Black-Horse" Harry, 195
Lee, Charles Carter, 219
Lee, Gen. Henry "Light-Horse Harry," 143, 192,
    218, 240, 267; death of, 193–195; disinterment,
    276
Lee, Gen. Robert E., 193, 195, 216, 219, 225; first
    Dungeness visit, 218; second Dungeness visit,
    240
Le Moyne, Jacques de Morgues, 19; on food
    provisioning, 50, 52–54, 56; on Native
    dwellings, 23; on Native religious ceremonies,
    44; on Native sport, 46; on Native warfare,
    31–32, 34; on shamans, 41; sketches, 29, 31;
    on Timucua customs, 20, 26–27, 37–38; on
    transsexuals, 39–41; wounding and escape in
    battle, 34, 59
Leturiondo, Alfonso de, 65, 87
Lewis, Winslow, 217
lighthouse, 164, 200, 215, 217, 227, 262, 322
Lincoln, Abraham, 232, 237; "Lincoln's Fleet,"
    222, 223
Little Cumberland Island, 3, 4, 70, 103, 118, 126;
    Lynch-Rose land purchase, 140; Greene land
    acquisition, 144, 158, 164; *Rambler* shipwreck,
    200; *Wanderer* landing, 215; Civil War, 219,
    227, 233; World War II, 322, 323; National
    Seashore, 330, 332, 333; Prohibition, 341;
    Spaceport impact on, 350
Littlefield (plantation tract), 175, 186, 205

Littlefield, Catharine. *See* Greene, Catharine
    "Caty" Littlefield
Littlefield, Edwin "Ned" Brinley, 171
Little Satilla River, 187
Little St. Simons Island, 86
Little Talbot Island, 11
Lockett, Rev. T., 255
loggerhead sea turtles, 16, 342
Long, Maj. Armistead L., 219
López, Antonio, 69, 70, 73
López, Baltasár, 66, 67, 74, 75, 77; letter to King
    of Spain, 78; San Pedro church rebuild, 79, 81;
    Father Andrés mention, 87
Los Pinales, 79, 82
Lynch, Thomas, 142, 145, 146, 155; Cumberland
    land purchase, 140; heirs of, 144, 156, 158, 197
Lynch Creek (Beach Creek), 4, 165
Lyttleton, Gov. William Henry, 134

Mack, Dan, 273
Mackay, Angus, 138
Mackay, Daniel, 129
Mackay, Eliza Anne McQueen, 170
Mackay, Capt. Hugh, 100, 106, 111; construction
    of Fort St. Andrews, 101, 103; construction of
    Barriemackie, 106; Fort St. Andrews mutiny,
    109, 110
Mackay, Lt. Hugh, 100, 106
Mackay, Patrick, 138
Mackay, Robert, 170
Mackay's Town. *See* Barriemackie
Macon Company, 271
Macon Row, 273, 275
Macon Volunteers, 271
Margravate of Azilia, 97
marriage customs, Native, 37–38
Marrón, Francisco, 66
Marsh Tackies, 235
Martin, Luther, 254
Martínez, Pedro, 63
Massias, Capt. Abraham, 191
mastodon, 3
Matanzas Inlet, massacre at, 60
Mayo, Robert, 341
McGiffin, James, 289
McGillis, R., 156
McIntosh, George, 140

McIntosh, Gen. Lachlan, 138, 140, 143, 145

McIntosh, William, 126

McKee, Louis, 339

McKinnon, John, 156, 248

McKinnon map, 156, 248

McNinch, J. L., 277

McQueen, Ann Dalton, 145

McQueen, Eliza Anne Mackay, 170

McQueen, John (later Don Juan), 144, 145, 170

Meléndez, Doña María, 82, 84

Mellon, Andrew, 322, 328

Mellon, Paul, 322

Menéndez, Pedro de Avilés, 62–65, 71, 353; appointed governor, 57; Fort Caroline attack, 59; French massacre, 60; arrival of Franciscan priests, 66

Menéndez, Pedro de Márquez, 66

Mercer, Brig. Gen. Hugh W., 219

Mercer, Johnny, 219

Merrow, Audey (Holzendorf), 341

Merrow, George, 260, 322, 332, 339, 341

Merrow, Nelson, 255, 260

mico, 19, 67, 70–71, 74, 76, 79

Mifflin, Warner, 151

Milanich, Jerald, 9, 14, 16, 19, 29, 44, 67, 92

Milledge, John, 139

Miller, Caty. *See* Greene, Catharine "Caty" Littlefield

Miller, Isabella, 262

Miller, L. A., 277

Miller, Mary, 262

Miller, Phineas, 157, 167; Greene secretary, 144; Mulberry Grove manager, 152; Caty Greene marriage to, 156; construction of Dungeness, 156–164; timber operation, 165–166; death of, 167

Miller, Tommie, 260

Miller, Walter, 200

Miller family, 326

Missoe, 11, 121

Mitchell, Amanda, 248, 251, 323

Mitchell, Catherine, 251

Mitchell, Douta, 251

Mitchell, Elizabeth, 251

Mitchell, Hester, 251

Mitchell, Irene, 251

Mitchell, Laura, 251

Mitchell, Primus, 248, 250, 251, 254, 255, 323

Mocama: dialect, 9, 11; name for Cumberland Island, 11

Molyneux, Eliza H., 240; heirs, 281

Montgomery, J. A., 273

Montgomery, Sir Robert, 97

Montiano, Gov. Manuel de, 111, 142; Spanish invasion, 113–119

Moore, Francis, 102, 103, 117

Moore, William, 143

Morris, Leander, 285

Morris, Lester, 334

Morris, Thornton, 326, 327, 329

Morrison, Rev. L., 260

mourning/burial customs, Native, 38–39

Mulberry Grove, 144, 149, 151, 152, 160, 154; sale of, 156; Ned Simmons at, 186, 237

Musgrove, John, 99

Musgrove, Mary, 99

Muskogean/Muskogee, 19, 99

Nanny "Nan," 185

Napoleon, Louis (enslaved escapee), 227

Napoyca, 76

National Aeronautics and Space Administration (NASA), 349

National Bank of Brunswick, 321, 325

National Park Foundation, 326, 331, 332

National Park Service, 282, 313, 328, 333, 350; Rayfield archaeological excavations, 236; coastal preservation surveys, 322; Cumberland Island property acquisition, 327, 336; National Park Foundation creation, 331; Ruckdeschel property, 339; animal population control efforts, 343; Kennedy-Bessette wedding, 347

National Parks Omnibus Bill, 332

Newall, Thomas M., 189, 190, 191

New Hanover, 128, 129, 130, 132, 135

New London, Conn., 204, 213, 242

Newport, R.I., 146, 196, 197, 219

Newport District, 125

Newport Harbor, 151

Newport River, 93

Nightingale, Bernard Nicolau, 175, 193, 240

Nightingale, Florence, 218

Nightingale, John Alsop King, 216

Nightingale, John Corliss, 156, 157, 160, 166, 167, 171

Nightingale, Joseph, 160

Nightingale, Louisa, 197, 198, 215

Nightingale, Mary Ray King, 197, 198, 215, 218, 230

Nightingale, Phineas, 193, 195, 205, 240; plantation management, 196, 197, 198, 209; Civil War, 216, 218, 231, 236, 238; freedman church, 248; hotel, 252, 260; Dungeness sale to Robert Stafford, 239; Davis purchase of Dungeness, 281; death of, 240

Nightingale, William N., 240

Nightingale, William S., 216, 240

Nightingale, Liles, Dennard & Carmical (law firm), 240

Nightingale Trail, 322

Nixon, Richard Milhous, 332

Nombre de Dios, 82, 94

North Georgia Mountains Authority, 327

Norwich, Conn., 214

Nova Scotia, 148, 182, 185, 191

Oakland plantation tract, 196, 197, 198

Ober, Frederick Albion, 120, 158, 193, 195, 235, 282; description of Dungeness, 164, 165

occupation of Cumberland Island: by British navy, 175–192; by U.S. Navy, 224–238

Ocmulgee River, 9

Oconee region, 141

Oconee River, 9

Oconee War, 150

Oglethorpe, James Edward, 78, 87, 92; rise to prominence, 97, 98; founding of Georgia colony, 99–100; expedition to Florida and naming of Cumberland, 100–104; skirmish with Spanish, 105; mutiny on Cumberland, 108–112; Spanish invasion and counterattack, 113–119; postcolonial years, 121

Oglethorpe Hotel, 266, 274

Okefenokee Rural Electrification Membership Corporation, 333

Olmsted, Frederick Law, 207

Olsen, Jim, 341

Olsen, Olaf, 323, 324, 341

Olsen, Olaf, Jr., 322, 323, 324

Olsen, Sonja (Kinard), 323, 324

Olsen, Thora (Kimsey), 349

Olsen's Yacht Yard, 324

Oriental House, 253
Osborne, Henry, 148
Otthelter, 130
Outina (Utina): customs of, 44; Laudonnière's downfall, 59, 60; territory of, 31; at war, 32, 34, 36

Page, Anne, 182, 183
Page, William E., 291, 294, 295, 302, 321
Page-Ladson sinkhole, 3
Palacios y Valenzuela, Gov. Lucas Fernando, 134
Paleoindian period, 2–4
Palmer, Frederick, 239
Panza, Sancho, 191
paramount chief, 10
Pareja de la Orden, Francisco: linguist, 19, 26; tribal lineages, 25; Native customs, 43–44, 53; catechism, 45; missions served, 66–67; Guale raid, 69, 73; petitions to governor, 75; later years, 84; Native epidemics, 92
Parris Island, 29, 57, 62, 106
Peabody and Stearns, 289, 302, 313
Peebles, Andrew, 285
Peeples, J. B., 326, 336
Peerson, Elias (Clubb), 253, 254
Pelham-Holles, Thomas, 102
Pennington, John, 339
Perkins, Coleman, 322
Peter (enslaved), 204
Petty, Fay, 277
Philip II, 62, 66, 67, 75, 78, 81; Menéndez appointment, 57
Philip III, 78, 81
Pinckney, Gen. Thomas, 189
Pine Island, 341
pirates/pirating, 64, 82, 127, 170, 197, 225; raids, 93
plants, medicinal, 65
Pleistocene, 3
Plum Orchard, 176; antebellum period, 209, 210; Carnegie era, 302, 313; Kennedy-Bessette wedding, 346
Point Peter, 76, 178, 330
Port Royal, 57, 62, 98, 160; Bryan plantations, 124; Samuel Francis Du Pont attack on, 224, 226, 227, 228
Porturiba, 14
Potano, 25

Powell, James Edward, 134, 135
Pratt, Charles, first Earl of Camden, 144
Privy Council, 128
Pulaski, wreck of, 197, 198, 215
Putnam, A. T., 270
Puturiba, 69, 70, 71, 73, 91

Quash, "Uncle," 245
Quin, Dr., 147

Raccoon Keys, 332
Rayfield, 175, 186, 205, 234, 236, 248
Readdick, Wilber, 326
Reynolds, Gov. John, 128, 129, 130, 134, 139
Reynolds, Maj. John G., 226
Rhynah (Nightingale nurse), 197, 198
Ribault, Jean: description of Timucua people and customs, 10, 11, 17, 19, 20, 21, 23; on Native alliances, 28, 29, 36; on Native customs, 41, 44, 46, 48, 50, 53, 57; return to Florida, 59; death at Matanzas Inlet, 60
Ricahecria (Chichimeco), 93, 94
Ricketson, Lucy "Miss Lucy" Carnegie (Ferguson), 315, 325, 326, 330, 339; biosketch, 333–337
Ricketson, Oliver G., III, 326
Ricketson, Oliver Garrison, 302, 315
Rockefeller, Lucy (Rice), 325
Rockefeller, Nancy, 325, 328
Rockefellers, 329, 333
Rogel, Juan de, 65
Rose, Alexander, 140, 142, 144, 145
Ross, Maj., 185
Ross, Ann, 266
Ross, Edgar Alfred, 264, 266, 269, 270
Ross, Mary, 19, 79, 84, 85
Ross, Mary Hermione, 264, 269
Royal Council, 127, 138, 140
Royal Marines, 176, 179
Ruckdeschel, Carol: biosketch, 339–343; Kennedy-Bessette wedding, 347
Ruíz, Pedro, 82, 84

San Buenaventura de Guadalquini, 11, 92
Sands, Phebe Littlefield, 162, 167
Sands, Ray, 162, 167, 191
San Marcos Phase pottery, 17

San Mateo, 60, 63, 64, 89
San Pedro de Mocama (San Pedro de Tacatacuru), 14, 62, 66, 64, 67; Guale raid, 69–70, 87; Yamasee settlement, 93
San Phelipe (Felipe) de Atuluteca, 93
San Phelipe III, 93
Santa Catalina. *See* St. Catherines Island
Santa Elena (Parris Island, S.C.), 57, 62, 64, 84, 106
Santa Maria River, 11
Santa María de Sena, 76
Santo Domingo, 56, 76
Sapelo Island, 57, 93, 125, 156, 189, 341
Sapelo River, 126
Saraby (Caravay), 11
Sarah, "Mom," 193
Sargasso Sea, 342
sassafras: indigenous name for Cumberland Island and medicinal uses of, 11; as trade crop, 81
Sassnett, W. R., 277
Satilla River, 14, 30, 117, 124, 200; Gray's Gang, 128, 129, 135
Saturiwa, Chief: domain, 11; meeting French explorers, 29–30; warfare, 31–36; hostilities toward Spanish, 60, 63
Savannah (culture), 16
Savannah, Ga., 87, 100, 106, 112, 119, 151; relocation of St. Augustine presidio to, 78; Yamacraw Bluff renamed, 99; colonial Georgian's population locale, 123; Darien road, 124; Bryan land purchase, 125, 138; Gray's Gang, 128–135; Land Tuesday, 138; Sons of Liberty, 139; Nathanael Greene estate location, 151; George Washington visit to, 152, 237; George Washington Greene burial, 154; Phineas Miller advertisement, 166; Caty Greene visit to, 171; George Cockburn's plans to invade, 179, 189; Louisa Shaw's horticulture expertise sought, 195; Dungeness advertisement, 196; *City of Austin* shipwreck, 200; Robert E. Lee in, 216, 218, 219, 225; Samuel Francis Du Pont in, 227; William T. Sherman's advance on, 237; rail service to Cumberland from, 260
Savannah River, 78, 94, 97, 124; South Carolina claim to Georgia land, 137

Sea Fencibles, 189
Seagrove, James, 148
Sea-Side House, 262, 264, 266, 269, 270
Seine River, 11
Seloy, 59
Seminole, 93, 95, 141, 145
Serendipity, 336, 339
Settlement, the, 255, 276, 322, 323, 326; NPS
    acquisition, 332; Carol Ruckdeschel at,
    339; dynamiting of, 341; Kennedy-Bessette
    wedding, 346, 347
settlements, African American, 245–260
settlements, Timucuan, 11, 14, 23, 73
Seward, Joyce, 323, 327, 329, 334
Shackleford, Lee, 271
Shaw, James, 172, 175, 182, 185, 193, 195, 196, 197
Shaw, Louisa. See Greene, Louisa Catharine
    Shaw
Shepard, Col. Joseph, 250, 251
Sherman, Gen. Thomas W., 224
Sherman, Gen. William T., 233, 237, 238, 250
shipwrecks, on Cumberland and surrounding
    waters, 200
Shoop, Robert, 339
Sidney Lanier Bridge, 70
Sierra Club, 333
Silva, James R., 205
Silver Bluff stage, 3
Simmons, Ned (Simons), 186, 191, 236, 237
Simmons, William, 124, 126
Sims, William, 277, 278
Skipwith, Peyton, 167, 171
Smith, John, 139
Somerville, Capt. Philip, 176
Spaceport Camden, 349, 350
Spalding, Isham, 204
Spalding, James, 203
Spalding, Thomas, 126, 189, 190, 191
Spanish moss, 6
Spartina grass, 6
Special Field Order 15, 237, 238
Spivey, Billy Ray, 323, 334
Sprague, William, Jr., 240
Stafford, Gov. Anson P. K., 274
Stafford, Clarissa, 204
Stafford, Elizabeth, 204
Stafford, Harriet, 204

Stafford, Lucy (Thomas), 204
Stafford, Mary, 204
Stafford, Robert, 203, 204
Stafford, Robert Thomas, 183, 198, 245, 248;
    birth, 204; description of, 213, 239; land
    purchases / enslaved ownership, 205;
    Planters House, 209; children of, 210, 213;
    New England properties, 213, 214; Union
    occupation and, 234–238; postbellum period,
    239–242; death of, 243; property purchase by
    Carnegies, 285, 289
Stafford, Susannah, 183, 204, 205, 243
Stafford, Thomas, 203, 204
Stafford, Thomas (son of Robert Thomas), 204
Stafford lawsuits, 300
Stafford Place, 302, 309, 321, 332, 334
Stafford Plantation (formerly Littlefield), 205
Stamp Act, 139, 140
St. Andrews, Scotland, 302, 306
St. Andrews Bar, 200, 275
St. Andrews Lighthouse, 217
St. Andrews Sound, 14, 84, 117, 215, 217, 270;
    Samuel Francis Du Pont occupation, 226, 227;
    World War II, 324
St. Augustine (San Agustín), 57, 60, 62, 63, 64,
    82, 88, 105; Saturiwa chiefdom, 11; naming of,
    59; 1597 Guale revolt, 71–74; caciques visit to,
    77; petition to relocate presidio, 78; plans to
    restore missions, 79; Father Pareja relocated to,
    84; Father Andrés shipwreck account, 88, 89;
    Jonathan Dickinson's shipwreck account, 90;
    mission contraction, 93; Timucua relocation
    to Cuba, 94–95; Oglethorpe's 1736 expedition,
    101–103; Oglethorpe siege of, 113; Spanish
    1742 invasion, 112, 116–117, 119; Gray's Gang,
    129–134; Yamasee guides for enslaved, 132;
    John McQueen relocation, 145, 170; Nathanael
    Greene visit to, 147–148; Phineas Miller visit,
    167; 1812 Georgia Volunteers advance on, 171;
    in Samuel Francis Du Pont laudation, 232
St. Catherines Island (Santa Catalina), 63, 67,
    84, 93
Steedman, Cdr. Charles, 231, 232
Stepney (enslaved father of Primus Mitchell),
    248
Stewart, Lt. Alexander, 118, 119
Stiles (Styles), Col. William Henry, 219, 221

Stiles family, 254
St. Johns River, 11, 28, 29; arrival of Huguenots,
    29, 31, 57; destruction of Fort Caroline, 59,
    63, 65; Franciscan missions, 66, 73, 84, 89;
    Dickinson party, 92; disputed territory, 95,
    100, 101; Oglethorpe expedition, 103; military
    ruse by Oglethorpe, 105; Fort Picolata raid,
    113; Bryan expedition, 125; proposed southern
    boundary for Georgia colony, 129, 134,
    141; Nathanael Greene's journey, 147–148;
    enslaved escape, 187; arrival of Staffords, 203,
    232, 237
St. Mary Parish, 138, 144
St. Marys (Amelia Island mission), 90
St. Marys, Ga., 29, 76, 121, 131, 135, 146, 148, 164,
    169, 341; harbor/inlet, 160, 169, 203; illegal
    trade, 169, 170; War of 1812, 173, 176–179, 189;
    mention in 1825 advertisement, 196; Robert
    Stafford and, 203–205; Civil War, 220, 221,
    224, 228, 232; hotel era, 250, 260; Carnegie
    era, 285, 302; ferry access, 330; landing strip
    for Lucy Ferguson, 334; Kennedy-Bessette
    wedding, 346
St. Marys River, 11, 23, 30, 63, 103, 113, 119, 123,
    124, 126, 132; Georgia-Florida border, 120, 137
Stockwell, Capt., 223
Stockwell family, 279
Stoddert, Benjamin, 166
St. Phillips, 90
strip mining (proposed), 325, 326
St. Simons Hotel, 271
St. Simons Island, 11, 16, 17, 63, 86, 102,
    142, 167; placement of mission, 92; Fort
    Frederica, 100; skirmish and meeting with
    Spanish envoy, 105; Spanish invasion, 112,
    117–118; Bryan expedition, 125–126; Gray's
    Gang, 129; Burr visit to, 169; War of 1812,
    182–191; Anguilla cotton production on, 203;
    lighthouse, 217; Civil War, 221–238; hotel era,
    271–279; World War II, 324–325; National
    Seashore, 330
St. Taffeys, 130
St. Thomas Parish, 144
Stuckey, W. S. "Bill," Jr., 329, 330, 331, 332
Suli-bul-Ali "Africa Tom" (Salih Belali), 188
Sunbury, 78
Swanton, John, 19, 36, 43, 46, 93

Table Point, 93, 205, 333
Tacatacuru, Chief, 11; domain, 17; visit by
    Ribault, 29; description of, 30; warfare, 31, 32,
    36; hostilities toward Spanish, 60; murder of
    Jesuit priests and raids, 63; death of, 64
Tacatacuru tribe: Cumberland settlement
    location, 9, 11; archaeological survey, 67
Talbot Island, 135
Talmadge, Herman, 332
Tama, 65, 70, 78
tattoos / body piercing, 19, 22, 66
Terrapin Point, 91, 101, 103
Thaw, Margaret Copley (Carnegie), 313
Thimagona, 29–31, 36, 60
Thiokol, 349
Thompson, David, 217
timber harvesting, 140, 146, 149, 204; French
    interest in, 154–156; Miller contract with U.S.
    Navy, 165–166; War of 1812, 191; Civil War,
    234; Carnegie era, 321, 322
Timucua, 2; belief system, 43–46; ceramics,
    16–17; domestic animals, 48; dwellings, 23–24;
    entertainment, 50; foodstuffs, 50–56; funerals,
    38–39; geopolitics, 28–36; household size, 10;
    language, 11, 26; marriage, 37–38; medicinal
    practices, 41–43; physical appearance, 19–23;
    population and territory, 9; social structure,
    25–28; tools, 46–48, 50; towns and villages,
    10–14; transexualism among, 38–40; warfare
    practices, 31–36
Tolomato, 67, 71, 94
Tolson, Lt. William, 117
Tomochichi, Chief, 99–104
Tonyn, Gov. Patrick, 141, 146
Toonahawi (Toonahowi), 99, 100; naming
    Cumberland Island, 102, 104
Townshend, Charles, 139
Townshend Acts, 139
Trapier, Gen. James Heyward, 226, 228

Treaty of Aix-La-Chapelle, 112
Treaty of Ghent, 188, 189, 190
Treaty of Paris, 119, 120, 137
Treaty of Seville, 112
Treaty of Utrecht, 104, 112
Trimmings, Charles, 254, 255, 276, 339, 341
Trimmings, P., 260
Trustees, Georgia Colony Board of, 98, 100, 105,
    106, 112; report of mutiny to, 108; Bryan land
    grant, 124, 125
Turner, Daniel, 166, 167
Turner, Henry, 171
Turner, William T., 254
Tuten, Russell, 329

Udall, Stewart, 326, 327, 329
University of Georgia, 219, 333, 343

Valley Forge, 142, 143, 192
Vandyke, Peter, 139
Vásquez, COMO Don Pedro, 148
Vector Launch, 349
Velasco, Diego de, 66
Verascola, Francisco de, 69, 70, 71
Vernal, Clemente, 82
Vosburgh, Francis, 239

Wadsworth, Jeremiah, 149
Wallace, W. W., 270, 341
Walpole, Robert, 106
Wanderer (slave ship), 215, 216
warfare, Native, 28–36
Warrenton, A. W. J., 281
Washington, D.C., 169, 225, 232, 281, 300, 334;
    burning of, 171, 173, 176, 182, 192
Washington, Gen. George, 142–147, 150, 152,
    165, 169
Washington, Martha, 142, 169
Washington County, 152

Wayne, Gen. "Mad" Anthony, 143, 151, 152
Weaver, Donna, 349
West India Regiment, 176, 183, 187
Westo, 93, 94, 132
Whitefield, Rev. George, 124
Whitney, Eli, 154, 156, 157, 167, 171, 173
William, Augustus. See Cumberland, Prince
    William Augustus, Duke of
Williams, Catherine, 242
Williams, Cornelia Stafford, 300
Williams, John, 129, 132
Williams, Capt. John, 170, 171
Williams, Thomas, 139
Williamson, John, 124, 126
Wilmington culture, 16
wine production, 151
Wirth, Conrad, 328
Wissoo, 11, 102
Wolf Island, 86, 87
Wood, Virginia Steele, 127
World War II, 322–325; sinking of cargo ships,
    323
Worth, John, 19, 60, 93, 94
Wright, Elizabeth, 121
Wright, Brig. Gen. Horatio, 226
Wright, Gov. James, 119, 135, 137, 138, 141
Wright, Margaret, 325

Yamacraw, 91, 99, 100, 103, 118
Yamacraw Bluff, 99, 124
Yamasee, 63, 91, 92, 95, 101, 105; raids, 93, 94;
    guides for enslaved, 131, 132
yaupon holly, 6, 10, 86
Yazoo, 156, 157
Ybarra, Pedro de, 81, 82, 84

Zabette. See Bernardey, Elizabeth "Zabette"
Zéspedes, Vincente Manuel de, 146, 147, 148
Zivulki, Charles Dieudonné (Cybulski), 239